THE REAL TRAVIATA

Frontispiece: Unattributed watercolour of Marie Duplessis, perhaps by Charles Chaplin.

THE REAL
TRAVIATA

THE SONG OF MARIE DUPLESSIS

RENÉ WEIS

OXFORD
UNIVERSITY PRESS

OXFORD
UNIVERSITY PRESS

Great Clarendon Street, Oxford, OX2 6DP,
United Kingdom

Oxford University Press is a department of the University of Oxford.
It furthers the University's objective of excellence in research, scholarship,
and education by publishing worldwide. Oxford is a registered trade mark of
Oxford University Press in the UK and in certain other countries

Published in the United States of America by Oxford University Press
198 Madison Avenue, New York, NY 10016, United States of America

British Library Cataloguing in Publication Data
Data available

Library of Congress Control Number: 2015931983

ISBN 978–0–19–870854–4

Printed in Great Britain by
Clays Ltd, St Ives plc

For my wife Jean

Preface

The research for this book was carried out in Britain, Belgium, France, Germany, Italy, Switzerland, and New York City. Much of the story of Marie Duplessis is intimately linked to her home in the Orne, Basse-Normandie, where the horse-pasturing landscapes in which she grew up survive almost untouched. Exploring her native villages of Nonant-le-Pin and Saint-Germain-de-Clairefeuille and the rolling hills between them and nearby Exmes, along with other villages connected to her family, proved illuminating time and again, and often in unexpected ways. It is still possible to walk in the footsteps of the future lady of the camellias in the solitary country lanes that link these Normandy hamlets. They bring to life what must have been the depth of her loneliness as she drifted through them during prolonged spells as a homeless child. I must thank the people in all the villages, particularly in Nonant and Exmes, who were prepared to listen to a stranger and help him with local lore.

I missed Jean-Marie Choulet during my visit to his museum dedicated to Marie Duplessis in Gacé but his subsequent correspondence and sharing of his collection's artefacts has been most gracious. The mairie of Nonant allowed me to consult their original ancient plans of the village on site as did the departmental archives in Alençon, where I searched extensively for the identity of the villainous Plantier of Exmes. To this day the tourist interested in the story of the girl who became 'traviata' can follow a well signposted track, the 'Circuit de la Dame aux Camélias', dedicated to various places associated with her.

Inevitably much of the real story now lies hidden in places that are far-flung. Thus poor Marie's mother's calvary ended in Clarens near Montreux on Lake Geneva. The Archives Vaudoises of Lausanne and the minuscule local history archive of Montreux were delightfully professional and attractive places in which to work, the latter not much more than a stone's throw from the place where the mother of Marie Duplessis has rested since 1830.

Cemeteries inevitably played an important role in my researches given the significance of the tomb of the lady of the camellias in Montmartre and the curious fact that in Paris major cemeteries are still guardians of their own records. I am grateful to the staff at the Cimetière de Montmartre for their forbearance and for letting me photograph their documents, which include extensive materials on the lady of the camellias.

Much of the Paris that Marie Duplessis knew, the city of Balzac, Hugo, and Lamartine, survives, including a number of its theatres, buildings, squares, streets, and locations such as Palais-Royal behind the Comédie-Française. It was here that Marie Duplessis used to walk and where she first became the plaything of a wealthy man; it was here too that she attended her last show ever. It seems fitting that the small but brilliant archive of the Comédie-Française, inside Palais-Royal, should have an important collection bearing on this story, and I am grateful to have been granted access to it and to reproduce two of its images in this book. Two theatres, the Variétés and the Gymnase, remain to all intents and purposes the way they were in the 1840s when she was a regular visitor; the Variétés in particular is almost untouched as we know from contemporary drawings of it. It is possible today to be seated its orchestra stalls and glance up at the very box where she used to sit. Doing so may not add directly to intellectual knowledge of her but it does feel like touching the face of history.

I am grateful to the Dumas Society for their help with trying to trace extant portraits of Marie Duplessis, to the library of Saint-Germain-en-Laye where Dumas *père et fils* spent much time and where *La Dame aux Camélias* was written, and to the archivists at Versailles, who accommodated my extended visits there. Following her round Europe to, among others, Baden-Baden, Spa, and Bad Ems, meant eavesdropping on seismic changes in European history. Some of the grand buildings of the old German spa resorts still stand, though almost none do now in Spa, one of the last two resorts visited by Marie Duplessis and where I must thank Mr Guy Peeters for his help with the Spa police records. I was well looked after in the tiny local history archive in Baden-Baden and similar courtesies were extended to me in Bad Ems. The *Fremdenlisten* ('lists of foreign visitors') in both, and particularly the *Badeblatt*, are almost complete and constitute invaluable records for researchers. In 1840s Europe these places rocked to the pulse of polkas, waltzes and power, a far cry from the Sleepy Hollows that they are today, although Baden-Baden can still seduce the modern visitor with its hidden charms.

If Marie Duplessis had wished, she could have allowed herself to be adopted and become the châtelaine of a grand manor house near Doncaster. The extensive papers of Sprotbrough Hall are preserved in the Doncaster Archives and await further exploration, perhaps even with regard to the story of Marie Duplessis.

In Italy I worked in Venice where *La traviata* first premiered in 1853, particularly in the Biblioteca Nazionale Marciana and in Casa Goldoni, and in Busseto where the Casa Barezzi, once belonging to Verdi's father-in-law, is today fully restored to its nineteenth-century glory. The whole town is redolent with Verdi memories as are his homes in nearby Roncole, where he grew up, and in Sant'Agata, where he was lord of all he surveyed at the time of *La traviata*. The guided tours in both places are instructive and revealing, and their atmospheric value, particularly in Roncole and in the church where he played the organ as a child, is hard to overestimate. While much of Verdi's *oeuvre* and correspondence is in the public domain, much of it similarly remains hidden from view. I was privileged to be granted access to the Verdi materials at New York University under the supervision of Francesco Izzo, scholar, pianist, and now friend. Francesco proved to be the most genial of hosts and an inexhaustible fount of information on Verdi and romantic nineteenth-century opera.

Inevitably most of the work for this book was conducted in major research libraries, particularly the British Library in London and the Bibliothèque Nationale de France in Paris, both at Richelieu and in Tolbiac. I am grateful to my own library at UCL, for its rich collections in the nineteenth century and its efficient Interlibrary-Loan system that allowed me access to almost anything from anywhere in the world on UCL premises. Not far from my office at UCL sits the University of London Library at Senate House, which houses one of the richest music collections in the capital. Other libraries and archives such as the Beinecke in Yale, the Wallace Collection in London, the Rare Books collection of the University of Virginia, the Wagner Museum in Bayreuth, all helped and dealt with my enquiries with courtesy and kindness.

I owe a huge debt to The Leverhulme Trust for freeing me from all major academic commitments for three years to research and write this book. It is a pleasure to thank Leverhulme for their generosity and their light touch monitoring; to be trusted may be the greatest spur of all. It is a privilege to thank my Leverhulme referees, R. I. Moore of the University of Newcastle, Denis Noble of the University of Oxford, and James Shapiro of Columbia

University. John Snelson of the Royal Opera House advised on Verdi's keys in *La traviata* and on much else; he was, as ever, the most generous of friends with his time, expertise, and his contacts in the world of music, putting me in touch with Mary Jane Phillips-Matz and Francesco Izzo among others. Bill Hamilton of A. M. Heath again gave me more of his valuable time than I had a right to expect, repeatedly pressing me to get ever more deeply inside the soul of Marie Duplessis, to understand why she never ceased to forgive all the harm done to her by men, whether it was this that ultimately made her Violetta.

I wish to thank my readers at Oxford University Press for taking much time over my manuscript and for all their advice. I learnt a great deal from them and have followed their suggestions to the letter wherever possible; and in spirit in the few other instances. Tom Chandler copyedited my book with impeccable professionalism and Matthew Cotton was the most genial of editors.

I must record my gratitude to my colleagues in the UCL English Department whose support and friendship mean a great deal to me. Neil Rennie stiffened my resolve at a crucial point and Greg Dart was ever ready with references to Stendhal, music, or French novels. Susan Irvine and John Mullan, both Heads of Department during the making of this book, have served their colleagues with selfless commitment for which I am grateful. Stephen Cadywold and the staff in the English Office at UCL add immeasurably to my sense of the Department. My debts to Rosemary Ashton, Dan Jacobson, Karl Miller, John Sutherland, Ross Woodman, Michael Worton, and Henry Woudhuysen stretch back over many years and are imprinted in everything I write.

In January 1980 I sat in the Amphitheatre of the Royal Opera House in London at a performance of *La traviata*. The role of Violetta was sung by Kiri Te Kanawa, conducted by John Pritchard, with Stuart Burrows as Alfredo and Renato Bruson as Germont. The production was by Luchino Visconti. It was one of those nights at the opera house when everything fell into place and the music and singers were allowed to work their magic. No recording survives of this but on that occasion Kiri Te Kanawa and the genius of Visconti joined forces to deliver to a London audience a near perfect version of Verdi's masterpiece. This book is among others a tribute to the memory of that night.

R.W.

Department of English
University College London, 2015

Contents

List of Illustrations

I

Prologue

A weekend in the country

La traviata is probably the best loved opera in the world. In three recent seasons the Royal Opera House in London staged no fewer than thirty performances of the opera, their Violettas including legendary sopranos like Renée Fleming and Angela Gheorghiu. All sold out almost instantly, proving that over 160 years on from its premiere in Venice, *La traviata's* ethereal melodies continue to move modern audiences like no other. And yet this transcendent musical melodrama, so much part of modern high culture, originated in a collision of real life prostitution, love, and artistic creativity.

La traviata may be as timeless as Mozart's *Nozze di Figaro* or *Don Giovanni*, but unlike them it is rooted in a true story that happened in Paris in the 1840s. Verdi's masterpiece would not exist if it had it not been for the life of a courtesan who died at the age of 23 in a Paris apartment in the Madeleine. The young woman was called Marie Duplessis. In a silver-tongued obituary, published a few weeks after her death, the poet and novelist Théophile Gautier reminded his readers of who she had been and why she had captured the imagination of the capital:

> More than once, on the boulevard des Italiens, at the opera, at all the shows where it is almost impossible to secure a seat, Parisians will undoubtedly have spotted, in the most desirable box in the theatre, a young woman of exquisite demeanour. They will have admired those chaste, oval features, her gorgeous dark eyes shadowed by long lashes, the purest arching eyebrows, a nose of the most exquisite and delicate curve, her aristocratic shape that marked her out as a duchess for those who did not know her. Her fresh bunches of flowers, the elegant taste of her clothes, the splash of diamonds, all underpinned this impression. She was a duchess but her duchy consisted of Bohemia...by a twist of fate she was born a peasant girl in Normandy.[1]

Conceding that Marie Duplessis was of the humblest birth, Gautier returned to the charge by claiming that her beautifully turned feet were never meant to be shod in anything other than the finest satin. Her soft skin was the texture of camellias, he rhapsodized, before she was ever called 'lady of the camellias', and it cried out for the finest lace and fabrics that could be had.[2] Such was her magnetism, he claimed, that whole diamond necklaces freely wound themselves around her neck, longing to rest on her soft bosom, while the best carriages and finest horses in town volunteered to carry her just as the most exclusive designers of Venetian mirrors in Paris relished the thought that she would admire herself in their furniture. Gautier's paean to Marie Duplessis stops short of turning her into a goddess. He wonders why none of the maverick young men who had haunted her apartment when she was alive had thought of

> spreading a handful of gold in front of a sculptor, and commissioning him to eternalize, in marble of Carrara or Paros, the beauty that was the glory and undoing of Marie Duplessis. That way at least her life would have served a purpose. Phryne [a legendary courtesan who modelled for Praxiteles] left a statue, and history has pardoned her. Who among us, thanks to Phidias and Praxiteles, has not unwittingly doted on some Greek courtesan.

If the great Attic sculptors Phidias and Praxiteles could not serve, Verdi's *La traviata* did. It is in the lyrics and music of Verdi's grand opera that Marie Duplessis achieved lasting and universal fame as Violetta Valéry.

The opera centres on a sweet-natured and glamorous courtesan, who is consumptive and therefore doomed. Her name is Violetta Valéry and she briefly finds happiness in the arms of an idealistic young man, Alfredo Germont, who loves her for her generous heart as much as her beauty. He knows what she does and he knows too that she is gravely ill, which is why he wants to save her by taking her out of the moral morass that is Paris, with its all-night balls, orgies of drinking, and promiscuity. She trusts him and allows him to transport her into a country idyll. In this pastoral bubble, Violetta and Alfredo enjoy days of bliss, the only shadow on the horizon being Alfredo's debts that Violetta is trying to settle by secretly selling off her most precious possessions. Alfredo has only just left for Paris to assume charge of his debts himself, when his father Germont appears. In the longest scene of the opera Germont *père* confronts Violetta with her past. He informs her of the fact that Alfredo has a virginal younger sister whose marriage will be jeopardized if her brother continues his liaison with a prostitute: surely she must appreciate that sooner or later he will tire of her and that therefore she might as well agree to leave him now before his sister's marriage prospects are ruined?

Violetta at first fights Alfredo's father but in the end she realizes that he is right, that there can be no respectable future for women like her and that she must leave Alfredo before his sister's life is wrecked in turn. Her self-sacrifice is unconditional and, to save Alfredo from despair, she pretends that she freely reverted to her former dissolute life in Paris by accepting an invitation to another Parisian hostess's party, her friend Flora Bervoix. That way he will despise her, she hopes, and suffer less from his loss, although one day, after she is dead, his father Germont will reveal the true reason behind her departure. That promise she extracts from Alfredo's father.

Alfredo, however, follows Violetta to the party at Flora's and confronts her after winning at the gambling tables. She refuses to explain why she left him. Incredulous, he asks whether she loves her previous keeper, the Baron. Realizing that such a profession of love, however far from the truth, may be the only way to keep her promise to Alfredo's father, Violetta replies 'Yes, I love him!' Outraged Alfredo flings his winnings at her, appealing to the assembled crowd to witness that he has settled his debts, paid his dues to a courtesan in cash, as befits women of her kind. Violetta collapses as Alfredo's father enters. He expresses shock at his son's insulting Violetta in this fashion, because he knows the truth about her noble heart. The last scene of the opera plays in Violetta's apartment during the Paris Carnival in February, the same month in which Marie Duplessis died. Alfredo is on his way to join her, as is his father, to ask her forgiveness and to be together in a happier future away from Paris. By now Alfredo knows all about Violetta's selfless love and greatness of heart. But it is too late and Violetta dies in his arms, after urging him to find happiness with a pure young woman while she will be praying for them both in heaven.

Many details of *La traviata* originate in the real life story of Marie Duplessis, because the opera was inspired by a biographical novel about her, *La Dame aux Camélias*. It was written by one of her lovers, Alexandre Dumas *fils*, and is far more memoir than novel. It is, at times, a barely disguised account of the life of Marie Duplessis and was written within months of her death. Verdi's opera premiered a mere six years later. It is hard to imagine that a work as intensely moving and idealistic as *La traviata* could grow out of the sordid world of nineteenth-century prostitution. Surely, one wonders, real life *traviatas* like Violetta do not exist. Or do they? One of the moral and imaginative challenges historically of Verdi's great opera was precisely that, and predictably the work was at first castigated for its reck-lessness, for daring to turn a demi-mondaine into a virtual saint.

It was a bold thing to do this in the middle of an era we call Victorian. During that period *La traviata* was never performed in the nineteenth-century contemporary costume that Verdi had intended. He had wanted his 1853 opera to be staged in the fashions of the 1840s and 1850s. This proved a bridge too far throughout his lifetime. But by the end of the twentieth century the story had become domesticated, while its power to move remained undiminished. Thus the 1990 film *Pretty Woman* not only artfully reimagines *La traviata* but inserts the opera itself into the plot when Edward Lewis (Richard Gere) takes Vivian Ward (Julia Roberts), a big-hearted Los Angeles prostitute, to see *La traviata*, aware of course of the fact that Vivian is a Violetta by another and rather similar name. In the great scene at the opera, Roberts's facial expressions guide our emotional responses to Verdi's music drama with consummate artistry. At first the joy and laugh-ter of the party in the opera's opening scene, with the flourishes of the famous brindisi ('Libiamo'), thrill her by their exuberance. She looks increasingly troubled by the crescendo of pathos during Violetta's anguished exhortation 'Amami, Alfredo', when she prepares to part from her lover to save his family's honour. As the opera ebbs away with Violetta's death, tears well up in Roberts's eyes.

By inviting a romantic prostitute to a performance of *La traviata*, the pro-ducers of the film indulged the fantasy of treating Marie Duplessis herself to an opera that is in essence all about her. What would she have made of the fact that she, who loved opera, who attended premieres in Paris, including probably that of Verdi's *Nabucco*, would one day be renowned throughout the world as the real life inspiration for the heroine of one of the most illustrious of all operas, Verdi's *La traviata*? Violetta's suffering and sorrows, the 'corsi affanni' of the famous Act 3 'Parigi o cara' duet, resonate as a percussive leitmotif in the opera. The composer never blames Violetta for her way of life. Rather, the opera is a celebration of Violetta and, by extension, of the young woman who rests under a sarcophagus in Montmartre. Neither Verdi nor his Venetian librettist Piave ever met her, although they were both her contemporaries. Her name as recorded on her tomb was Alphonsine Plessis which she later changed to Marie Duplessis.

What follows is the true story of the young woman whom the world knows as Violetta in *La traviata*. Marie Duplessis may have been a courtesan but she was as much in touch with grace, beauty, and illness as the heroine of the opera. Her unconventional and tragic existence inspired Alexandre Dumas *fils* to write his scandalous novelistic memoir. He christened her 'la dame aux camélias'. The suggestive name stuck: it conjures up a mysterious life, turning a mundane, and at times tawdry, existence into the magical world of a mythical flower girl. She did, it is true, love camellias in real life as one of her surviving shopping lists proves. An invoice of 9 November 1843 from her supplier of flowers, Ragonot of 14 rue de la Paix, overwhelmingly features different arrangements of camellia, in this particular case white ones, it seems.[3] Camellias were her calling card: a red camellia meant that she was sexually unavailable, while a white one signalled the contrary. Dumas reports that she wore a red one during four days every month and a white one during the other twenty-four: no-one, he remarks with goading disingenuousness, ever grasped what this meant.

A good place to begin the tale of Marie Duplessis is on a balmy weekend in provincial France during the summer of 1841. It occurs at an important turning point in her life and was recorded in minute detail by someone who was actually there and who, in the course of this visit, became her friend and confidant. He will play a significant role in the unfolding of her story precisely because of the trust she placed in him and the care with which he recorded their conversations. It is largely through this friend that we get to know what Marie Duplessis said and thought. Other people in the story are mere eyewitnesses who recorded what they saw of her and what she did rather than telling us what she herself thought and felt.

It was around noon, on Saturday 10 July 1841, when the stagecoach from Paris pulled into the courtyard of the coaching inn of the village of Nonant in Lower Normandy. Two young women, a lady and her maid, alighted. They were both around 16 or 17 years old. The mistress, of medium height, svelte, and with abundant chestnut hair, exuded an aura of elegance, her features moulded into a gently oval curve and dark eyes that seemed pools of melancholy tenderness. She had flawless skin and perfect white teeth, and she wore stylish, artfully understated clothes. On her head sat a coquettish lace bonnet with fluted frills.

The two women, followed by their luggage, made straight for the Hôtel de la Poste where they would lodge. This aroused some interest because not many people stayed in Nonant, which was a transit post where travellers enjoyed refreshment breaks before pushing on north to Rouen or south to Alençon, the departmental capital of the Orne. The grand stud of Haras-du-Pin lay five miles to the west. If the great Bordeaux to Rouen road had thrust Nonant into a strategic position, the stud was the economic power-house of this horse-pasturing region. Here some of the richest families of France and Britain met regularly to foster the burgeoning equestrian culture that the English had transplanted to France in the wake of their victory at Waterloo. The Haras-du-Pin was linked umbilically to the riding hubs of Paris, notably the exclusive Jockey-Club, which will play an impor-tant part in this story. For a small place like Nonant, with 878 inhabitants in 1841 (it has a fraction of that today), the coaching inn was an impressive affair, stabling as many as a hundred horses. The staging post also doubled as the mail office of the region. The entire range of the 'Hôtel de la Poste', stables, and post office were owned and serviced by a prosperous local fam-ily called Vienne. Monsieur Vienne, a deputy mayor of the town at the time, looked after the stables, horses, and coaches while Madame ran the inn (Figure 1.1).

The two weekend visitors commandeered the best rooms of the house. Then they retired to rest and recover from the rigours of the journey from Paris. At about 5 o'clock that afternoon, the young mistress, now refreshed, descended the stairs. She went straight up to the owner with 'Madame

Figure 1.1 The site and remains of the Viennes' home in Nonant.

Vienne, don't you recognize me? But you know me well; I am the little Plessis girl.' The hostess replied 'Oh, of course! My poor little girl—I certainly wouldn't have recognized you: will you stay the night?' The 'little Plessis girl' was Alphonsine Plessis. As a child she had briefly lived in a modest rented house two minutes' walk away from the Hôtel de la Poste. Madame Vienne addressed the young Miss Plessis with 'poor girl' for good reason, because her father had died a few months earlier in the neighbouring hamlet of Ginai. Alphonsine was an orphan. She had not attended her father's funeral in February, because she had been indisposed in her new home of Paris. It is true that she had been unwell, but only her elder sister, who lived locally, knew the true reason for her fragile state of health which had caused her absence. Now, as a minor and orphan, she had come ostensibly to meet her guardian, her great-uncle, and also to recover her health. She asked to keep the room in the inn for a couple of nights. Madame Vienne agreed. She also acceded to Alphonsine's request to join the Viennes' family table in their dining area.

Throughout the dinner conversation Madame Vienne's 24-year-old son Romain was present. He was pursuing business studies in Paris and had last seen Alphonsine five years earlier. He noticed that she was uncommonly handsome, with polished manners, charm, animated conversation, and a mischievous sense of humour. Alphonsine seemed to have grown up with astonishing speed and had clearly done well for herself, if her clothes and general demeanour were anything to go by. Whether she reverted to her regional dialect out of courtesy to her hosts, or whether she spoke in the perfect Île-de-France accent that she had acquired since leaving the region, is not recorded. Romain Vienne was bewitched by their young guest while she found him congenial. They knew many of the same people in Nonant and the surrounding hamlets, but as they were eight years apart in age, they had not been at school together. Moreover her elementary schooling had been in the neighbouring parish of Saint-Germain-de-Clairefeuille, while his had been at Nonant.

After dinner she asked to see the extensive gardens of the inn, an expanse of land and orchards that can still be glimpsed behind the ramshackle buildings that remain of the former staging post. Beyond them fertile pastures roll away towards Saint-Germain-de-Clairefeuille, a place close to Alphonsine's heart as the home village of her mother. Vienne picked a bunch of flowers for his fair guest in his parents' garden and relished steering their conversation in the direction of, as he put it, 'Rabelaisian chat', that is talk laced with sexual innuendo. It had not taken him long to realize that his beautiful companion worked in the lucrative Paris sex industry; perhaps he already knew because rumour travelled fast and Nonant and Paris were not that far apart even in the sunset years of the stage-coach.

The following day was Sunday. Alphonsine rose early and set off for mass at the parish church of Saint-Blaise. She was barely halfway along when she ran into an old acquaintance, a young farmhand by the name of Marcel. They knew each other well. She warmly greeted him and invited him to join her for lunch in her inn. Then she proceeded on to mass. It was her first time back in Nonant in over six years. We will never know for sure what she thought as, to the sound of high mass bells, she filed into the church with the crowd of worshippers, through the insalubrious water-logged cemetery and past the majestic elm tree that thrived in it. Her only happy times in Nonant had been moments spent with her mother who was trying to scrape a living from the meagre proceeds of their corner shop. But perhaps her mother was never far from Alphonsine's mind and heart, even though she was only 4 years old when, twelve years earlier, her gentle parent had fled in fear of her life. She would never see her again, although her mother was destined to appear in her life one more time, spectacularly so, and in circumstances stranger almost than fiction could fathom.

There was a more pressing reason why the pensive young woman might have been day-dreaming about her mother in church on this Sunday morning: she had herself been delivered of a baby boy only two months earlier. The birth had been protracted and had seriously affected her health. This is how she came to be visiting Normandy now, on doctor's orders, on the assumption that the country air would restore her health. A wealthy man, the father of her baby, was looking after her. During the period of her confinement she had wanted for nothing materially. She may have pondered this as she sat among these industrious, mostly poor, men and women, whose livelihoods depended on unreliable crops and the robber barons who ran the stud at Haras-du-Pin. Some of these wealthy men she had come to know in Paris, a fact that would have astounded most of the flock on this Sunday morning who shared her humble background.

At Sunday lunch, back in the Viennes' inn, Alphonsine and her maid Rose were duly joined by Marcel, who presumably was impressed by the fine wines that the women reportedly ordered. On this occasion the Viennes were taking their Sunday lunch in a room apart from the main dining area. Towards the end of the meal Alphonsine ordered champagne, her favourite drink along with Burgundy wine from Pommard, and sent for Romain Vienne, suggesting that he join their threesome.[4] He did and noticed, disapprovingly, that Marcel paid rather a lot of attention to the buxom maid, probably because the mistress had evidently outgrown the rustic Marcels of the Orne. In the afternoon Alphonsine set off to visit her sister, family and friends, who all lived within two or three miles of the coaching inn. At seven that evening she was back for dinner and again ate with the Viennes. Romain Vienne later recalled that she sat on his left while her maid faced him across the table. He was keen to stress that this reflected his abstracted state of mind: heaven forbid that his readers should think that he, like the rustic Marcel, should be attracted to either mistress or maid.

By eight o'clock dinner had finished. Picking up two chairs, Vienne invited Alphonsine to accompany him outside. It was a glorious summer's evening. The sky had turned a flaming red and the scents of flowers were wafting across to Vienne and Alphonsine from the gardens and adjacent meadows. So too may have been the acrid smell from smoking by several male travellers who had taken over the main bench outside the restaurant. No sooner had they spotted Alphonsine than two of the young men pounced on her and Vienne, interrupting their conversation. As the innkeeper's son Vienne felt unable to remonstrate with them over their boorishness. So he rose and walked towards the garden where the young woman presently joined him. Hooking her arm into his she asked whether he would join her for a late evening walk on the Paris road? He would, at which point she remarked gratefully that it would provide an excuse to give the slip to the bumptious young men and their clumsy compliments.

They turned left out of the inn's courtyard and made their way up the hill on the main artery linking Nonant to Paris seventy miles to the east. As they were strolling along in the golden light, they encountered a festive party heading towards them from the neighbouring village of Le Merlerault. Some of the group were singing. It consisted of a young couple and of their immediate family and friends. Forty-seven years later Vienne misremembered them as newly-weds. Marriages could not be contracted on a Sunday, so the party was not returning to Nonant from a wedding breakfast. Nevertheless Vienne's memory was essentially right about the link to a wedding, because the party that he and Alphonsine encountered had in fact been celebrating the first reading of their banns at noon that day in the church of Le Merlerault. They were a prospective bride and groom and their families. To be precise, the future 'dame aux camélias' and her friend Vienne met Hégésippe Gautier and Marie-Louise Alcaume from Le Merlerault, who eventually married on 31 July 1841.[5]

Alphonsine and Vienne chatted briefly to the banns party before proceeding up towards the crest of the hill of Pont-Rouge, as this stretch of the road was known at the time. She was touched by the excitement of the betrothed couple: 'How much they love each other!' she exclaimed, to which he replied, 'They will soon love each other even more.' 'You think so?' she retorted in an unexpectedly barbed voice, as if wondering how anyone could presuppose that marriage underpinned affection, unless they were naïve. To change the topic, and perhaps to mollify her host, she then congratulated Vienne on a recent career success. Encouraged by this, Vienne started asking her about her life in the metropolis and her past in these very hills and pastures. She was remarkably uninhibited about Paris, talking frankly about her life since leaving the Orne, the pleasure trips to the Bois de Boulogne, her friendships with other girls who did not relish lives of hard work and deprivation, her lot as a courtesan—what her interlocutor prudishly set down as 'the story of our grandmother Eve'.

Now that she had started talking Vienne felt emboldened to enquire after her recently deceased father. Much to his surprise she burst into tears at the mention of him. After all, he thought (although he probably did not share this with her), she could not conceivably mourn the passing of a monster, who had been feared and loathed locally for what he had done to his wife and two daughters? The village was rife with rumours and true stories about him, and the two most scabrous of all concerned the young woman who walked beside Vienne. And yet she not only seemed to defend his memory but imperiously ordered Vienne to drop the subject, as it upset her too much.[6] She then revealed to him what she had already told his mother earlier in the day, that she had given birth to 'a beautiful baby boy' in May. Then she expanded on the topic of the baby's father,

> her liaison with the Vicomte de Méril. 'But', I said to her, 'it seems to me that a Monsieur de Méril was appointed, a few weeks ago, sub-prefect of a city in the East: is this same Monsieur de Méril your lover? He possesses an illustrious name.' 'Himself, and I will provide you with proof of it one of these days by showing you the letters that I will receive from him.'[7]

As it is, Vienne had just recently, on 13 June 1841, seen that very name in the influential paper *Journal des Débats*, which reported that the alleged father of her baby had, by ministerial decree, been appointed to the 'conseil général d'agriculture' as of 2 June 1841. Could it really be him? Vienne asked after the baby. She told him that her lover had decided to take the infant away with him to his new posting in 'Burgundy' to have him brought up there. Whatever maternal feelings she may have harboured were, it seems, set aside of necessity. How much did Alphonsine really know about the fate of her child as she walked with Vienne? She seemed too relaxed to be aware of the truth, and although she used to joke about lying as a most effective whitener of teeth, it is doubtful that she was lying now or knew what had really happened to her child. At this point in the conversation Vienne backed away from further questions. He was no fool. He knew well that she could not cope with a baby in her chosen 'profession', and he may have assumed that she was telling him euphemistically that the baby was given up for adoption by his rich father. The rest of their walk passed in amiable banter about Paris and people they both knew. Alphonsine playfully threatened to introduce the somewhat stiff Vienne to some of her girlfriends when they were both back in Paris, presumably in response to his keen, if not salacious, interest in the company she kept. It was dusk when they reached the top of the slope. Vienne stepped into a field and picked a bunch of cornflowers for his companion. By the time they returned to Nonant the moon was out, suffusing, in Vienne's words, 'the pale crepuscular glimmers with gentle clarities'. It had been an idyllic weekend and Alphonsine had rested well.

The following Monday her maid Rose returned to Paris while the mistress rejoined her guardian, her great-uncle Louis Mesnil, and her aunt Julie in the hamlet of La Trouillière, two miles up the hill to the north of Nonant. The Mesnils and their home occupied a very special place in Alphonsine's heart. She was barely 4 years old when her traumatized mother sought shelter here with her two daughters. The Mesnils warmly welcomed her now. They had prepared a comfortable bed and even set aside a small room off their kitchen range for her. It is not impossible that theirs was the ancient, timber-framed crooked house that still stands here; this was certainly a building that Aphonsine's relatives would have known well even if it was not necessarily theirs.[8] Thirteen years earlier she and her sister had been a drain on the Mesnils' scant resources but now she was the prodigal daughter returned home, had money, and paid handsomely for staying with the Mesnils. Much had happened since that bleak January of 1828 when the girls' mother was nearly murdered. With their father gone, it looked as if the family, all of them on the girls' mother's side, could start again. Alphonsine's affluence was compounded by an astonishing, brand-new, education; not just in the ways of the world, but in all the more traditional senses of the word 'education'. How far she had travelled constituted a tribute to her sheer intelligence and native wit. She spotted an opportunity and she grabbed it. Her lot before leaving Normandy had been desperate enough for her life in Paris to be not just tolerable, but clearly also enjoyable.

2

A mother and daughter

1824–1837

The baby girl who would one day become 'la traviata' was born Alphonsine Plessis in Nonant at 8 p.m. on Thursday 15 January 1824. Her mother was Marie-Louise Michelle Deshayes, also known variously as Marie Anne, or Marianne. On Alphonsine's birth certificate issued on this day, her mother is called 'Marie Deshaies' from Saint-Germain-de-Clairefeuille, born to Louis Deshayes and Madeleine Louise Marre. In what follows she will be called 'Marie' because her daughter Alphonsine would eventually adopt her mother's first name from her birth certificate: if she thought of her mother as Marie, so should we. On the day Alphonsine was born, her mother was 29 years old and her father 34; by coincidence he shared a birthday with his new daughter. The following Tuesday Alphonsine was christened 'Rose Alphonsine' in Saint-Blaise, at a baptismal font that still graces the entrance of the church, proudly proclaiming its association with the future lady of the camellias. Her aunt Françoise-Julie and her uncle Pierre Saulnier stood as godparents. Alphonsine was the second Plessis child; a sister, Delphine Adèle, had been born two years earlier, in February 1822.

By the time of Alphonsine's birth her family had moved from the mother's home village of Saint-Germain-de-Clairefeuille to a small corner shop in neighbouring Nonant (Figure 2.1). It is clearly visible as plot 146 on the 1811 survey map ('cadastre') of Nonant, to the north of the toll gate that straddled the junction. It was the last house at the eastern end of the Grande Rue that traverses Nonant. It was obliterated during the widening of the Alençon–Sées–Gacé road, which sliced off the bottom tip of the little escarpment that to this day forms an attractive courtyard on an otherwise soulless junction with two desolate rival petrol stations.

Figure 2.1 Nonant in the Orne, the home village of Marie Duplessis as it is today.

The Plessis family had moved here because their shop at the junction was strategically positioned for trade. Saint-Germain-de-Clairefeuille, though less than a mile away, was a mere hamlet compared to Nonant, which not only boasted several public houses but also the vast coaching inn of the Viennes, its own gendarmerie, opposite the Plessis family home (the police station can still be seen in nineteenth-century postcards of Nonant), and fairs and an important market on Fridays. By the time the family set up home in Nonant in 1823, they were, however, struggling financially and their marriage was falling apart. Life was hard at the best of times in rural France in the 1820s, in a country that had gone through the cataclysms of social revolution and wars in the three decades preceding it. While his genteel wife did her utmost to keep a home, Plessis became an increasingly violent drunk. He had not learnt any trade even though he could write. Instead he earned his crust as a pedlar, selling whatever his wife managed to produce in her shop.

They seem to have met while Plessis was hawking his wares in the village of Courménil where the mother of the future lady of the camellias resided at the time. She and her widowed father had moved there from his native Saint-Germain-de-Clairefeuille and now inhabited a spot called 'Plessis'. When Marie Deshayes and her father were asked to give their address, they would declare that they hailed 'from Plessis in Courménil'. The importance of this to the story will become clear later. Marie was 26 years old and Marin Plessis 31 when they married. She was beautiful, with long black hair, blue eyes, and a daintily sculpted nose that her daughter Alphonsine inherited. She was intelligent and sweet-natured: in the words of Romain Vienne, 'she was blessed with all the gifts'. The Deshayes may have been distantly related to one of the grand families of the region, an assertion frequently made in the past without basis in fact, though often adduced to account for her refinement and, above all, for the way in which she was rescued in extremis from her husband. By all accounts the Deshayes family was respectable. Even if Marie was not necessarily her husband's superior socially, she certainly was in every other way. Although she, like both her parents, was born in Saint-Germain-de-Clairefeuille, she and the pedlar were married in her father's adopted village of Courménil on 1 March 1821.

Unlike his wife, Marin Plessis was illegitimate. His mother was a drifter by the name of Louise-Renée Plessis. His father had been a lazy and unprincipled priest called Louis Marin Descours, vicar eventually of the village of Lougé-sur-Maire just at the time when his unacknowledged son was growing up there. From inauspicious beginnings Marin Plessis went from bad to worse. What he had been gifted by way of looks and charm quickly evaporated while Marie Deshayes needed to devote ever more time to the rearing of her two baby daughters, Delphine and Alphonsine. Keeping her shop going as a small business at the same time was almost impossible. Her father Louis Deshayes and also, it seems, her sister, were helping out as much as they could.

If the arrival of little Alphonsine drew the couple together in a truce, it was inevitably short-lived. Soon they were unable to run the business in Nonant and became insolvent. So Marie and Marin moved to a cottage or barn in a hillside hamlet known as 'Les Orgeries', halfway between Nonant and Exmes (pronounced 'èmes' and meaning 'elevated place'). Marie must have dreaded this move. At least in Nonant the gendarmerie were her neighbours, and they might just have intervened if her husband's temper got the better of him. Now they were cut off and the poor wife reeled between bouts of terror and beatings. How the doomed couple managed to feed their children in the three years leading up to January 1828 is hard to imagine. Not only did Marin batter his wife, he also once hurled little Alphonsine across the room. By a miracle she landed on a straw mattress and survived. Her mother's only comfort may have been the thought that her sister lived in neighbouring La Trouillière, ten minutes on foot, along with her great-uncle Louis Mesnil, her mother's uncle. As long as family were somewhere nearby she might be safe, however precariously.

No-one tolerated the Plessis as tenants for long. Eventually they fetched up in a house two miles above Nonant close to the Rouen road, in a place called la Castelle. The 1811 survey plan shows just three habitations here, one on the Ménil-Froger side down towards Le Merlerault and two on the Croisilles side. A little further down the track, some hundred yards or so away from the main road, sits a tiny isolated hovel. This is probably where they lived when, shortly before Christmas 1827, Romain Vienne spotted Marie Deshayes in Nonant. It was the last time she appeared in the village. It was market day and she had come to sell threads, ribbons, and other haberdashery in the covered 'Halles' in the Place du Marché, on the site of today's municipal car park opposite the church.[1] In Vienne's own words,

> Her features have stayed engraved in my memory. She had lost none of her remarkable beauty or her virginal freshness. I was nevertheless struck, without knowing why, by an indefinable alteration of her traits, her resigned expression, her pallor and the gentle melancholy in her large blue eyes. Across her glorious forehead floated a few locks of her magnificent hair, jet-black. She repeatedly hugged me tenderly while talking to my mother. I was struck by how pained and pensive she looked. I have never been able to forget it.[2]

Not long after this, things came to a head in the miserable cottage at la Castelle. It was the night of Epiphany, 6 January 1828, nine days before Alphonsine's fourth birthday. It was bitterly cold. Marin arrived home, blind drunk and frozen. When he flung excessive wood on the fire, his wife remonstrated with him over such reckless profligacy, as they were nearly destitute and every little bit counted, including the wood. In response he grabbed her: if they could not afford fuel he would burn her as substitute, he screamed! A terrible struggle ensued. She fought him, desperately clinging to the table and bed, to stop him from dragging her into the flaming hearth. Her two little girls must have been terror-stricken during the ten minutes the vicious drunk was trying to murder their mother. The other houses at la Castelle were too far away for her screams to reach there, the more so since everyone had buckled up their homes against the deep frost.

She would have died that night if her screams had not been heard by Henry Aubert, a 25-year-old postman and innkeeper from Nonant, who on this cold night was returning from Rouen. He stopped his carriage, charged into the house, and flung himself on Plessis. Plessis was no match for the gentle giant Aubert. Almost sober now, he cowered while Aubert instructed Marie to take her children down the hill into Nonant and wait there for him: 'as for you, miserable wretch, if you so much as move towards the door I'll break your bones.' Henry Aubert has no role in either *La Dame aux Camélias* or in *La traviata*, but on this terrible Twelfth Night in a hamlet in the Orne he saved not just one life but probably three, as Plessis might well have murdered his children too if he had succeeded in mortally wounding their mother. By not looking the other way, Aubert played a significant part in the complex hybrid trajectory of life and art that eventually resulted in *La traviata*.

That night Marie and her children were entrusted by Aubert to a reliable friend in Nonant. The following day the battered mother, after learning that Marin Plessis had left their abode for the time being, returned to her home; or what was left of it, because the villain had trashed it out of sheer frustration. She wept. She had tried everything to make a home even in these dreadful circumstances, but the night before she had come close to being killed; and now the few remnants of her home were destroyed. She collected what she could of her own and her children's clothes. Then she fell to her knees and prayed for forgiveness for what she knew she needed to do now.

With her children in tow she proceeded to the hamlet of La Trouillière, some 300 yards down the hill where her uncle and aunt lived. What happened next must have been the hardest moment in her life. She knelt and, holding her two little girls in her arms, showered them with kisses. Then she entrusted them to the safekeeping of her family. She realized that Plessis would search for her everywhere, intent on beating her to death. Her family knew where she would hide but her little girls could not be told. They remained unaware that for the whole of the next month their mother was sheltering in a loft fewer than five miles away. How they must have missed her in those early days, particularly after witnessing how she had been hurt time and again, and almost fatally on that Epiphany night.

They never saw her again. From now on the girls' lives were defined by their mother's absence. Hers would similarly revolve around missing them, although she probably heard how they fared through the very family who would protect her over the next two years. Quite how deep and tragic her yearning for them was would be brought home to the two sisters many years later. Initially Marie Deshayes sheltered in a place called 'la ferme des Loges', an outhouse barn attached to the 'Manoir des Loges' at Avernes-sous-Exmes which borders on Courménil. It would appear therefore that she sought refuge at her father's at first, because that is where he lived, and that he and family friends by the name of Dupont hid her. The 'Ancien Manoir des Loges' dates from the seventeenth century and is still there.[3] She was safe here for a month but then was spotted by a notorious gossip. She had to move and so, under the cloak of night, her friends and family spirited her away, first to the Duhays manor at 'Le Mesnil' in the woods behind Saint-Germain-de-Clairefeuille, and from there, with the help of the Duhays, to a house, still there today, next to the church of Saint-Germain (Figure 2.3). Here she sheltered for a week before being smuggled onto a coach bound for Paris by Romain Vienne's father.

In the end Marie Deshayes escaped through powerful local connections who rallied to her help. All this time the pedlar Plessis was roaming the region looking for her. But the children did not know where she was and he did not dare lay a finger on the aunt and uncle who fostered the two girls, perhaps because of the uncle's official rank in the village (he is referred to as 'capitaine') and because he may have heard that his wife now enjoyed aristocratic allies. She did indeed, and why and who they were will become clear shortly. For little Alphonsine these first few months of 1828 must have been among the hardest of her life, but at least she and her sister now enjoyed a respite from violence and screaming. Perhaps the Mesnils managed to reassure the little girls about their mother, explaining that it was better this way, that their mother would come back to collect them once she was safe, that she never stopped loving them.

The years 1828 and 1829 came and went. The two little girls at La Trouillière were a burden, undoubtedly, on the brave Mesnils, but they somehow managed to feed these two additional mouths, with some support probably from the Marre families of Saint-Germain-de-Clairefeuille, cousins of Alphonsine's mother whose own mother was née Marre. What happened next, in a place far from Normandy, would plunge the families of Nonant and Saint-Germain-de-Clairefeuille into turmoil. In the evening of 30 September 1830, at 8.30 p.m., the register of the dead at Montreux in Switzerland records:

> On 1 October 1830 Doctor Buenzod, visitor of the dead of the parish of Montreux, noted that 'Marianne Deshayes', aged 33, chambermaid from Courménil in the Department of the Orne, daughter of Deshayes, wife Duplessis, died in the parish of Châtelard on 30 September 1830, at 8.30 in the evening.
>
> Pastor Bridel[4]

Four days earlier Marie had in fact turned 36, not 33 as the register mistakenly states. In Montreux on Lake Geneva she languished a very long way from where her heart must have been with her little girls in the Orne. An aristocratic woman sat with her as she lay dying in a property owned or rented by that family on Lake Geneva. In Vienne's words, 'as death approached, she took the hand of the baroness, wet it with her tears and movingly appealed to the lady's compassion on behalf of her two orphaned girls in Normandy. Lady Anderson promised that she would look after them.'[5]

That at least is what Vienne claimed and there is no good reason to doubt his word. Châtelard, the place where Marie Deshayes's death was recorded, is in Clarens, a village that stretches from the edge of the lake up the slopes towards the vineyards that huddle around the château de Châtelard (Figure 2.2). In the late 1820s when Alphonsine's mother briefly lived in this grandiose cadre, Clarens was the most celebrated spot on the whole lake. Two great writers had rendered it so: Rousseau and Byron. It was in this very village that, in 1761, Rousseau set his novel *La Nouvelle Héloïse*, thereby propelling a humble hamlet in the gulf of Montreux into the eye of the first European tourist storm. The original title of the novel, *Lettres de deux amans habitans d'une petite ville au pied des Alpes* ('Letters between two lovers living in a small village at the foot of the Alps'), melded the lovers' fictional story and the place in which it was set. Such was the success of Rousseau's novel that the publishers could not keep up with the printing, as hordes of readers made for Clarens in search of the 'bosquet de Julie', the very place where Julie and her teacher Saint-Preux first kissed.

A copy of Rousseau's *La Nouvelle Héloïse* was found among the possessions of the lady of the camellias after her death, along with *Manon Lescaut*. That the illicit *Manon* should be high among the favourite books of a literate

Figure 2.2 The hamlet of Clarens near Montreux, famous through Rousseau and Byron, where Marie Duplessis's mother died.

courtesan need not come as a surprise, but her reading of the long and demanding *La Nouvelle Héloïse* may have been attributable to her mother's time at Clarens. One wonders whether during one of her visits to Chamonix and other mountain resorts—we know from a stamp in her passport that she visited Bagnères-de-Luchon in the Pyrenees and so, probably, did Alpine resorts too—she did not descend on Clarens to visit her mother's tomb? Certainly by late 1845 she knew all about her mother's final resting place; in fact she may have learnt about it long before then from another source much closer to home.

   While the presence in Châtelard and Clarens of the mother of the future lady of the camellias is firmly established by her death certificate, neither she nor, more surprisingly, her aristocratic English patrons—Vienne calls them 'Anderson'—appear to have left any other trace in the recorded history of the area. Byron's visit to Clarens a few years before the arrival of Marie Deshayes may help throw some tangential light on this, because his stay there is not only well documented but has been extensively researched. He loved *La Nouvelle Héloïse* so much that fifty-five years after its publica-

tion he visited Clarens 'with Rousseau in hand', as he put in a letter of 23
June 1816 to his friend Hobhouse.[6] He spent two nights there, one with
Shelley in June 1816 and another, a few months later, with Hobhouse. He
glowingly apostrophized the village in *Childe Harold*, with particular reference to Rousseau's love story. The Clarens stanzas of Canto III (99–104)
rhapsodically evoke the grandeur of the village's setting at the foot of gla-
ciers, including the vineyards that to this day surround Châtelard, 'vines /
Which slope his green path downward to the shore'.

As one of the most fashionable poets of the age, Byron too featured in
Marie Duplessis's library. He preceded her mother in Clarens by twelve
years and had stayed in two inns, owned by the Dufour (25 June 1816, with
Shelley) and Pauly (18 September 1816, with Hobhouse) families.[7] Since
Marie Duplessis's mother was called 'femme de chambre' on her death certificate, is it not inconceivable that she worked, at least some of the time, for
one of these two inns, both of which enjoyed a long history in Clarens until
the late 1840s.[8] In 1845 one of Clarens's most renowned sons, the poet and
scholar Alexandre Vinet, died in the Dufour house, in the same room once
apparently occupied by Byron, at 8 Rue des Artisans. Did Byron's links to
Clarens account partly for Marie Duplessis's interest in the English poet?

Questions about her mother's employment in Clarens only arise because
her rich patrons left no mark in the records of the village, at least none that
can be recovered. The registers of the regional police granting visas to foreign visitors are silent on this matter and the Liste des Étrangers, such a
boon to researchers of mid-nineteenth-century European spa towns, only
starts in 1892. There is no mention of the Andersons in the local tax records,
nor is there any reference to property owned by them in various related
surveys. It all seems a bit of a mystery unless, contrary to Vienne's assertion,
they did not after all own a property there but instead rented, for extended
periods, the château perching on top of the tor of Clarens. Were the
Andersons the brand-new *lessees* of the château of Châtelard to whom
Byron refers in his letter of 18 September 1816 when he stayed again in
Clarens, this time with Hobhouse:

> arrived the second time (1st time was by water) at Clarens beautiful Clarens!—
> went to Chillon through scenery worthy of I know not whom—went over
> the Castle of Chillon again—on our return met an English party in a car-
> riage—a lady in it fast asleep!—fast asleep in the most anti-narcotic spot in the
> world… After a slight & short dinner—we visited the Chateau de Clarens—
> an English woman has rented it recently—(it was not let when I saw it first

[June 1816]) the roses are gone with their summer—the family out—but the servants desired us to walk over the interior—saw the table of the saloon—Blair's sermons—and somebody else's (I forgot who's—) sermons—and a set of noisy children—saw all worth seeing and then descended to the 'Bosquet de Julie'...[9]

Perhaps Romain Vienne's 'Andersons', the benefactors of Alphonsine's mother, were the very English people Byron and Hobhouse passed on their return from Chillon (which may be why they were 'out'), the place that inspired Byron's 'The Prisoner of Chillon', a poem about François Bonivard's six-year ordeal chained to a pillar in the dungeon of the Montreux–Chillon castle.[10] Byron's ode to Clarens in *Childe Harold* and his subsequent prestige inevitably meant that, in time, everyone locally wanted to have known the great poet. A measure of healthy scepticism about some of the more inflated claims made about the poet's stay in Clarens is advisable.[11] Nevertheless, accounts by serious local historians such as Eugène Rambert, born near Clarens in 1830, fourteen years after Byron's stay in Clarens, cannot be dismissed out of hand.

Rambert was appointed to a chair at the University of Lausanne at the age of twenty-four, after studying in Paris. His perceptive pages on the 'Doyen Bridel', the very pastor who buried Marie Duplessis's mother, immediately precede those on Byron and show a cultured intelligence, as one would expect from a scholar of his background and a friend of the great Swiss novelist Gottfried Keller. He would not have been taken in by locals boasting about their eminent visitors. That they were embellishing he would have suspected, but not to the point of inventing entire stories. Here is what Rambert records about the poet's two visits in a book published in 1877:

One still points out at Mr Dufour's in Clarens a room where he [Byron] lived...He also lodged in another house, where lived a lady by the name of Pauly, who thought highly of him, because of his good manners, his guineas, and his fame. Perhaps she imagined that some of it would rub off on her. In any case, she thought he was a great original, a kind of madman, who 'paced up and down all night in his room.' I had that from her own mouth. One day she was squatting in her garden, in very ordinary clothes, in the process of scraping her cabbages...when she heard someone call her name with a great burst of laughter. It was Byron who had arrived unannounced and was watching her over the hedge. She wanted to flee but was restrained. They insisted that she squat again in front of her cabbages until one of Byron's companions, Hobhouse I believe, could sketch her in his album. 'Never', she told me, 'did I feel more embarrassed.'[12]

Would this respectable historian and professor really make up a conversation with Madame Pauly? By the time she spoke to Rambert, she must have been well into her sixties if not seventies, while Rambert was almost, though not quite, a contemporary of Byron's.[13] He knew the Dufours and the Paulys of Clarens and he knew the pastor who had tended the dying mother of the future lady of the camellias. The detail of the cabbage patch, the hedge, and perhaps above all Hobhouse's sketch book—in 1818 Hobhouse published *Historical Illustrations of the Fourth Canto of Childe Harold*—all ring essentially true. Rambert grew up within a mere fifteen minutes' walk from the two Clarens inns and must have known them well. He does not mention famous foreigners other than Byron, largely because he is interested above all in the Vaudois region's history and its topography.

It is a pity that he does not say more about the Dufour inn because Byron mentions it and it was a favourite haunt of the redoubtable Lady Frances Compton, of whom Sir Walter Scott wrote that she was 'a spirited old lady, fond of dogs and horses, and had a pair of loaded pistols to defend her house in person when it was threatened in the corn bill riots'. She was also, it seems, a great traveller abroad. A later important historian of Montreux notes that 'One of our first foreign guests was Lady Compton, sister of the Duke of Northampton, who stayed at the minister Dufour's, formerly a tutor to the family of the Duke; and so the small lounge of the minister became, in some measure thanks to the presence of Lady Compton, a centre of social gathering for the first visitors to Montreux... the first two hotels opened around 1835.'[14]

Gabriel Dufour of Châtelard died at the age of 93 in June 1828. His death notice, certified by the same doctor (Buenzod) and priest (Bridel) who also attended to Marie Deshayes two years later, states that he had been a minister at Mulsoe Manor which belonged to the Earls of Northampton until 1801. At the time of the nonagenarian Dufour's death, which coincided with the arrival at Clarens in the summer of 1828 of Marie Duplessis's mother, Lady Compton was herself 70 years old. She and Dufour went back a long way and were close enough for Dufour to name his son Charles Gabriel Spencer, after Lady Compton's father, Spencer being one of the Northamptons' preferred first names.[15] Links between members of the English aristocracy and local families and innkeepers of Clarens reach back, it seems, into the late eighteenth century, and may inadvertently, through her mother, connect the lady of the camellias—if distantly—to Byron. It stands to reason that, as a friend of Walter Scott's, Lady Compton probably knew Byron and

she may have met Byron at the Dufours' in 1816, although he does not say
so specifically in his letters. She probably spent most of her last years here
because, when she died on 20 February 1832, the *Registre des Décès* duly
records that, while she was born at Castle Ashby, she lived 'aux Planches',
close to the centre of modern Montreux. It is inconceivable that Lady
Compton and the Andersons, both horse-mad British aristocrats, would not
have known one another in Châtelard–Clarens, which boasted a very small
expatriate community among its 2,055 inhabitants in the 1831 census. If they
did, they must have spoken about Byron, who was then the best-known
Englishman alive and who had stayed in their tiny and remote expatriate
corner only fairly recently.

The full name of the good English Samaritan who sat with Marie
Deshayes in her final hours was Lady Charlotte Anderson Pelham Worsley
Yarborough, born on 20 October 1810, the youngest child of Sir Charles
Anderson Pelham, Baron Yarborough, and of his wife Lady Henrietta.
Lady Henrietta died in June 1813 so that Lady Charlotte Anderson lost
her mother before she was even 3 years old. Many years later this shared
tragedy, the fact that they both lost their mothers when they had been
3 and 4 years old respectively, would consolidate the bond between her
and the lady of the camellias. Charlotte Anderson was 17 when Marie
Deshayes joined her family in Paris, to become their chambermaid first
and then a confidant. The battered wife of Plessis and the female scion of
the Yarboroughs met through the intermediary of the Duhays family and
their connections to the stud at Haras-du-Pin. The link was an English
jockey by the name of Augustin. He had ridden for the legendary house
of Médavy, true-blue equestrian aristocracy, and had retired to Paris where
his wife, then widow, tutored a grand English lady, who can only have
been the then teenage Charlotte Anderson.[16] The Duhays had kept in
touch with Augustin's widow and told her about the plight of Marie
Deshayes; she in turn passed this news on to Lady Anderson, who offered
to take in Marie.

Why would she be so charitable to a complete stranger and did the
underage and unmarried Charlotte Anderson have the authority to employ
a stranger on her own? According to the more authoritative source of two
on this, one written many years after the event by Charles Duhays, a direct
descendant of the Madame Duhays who arranged Marie's safe passage in
1828, 'Lady B. [*sic*], recognizing in the fate of this unhappy woman a strong
similarity to her own, was keen to take her in'. The 'similarity' can hardly

refer to a violent husband as Charlotte Anderson was not married and had no children at that stage. It may have been the early loss of her mother that made her feel so spontaneously charitable towards Marie who had been forced to forsake her children.

Among the Andersons, Marie's life changed in every sense. Her sweet nature and well-bred manners instantly, it seems, won over her employers who became her friends and, indeed, seemed to adore her. Her relationship was primarily with Charlotte Anderson. Although Charlotte was sixteen years younger than Marie, the two women grew very close. They must have been temperamentally similar. Certainly Charlotte's testament many years later, and indeed that of her future husband too, suggests that she was an exceptionally warm and generous person who, like her husband, cared deeply about her servants' welfare after her own death and rewarded them accordingly.

Her employers took Marie Deshayes, the mother of the future lady of the camellias, with them everywhere, perhaps because Charlotte could not bear to be parted from her chaperone. In Paris the Andersons lived, or rented, in the exclusive Faubourg Saint-Honoré, close to the British Embassy. One Sunday they took Marie along to mass in the Sainte-Chapelle when the King, Louis-Philippe I, was present. He spotted the pretty, melancholy Deshayes woman and, according to Charles Duhays, whose family had arranged for Marie to flee the Orne, only had eyes for her. The magnetism of the future lady of the camellias evidently stemmed in large part from her mother.

The Andersons divided their time between Paris, Lake Geneva, and Britain, while also patronizing the spas of Europe. One of these was Chamonix in the Alps, not far from Clarens. The leading Parisian fashion magazine *L'Illustration* described it as 'the meeting-point of the entire *beau monde* of London and Paris; the English above all visit here in droves'.[17] It was during a visit to Chamonix that Lady Charlotte Anderson had her friend Marie Deshayes painted by a local artist, not once but twice. One of these miniatures survives in the Musée de la Dame aux Camélias in Gacé and is reproduced in this book; the other, probably identical, may still be in the possession of the Anderson Yarborough families, unless it was sent by them to Alphonsine's sister Delphine after the death of the lady of the camellias. That Charlotte Anderson was devoted to Marie Deshayes is not in doubt, but to have a favourite servant drawn by a painter seems an almost excessive act of affection. The most plausible explanation is that Marie longed to have two pictures of herself to send home to her girls back in Normandy, to let each of them have an image of her to cherish. Marie clearly confided in Charlotte over time and eventually the gentle Lady Anderson would have learnt the whole truth about the events in Normandy that had triggered Marie's flight.

Marie Deshayes lived with the Andersons for two years and eight months before she died. They cannot have been happy times because she was separated from her girls, but at least she was esteemed and, it seems, loved. Vienne claimed that Marie died of a broken heart, but galloping phthisis is a more likely cause. It is cited by Dumas's heroine who declares: 'My mother died of consumption.'[18] Marie was almost certainly buried in the Clarens cemetery high above Lake Geneva, in one of the loveliest panoramic spots of this region of epic landscapes. Nabokov and Sidney Chaplin now keep her company as do most of the people whose paths she crossed during her short stay here. No Andersons or related names are recorded as dying in the Montreux or Clarens records, apart from Lady Compton. The 26-year-old Herbert Pelham who died in Clarens on 30 May 1881 is probably not related to the Yarborough branch, even though it includes the Pelham name.[19] If Marie Duplessis did at some point make it to the place where her mother died in 1830, she might have taken heart from the idyll that the country churchyard of Clarens is to this day.

If she visited, she may never have told Vienne about it as he would have been bound to mention it. As it is, Marie Duplessis may have known much more about her mother's time in Clarens, and far earlier, than is commonly supposed. The clue is a mystifying afterthought in one of her letters to her uncle after her return to Paris, a letter dated 25 November 1841. The letter itself is reproduced later in its proper chronological place. Its postscript is what really interests us here. It reads 'Bien des amitiés pour moi chez l'anglais', which would seem to mean 'Please pass on my best wishes to the Englishman'. Her French usage 'pour moi' is not entirely idiomatic and could mean that, rather than sending her regards, she is instead telling her uncle that she was treated warmly by the English family.

Biographers of the lady of the camellias have all along taken it for granted that her reference to an unlikely English neighbour in Nonant, Saint-Germain-de-Clairefeuille, or Trouillière must somehow refer to the Andersons or friends of theirs, even though no English names feature any-where in the registers of the état civil of the region. But what if she did not mean to write 'l'anglais' at all, but 'Langlais'? Or, more accurately perhaps, 'Langlois'? The registers for Saint-Germain-de-Clairefeuille for the years

1833–42, the ones that most concern us, consistently spell the local family name 'Langlois', almost certainly the correct orthography, even though the consolidated 1820 index of names, the so-called *liste nominative*, spells 'Langlais'. Common sense suggests that in her postscript Marie Duplessis is referring to the Langlois (Langlais) family and not to non-existent English people. If it had been the Anderson family, or indeed the English jockey Augustin who forged the link between her mother and the Andersons, she would have used their names.

The Langlois were an old Saint-Germain-de-Clairefeuille family as was that of the mother of the future lady of the camellias. They must have known each other well and the links between the Langlois and Deshayes would have been tribal and, possibly, family. My researches in the Archives Vaudoises in Lausanne in May 2013 and in the local history archive in Montreux, which includes Clarens, suggest that there may be a more immediate, less circumstantial, reason for Marie Duplessis's fondness for Langlois, one connected directly to her mother's stay in Montreux. It may constitute an important piece of evidence as it would appear to suggest that she knew much more about her mother's life, and perhaps her death too, than is usually assumed, and that as early as the summer of 1841, if not before.

Marie Deshayes probably arrived in Châtelard in the summer of 1828. At just that time, on 19 June 1828, the police records for Lausanne state that a 'Pierre Langlois' was granted permission to reside in Lausanne.[20] That this was a French Langlois is without doubt, as the police checked only foreign passports and visas, and scrupulously so, as Byron discovered to his chagrin when he was challenged about his lack of identity papers on Lake Geneva. It could be a coincidence that a Langlois turned up in the area at that very time and that he was not related to the Ornois Langlois family of Saint-Germain-de-Clairefeuille. But it is more likely that his presence here was connected to that of Marie Deshayes, that they were friends abroad from the same village, and that he had returned to Saint-Germain-de-Clairefeuille by the time Marie Duplessis visited her family in the summer of 1841. If this train of thought is largely accurate, it would mean that the two sisters early on were well informed about their mother's time in Clarens. Certainly Marie Duplessis's letter to her uncle not only suggests that she was fond of Langlois but also that her uncle knew the Langlois well enough to pass on his niece's regards.

Many years later Montreux and the lady of the camellias would one last time connect when the great actress Sarah Bernhardt appeared as Marguerite

Gautier, the heroine of *La Dame aux Camélias*, in the Kursaal in Montreux. Her performances in the role had become legendary, eventually overtaking even Eugénie Doche, the triumphant original actress in the role, and attracting the attention of Dumas *fils*. What rendered the 1892 Montreux performance a milestone was that it marked Bernhardt's 1000th appearance in the part. Did she or anyone involved in the show that night know that the earthly remains of the mother of Marie Duplessis rested just up the hill from the Kursaal? Or, perhaps, was that the very reason why Bernhardt chose to star in one of her signature roles in Montreux? She after all knew well two of Marie Duplessis's lovers: Dumas *fils* and another man, the father of her baby who was also the lover of Bernhardt's aunt and who has even, sometimes, been thought to be Bernhardt's father because he paid for her education. He is the Pygmalion of this story, in more senses than one.

The young Lady Anderson was 19 when her friend died. She could have posted the portraits to Normandy, or indeed she might have sent for the two semi-orphaned girls, but this did not happen. We will never know why, but it would be a source of regret and sorrow to Lady Anderson in later life, never more so than when she in turn had to confront a terrible bereavement. If Lady Anderson's promise to her friend came to nothing, it may be because, not long after the death of Marie, she met Joseph William Copley of Sprotbrough Hall in Yorkshire. They married by 'special licence' on 19 November 1831 at Brocklesby, the Lincolnshire country seat of the Yarboroughs. Charlotte may have been pregnant at the time, hence the dispensation. Either way, whether conceived out of wedlock or after the marriage, her baby, a girl, would have been born in the course of 1832. It has, unfortunately, not been possible thus far to trace this daughter's birth. All we know is that the baby was a girl.

The news of their mother's death may not have been revealed to Delphine and Alphonsine at the time it happened. However shocked Marie's relatives were by what they heard, they had to protect the two children above all: as long as their mother was thought to be alive the children would enjoy the same influential protection from their monstrous father as their mother. There was no getting rid of Marin Plessis. He continued to haunt the region. Where could he go? Paris? He may well have tried that because he had relatives in the capital and knew how to get there. But in the end he stayed put. In the 1840s rural France remained deeply traditional with little inward or outward migration. All that would change with the imminent arrival of the railways, but in the early 1830s the only travellers among the rural poor were the Roma people or gypsies, who had been moving around since the Middle Ages. Victor Hugo's contemporary portrayal of the gypsy girl Esmeralda in his novel *Notre-Dame de Paris* captures the double-edged fascination the Roma exerted over the rest of the population. The 16-year-old Esmeralda may be fittingly 'bewitching' and kind-hearted, but she is accompanied constantly by a mysterious goat, Djali, who performs tricks on her mistress's tambourine. The Roma people were associated with magic, the black arts and, more commonly and sinisterly, with the kidnapping of children. Plessis knew gypsies, of course: as a roving pedlar he was almost one himself, though the Roma were tribal while he was a loner. When he needed them, though, they would be ready to help him out.

In 1832, when Alphonsine was 8 and her sister 10, the two girls were split up by their family. Looking after them now that the elder was on the threshold of her teens was becoming too much of a burden for Louis Mesnil and his wife, who were into their sixties. In any case, it is likely that throughout the rearing of the girls they were assisted by Agathe Boisard from the neighbouring hamlet of La Porte, some fifteen minutes further down the hill towards Nonant. Agathe was another cousin of the girls on their mother's side. She had been born Françoise Agathe Marre, like Marie Deshayes whose own mother was a Marre. So it came about that the elder sister, Delphine, stayed on at La Trouillière while little Alphonsine now joined the Boisard household. By then the Boisards had three children of their own, aged between 3 and 8 years. It is likely that they expected Alphonsine to assist them with their child-rearing while providing her with a roof over her head. Her father Marin had promised to contribute to the cost of rearing her, but he never paid the family a penny. That he should be involved at all comes as a surprise, but he probably kept a close eye on the girls knowing full well that if their mother reappeared in the Orne her daughters would act as a magnet. By now this nomadic character had temporarily settled in Saint-Germain-de-Clairefeuille, less than twenty minutes across the pastures from Alphonsine in La Porte. The area was criss-crossed by well-kept paths that rendered moving between the villages much easier than it is today.

Little Alphonsine may not have been happy at the Boisards, well-meaning though they seem to have been. This is suggested by the fact that she did not immediately visit them, if she did at all, during her return to Nonant in July 1841. In the end Agathe Boisard could only provide so far for her new charge. It was she who organized her primary education in the school at

Figure 2.3 The church in Saint-Germain-de-Clairefeuille, where Alphonsine Plessis took her first communion and in which her sister Delphine was married. The house visible beyond the church is where her mother hid before fleeing Normandy.

Saint-Germain-de-Clairefeuille. It was here too that Alphonsine was prepared for her first communion at the age of 9.[21] The 'école des filles' that she joined was in the charge of the 'sisters of Providence from Sées', the region's most important bishopric less than twenty miles away. One particular nun who taught Alphonsine was Sister Françoise Huzet: she is listed as 'institutrice' for Saint-Germain in 1831 and later spoke warmly about the little girl she once tutored years earlier.

In the spring of 1833 Alphonsine took her first communion in the church of Saint-Germain (Figure 2.3). How aware was she, if at all, of the celebrated Flemish artwork in the choir as she processed down the aisle with the other little girls? She who later loved art and all things beautiful to the point of being almost a connoisseur can hardly have been impervious to the stunning interior of this exceptional church, even if other thoughts crowded her mind then. Her mother ought to have been present for this first important public ritual. In 1834 Alphonsine was 10 years old, a child without a childhood and nothing to exercise her quicksilver intelligence. News of the loss of her mother became public knowledge in March 1834. All hope must have seemed forever dashed when she heard this announcement. It is possible that the death of Marie Deshayes had remained a secret to all but a few of her closest relatives until an official extract from the 'registre des décès' of Montreux arrived in Courménil. It is an almost identical copy of the original cited above and reads

> died in the parish of Châtelard (Montreux), Des Hayes,
> Wife Duplessis, Marianne
> Profession: chambermaid.
> Born Curménil [Courménil], Department of the Orne, France
> Residing at (residence not indicated)
> Aged thirty-three [sic: she was in fact 36]
> Daughter of Des Hayes
> And Official status: wife Duplessis[22]

It is not known who requested this document. Marie Deshayes's father was still alive in Courménil at this point but he almost certainly learnt of his daughter's death shortly after her decease in 1830. If he did indeed have a hand in hiding her when she first fled, he must have kept in touch with either the Duhays or Anderson families, or both. Also, he would not have done anything to jeopardize the welfare of her two girls, unlike this document which *de facto* conferred to Marin Plessis sole authority over them as the surviving parent and guardian. The most likely explanation for the news breaking now, after nearly four years, is that Plessis heard a rumour about the death of his wife and asked the parish priest of Courménil, who had married them, to find out on his behalf. It was not that he was illiterate. On the contrary: to judge from his signatures he was able to write 'Marin Plessis' very clearly and even attractively, but an official request by the priest of Courménil for a death certificate would carry more weight than a pedlar's letter.

Plessis was undoubtedly horrible, but he may have been more complex than this narrative suggests, overlayering his story, as it does, by drinking and abuse. Perhaps from time to time, as he ranged through the hills and plains of the region, even he was pained at the thought of his lost wife. They had once loved each other after all and, like many violent drunks, he may have been haunted in his more lucid moments by what he had done to the woman who had married him. If he had been Bill Sikes to Nancy, he also needs to be seen, at least in part, through the lens of his younger daughter's loyalty to him, in spite of everything he had done to her mother and also to her. In the end he probably sinned against Alphonsine more than against anyone else; and yet, from a recessed corner of her hurt nature, she glimpsed something in him that made her forgive him.

The formal request from Courménil had elicited an official answer.[23] Now everyone knew that Marie Deshayes had died, including her daughters. Six years and two months had passed since they had last seen their beloved mother's face. Whether they learnt anything about what had happened to her after her flight from Normandy we will never know. But it is highly probable that the Duhays family from 'Le Mesnil' in Saint-Germain-de-Clairefeuille kept the family informed throughout and that Alphonsine and Delphine were told too about the English baroness as they grew up.

To make matters even worse, and perhaps because her mother's death released them from immediate family links to her, the Boisards now told Alphonsine that they could not continue feeding her: she would henceforth have to fend for herself. If by this drastic act the Boisards hoped to force her father's hand, they were wrong as he resolutely refused to provide anything towards her upkeep. Over the years other cousins had helped out sporadically, but the family could barely survive even without her additional mouth to feed. From now on little Alphonsine would be welcome only to sleep at the Boisards at night, but she could no longer eat there.

How could this 10-year-old possibly cope with this? She must have felt utterly rejected. Nor did she have, it seems, the option to rejoin her great-uncle Louis's home at La Trouillière where her sister lived. Why she remained loyal to the people at La Trouillière is a mystery. Whatever the reason why they could not take her in, she must have accepted it absolutely. Her desolation that spring and summer of 1834 is hard to imagine. At one stroke she had become the goose girl of the Grimms' fairy tale, a motherless waif adrift in the hills of Nonant and Saint-Germain in utter inner solitude and reduced to the ultimate humiliation of begging. Few pictures render Alphonsine's predicament more poignantly than the 'Little Beggar Girl' ('Petite Mendiante') by William-Adolphe Bouguereau (1825–1905), an artist contemporary with her. The child's wistful hurt expression and rich cascade of hair could be Alphonsine Plessis's, as could the little girl's gypsy clothing (Figure 2.4).

Hunger now cruelly shaped her life to the point where, if she could not find food, she might starve to death, particularly at the onset of winter. She started roaming the pastures in search of food, wandering forlornly through

Figure 2.4 *The Little Beggar Girl (Petite Mendiante)* by William–Adolphe
Bouguereau, an artist contemporary with Alphonsine Plessis.

the hills, copses, and meadows between Nonant and Le Merlerault in the
south and Exmes and la Castelle in the north, asking for work and begging
at local farms. Sometimes when she was hungry and could not find anything, she sought out her sister's home at La Trouillère, but usually she called
on other members of her extended family for bread and water.

Then, as summer turned to autumn and the haymaking and harvest seasons, she joined in as best she could, thus earning handouts here and there.
Every little bit helped and the farm labourers, many of whom felt sorry for
the child, shared their meagre fare with her, their soup, bread, and cider. At
a price though, because before long she became their plaything. She thought
nothing of it but enjoyed the attention and, it appears, their inevitable
caresses, as she later confessed to a friend. The way the men talked and acted

infected her and soon she shed all reserve and control. If not exactly a feral child, she became precociously sexual, unaware, in the words of Romain Vienne, that clothes were not just for keeping her warm but also meant to cover nakedness and thus restrain sexuality. Quite how long this desolate and dangerous period of her life lasted is not known. It was one thing to be out in the open all day during the summer and early autumn months; quite another to drift over the exposed hills of the Orne in the dark, wet, and often icy winter months. It is possible that her periods of begging and drifting were confined to the summer months. There was no mandatory school to structure her life so that from now on Alphonsine was immersed in a world without boundaries. It seems that she lived this chaotic life for at least two years, a rural cider-drinking waif straight out of Fagin's soup kitchen, but with sex; a prepubescent Nancy rather than a saintly and sexless Oliver Twist, although in truth Alphonsine was always both Nancy and Oliver. If her first sexual awakenings were natural, their context was sordid and exploitative in a world of shepherds, farmers, pedlars, and drifters.

As the men fondled her, she saw what they did and what they liked. One day, perhaps inevitably, she went further and propositioned a teenage farmhand by the name of Marcel, the same Marcel she invited to lunch with her at the Viennes' five years later. She fancied him: she was 12 while he was 17½. In her own words later, she seduced him with 'Come on, I will do like Josephine and you, you will do like Alfred', obviously referring to two people she had watched having sex. It was her first time. In the light of what would happen to her shortly, it is appropriate to wonder whether she was hurt and whether the two of them really did have full intercourse. If they did she must have bled, in which case her hysterical reaction later over her first period makes little sense. On the threshold of her teens she turned into a pretty girl. The more attractive she became, the easier, she realized, it was for her to feed herself by using her looks, even though she was still only a child. Sex with Marcel was probably followed by other such encounters. Did she ever, during this time, run into her father who was combing the same fields at that time? Many of the men with whom she consorted during these forays in the woods and hills around Nonant and Exmes would have known the pedlar Marin Plessis. Because of his reputation for violence and his nickname of 'sorcerer', they may have been wary of tangling too much with his daughter. For once he may, unwittingly, have done her a favour in that she may have been marginally safer from abuse once they knew whose daughter she was.

Rumours of the little girl's promiscuity finally reached the ears of her aunt Agathe Boisard. Appalled by what she learnt and not wanting to remain responsible for her, she took Alphonsine to her father in Saint-Germain-de-Clairefeuille where he lived at the time, demanding that at last he must do his duty. She appears to have thought that he could rein in the little girl's sexuality before she reached puberty and became pregnant. She might as well have entrusted Little Red Riding Hood to the Big Bad Wolf. The degenerate Plessis instantly spotted an opportunity for making money from his youngest child's blossoming looks, although even he held off briefly before taking that final step and turning her infant sexuality into cash.

At first he placed her with a laundry business in Nonant run by a Madame Toutain, someone who, against the odds, would be kind to the sorcerer's daughter, for the sake of her mother and probably because she understood the child's precarious predicament and liked her. Also, she proved to be an industrious and capable worker. Alphonsine would stay loyal to this employer in later life. So it came about that she worked, and presumably lodged, in Nonant for several months. During this period she regularly called on her father for her weekly Sunday visit which, according to Vienne, usually lasted an hour. Since these happened on Sundays we may assume that it had to do with her attending mass in her first communion church. Perhaps the Toutains were trying to implant some kind of moral structures in the little girl's life after two years of anarchy and drifting. Plessis could hardly fail to notice during these visits how pretty the lissom Alphonsine was becoming, if she did indeed see him on Sunday, before or after church, for it is impossible to imagine the sorcerer at worship. He must have been penniless and desperate, because he now decided to make money from pimping for his own daughter. She was his after all, he must have reasoned, and plenty of men seemed to want her; also, she appeared to have sex on the brain, so he was only letting her follow her instincts. He would start by lending her to a 'friend' who had more money than sense and who had, it seems, expressed an interest.

3

L'affaire Plantier

Exmes 1837

So one Sunday in August 1837 Plessis took the 13-year old Alphonsine to the village of Exmes above Haras-du-Pin, a substantial hamlet with a hybrid cathedral church. He introduced her to her new special friend, a wealthy septuagenarian shoemaker by the name of Plantier, who lived in a mean and dreary cut called 'Four Banal', that is 'communal baking-oven', after the site of the village's bakery (Figure 3.1). Four Banal links the church square to the village's main street, at the corner of which stood Plantier's house. Jean-Marie Choulet, the curator of the local museum of the lady of the camellias, knows this part of the world and its connection to Alphonsine's story better than anyone. According to him, Plantier's 'small house and courtyard' belonged to the local wigmaker Jean-Pierre Chéron, 'dit Plessis'.[1] The deal that Plessis and Plantier had struck was that the sorcerer's daughter would 'entertain' the old satyr in return for a certain sum of money that would be paid out to both of them every weekend.

Quite how aware she was of what was going on is hard to determine. She probably understood full well that it was her body and sexuality that the two men were bartering over. It was the link between body and money that must have baffled her at first. So far no-one had ever paid for her favours in any way other than with food. Money must have been a hard concept to grasp because she had been too small when her mother was trying to earn it, and the link between it and food was not necessarily one that she had encountered before. But now she did so with considerable alacrity. If she was afraid of the old lecher she was not so for long, it seems, for on her return to Madame Toutain's after her first weekend in Exmes she proudly displayed to her the cash she had collected in Four Banal.

Figure 3.1 The close of 'Four Banal' in the village of Exmes, where Alphonsine Plessis was kept in sexual servitude by old Plantier in the buildings on the left of the picture.

This went on for several months. Alphonsine's work as a laundress started to suffer, presumably partly because her wages were far inferior to what she received from old Plantier. Eventually, one Monday, she failed to show up for work in Nonant. When a couple of days later she did, her demeanour and cavalier attitude caused Madame Toutain to confront her: what was going on in Exmes, she wanted to know, to which Alphonsine replied that she and Plantier 'amused' each other: that was all. But her employer already suspected that something rather more sinister was afoot. After all the two villages were only three miles apart. Its cathedral notwith-standing Exmes was a smaller place even than Nonant and the locals had started to talk. They knew full well who the little girl was and undoubt-edly had a pretty good idea about what was going on at the bachelor Plantier's. There were moreover Toutains in Exmes, relatives of the Toutains of Nonant. They had probably tipped their cousins the wink since the Toutains were running a successful family business that could not afford to be contaminated by the paedophile machinations of the two miscreants.

But their racket was about to be exposed by nature itself which intervened to save Alphonsine.

Suddenly one day she fled Plantier's house. When shortly afterwards local people found her, the little girl was hysterical, wandering aimlessly in the meadows around Exmes. Something dreadful, it seems, had happened to her: according to Vienne, 'she had become a young woman...a sudden terror had taken hold of her at the onset of puberty.' Tragically she learnt precociously that sex could be traded for money before she knew about her body's most basic biology. She had no mother to tell her the facts of life. On the very day she reached puberty she resided in the house of the first person ever to pay her for sex: Old Plantier was her first client and her father her original procurer. She was 13 years and 8 months old, and could be expected to be menstruating by then, as is made clear by Ambroise Tardieu, the chief forensic scientist of nineteenth-century France, who expressed concern when examining a well-developed 13-year-old girl who had not yet started her periods.

She later confided in Vienne that her panic at her first period stemmed from a belief that her bleeding was divine retribution for her sins with Plantier. No prosecution ensued when she was found and no judicial documentation of the affair survives, even though the police and local magistrates did, it appears, investigate. Nothing could in the end be proved against the two villains. In the meantime the little girl was placed with a caring family of innkeepers a hundred yards or so up the main road from Plantier's house. Here, in a building that still stands today, she worked for several months as a chambermaid for the Denis family (Figure 3.2).[2] To ensure that Alphonsine was safe, Madame Denis slept in the same room as her new charge, who was diligent and grateful. The proximity of old Plantier's cottage may be more disconcerting to the modern reader than it was to the little girl, who seemed not unduly afraid of the old abuser. They must have met repeatedly during this period, if only in church on Sundays, but we may be sure that Plantier kept a low profile, so low in fact that all trace of him seems to have disappeared from the official records.

While all writers on the story of the lady of the camellias confidently refer to him, the fact is that no Plantier is listed anywhere in the *état civil* or any other records of the period relating to Exmes. Why this should be so is unclear. He would certainly not have been expunged for molesting a little girl. Things did not work that way. There is really only one possibility, namely that the only source of the affair, Romain Vienne, altered the name.

Figure 3.2 The Denis inn, Exmes, where Alphonsine Plessis sheltered after escaping from Plantier.

Although Plantier is a name found in the region, none existed in Exmes. The question is why Vienne would want to disguise the name of a villain who had probably been dead for fifty years by the time his book appeared in 1888. The obvious excuse for a pseudonym is that Vienne and his family lived locally in Nonant at the time of publication and Exmes is a neighbouring village. It is quite possible, indeed probable, that members of Plantier's extended family (he was a bachelor) still lived there. It is worth pausing over this because parts of Vienne's book read like an encoded memoir. Some of the time he offers up the real names of people, as for example with the nun who taught Alphonsine at school. For all her important lovers, however, he hints at names that only those who were privy to certain details of the story could identify. The genealogies of Exmes are hardly complex or extensive. If Plantier is not the real name of the culprit, could we not guess at his identity from the extant records of the village? It ought to be possible, but successive researchers have signally failed to do so. This is the more surprising as the records for Exmes are fairly full and the village was small enough in the 1830s to allow sleuths to sift through all the likely suspects who fit the profile of the offender with regard to age and unmarried status. What further muddies the waters is that while Vienne appears to be squeamish about naming the real Plantier, he is quite specific about where the blackguard lived. Even fifty years after these events, many people in Exmes would have known exactly who had inhabited the corner of Four Banal in years gone by.

Alphonsine had sheltered in the Denis inn for a few months when her father showed up once again. It was October 1838. The Denis angrily showed him the door but the following day he dragged his daughter away anyway and took her up the road to neighbouring Gacé, the largest town of the region. Here he put her to work in a factory that produced umbrellas, not far from the old château which today houses 'Le musée de *La Dame aux Camélias*'. The business was owned by one Louis Fremin; Vienne calls it 'la maison Firmin'. In the factory the 14-year-old Alphonsine was befriended by a woman who worked in the same building and who, it seems, eventually joined her in Paris. She has never been positively identified but Vienne asserts that she returned to Gacé in later life and that she died there. A Prudence Zélonide Saussaie died in Gacé in 1871 at the age of 52, making her nearly five years older than Marie Duplessis. She would only enter the frame because in *La Dame aux Camélias* Marie Duplessis's procuress is called 'Prudence Duvernoy', who is however unequivocally based on the real life Clémence Pratt, Marie Duplessis's neighbour in the Madeleine. It is more likely that, if a Gacé girl did indeed fetch up with Marie in Paris, it would have been her chambermaid Clotilde.

Around Christmas 1838 the restless Plessis reappeared. He had decided on a whim to take his younger daughter to Paris, to apprentice her as a laundress ('*blanchisseuse*') in a small business run on the outskirts of the city by one of her mother's many cousins. Before setting off for the capital, father and daughter sheltered in a barn near Exmes where he was living rough at the time. What happened next is reported with outrage by her two most reliable contemporary chroniclers, Charles Duhays and Romain Vienne. Both agree, independently, that over the next fortnight Plessis repeatedly engaged in incestuous sex with his daughter. She was barely past puberty; her wretched father was raping a child. This information can only have come from Alphonsine herself. Years later, during the Saturday evening walk with Vienne in the summer of 1841, she nevertheless defended her appalling father. Was this the sign of a desperate collusion of abused with abuser? Was the daughter as attracted to the reckless charmer Marin Plessis as her poor mother had been, and to such an extent that there was nothing she could not forgive him? There is a further possible explanation for her apparent forgiveness, namely that after serving her 'apprenticeship' in the sex trade in Paris she believed that most men were equally vile and that her father was not that different from the men who paid her for sex in the big city. They were richer and vastly more urbane, but in the end they desired her in the same way as Plantier and her father had. Not since her mother left had she known love or tenderness; what others called love she had only ever experienced as sex.

A wretched childhood marred by sexual abuse was one that she inevitably shared with many of her contemporaries. The victims were almost invariably little girls at the mercy of men, including their fathers. A doctor born in 1818, six years before Marie Duplessis, eventually lifted the lid on this nightmare of hidden sexual assaults—secret by convention, shame, and taboos against incest. This was Ambroise Tardieu whose book *Étude Médico-Légale sur les Attentats aux Mœurs*, published in 1857, was the first systematic study of what is now termed child abuse. Tardieu's *Étude* went through several more editions after 1857, including an ever increasing number of case histories, which he called 'Observations'. They make devastating reading, because of their content, of course, but also because Tardieu uses a doctor's clinical language, stripped of any euphemisms. His steely anatomical language leaves nothing to the imagination. The examination of little girls in his 'Observations' is conducted in the anatomically specific terms of modern gynaecology. He wants to tell the truth, no matter what it takes. One can imagine the agony that the children and young teenage girls underwent at the time—first the horror of abuse and then the shaming aftermath of examination—when so much of the human body remained officially uncharted territory, let alone needing to confront it in the context of sexual abuse and venereal infection.

Many of Tardieu's 'Observations' resonate with the fate of little Alphonsine, but one does more so than most given her predicament at Plantier's. It concerns a 71-year-old schoolmaster who regularly abused an 8-year-old girl by the name of Adéline (also called Élise) Beaunise. Eventually the little girl started suffering from serious discharges, which her mother spotted on her sheets. She notified the authorities, which is how Tardieu and his colleagues came to examine her. The little girl was furtive and slight, they record, and her eyes had unnaturally dark rings for someone so young, which the doctors interpreted as a sign of extreme mental stress. They could not get her to collaborate fully, but they noticed that she was still a virgin, even though the old schoolmaster had repeatedly abused her. He would hoist her up on a stool, spread her legs, and slide a finger inside her. On some occasions it was something else—the little girl did not say what—and he rubbed against her. Once she felt that her legs were all wet. He never hurt her physically and she did not hurt when she urinated even though her insides were inflamed. The doctors concluded that the old abuser had passed on a venereal infection to the little girl, because he 'suffered from a massive double inguinal hernia, genital warts, and considerable urethral discharges, venereal in origin and contagious', and that his rubbing his member against her vulva was the reason for her infection.[3] The degenerate schoolmaster had been careful not to rupture his victim's hymen. Had he done so, he might have laid himself open more readily to a charge of rape, regardless of whether or not the terrified little girl was prepared to testify. Perhaps Plantier was similarly careful not to penetrate little Alphonsine fully, because he suspected that she too was a virgin. That Alphonsine was not as yet 'réglée', in Tardieu's word, probably saved her when she was sold to Plantier. The old man may not have known that she had already engaged in pre-pubescent sex. Perhaps she held out on this because she knew full well what he would do if he knew that she had already had sex.

Rape was notoriously hard to prove, as Alexandre Jean-Baptiste Parent-Duchâtelet noted in a ground-breaking study of prostitution in Paris that appeared in 1836, the year before Marie Duplessis was hived off to Plantier. His two-volume report was entitled *De la Prostitution dans la ville de Paris: considérée sous le rapport de l'hygiène, de la morale*. Parent-Duchâtelet was a doctor who had made his name with the first ever serious scientific research on the sewers of Paris and the danger posed by noxious and toxic gases rising from untreated human waste left to rot in the open air.[4] From the material detritus of the big city, he progressed to its moral sewer, prostitution, complementing his medical training with an assured grasp of the sociological issues involved. Parent-Duchâtelet paved the way for Tardieu by first daring to be fully explicit about the anatomy of female sexuality. It was possible to do this primarily because the women in question were prostitutes. After extensive research, Parent-Duchâtelet concluded, with consternation, that rape was much more common than was usually supposed but that the victims' parents often covered up the offence to save their daughters' honour and thus let the guilty off the hook.[5]

The extent to which young women were fair game for sexual predators can be gleaned from the account of an attempted rape in the autobiography of the celebrated Parisian dancer Céleste Mogador. Her real name was Élisabeth-Céleste Veinard, later Comtesse de Chabrillan; she was born the same year as Marie Duplessis. Her multi-volume *Mémoires de Céleste Mogador* (1848) provides a relentlessly candid perspective on the world in which she grew up. There may be nothing quite like it in nineteenth-century writing by women. Her story charts the slide of an assaulted teenage girl into prostitution, her survival, and, eventually, her successful emergence into respectability and esteem.

Élisabeth-Céleste was 15 when she found herself alone in a house in the Marais in Paris with her mother's lover Vincent, who had known her since she was a child. One night when her mother was away for a few days, to nurse her ailing father, Vincent assaulted Élisabeth-Céleste. She pleaded with him, pointing out that she was virtually his daughter, but to no avail. Picking her up he held her with 'Shut up, give yourself freely or I will take you by force.' Recoiling at his touch and his 'damp mouth' she thought she was lost: 'My struggle was futile when, on a sudden inspiration, I bit his arm so fiercely that he screamed and let me go.' What saved her in the end was the breaking of a glass pane which attracted the attention of neighbours and caused him to flee. Élisabeth-Céleste drifted out of the house and into the night. Shortly afterwards she was arrested and taken to a women's prison where she met women younger than herself, female children, who were locked up for begging and soliciting. Presently an intense friendship blossomed between Élisabeth-Céleste and a young prostitute by the name of Denise. When Élisabeth-Céleste was released back into her mother's keeping and that of the degenerate Vincent, her mother refused to believe her daughter while the lover brazenly accused the daughter of being a jealous fantasist. In the end Élisabeth-Céleste fled home to rejoin her friend Denise in a brothel.[6]

Horrendous as it may seem, Paris had a number of child prostitutes. They caused particular grief to scrupulous doctors like Parent-Duchâtelet who found 'examining young, prepubescent prostitutes who are physically children' profoundly distressing. While the textbooks were categoric about the symptoms of rape, experience on the ground was very different, to the point where, as Parent-Duchâtelet concludes, some girls who had worked as prostitutes for ten or twelve years were so pristinely preserved sexually as to make the doctors wonder whether they were not virgins. From his extensive forensic work in prisons and hospitals he concluded, when talking about rape and pre-pubescent prostitutes, that even in cases of rape it was often difficult to establish clear intimate physiological differences between victims and other women. Villains like Plantier and Plessis did not know this. They may have presumed that as long as her hymen was intact no-one could prove abuse, unaware of the fact that legally much more than a broken hymen was required to prove rape. Alphonsine's predicament at Plantier's may have been even worse than little Adéline's, although at least she was not obviously frightened of him when they were alone in his house in Exmes. The difference is that Adéline had parents who loved her and wanted to protect her, while the girl from the Orne not only did not have a mother but was prostituted by her own father. We will never know what happened to little Alphonsine at the mercy of her barbarous father, but it was probably not that different from the stories related here. Her trajectory from abused child to kept woman and courtesan has its own predictable logic. From the shepherds of her native Orne, and from Plantier and Plessis, she gleaned that men wanted women in ways that she could never have imagined during the days when her mother was still there to look after her and her sister.

In January 1839 Plessis escorted Alphonsine to Paris. He was too poor to afford the stage coach from Nonant. Instead he prevailed on some of his gypsy friends to give him and his daughter a lift to Paris. Once they arrived in the capital he took her to a relative of her mother's family, one Madame Vital, who secured her a place in a small laundry business in the rue de l'Echiquier near Porte Saint-Denis in the 10th arrondissement. There he left her to earn her living as best she could. When Plessis returned to the Orne a few days later on his own, the local people began to suspect that he must have sold his pretty girl to the gypsies. Her sister Delphine and other members of her family also demanded to know whether Alphonsine was safe. It was only when other Orne visitors to Paris reported that the younger Plessis girl was alive and well, that their father was off the hook.

4

Working girls in Paris
1839–1841

After a brief spell as a laundry woman, Alphonsine joined a firm of milliners (*modistes*). The business, 'un petit magasin de modes', was owned by a friend of Madame Vital, a certain Mlle Urbain, of 8 rue de Louvois in a building that still stands, in a small square bordering on the Bibliothèque Nationale Richelieu and ten minutes away from Palais-Royal. The future lady of the camellias now became a seamstress (*couturière*), an occupation closer to her heart than doing the laundry for demanding Parisian hotels.

From that very time an extraordinary glimpse of Alphonsine, on the eve of her meteoric rise, survives. She was working at Mlle Urbain's when she was spotted on the Pont-Neuf by Paris's leading theatrical entrepreneur, Nestor Roqueplan, king flaneur of the boulevard and director at some point or other during his illustrous career of the legendary Variétés theatre as well as of the Paris Opéra.[1] In the late 1830s Pont-Neuf was renowned for its coffee huts ('baraques') and chip vendors who were trading from makeshift stalls.[2] Roqueplan was people-watching, a leisurely pursuit indulged in with relish by dandies like him, when he noticed a ravenous, waif-like creature eating a green apple while staring intently at the sizzling chips. She was so obviously hungry that he took pity on her and bought her a portion. She greedily devoured the chips without saying a word. Whether he really acted out of charity or whether he expected something in return, he does not tell, but as Roqueplan seems rarely to express an erotic interest in women we may suppose that this was an innocent act of kindness.[3] Three years after this encounter on a Seine bridge, he ran into the same young woman again in the Ranelagh, Paris's most fashionable and aristocratic pleasure garden in the 1840s.[4] She was virtually unrecognizable: dressed in the finest fabrics of the

Figure 4.1 A rare photograph of Paris in 1852, five years after Marie Duplessis's death, showing Notre-Dame de Paris and the adjacent hospital Hôtel-Dieu, taken from the boulevard Saint-Michel.

capital, well spoken, the distillation of elegance and style, and on the arm of Agénor de Guiche Gramont, one of the most eligible young aristocrats in Paris. She had become demi-monde royalty: a virtually illiterate country girl had metamorphosed into the most sought-after woman in the capital, openly maintained by rich and powerful lovers.

Around the time of her Pont-Neuf meeting with Roqueplan, Alphonsine became good friends with two other young women at the milliner's. Together the threesome started to frequent the neighbouring arcades of Palais-Royal, the autumn fêtes at Saint-Cloud, the Fête des Loges at Saint-Germain-en-Laye, and the 'Bal Mabille' on the Champs Élysées, the preferred dance venue of Parisians of all classes in the 1830s and '40s. It occurs repeatedly in Balzac's novels, while its chief claim to fame today is that the *cancan* was born here. In *Mémoires*, Mogador recalls visits to Mabille:

> It was nine o'clock when we arrived at the Allée des Veuves... Mabille used to be a litte country ball, illuminated by oil lamps... one paid half a franc entry fee... it was the preferred meeting place of footmen and

chambermaids at a time when they were less elegant than their masters and mistresses. [I]t was a modest garden...jolly working girls and milliners could tell us all about it...the Ball was making progress...one now paid a franc for admission.[5]

Hers was the perspective of a female *artiste* at the most popular public venue where social classes mingled freely. Male stories about working girls dancing at Mabille were rather different. As it is, one of the most illustrious names in France left us his account of routine visits to Mabille: Edmond de Goncourt, joint founder with his brother Jules of France's most esteemed literary prize. He was two years older than Alphonsine and frequented many of the same places at the same time as her. That the Goncourts knew her is clear from a review they wrote of Dumas's play *La Dame aux Camélias*.[6] He left an unforgettable record of the world of predatory sex into which Alphonsine now ventured, a world in which young men picked up women without, it seems, the slightest scruple. What follows is not a story about rape, but it could almost be about just that. The guilty party is one of France's most revered literary figures to this day:

> I was twenty-four, I think, and at that time I often went to Mabille, where one evening I met a girl of sixteen or seventeen, accompanied by her mother, a woman with the head of a procuress. The girl had big, sky-blue eyes, set close to a long aquiline nose, and she was tall, thin, flat-chested, and dressed in the humble clothes of a grisette.[7]
>
> I danced with her that evening—people danced in those days. Then I met her again the following nights, and after seven or eight evenings spent almost entirely dancing quadrilles and polkas with her, she readily granted the rendezvous I asked her for.
>
> I took her to a little apartment occupied by one of my young cousins at the bottom of the rue d'Amsterdam. And there, intimidated by her silence and the angelic look in her eyes and impeded by what I took to be physical malformation, I muffed her twice. Finally the second time, as she was getting ready to go, I threw her on to a sofa in the ante-room; and while I was on my knees, taking my pleasure with her, I heard something like the sound of a toy drum bursting, and I saw tears come into her eyes, though she did not utter a single cry, a single groan, a single sigh. And when she got up, her thin summer dress was stained with blood...That habituée of Mabille was a virgin. I would never have thought it possible.
>
> She was a strange creature, that girl, with the ecstatic pallor of her face when we made love together, the inert passivity of her body, in which nothing was alive but the pounding of her heart, and the expression in her big blue eyes,

which occasionally gleamed with the perversity of an angel cast out of Heaven. Ah, those eyes! I have seen them since at Florence, in that snake-eyed angel in Simon Memmi's Annunciation.

I cannot say that I was in love with her; but I felt a sort of curiosity, an affectionate curiosity about the secretive, enigmatic creature that was inside her, together with a little of that proud gratitude that any man feels towards a woman who has given him her virginity.[8]

It is not clear from this whether Goncourt paid the young woman he had so brutally possessed. He does not mention money, but he does assert that her mother resembled 'a procuress'. The chaperoning of young women by their mothers was not uncommon in the period, and sometimes they were indeed their procuresses, as in Alfred de Musset's poem *Rolla*, first published in 1833. Alphonsine Plessis was 9 years old when the poem appeared; eventually, as Marie Duplessis, she too would have a guardian matron in the form of a middle-aged former courtesan, who shadowed her at the opera and theatre and arranged for meetings with her charge. Not only that, but this companion, who ran an impressive legitimate business alongside her pimping, dragged her real daughter to shows with her for cover. Even the mother–daughter bond could not resist the pounding juggernaut of sex and greed that was bearing down on the roaring Paris of the 1840s.

As an intelligent, alert young woman, Alphonsine must have been acutely aware of the dangers of the world of Parisian prostitution, a swamp of syphilis, poverty, and violence. These were starkly set out by Parent-Duchâtelet, who records that

> Every day one encounters, whether in hospitals or in the infirmaries of prisons, young prostitutes, barely launched in their professions and as yet childless, whose vaginas are further dilated than the sex organs of married women who have undergone five or six childbirths. At the same time one here meets women who, after twelve or fifteen years as prostitutes and while exhibiting on their faces and figures the hallmarks of serious decay, have vaginas which show no sign of alteration. My attention was drawn one day, in the Prison des Madelonettes [a women's prison in Paris], to a 51-year-old streetwalker who had worked as a prostitute in Paris since the age of 15 and whose sex organs were so pristine that they could have been mistaken for those of a virgin having just come through puberty.[9]

From his countless examinations of streetwalkers, Parent-Châtelet concluded that there was no anatomical way *other than syphilis* to tell honest women from prostitutes. Parent-Châtelet died at the age of 46. Had he lived, he might have joined the ranks of the Louis Pasteurs of medicine. His suggestion that syphilis could be a sexual barometer provoked a strong response from another specialist in the field, as we will see presently, someone who was well aware of the fact that, by transmission, this terrible and contagious curse afflicted the guilty and the innocent alike. This other person, one of Paris's most senior police officers, not only campaigned for research into palliative and hopefully curative treatment of the nineteenth-century disease, but was anxious too that a cure for syphilis should not be seen as a passport to a licentious lifestyle. The fact that prostitutes and promiscuous men were the chief sufferers must not, he argued, mean that the state should therefore go easy on the search for a cure.

What Alphonsine needed to do, if she wanted to live free from hunger and rise above the casual cruelty of men like the Goncourts and a life of utter drudgery, was to use her looks and her intelligence to find a protector, a lover who paid for sex but who would keep her free from any kind of indigence while allowing her a measure of freedom; and without her having to endure the suffering and dangers of a professional street prostitute. By joining Mlle Urbain's she had not only moved into the centre of the big city and into the immediate vicinity of the glamorous and seedy hub of Palais-Royal, but she had also escaped the constant scrutiny of her increasingly disapproving relative. She still returned to Madame Vital at night to sleep; but not always. Before long, inevitably, the two women fell out. At first Madame Vital tried to warn Alphonsine, troubled by how the beauty of the girl from Nonant inexorably drew men towards her; the wrong kind of men, men who were looking for women to keep as paramours.

Just such a man, an affluent bourgeois whom Vienne names as 'Nollet', a widower and owner of one of the restaurants in Palais-Royal, started courting the *modistes* of Mlle Urbain; the Three Graces, as the young women were known to their friends. The central location of Palais-Royal, its enclosed park, galleries, and restaurants, including the Véfour (now Le Grand Véfour) in which Alphonsine Plessis ate later with her powerful friends, acted as a magnet that drew into its ambit Paris's aristocrats, gamblers, cruisers, and young women like Alphonsine and her friends. It was the trendiest place in town until 1840 when new legislation banned 'les jeux publics' at Palais-Royal. Here, it was well known, young women plied their trade. A contemporary witness records that 'Palais-Royal owed its splendour to its gambling houses and to the young women, as frivolous as they were charming, who had here pitched their tents.'[10]

In the late summer of 1839 this 'Nollet' set her up as his mistress in a small love-nest apartment in the rue de l'Arcade. The fact that he was wealthy enough to afford a mistress in a small central Paris apartment makes one wonder whether he was not in reality M. Collot, who then owned the acclaimed restaurant Trois Frères Provençaux in the Galerie de la Rotonde, Palais-Royal, nos. 96–99 (later called Galerie de Beaujolais) on the same side as Le Grand Véfour at nos. 81–82, a place that she and members of her circle such as Lola Montez later patronized; or M. Questel, who owned the equally sought-after Café de Foy, also in Palais-Royal. But Collot is the more likely candidate: his name agrees more readily with Nollet and thereby accords more with Vienne's practice of using pseudonyms that phonically evoke the hidden names behind them. In a revealing survey about the cafés and restaurants of Palais-Royal, the former doctor and eventual grandee journalist and director of the Paris Opéra, Louis Véron, notes about the Trois Frères Provençaux that Collot 'for the last fifteen years managed to retain that house's brilliant reputation and prosperity'.[11]

After years of being shunted about, the 16-year-old Alphonsine now had a home of her own. She was fed and looked after by a lover who paid all her bills. It must have seemed a worthwhile bargain. Of course she would have known that she might never be allowed back into proper society. But respectable 'society' was hardly something she could ever aspire to as a laundress or 'modiste', and what other opportunities were open to her? In the early stages of her affair with Nollet, Alphonsine failed to return to her relative Vital's house one night. She stayed away for several days and then wrote to Madame Vital to explain that she had found a 'protector': could Madame forgive her and would she receive her the following Sunday when she was hoping to call? The response was swift and clear: 'If you ever set foot in this house again, I will chase you out like a piece of vermin.' The two women never met again although years later Madame Vital would attend Alphonsine's funeral. Alphonsine also called upon the rather more gracious Mlle Urbain for a tearful farewell. She had been a good employer and refused to judge her young charge, who in return cherished her for the rest of her short life.

By letting Nollet set her up in a home in which she was comfortable enough and where she would be visited for sex by her bourgeois lover, Alphonsine became a kept woman, an amateur prostitute not unlike the London women Stendhal reminisced about in his *Souvenirs d'Égotisme*. Stendhal's memoirs chime with Goncourt's, though they refer to another city during the decade before this one. Stendhal died in 1842, at the height of Marie Duplessis's 'reign' in Paris, and today rests a mere hundred yards up from her in the Cimetière de Montmartre, neighbours almost with the nearby young Dumas who had been her lover. The author of two of the greatest French novels of the nineteenth century, *Le Rouge et le Noir* and *La Chartreuse de Parme*, records visiting young prostitutes in London in a similarly unsentimental, matter-of-fact vein as does Goncourt, though without the unconscionable cruelty of the former. It is revealing about the men's casual attitude to what they were doing, but it above all highlights the almost banal domesticity of the amateur, freelance prostitution that was rife in all the major European cities.

Stendhal was staying in London with two friends, called 'Barot' and 'Lussinge'. When the Frenchmen complained about not having pleasant company in London, their English valet fixed them up with young women, promising them a good time. 'Our young women lived in a lost part of the city, Westminster Road, perfectly positioned for four heavy sailor pimps to beat up Frenchmen.' The Frenchmen were warned by English friends not to venture down to this rookery in Southwark as it was bound to be a trap. But Stendhal—he was 38 at the time and already suffering from the syphilis contracted during his time in Bonaparte's army as a young man—and 'Barot' (his friend Nicolas-Rémy Lolot) went anyway. It was late at night when a cursing coachman deposited them outside a pint-sized cottage of three floors no less, a mere 25 feet high at most, a veritable dolls' house. Three young women welcomed the two Frenchmen in. Stendhal's account of what followed next takes us right into the heart of a freelance brothel in the same gothic city evoked by Dickens in *Oliver Twist* seventeen years later:

> I had expected to see three degenerate sluts. Instead, they were three slight little girls with beautiful chestnut hair, rather timid, very anxious to please and deeply pale.
>
> The furniture was ridiculously small. Barot was fat and large, me just fat. We found nowhere to sit properly, because the furniture all seemed designed for dolls. We were worried about breaking it all. Our little girls spotted our embarrassment which only rendered theirs even more acute. We were wholly lost for words. Luckily Barot thought of asking about a garden.
>
> 'Oh, we do have a garden', they said, not exactly with pride but just a hint of the pleasure of having something worthwhile to show us.
>
> We descended into the garden with candles, to see it. It measured 25 feet in depth and was ten feet wide. Barot and I burst out laughing. There sat all the

tools of the poor girls' domestic economy: a small basin for the washing and another one with an ellyptical appliance to let them brew their beer.

I was touched and Barot was disgusted. In French he whispered to me 'Let's pay them and go', to which I replied 'They would be so humiliated then.' 'Never mind—humiliated?! You know them. They will send for other punters, if it is not too late, or their lovers, if things happen here as they do in France.'

The truth of all this left me cold. Their poverty, all those tiny bits of ancient but spotless furniture, had touched me. We had not even finished taking our tea before we were cosy together to the point where we confided in them, in poor English, our initial fear of being assassinated while there. They were much troubled by this....

No door in the house had a lock on it: another matter for anxiety as we got ready to go to bed. But what good would doors and sound locks have been anyway in a place where, with a punch of one's fist, one could have knocked over the flimsy brick walls. The slightest noise was audible anywhere in the house. Barot, who had ascended to the second floor to a room above mine, called out to me: 'If you are murdered, call me!'

I wanted to keep the light on. The '*pudeur*' of my new mistress, so surrendered and sweet otherwise, could not bring herself to agree to this. She shuddered with fear when she watched me laying my pistols and dagger on the bedside table opposite the door. She was charming, slight, well made, pale.

No-one killed us.

That morning the two Frenchmen sent off for meats and wine to share with the girls. They promised to return that night. Indeed, as Stendhal records, he was looking forward to the night all day, so much so that even the show they saw that night in Covent Garden seemed long to him.

> Finally Barot and I arrived at our little house. When the young women saw us laden with bottles of claret and champagne the poor girls' eyes widened. I readily believed that they had never seen an as yet unopened bottle of real champagne.
>
> Luckily the cork of ours popped. They were absolutely delighted, but even then maintained a tranquil and decent decorum. In fact nothing was more decent than their conduct, but then we knew that already. [12]

The men had worried, unnecessarily, about the girls' pimps. It seems that there were none or, if there were, they were their lovers or boyfriends. So many women of all ages made ends meet by selling themselves, an open secret that many years later thrust itself to the fore in London when the Whitechapel murders of 1888 forcibly alerted the country to the sheer scale of casual sex for money in the capital. [13] The myth of a classless Victorian respectability was another victim of the infamous East End murders. While France, and Paris in particular, was superficially more tolerant, more sexually sophisticated than the huggermugger sexuality of 'Victorian' England, re-rooting itself in the country's Puritan heritage, urban prostitution in Paris took multiple forms and exercised the country as much, though not as morally, as it did Britain. Indeed, as one expert on this topic notes, 'no law on prostitution was passed in France during the entire course of the nineteenth century', even if there was plenty of concern about it.[14]

The teenage Alphonsine, barely 16 years old, more than anyone else perhaps resembles the young prostitute 'Marie' of Musset's poem *Rolla*, a sulphurous invective against Voltaire whose free-thinking Musset blames for the moral collapse and debauchery of the present time. Marie is 15 while her lover, Jacques Rolla, is a *roué* and sexual wastrel (Paris's 'plus grand débauché'), though he is not without tenderness to the point where he spends the last night of his life with the ever innocent Marie before poisoning himself and dying in her arms. Alfred de Musset was one of Marie Duplessis's most celebrated contemporaries, whose reputation endures undiminished to this day. He and she frequented the same set of people; she probably also knew the beautiful tobacconist on whom he had a notorious crush. She worked in the *Tabac* wedged between the Maison Dorée and the Café Riche (Figure 7.2); Claudin described her as 'a certain blonde young woman with flashing eyes' whose cigars, like her looks, were vastly superior to any others.[15]

This is how Musset sets the scene in *Rolla* by taking us into a bedroom in a house in Paris:

> It is a child who sleeps here—on her parted lips
> There flits from time to time a soft and gentle sigh...
> A child sleeps behind these thick curtains,
> A fifteen-year-old child, almost a young woman;
> Nothing is as yet fully formed in this delightful creature....
> She sleeps; look at her noble front, so innocent!
> Everywhere, like pure milk on a limpid wave,
> Heaven on her beauty spreads her chastity.
> She sleeps completely naked with her hand on her heart...
>
> If it is not your mother, o pale young girl,
> Who then is that woman sitting at your bedhead,
> Who watches the clock and the spitting hearth,
> Shaking her head and with such an air of concern?
> What is she waiting for so late?—For whom, if she is your mother

Did she go and open, a few moments ago,
Your door and balcony window—if not for your father?
But your father, Marie, has been dead for a long time.
So for whom are these bottles, this set table...
Silence: voices can be heard. Unknown women
Have opened the door, and others, half-naked,
Their hair dishevelled drag themselves along the walls,
Passing sweat-drenched through dimly lit corridors.
A light moved—the last flickers of its gloomy shine
Reveal the remains of an orgy at the end of a hidden boudoir....

The poet pauses before returning to the charge: it can surely not be that his vision is that of a brothel, a whorehouse of naked women engaged in wild orgies! Must this not be a nightmare while the 15-year-old Marie innocently sleeps, watched over by her mother: 'Everything rests, everything sleeps—that woman is your mother', he reiterates, but to no avail. He knows that even this most sacred of bonds is no match in the end for the chief corrupter of all, whom he now apostrophizes:

Poverty! Poverty! You are the courtesan.
It is you who pushed this child into this bed...
It was you who, whispering in the blowing wind,
In the midst of sobbing during bitter sleeplessness,
Came one gentle night and murmured to her mother:
'Your daughter is beautiful and a virgin: all that can be sold'...
Poor girl! At fifteen her senses were still dormant,
Her name was Marie...
                              As she is now,
Behind the shameful curtain of this hideous lair,
In this heinous bed, she gives to her mother,
As she returns to her abode whatever she earned there.

Musset's poem inspired the notorious painting by Henri Gervex (Figure 4.2), which scandalized contemporaries as much as Manet's more restrainedly nude *Déjeuner sur l'Herbe* had done fifteen years earlier. The painting, curiously unerotic for all its alluring nudity, captures the moment before the final lines of the poem when, after one last night with Marie, the bankrupt Rolla takes poison at dawn and dies in her arms:

Rolla turned round to look at Marie.
She was tired and had fallen asleep again.
So they both fled the cruelty of fate:
The child into sleep, the man into death.

Figure 4.2 *Rolla* by Henri Gervex, a powerful and controversial illustration of the last scene of Alfred de Musset's poem 'Rolla', about the sorrows of debauchery and prostitution. The young courtesan on the bed is the 15-year-old 'Marie'.

In 1839, the very year Marie Duplessis arrived in the capital city, another book on prostitution appeared. It was called *Les Filles Publiques de Paris*. The author was one F. F. A. Béraud, a former Paris police commissioner, who had been the city's 'special superintendent of the active engagement with the Office of Moral Behaviour'. He was well placed to comment on prostitution. Like Musset in his poem 'Rolla', he knew that the root causes of prostitution lay all too often in poverty. Béraud's seminal book is the work of a well-intentioned crusader who refuses to point a moral finger. The chief thrust of his tome is to urge the government of the day to invest heavily in research into a cure for syphilis. His book contains a collection of 'true' stories from the twilight zone of Parisian prostitution as he encountered it while serving the city of Paris. Its tone is understanding and compassionate.

One story that stands out is the tale of Emma and Tullie. Its analogies with that of Marie Duplessis and her eventual domestic arrangements, which included living next door to the woman who was managing her sexual affairs, are disturbing. It reads like a Dickensian parable about the corruption of innocent youth, but it does not have a happy ending. Béraud changed only the names. 'Emma' was a 16-year-old actress who lived with her mother: 'The little dancer only took minor roles in one of the more insignificant theatres and her remaining hours were spent with her mother whom she helped colour in designs on envelopes destined for perfume shops.' A reckless gambler by the name of 'Casimir', the estranged lover of a former actress and procuress called 'Tullie'—they parted when he was gaoled for debt—saw Emma at the theatre and became obsessed with her. Since parting from Tullie he had made money from servicing the desires of an old woman. Now solvent and even rich, he was welcomed back by Tullie who, for a handsome reward, promised to deliver the virginal Emma into his bed. The way to Emma lay through her mother and Tullie set about wooing the mother by holding out the prospect of a gilded future for her daughter. After Emma's mother died, Tullie rented a small apartment for Emma adjacent to hers, while all the time allowing Casimir to shower the young woman with gifts. The apartment was lavishly appointed by Emma's 'fiancé' who was biding his time until the moment was right for the seduction:

> I will not linger over all the details of that fateful day that saw the perdition of the poor orphan girl... the measures put in place by the procuress and her sordid Don Juan were so well honed that the wretched Emma could not escape the hidden snares that surrounded her everywhere. After losing her virginity she unwittingly became a party to her own dishonour by throwing herself into the arms of her seducer, believing that she was tied to him just as surely as if religion or the law had sanctioned their union. The two scoundrels left her in this blind faith until the very last.
>
> Less than a fortnight had passed before Emma started to experience those bouts of sickness that told her that she would be a mother. But this was not the worst blow that fate had dealt her. Casimir, not fully recovered from a pernicious and congenital syphilis, passed on to the poor child this dreadful disease.
>
> Her first symptoms, as familiar to the procuress as they were unknown to the victim, launched a train of thought in the pimp that she kept well to herself. Instead she reassured her and told her that her pains stemmed from her transition from virgin to woman and that they would all be over by the time she got married. This was always the solace offered her and Tullie appeared to be looking after the unhappy orphan when in fact she did nothing to stop the spread of the disease.

Eventually poor Emma, still only 17 and as innocent as Adéline Hulot in Balzac's *Cousine Bette*, died, deluded to the end about the true characters of her seducer and the procuress who had delivered her into his arms after lulling her mother into a false sense of security. Tullie's reason for not having Emma treated sooner was sheer greed, her predatory desire to inherit the furniture and possessions left by Emma and her mother.

While excoriating misfits like Tullie and Casimir, Béraud's chief concern was to save the victims from a fate even worse than unwanted pregnancies: syphilis. Béraud urged the government to push for a vaccine against syphilis: why, he asks, 'in this century of progress', will it not spur on doctors and biochemists, by financial inducements and honours, to combat the ravages of syphilis just as in earlier times it had fought and overcome smallpox? The horrors of smallpox were many, he notes, and included the blinding of children, a huge infant mortality and yet 'today [1839] this disease passes unnoticed; smallpox is no longer an issue, remaining only as a memory in our dictionaries'. He was well aware of the argument that syphilis was widely perceived to be a disease contracted by 'libertinage', and that this was one of the reasons why many people were reluctant to invest massively in the fight against a perceived excrescence from immoral behaviour. But it was not just the guilty who were infected:

> Are they guilty, the unfortunate victims of a straying husband, father? Is it not the most resounding injustice to condemn them to suffer the consequences of libertine behaviour of which they are completely blameless? I ask mercy for them rather than for him, because I do not want a wife or children to have to suffer the dreadful consquences of a fault that was never theirs.[16]

5

A fair lady meets Pygmalion

1840–1841

Alphonsine did not last long as Nollet's mistress. Perhaps it was the smarter clothes that she was now wearing that attracted her next lover, possibly during one of her forays to Palais-Royal. She was not quite 16 in January 1840 when she encountered one of the most sophisticated men in the capital, a grand aristocrat with almost unimaginable connections to power and society. He was twelve years older than her. The gulf between the teenage country girl, the mistress of a petty striving bourgeois, and the stylish aristocratic playboy could hardly be wider. He possessed one of the most eminent names in the country but that would not prevent her from mesmerizing him to the point where he could not live without her. It says much for her confidence, charm, and brilliance and for her instinctive grasp of the power of her sexuality. She already knew that, but now it was proven to her exponentially.

Her new lover set about transforming the girl from Normandy into the queen of Parisian courtesans. He exposed her to a barrage of teachers, each the best in his discipline in all of Paris. If she could just about read and write at the start of this relationship, by the time it had run its course eighteen months later she owned a library, played the piano, and had shed all trace of a regional accent.[1] She now appreciated opera and her instinctive refinement and good taste in clothes were given their head fully. By the time she died her library included volumes by Byron, Châteaubriand, Hugo, Lafontaine, Lamartine, Marivaux, Molière, Rabelais, Rousseau, and Scott. One of her friends later commented admiringly on her 'prodigious memory'. She especially loved the novels by Dumas *père*, whom she courted briefly in support of an acting career, and she would avidly read Eugène Sue's violent epic about the underbelly of the capital, *Les Mystères de Paris*, when it was serialized in the *Journal des Débats*. Her favourite novel was a scandalous eighteenth-century romance, which also became the subject of a great nineteenth-century opera, *Manon Lescaut*, a work that celebrates the madness of illicit love and sexual licence. It is no coincidence that Alphonsine's lover Dumas *fils* later used this particular novel in *La Dame aux Camélias* to provide the crucial plot link between the narrator and the character of Armand Duval.

During the first eight months of 1840 Alphonsine learnt much about the social rituals of becoming a leading metropolitan demi-mondaine. Despite a background deprived of every material and emotional support, she now found herself propelled to the top échelons of Parisian society. Undaunted, it seems, by her meteoric advancement, Alphonsine grabbed the extraordinary opportunity that was gifted her. She was fiercely intelligent, desperate to learn, and determined never to starve again. So who *was* this Henry Higgins who turned the 'country lass' Alphonsine Plessis into the ultimate 'fair lady' Marie Duplessis, to use the name she adopted in 1842? The only contemporary source about his affair with Marie Duplessis, Vienne, refers to him as the 'Duc de R——', calling him 'la perle des protecteurs', that is, someone with exquisite taste and discrimination in the erotic art of keeping women. Clearly he cared very deeply about her to go to so much trouble and expense over a young woman who was in the end merely a 'grisette' and budding 'cocotte'.

The simplest explanation is probably the truest: he had fallen in love. Her extraordinary charm had bewitched him; he had recognized quite how special she was. This rich, powerful aristocrat more than anything desired her company, yearned to be seen in public with her, to show her off with pride at the opera and theatre, among his friends in high society and at the races of Chantilly. This was not an affair of furtive sex in a rented hotel bedroom à la Goncourt; perhaps he was even hoping to marry her. Years after their affair he remained faithful to her memory. Such was the ardent loyalty she inspired. The identity of her Pygmalion has remained shrouded in mystery until now. He was in fact the patrician Charles Auguste Louis Joseph de Morny (1811–65), the illegitimate son of the Napoleonic general Charles de Flahaut and Hortense Bonaparte, stepdaughter of Napoleon I and wife of Bonaparte's brother Louis-Napoleon, King of Holland (Figure 5.1). Queen Hortense had a legitimate son, Charles Louis-Napoleon Bonaparte, who in 1848 became the first President of the Republic and eventually Napoleon III. Charles de Morny was therefore a true-blue Bonaparte and

Figure 5.1 Charles Duc de Morny, a Bonaparte and half-brother of the
President-Emperor Napoleon III. In 1852 he issued the licence for *La Dame aux
Camélias* at the Vaudeville theatre.

half-brother of the President-Emperor Napoleon III. The entire French
governing class knew his pedigree despite an elaborate cod story about his
alleged parentage and birth. When eventually Napoleon III called upon him
to serve in his cabinet, Morny responded enthusiastically. He proved so
adroit at politics that it was widely thought that he would make a better
president than the legitimate ruler.

During a heady spell from 1837 to 1842, the 'five missing years' according
to his biographer, who was unaware of the relationship between his subject

and the lady of the camellias, Morny was sowing his wild oats. His boon companions were almost all drawn from the Jockey-Club to which he was elected on 28 January 1837. The head of this rich Anglo-French cabal, founded in 1833, was an eccentric French Englishman (he never visited Britain and his English was poor), a Croesus by the name of Lord Henry Seymour. To most Parisians he was known by the sobriquet of 'Milord l'Arsouille' or, in the English that Seymour did *not* understand, Milord Arsehole; literally a carnivalesque figure in the first instance cheerfully grafted onto the flamboyant figurehead of the Jockey-Club.

In his memoirs, one of his acquaintances, also unaware of Morny's liaison with Marie Duplessis, commented on Morny's 'obsessive tendency to lecture those closest to him constantly on their dress codes, language, and general demeanour and manners. It was a monomania of his.'[2] His own manners were said to be flawless and were attributed to the women who had brought him up. It was these character traits that focused on making Alphonsine into the most famous courtesan of the 1840s. Even his best friends, who might have told us more about his romantic life during this period, kept their counsel. One of them writes that 'we know almost nothing about the flower of his carefree youth other than that he was charming, lost his hair early on, and loved thoroughbred race horses ... let us therefore dream that out there somewhere are whole bundles of letters addressed to Zoe, Mathilda and Juliet.' For those three names one needs only to substitute Alphonsine. His close friend Alton-Shée, one of the founders of the Jockey-Club, describes Morny as follows:

> Without being truly handsome, he appeared wholesome and benign, elegant and distinguished. He was impressively proportioned, excelled at sports and was one of our best 'gentlemen riders'; friend and, occasionally, happy rival [in love] of the Duc d'Orléans, he was hugely successful at romances with women. Cultured for a socialite, with a taste for lazy luxuriating and a talent for work, with absolute self-belief, audacious, intrepid, calm and controlled, sound judgement, spirited, gay, better at camaraderie than friendship, better at protecting than devotion; in love with pleasure, keen on luxury, prodigal and greedy in equal measure, player rather than career climber, personally loyal but deferring to no higher principles of humanity or politics, nothing restrained the freedom of his movements. He enjoyed certain princely characteristics, such as deviousness, thoughtlessness, a contempt for his fellow men at the same time as a desire to please them. For him the end justified the means, not for the sake of a religion or a political idea or an ideology, but for his own self-interest.[3]

Figure 5.2 No. 28 rue du Mont-Thabor, a street parallel to the rue de Rivoli, close to the Tuileries and Place de la Concorde. Alphonsine Plessis was moved here by Morny.

The young Morny was tutored in the de Souza household by the same Gabriel Delessert, the future head of the Paris police, whose son would later become involved with Marie Duplessis and walk in her funeral cortège.[4] Morny's passion for horses was well known. Like others among Marie Duplessis's rich lovers, he was a daredevil who took part in the steeplechase as soon as it was founded. In the fashionable neologism of the time, he was a 'gentleman rider' and the legendary racecourse at Deauville in Normandy was his creation. It seems that he may also have coached Marie Duplessis. We know that she was a hugely accomplished horse-woman and she had grown up in the most horse-loving region of France.

That by itself though did not turn her into a rider. It can only have been Morny who first fed, and then nurtured, her love of horses and her equestrian skills. During the last summer of her life she returned to the Orne to ride and rest, hoping against all the odds that she might yet be saved by country air and exercise.

Morny was certainly sowing his wild oats then, because in August 1840 he made Alphonsine Plessis pregnant. He was already the father of an illegitimate 2-year-old daughter by an aristocratic woman, the wife of a diplomat. From the small apartment in the Rue de l'Arcade where Nollet had hidden her, Morny moved Alphonsine to 28 rue du Mont-Thabor, a street parallel to the rue de Rivoli, a mere stone's throw from the Tuileries and Place de la Concorde (Figure 5.2). This tall block of rooms and apartments with an inner courtyard stands today largely unaltered. It was here that she spent her first Christmas as an expectant mother.[5]

We will never know what passed between her and her lover during these days of counting down towards her delivery in May. It was hardly an untroubled time for her, and in February 1841 news from Normandy reached her that her father had died. Marin Plessis's death occurred at 3 p.m. on 8 February 1841 in the house of one of his neighbours in Ginai near Exmes. He was 51 years old. It seems that his last weeks were spent in agony as he was afflicted by a dreadful skin disease. The local people avoided him like a leper and Vienne recalls that only his (Vienne's) own brother-in-law, a doctor, and a local priest were charitable enough to feed the pariah from time to time as he lay dying in a hovel. Syphilis has been surmised as the cause of his death, but we cannot be sure. He had abused, perhaps raped, his daughter Alphonsine, but even that had not set her against him. Did she grieve for him? It seems that she did but she was also out of his clutches now.

6

The baby of a traviata

Versailles, May 1841

In March 1841 Morny installed his teenage lover in a well-appointed apartment in Versailles, at 9 rue du Marché Neuf (Figure 6.1). At no. 7 next door resided a midwife, Dlle Marie-Louise Giffault, who was thus able to give Alphonsine her almost undivided attention. The same buildings still flank each other today, essentially unaltered from the way they were in 1841, notwithstanding the hideous stucco incrustation of no. 9. Her baby remains the most closely guarded secret of the lady of the camellias to this day. He has not only been shrouded in mystery until now, but his very existence has been questioned by most of her biographers. But she did have a baby and he was not very difficult to trace.

We know from Alphonsine's conversation with Vienne during their walk on 11 July 1841 that the birth had been difficult. But her lover had ensured that she was comfortable during her confinement, in striking contrast to a story related by her contemporary Céleste Mogador, whose autobiography tells a harrowing tale of a cast-out pregnant young woman's ordeal in the Paris of the period. It is worth pausing over this for a moment, as it is representative of the fate that could have befallen Marie Duplessis. It may go some way towards explaining why she preferred a life of genteel prostitution to abject honest poverty. The young woman in question was none other than the Mabille dancer known by the sobriquet 'Reine Pomaré', whose real name was Élise Rose Sergent.[1] She was a direct contemporary of Marie Duplessis and died the year before her, at the age of 22. The two women would almost certainly have spotted each other at Mabille as the 'Reine' was, briefly, the most celebrated of all the polka dancers at the Jardin Mabille.[2] Sergent came from a wealthy family and was expensively educated. Then, one day when she was around 17, her father lost everything

Figure 6.1 No. 9 rue du Marché Neuf, Versailles where Alphonsine Plessis gave birth to her baby. At no. 7 next door (to the left) resided a specially retained midwife.

when his uninsured business went literally up in flames. Not long afterwards she became pregnant by a shiftless lover. She went to see a doctor whom she knew when she started to be sick and faint: 'You are pregnant. It is not dangerous', he informed her.

> I went downstairs determined to throw myself into the river as soon as it was night. I ran to the man who had lost me. He could think of only one way to save me: to destroy my baby. I stared at him in horror: my contempt for him was bottomless.[3]

The traumatic story of her pregnancy and baby is related by her friend and dance rival Mogador. The account of giving birth in a miserable workhouse is heart-breaking as is Sergent's terror about being too undernourished to nurse her little boy once he was born. Her anguish over the little creature floods the pages of the narrative:

> After dreadful pains I was delivered. I had given birth to a boy. I asked God's forgiveness for his birth and begged Him to save his life and to take mine

instead. He was so delicate, the poor angel, that I constantly listened out for his breathing.

They tried to stop me feeding him, but I would have none of it. The time had come when I had to leave the maternity hostel. They gave me a little bit of money, some baby clothes, and I left with my treasure in my arms.

I arrived at the hotel [where she had stayed until her labour was imminent]. I was not too badly received. I returned to my cubbyhole and did a little work. My poor child was alarmingly pale. He was ten months old, he smiled at me and he held out his tiny hands to me. I was happy. That happiness I had not deserved, and it was short-lived.

Convulsions, that terror of all mothers, convulsions put my baby's life at risk. However closely I hugged him to me, his little limbs were twisting and his face turned blue. I covered him with kisses, I warmed him with my breath, I told him with my hands folded in prayer 'Be quiet, your screams are killing me', and I prayed. He relaxed and rested for a few hours. Then the convulsions returned, worse than before.

This dreadful struggle lasted eight days. It finally came to a head and then he relaxed. I thought he was resting. I prayed to the Virgin Mary to put an end to his suffering, by saving his life or by taking mine, rather than let him continue to suffer like that. I had no strength left to watch him suffer any more.

I waited a long time for him to wake up. I picked him up. He was stiff and icy. I dropped him, then took him in my arms, unable to shed a tear. 'You miserable wretch', I said to myself, 'you killed him. Did your prayers fly up to heaven?' I raced down the stairs, screaming that I needed a doctor, that my child could not be dead without me.

They managed to take the corpse of the poor little angel from me. One of the young men in the hotel paid for his funeral.

I followed the body of my son to Montparnasse. I arranged for a marker to be attached to his bier so that I could claim him back from the paupers' common grave ('fosse commune') once I had the money to buy him a cross and his own grave.

I spent the next fifteen days in a mad, desolate trance. I did not again climb back to the room where he had died. Everyone in the house offered me their hospitality.

'Come on', said one of the good-hearted young men, 'you cannot go on like this. You need a bit of distraction.'

They made me eat, drink, and took me to Mabille.[4]

Such was the common lot of poor and unmarried teenage girls giving birth in the slum workhouses of Paris in the 1840s. After listening to Reine Pomaré's account, Mogador remarked 'The Reine Pomaré disappeared and in her place I now saw a poor girl who was even more wretched than me.'[5] Élise Sergent survived her child by barely four years. From Mogador's account of her loss and subsequent life of manic partying, drink, and desolation, it appears that she may not have wanted to be parted from her 'little angel' any longer.

The teenage Alphonsine Plessis's lot was exceptionally fortunate under the circumstances. She was not alone, cold, or hungry, even if all were privations she had experienced only fairly recently. The only references to her baby are in Romain Vienne's chronicle and in a reported conversation with the wife of Alexandre Dumas *fils*. Vienne records that at one point during her visit to Nonant in the summer of 1841 Alphonsine was berated by her sister Delphine for the ignominy of having an illegitimate baby. Apart from this, there is only one further credible allusion to her baby. It dates from several decades after these events, when the younger Dumas's widow confirmed that Alphonsine had confided in her husband that she had indeed been a mother. According to the author Georges Soreau, who knew Dumas's wife, 'Mme Henriette Alexandre Dumas informs me that her husband frequently asserted in front of her that there had been a baby.'[6] In the late 1890s Soreau wrote to the Mairie de Versailles and asked them to check their records for a baby born to Alphonsine Plessis. They replied categorically that no such baby appeared in the registers for 1830s or 1840s. It is true that nowhere in the archives of the *état civil* in Versailles is there a record of a birth that would seem to be connected by name to Alphonsine Plessis, or to any of the likely fathers of the child. But this ought not to come as a surprise, since the baby was illegitimate and his father a peer of the realm keen to remain anonymous.

The waters are muddied further by the fact that Versailles boasted a charitable institution that, unintentionally, helped to sever the links between children and their parents. This was the Asile de Vieillards hospital on the rue Duplessis where illegitimate children were regularly abandoned at night. It is an unsettling thought that the hospital in Versailles fronts onto a street called 'Duplessis', the same name that Alphonsine would eventually adopt. When I noticed this, I wondered at first whether she took the name Duplessis out of loyalty to her baby; in fact, her likely reason for assuming this name was, as we shall see, similarly sentimental. Foundlings, the so-called 'enfants trouvés', could not be traced back to parents and were named by the staff at the hospital. If, like so many others, Alphonsine's baby had been left on the steps of the hospital's gatehouse, his identity would indeed be lost forever. Four babies were 'found' on its doorsteps in May of 1841 alone, but the Versailles *état civil* also lists a number of illegitimate children during that period.[7]

The standard line on the baby of the lady of the camellias has long been that he was born probably in or near Versailles and that she may have lied about his early death; if not his very existence. But why would she do so? In fact, she did not lie about either. In trying to trace the infant it is worth looking again at what exactly Vienne says. According to him, in around March 1841 the 'Vicomte de Méril' moved the pregnant Alphonsine Plessis to Versailles and put her up

> in a modest but comfortable apartment, adjacent to that of a midwife to whose care he entrusted her. During the first days of May she gave birth to a beautiful boy who was handed over to a wet-nurse and fed at the breast. The young mother stayed on in Versailles until the end of June, to rest and to recover her health, which had been gravely affected by a prolonged birth. Then she moved back to her small apartment in Paris, but her doctor prescribed, and even ordered, her to sojourn in the country, notably to breathe her native air, for three months. She complied with this wise counsel and left for Normandy around 10 July.

At the time of the birth in May 1841, Alphonsine was 17 years and 5 months old.

Contrary to what is invariably claimed, there is in fact an infant listed in the archives of Versailles who fits *all* the important details provided by Vienne; and particularly the two clues about the confinement apartment being '*contigu*' (next door) to that of the midwife and the assertion that the child was born during the first days of May. This baby's name is Charles-Yves Deschamps, sharing his first name 'Charles' with both his father and grandfather. He was born on Wednesday 5 May 1841 at no. 9 rue du Marché Neuf, Versailles. The little boy's mother gives her name as 'Louise Victorine Deschamps couturière' and her age as 19. The baby is described as 'fils naturel' and his father is listed as 'unknown'; so is his mother's father while her place of birth is given as Versailles, a necessary lie if the baby was to be born in a district that was a place favoured by the aristocracy for disposing of illegitimate children. The original entry on the birth register in Versailles reads:

> Saturday 8 May 1841 at 3 p.m. The official record of the birth of Charles-Yves, male, born on 5 May at 8pm at *his mother's home at 9 rue du Marché*, the illegitimate son of Louise Victorine Deschamps, seamstress, aged 19 and born in Versailles of an unnamed father... On the presentation of the child and the testimony of D^lle Marie-Louise Giffault, *midwife of 7 rue du Marché Neuf*, who signed alongside the witnesses and us, the mayor of Versailles... [my emphases]

By giving her occupation as milliner or seamstress, Alphonsine Plessis, alias 'Louise Victorine Deschamps', was simply using her last job at Mlle Urbain's. She could hardly declare her employment to be that of 'courtisane' or 'cocotte'. As for the witnesses to the baby's arrival in this world, they were, one imagines, easily paid off by the father whose own official paternity had been an elaborate hoax. Versailles had featured in that too and had involved a luckless soldier by the name of Morny, who had been willing to lend his name to an offspring of the Bonapartes.[8]

Charles-Yves Deschamps deserves to join the ranks of illegitimate Bonaparte babies. Had he lived, he might well have prospered. Both his parents were highly intelligent and ambitious, and his father eventually became the second most powerful man in France. As for Alphonsine, giving birth to a Bonaparte baby was a matter of such pride to her that she could not keep it to herself. That is the reason why she told Vienne about the birth and the father. When he looked incredulous, she promised to prove his identity from the letters he was sending her to Nonant *poste restante* at the Viennes' post office. At the same time she urged him to be discreet around their friends in Paris as her sexual drawing power and commercial value as courtesan would inevitably be diminished by giving birth. But whatever prospects her little boy might have enjoyed as a Bonaparte, he had also trag- ically inherited his mother's genes which seemed to predispose the Deshayes women to phthisis even though tuberculosis is not hereditary.[9] A mere thirty-five days after his birth, he died around noon, on Wednesday 9 June 1841, in his wet-nurse's home in Versailles at 9 rue de l'Orient, a street across the square where he was born. The register duly records the death of

> the illegitimate son of Louise Victorine Deschamps . . . residing ('demeurant') at 9 rue du Marché Neuf and of an unnamed father. The witnesses are Messirs Nicolas Martin . . . also living at 9 rue du Marché Neuf, and René Guichet . . . innkeeper in the same street . . . who signed alongside us, the Mayor of Versailles, in the execution of our duty as public officials of the *état civil* after appropriate checking and noting the death.

The formulaic entry gives the mother's address as 9 rue du Marché Neuf, as it was at the time of the birth. It is not clear from the wording whether she was still living there when her baby died. The remainder of the entry rather suggests that she was not. Hence the presence of two witnesses: one of whom, Martin, was a pedlar ('bimbelotier' = seller of trinkets) who resided at 9 rue du Marché Neuf at the time the baby died, while the other one, Guichet, was an innkeeper in the same street. The two men presumably testified that the dead child was indeed the baby born at that address a few weeks earlier; the two witnesses who had signed the birth register did not come from 9 rue du Marché Neuf; there was no need then because the midwife testified to that address.

It would seem that Alphonsine Plessis left her baby behind soon after he was born. Her conversation of 11 July 1841 with Vienne implies that she was wholly unaware of the fact that by the time of her return to Nonant her little boy was already dead. Assuming that she told Vienne the truth, we must conclude that she returned from Versailles to Paris at some point towards the end of May, certainly well before 9 June. There is no reason to read anything sinister into this. For better or worse she was a 'working girl' who could not possibly look after a baby while plying her trade. The fact moreover that her powerful protector apparently promised to take the baby boy with him to new pastures in the 'east' of the country—Clermont-Ferrand which, though in the centre, lies south-east of Lower Normandy where the reported conversation about the baby took place—to raise him in a manner befitting his station, will have reassured her and exonerated her from too much guilt.

Nevertheless, giving up her baby and not yet knowing what had become of him must have affected her deeply. She was barely back in Paris after her confinement when her son was buried in the nearby Cimetière Saint-Louis in Versailles (Figure 6.2), where an entry in the cemetery's register duly records his interment.

For whatever reason his father failed to inform her of their baby's death until a year later. He must have known, because he paid for the wet-nurse. Perhaps he was worried about her fragile health after the birth, or else it suited him to keep her in the dark, to leave her under the illusion that he would be taking the boy with him to pastures new. Did he encourage her to depart for Normandy for three months to keep her out of the way and screened from any gossip? She attributed her decision to move to the country to her doctor. This is certainly possible because she was frequently in the care of doctors in Paris at the time. On the other hand she could hardly absent herself from Paris for the entire summer of 1841 without the financial backing and agreement of her wealthy lover.

In the months after the birth, she and Morny stayed in touch and on affectionate terms. At least, that is what she indicated to Vienne during their evening amble out of Nonant, an episode that in retrospect seems almost too carefree to be true. It would seem inconceivable that she knew what

Figure 6.2 The Cimetière Saint-Louis in Versailles, where Alphonsine Plessis's little boy, Charles-Yves, is buried.

had really happened to her little boy. She could hardly have been flirtatiously enjoying herself with Vienne if she had been aware of the fate of her baby. Rather, it may be that she was under the firm impression during her stay in Normandy that her child was alive and thriving. Vienne reports that, at her invitation, he perused one of the letters posted to Nonant by her lover. There was, he later recalled, 'everything in that missive: much affection and details about the child, who was in strapping health in every respect, except for love'.[10] If this letter was posted, as Vienne alleges, shortly before her departure from Nomandy back to Paris in late September, it would seem to be shockingly mendacious; a cynical fiction intended to mislead her and buy time for the father. Perhaps she was dispatched to Normandy not so much to recover her health, a convenient pretext, but to be out of the way, as the last thing Morny would have wanted was a courtesan mother nursing his baby and showing off the baby to her peers. It was one thing to father an illegitimate baby with a countess, quite another to do so with a teenage prostitute. Whatever his plans for their baby were, they were pre-empted, conveniently for Morny, by his tragically premature demise.

In July 1841, still not fully recovered, Alphonsine set off for her old home of Nonant. Not exactly a prodigal returning to her roots, but nevertheless a transformed young woman whose meteoric rise would continue unabated. The little, illiterate peasant girl from the Orne was now a rising star in Paris. So much had happened since she had been taken away from this very place by her father and his gypsy friends a mere two and half years earlier.

Rumours about her baby seem to have emerged at some point from her lovers, if not directly from her family: Dumas *fils* knew, and long before him others did too: not just Vienne and his mother, clearly, but also her sister Delphine. Vienne was wary of her account of the baby, and he was sceptical when she told him a year after their long walk that the baby had died of pneumonia. Had she asked to see his death certificate, he enquired: 'I didn't ask for anything at all,' she replied with finality. He wisely backed off but wondered whether the baby had after all survived, that his 'death' was a convenient fiction. Two independent accounts, reported by him, consolidated his suspicion. One comes from Charles Duhays, from the same Duhays family of the manor of Saint-Germain who had assisted Alphonsine's mother's flight from her husband. Writing in 1885 to one Gérard de Contades, author of a seminal article on the lady of the camellias, Charles Duhays asserted that her son was alive and that he had met him in his offices: he had become one of the grand names of the 'Stud Book', that is a member of the equestrian aristocracy that controlled the economy of the Orne not least through its links to the Jockey-Club in Paris, of which Contades's second cousin, himself once among her lovers, had been a luminary. According to Duhays, 'he [Alphonsine's son] is, I assure you, alive at this moment.' Duhays was certain of his facts because the man in question bore a striking resemblance to Alphonsine Plessis. That he would be a member of the National Stud seemed entirely natural because almost all his mother's aristocratic lovers, including his likely father, were involved with the Stud and its satellites throughout the country.

The second alleged sighting comes from another source close to the lady of the camellias. It is again reported by Vienne and once more it involves someone he knew well; indeed, very well by the time he wrote his book. This was Alphonsine's sister Delphine. She told Vienne of a mysterious visit she and her family received in their home in Saint-Evroult-de-Montfort near Gacé in 1869. A 28-year-old young man (and therefore born in 1841) had presented himself at their door and, with 'exquisite manners', asked to see a portrait of the woman who was known by then as Marie Duplessis.

Delphine obliged and noticed that, as he held the portrait, he gazed at it for a long time in silence, deeply moved and unable to suppress the tears that were welling up in his eyes. When he left he passed them a card with the name 'Judelet, businessman, Tours' on it.

No sooner had he gone than Delphine exclaimed 'Good God, how he resembles my sister!', to which her children added that he did indeed look like the portrait of their aunt. The following day Delphine started enquiries in local hotels and, when she drew a blank, she contacted the mayor of Tours, who replied that no such person could be traced anywhere in the city. This convinced the family that they had indeed met their nephew, who had come to see his mother's portrait while using a fake identity. There is no reason to doubt the essential truth of Delphine's account as reported by Vienne, but two details might nevertheless make one wary. The first one concerns the information about the caller's age, which turns out to be the exact age Marie Duplessis's son would have been in 1869. Is it plausible that Delphine's visitor would have told her his age when he called? What should be an important authenticating detail may well be information written back into the story by a Romain Vienne keen to consolidate his account, which leans towards supporting the view that her little boy survived into adulthood. The second reason relates to the Loire town of Tours. The only link between the story of Marie Duplessis and Tours is to be found in La Dame aux Camélias where Tours is the place in the country where Armand Duval lived with his family before coming to Paris and getting involved with Marie Duplessis. Vienne, it seems, is remembering Tours from Dumas; in his memory, reality and Dumas's fiction have merged to play a trick on him.

As regards the portrait that the stranger asked to see, this was indeed in the family's possession at Saint-Evroult-de-Montfort. It was drawn repeatedly from memory in the nineteenth century before surfacing at a radio auction hosted by the well-known French broadcaster Pierre Bellemare in 1960. It was immediately photographed as a record for posterity (Figure 16.3). It turns out to be remarkably close to the reproductions that were circulating in the intervening years between 1847, when it was sold to the family at auction, and 1960, when it was again auctioned only to disappear from view once more. In view of Duhays' and Delphine's impressionistic, anecdotal testimonies, the usually sceptical and astute Vienne concluded that his friend's baby probably survived, notwithstanding her categoric assertions to the contrary.

A question that has never yet been asked is whether Vienne enquired after her baby's name. It would seem to be the most obvious thing to do. Moreover his book repeatedly plays onomastic games with its readers, littering its narrative with hints that may, or may not, provide clues about the real life characters hidden by names that Vienne encodes with various kinds of clues. Both Vienne and Alphonsine would have been well aware that there were Deschamps in their immediate Orne neighbourhood (just as there were in Versailles), and a Louise Deschamps, the name borrowed by Alphonsine, had died in Nonant in March 1838. But what of the baby's first name, Charles-Yves? His father Morny's first name was Charles, but 'Yves'? There are no real-life Yves in the story of the young courtesan, but the most important man in her life is disguised by Vienne under the name of 'Robert de Saint-Yves', alias Vicomte Édouard de Perrégaux. To assume the name of her husband, 'Saint-Yves', to allude to her secret baby's name, 'Charles-Yves', is just the kind of private game that Vienne enjoyed playing against his readers. His name for her husband, unlike almost any other in his account, is not connected in any way to his real name; the only clue and link is with her baby.

Vienne's calling Perrégaux 'Saint-Yves' does not necessarily mean that he knew the full truth about her baby, but it does provide incidental support for the view that he knew her baby's real name. By transferring the baby's name to his mother's most important lover, and prefixing it with Saint, Vienne may not only have flaunted his knowledge of her most intimate secret, her son Charles-Yves, but may also have wanted to bond mother and son, whether alive or dead, together in his book.

7

Stallions and flaneurs on the boulevard des Italiens

1841–1842

M arie Duplessis remained with her family at La Trouillière for most of the summer of 1841, until the end of September. She spent her time visiting friends, like the Adams in Nonant, and regularly called in at the Viennes' post office to send mail and to collect post from Paris. Every week, it seems, Morny sent her a money order for 100 francs. He wrote too and so did Alphonsine's girl friends from Paris. On her walks down into Nonant she was occasionally joined by Delphine who was now living at their cousin's home in Saint-Germain-de-Clairefeuille, a family called Lanos.

It was the first time the girls had spent any time together since they were separated ten years earlier when Alphonsine was temporarily adopted by the Boisards. From time to time Vienne accompanied the two young women back from his parents as far as the junction of La Corbette at the end of the lane leading out of Saint-Germain. Alphonsine would push on to La Trouillière from here while Delphine doubled back to the church at Saint-Germain. The two sisters could hardly have been more different in appearance and temperament. Whereas Alphonsine was possessed of a languid beauty and a seemingly unassailable even temperament, the elder Delphine was plain, prickly, and jealous. As the two were growing up, nature only accentuated these differences further. Maybe it was a smouldering resentment that caused Delphine to let fly at Alphonsine one day when her sister tried to lure her away from Normandy to the luxuries and fleshpots of the capital. By then Delphine was engaged to a young local man. She was in no mood to be wooed away into a life of genteel prostitution in which she would anyway be bound to fail for lack of good looks. So an affronted Delphine furiously turned on her sibling and berated her for being a whore and the mother of a bastard. Alphonsine had undoubtedly been tactless by not appreciating the gulf between herself and her lacklustre sister, but she was unprepared for this bottled-up furious outpouring. According to Vienne, who witnessed the confrontation, 'Alphonsine, wounded to the core of her being by this violent outburst, reeled and for a moment seemed set to turn her back on her sister.' But Vienne, reproving both of them, somehow managed to calm the situation. That afternoon he and Delphine walked Alphonsine back all the way to la Troullière, presumably to make up, before returning to Saint-Germain where he parted from Delphine at the home of her aunt Lanos near the church.

Rumours must have been rife about Alphonsine. Local people were no fools. They guessed the source of her affluence, and her looks and clothes too spoke volumes even if she managed to dress modestly during her stay. She helped out at her Mesnil family in La Trouillière as best she could and she probably visited her father's grave at Ginai, a twenty-minute walk across the wold from their home. As summer turned to autumn, the most important holiday in the Nonant calendar, the feast of Saint Matthew held on 21 September, loomed ahead. In the words of the village's chief local historian, the precise Charles Vérel whose Nonant was essentially the same as Alphonsine's, 'One waited for Saint-Matthew's Day to buy umbrellas, soaps, crockery, and clothing... Young women in turn awaited the Saint Matthew's to have their ears pierced for wearing golden or silver pendants; their fiancés would buy golden trinkets for their betrothed, while farmers found here all the tools necessary for working the earth.' The whole of Nonant and the surrounding hamlets converged on the Halles near the church. So did Alphonsine. Did she stroll from stall to stall with Delphine, or Vienne, or any of her former schoolmates? Whatever she did it may have been one of her last appearances in Nonant that year. Or perhaps it was the last one her chronicler remembered. Vienne assumed that she returned to Paris around the feast of Saint Matthew. In fact, she stayed on for almost another six weeks, because two of her letters survive from that November. They were written after she returned to Paris. The first one is dated 12 November 1841 and is addressed to her uncle at La Trouillière:

My dear uncle,
I arrived safely in Paris but I am still in rather poor health. During the last few days I have again needed to call out the doctor. I trust that this letter finds you in better shape than me. I have just received a letter that you forwarded to me and it is a cheque that needs to be cashed in at the post office in Nonant. I am

enclosing it herewith. Could you kindly cash it in on my behalf as it needs to be signed by you as my guardian? You will receive 100 francs: could you kindly give ten to my sister and send me the remaining 90 by post? I sent you a night-shirt through the mail coach. It will be waiting for you at Madame Adam's in Nonant. I fervently hope that my beloved aunt is feeling better. I hug you with all my heart and am forever your devoted niece.

Alphonsine
12 of 9th [November] 1841[1]

It is evident from this that the young woman did not return to Paris until November, after nearly four months recuperating in the Orne. The money to which she refers comes from Morny. It arrived for her every week while she was away from Paris. By local standards it was a princely sum.

Worryingly she was still ailing, and she was oddly confused too about the 'chemise' which, it turns out, she had not posted at all.

On 25 November she was writing again:

My dear uncle,
It is not through forgetfulness that I have taken so long to write. Rather I returned to work in the store which I mentioned to you. I have had so much to do that I have not had a moment to write. I am sending you the parcel that I thought I had sent earlier. It contains a nightshirt for my aunt and another one for you. Could you kindly forward my linen to me as soon as possible, as I need it?

I received the money that you sent me. Thank you for going to all that trouble on my behalf. I wish it were already next summer to have the pleasure to see you again in Paris. Write to me with news of your health and of that of my beloved aunt whom I hug, as I do you, with all my heart.

Your devoted niece,
Alphonsine

By the time Alphonsine Plessis returned to Paris, Charles de Morny had left to take up an official government agricultural appointment in the Puy de Dôme region where he duly consolidated his power base by making a for-tune from sugar beet ('betterave à sucre'). Did he mourn for the dead little boy from Versailles? By the time Morny fell in love with Alphonsine he had already fathered a daughter with a rich society hostess, Fanny Mosselman, the wife of the first Belgian ambassador to France, Comte Charles Le Hon. She had been a great beauty. Balzac called her the 'ambassadress with the golden locks'. He too was as smitten with her just as much as the young aristocrats, who danced the polkas and mazurkas at the great balls thrown at the Belgian embassy at 7 rue de la Chaussée d'Antin.

The illegitimate daughter of Morny and the lady ambassador, the half-sister of Alphonsine Plessis's little boy, was called Louise Le Hon. She was born in 1838, and through her marriage to Stanislas Poniatowski she would create a political dynasty with tentacles reaching into the modern era of French politics. Morny's womanizing and multiple conquests produced further illegitimate children, including perhaps Sarah Bernhardt who so excelled at playing the lady of the camellias that years later Dumas *fils* presented her, as a gift of his esteem, with his parting letter to Alphonsine Plessis. Multiple paternities were the inevitable lot of restless philanderers like Morny. If he was indeed, as has been rumoured from time to time, the father of Sarah Bernhardt, then the famous actress would be the half-sister of Marie Duplessis's son! She may therefore have made her career partly by playing her half-brother's mother in *La Dame aux Camélias*.[2]

But the way Morny cared for Alphonsine Plessis in her hour of need, just as he did for little Sarah Bernhardt later by overseeing *her* education, suggests that this rake attracted women not only because of his charm, manners, and powerful connections, but by a generous and oddly loyal nature untarnished by his promiscuity. Charles de Morny *alias* Bonaparte had been introduced to Fanny Le Hon by his best friend, an inveterate reveller by the name of Fernand de Montguyon, his senior by three years. Such was Montguyon's devotion to Morny that he apparently considered committing suicide on hearing the news of his death. Montguyon too had been a leading light of the Jockey-Club from the start and, again like Morny, was a keen rider and owner of highy prized horses. They were the Castor and Pollux in the Paris of the 1840s and shared everything, including, it turns out, their women. So it need not come as a surprise to discover that Montguyon now took up his friend's place in Alphonsine's bed.

He inherited a shepherdess remoulded as princess. The more the pity then that he was never in Morny's league when it came to dealing with women, even kept mistresses. Montguyon's chief claim to fame in the Paris of the time was the fact that in 1836 he had founded the infamous 'hell's box' ('loge infernale') at the Le Peletier Paris Opéra, behind the boulevard des Italiens. 'Box 1', as it was known, was reached directly from the Jockey-Club, at the corner of rue Drouot, by a covered passage that connected the Club to the Opéra.[3] The 'lions' of the Jockey-Club used this box for assignations with the dancers and chorus girls of Paris's grand opera house, the Opéra Le Peletier, the same girls who were painted by Manet and Degas.

Montguyon's connections were impeccable: as equerry to the heir to the throne, Ferdinand Philippe, Duc d'Orléans, he belonged to the upper échelons of French society. Both the Crown Prince and his brother the Duc de Nemours were of course members of the Jockey-Club. None of this impressed Montguyon's contemporary, the splenetic diarist Horace de Vieil-Castel of the Louvre. In his view, Montguyon was merely 'a tiresome hack from the opera and habitual hanger-out at the theatre, a bad egg always game for mischief', a facile whoremonger who 'spent his life slipping in and out of the beds of dancers and singers, putting in appearances at the Jockey-Club, and fighting with other worthless imbeciles over the affections of some trollop or other'. One such 'trollop', though not one ever fought over in a duel, was Alphonsine Plessis. In the autumn of 1841 she was Montguyon's junior by sixteen years. He knew her well from meeting her repeatedly on the arm of his friend, not least during their visits to the opera. He probably also knew about the baby. Morny had invested a fortune in his young concubine over many months, to make of her a companion to be envied by others. He had been the first of her lovers to parade her as his trophy, and she could only be a trophy if she was beautiful, witty, and charming above all the other demi-mondaines of Paris.

Now it was Montguyon's turn with Alphonsine Plessis and he did not keep her a secret either. It seems that he took her right into the inner sanctum of the rakes' headquarters, the ultra-masculine Jockey-Club, and he did so moreover when Morny was back in town from farming in the Puy-de-Dôme. We know this because at some point between 28 February 1842 and 13 July that year she signed a cheeky petition in the 'Suggestions' ledger of the Jockey-Club. It concerned the nightly disappearance from its premises of the *Globe* newspaper to which the Jockey-Club subscribed. The note urged that the culprit, 'M. de V.', might consider taking out his own subscription if he liked the paper that much. The grumbling signatories included Morny, Montguyon, and the dissolute playboy Emilio Belgiojoso, who owned a house in the Madeleine in Paris which he shared with his estranged wife Cristina, a famous society hostess and Italian patriot.

The last signature, in feminine handwriting, reads 'Marie Duplessis', the name adopted by Alphonsine Plessis in the course of 1842. It was obviously inappropriate for a 'cocotte' (a euphemism for 'tart') to sign anything in the Jockey-Club while at the same time the habitués of that exclusive club were exactly the people who could be relied on to hang out with courtesans. The unofficial historian of the Jockey-Club notes that 'a joker ('farceur') closed the list of signatories by signing, in a feminine hand, with Marie Duplessis!...the future lady of the camellias.'⁴ Was she inside the Jockey-Club that night, perhaps after a night at the opera, fetching up in the club through the secret rakes' passage, led by Montguyon and Morny? If she was there, she was in the company of her two most recent lovers. Not only was Morny back in town, but he was evidently content with his friend having Alphonsine Plessis in tow. There can have been no secrets between these three, which is how she discovered probably now, if she had not done so before, that her baby was dead. The two men must have known all along exactly when he died while she probably did not. Did she ever make her way back out to Versailles to see his grave?

She was fast becoming the mascot of the Jockey-Club. She who had grown up in horse-breeding country now found herself owned by the thoroughbred denizens of Paris's most exclusive stable. And among these Montguyon was the ultimate horse's ass, to use an appropriate modern slang expression. He was a 'brilliant loafer', according to his friend the Comte Edmond d'Alton-Shée, who much preferred Morny. Montguyon may not have been entirely to Alphonsine Plessis's taste either, but Paris and his upper-class rich cronies clearly were. The goose girl from Nonant was now hobnobbing with the kingpins of the capital. The rustic swains and paedophiles of the Orne henceforth belonged to a different world altogether.

On 28 February 1842 Alphonsine Plessis wrote to Delphine. Once again she urged her sister, and now also one of her cousins, to come and join her in Paris: 'If you could only once see and experience the pretty town of Paris, you would never again want to leave and you would soon get used to it', she writes with verve, spurred on further by the thrilling prospect of a visit to the spas of Germany, all part of the chic Paris experience. Who the protector was who would spirit her abroad she did not reveal. That it was Montguyon can be extrapolated, however, from the consequences of a tragic event that happened at that very moment, one which affected the entire nation and would impact directly on Alphonsine's plans for Germany. Her letter to Delphine shows her unrepentant about her love of the fast life of the capital and still hoping to attract her sister to Paris. She seemed unfazed by the manifest, if unintended, contempt her letter showed for Delphine's life of hard, honest work. But the most interesting aspect of her letter is that she still signed herself by her real name of Alphonsine Plessis. This was about to change.

Something else happened during the spring of 1842, an event that helped shape the destiny that turned Alphonsine Plessis into the traviata of Verdi's opera. It concerned a 26-year-old, horse-obsessed aristocrat by the name of Édouard de Perrégaux, one of the two sons of Napoleon Bonaparte's Governor of the Banque de France. On 3 April 1842 he was elevated to the ranks of the Jockey-Club. The minute of his admission records that he was 'Officier de cavalerie. Propriétaire d'une écurie de courses. A monté en courses'. He was wealthy enough to own race horses, rode himself, and within a few months of joining the Jockey-Club stood to inherit half of his father's vast fortune. His mother had died many years earlier while his father passed away in June 1841.

Once the estate was settled, as it would be in August 1842, young Édouard de Perrégaux was free to borrow and spend to his heart's content in the expectation of a huge inheritance. Only it would turn out not to be quite that straightforward because his father, together with his lawyers and financial advisers, had set up a trust to control his two sons' profligacy, which he may have had good reason to suspect. His confidants were one M. Delisle, his adviser, and a M. Carlier, the manager of the Perrégaux empire. Both their counter-signatures were required for any major financial deals by Édouard de Perrégaux. One of these, probably Delisle, would act as the family's factotum when they intervened in his eventual relationship with Marie Duplessis.

The chief guardian of the estate was Édouard's aunt, a redoubtable matriarch by the name of Duchesse de Raguse, née Hortense Perrégaux, who lived at 49 rue Paradis-Poissonière, today's rue de Paradis, in a grand house that is still standing. She was one of the most formidable figures in Paris, instantly recognizable by her artificial nose, rendered necessary by cancer or perhaps congenital syphilis. She would play a significant part in the story of the Perrégaux fortune, particularly when it came into contact with the young courtesan from Nonant.

Perrégaux *père*'s provident stewardship of his estate was tested swiftly after his death when, in the spring of 1842, around the time of his admission to the Jockey-Club, Édouard de Perrégaux launched into a passionate affair with one of Paris's most celebrated actresses, Alice Ozy. After the lady of the camellias, Ozy was the most expensive woman to keep in Paris. The lives of the two young women are in many ways comparable, as might be expected of two beautiful, sought-after and spirited courtesans. When Ozy turned up in Paris and trained as an actress she entered a shadowy world frequented back-stage by rich and powerful men who kept women in love nests. Her world was not that different from Marie Duplessis's.

Early on Ozy became involved with the painter Théodore Chassériau and probably modelled for his daring nude painting *La toilette d'Esther*, which was exhibited in the Louvre in 1841. She modelled again for the superb painting *Baigneuse endormie près d'une source* (1850) (Figure 7.1).

Chassériau was a close friend of the poet, novelist and reviewer-in-chief Théophile Gautier, who had been an early admirer and supporter of his paintings. He may well have met Alice Ozy in Chassériau's studio. It was probably her modelling that prompted Gautier to ask her to let him draw her naked when she went to see him one day to solicit his patronage for a part she was hoping to play. Gautier was a rogue, though by all accounts a largely harmless one. He loved women almost as much as he loved hashish, as befitted the founder of the legendary 'Club des Hachichins' at the Hôtel Lauzan—in *Les Paradis artificiels* Baudelaire, a regular user, calls it by its other name of 'Pimodan'—at 17 Quai d'Anjou, on the Île Saint-Louis. Gautier's brilliant obituary of Marie Duplessis is quoted in the Prologue of this book. He who so longed to freeze the passage of time and its decay by art may well have asked the same nude favour of Marie Duplessis, if only to view

Figure 7.1 Alice Ozy in the *Baigneuse endormie près d'une source* by her lover Théodore Chassériau. She was Marie Duplessis's rival and the mistress of Prince Henri d'Orléans. She also modelled nude for Théophile Gautier.

her as an aesthetic object, for art's sake and to satisfy his curiosity. Alice Ozy obliged, although she and Gautier did not, it seems, engage in a casting couch affair. Rather, he drew her as she fell asleep, naked. That at least is the canonical version of this event. Gautier's drawing of a naked Alice Ozy asleep, infinitely less accomplished than Chassériau's, has survived.[5]

It may have been the supreme accolade of membership of the Jockey-Club that emboldened Perrégaux to initiate an affair with Alice Ozy at a time when she was the mistress of Henri d'Orléans, Duc d'Aumale, one of the younger sons of Louis-Philippe I. Aumale was deeply in love with Alice; even so Perrégaux succeeded in wooing her away. Perhaps she was disenchanted with the prince because he was too committed to his military career in Northern Africa and did not have enough time to live to the full a life of leisure in the capital. Or else Perrégaux proved irresistible, maybe by doting on her even more than his princely rival. As one of his contemporaries noted, Perrégaux kept on falling in love with women. He was as romantic as he was hopeless with women; a daredevil rider, like almost all Marie Duplessis's rich lovers, and physically fit if feckless to a degree, and pathetic in affairs of the heart. And yet, with all his shortcomings, Édouard de Perrégaux would become by far the most important man in the life of the lady of the camellias. He it is whom Verdi immortalized as Alfredo, Violetta's lover.

In the spring of 1842 Paris was as buoyant as it would be fifty years later during the Belle Époque, when the city rocked with art and inventiveness. Even today the French capital occasionally still gives off an aura of vernal romance and excitement, although modern Paris is a spectral reflection of its vibrant past. It too has succumbed to the corrosive torpor of global blandness and uniformity. But for much of the nineteenth century Paris was the most seismic city in Europe, brimming with political activity and, occasionally, erupting ferociously. The city on the Seine lurched from Revolution to Empire at the start of the century, to more revolutions, culminating in 1848 and the catastrophe of the Commune in 1871, when civil unrest and foreign invasion nearly destroyed it. It certainly reduced all its written genealogical records to ashes when arson incinerated the Hôtel de Ville where they were stored, a conflagration whose long-range fall-out haunts researchers of the city to this day.

By comparison the nine years Marie Duplessis spent in Paris between 1838 and 1847 were calm politically but socially and artistically roaring, a period of compulsive hedonism and 'gaieté', a word used by Gustave

Figure 7.2 The boulevard des Italiens, north side, the hub of 1840s Paris, from a drawing of the period: from left to right are the Café de Paris, Tortoni's, the Maison Dorée, and the famous Tabac frequented by Musset.

Claudin who, in his memoirs, brilliantly evokes the magical years of the boulevard leading up to 1848. Marie Duplessis missed the Paris of the July Revolution of 1830 which propelled Louis-Philippe I to the throne, and she died before the barricades rose again in 1848. The febrile creative energy of Paris in the 1840s is a remarkable by-product of political stability in the city of Balzac, Victor Hugo, Lamartine, Dumas *père* et *fils*, Gautier, and Charles Baudelaire, to mention only a few of its luminaries who converged on the boulevard des Italiens, the hub of the capital's café culture (Figure 7.2).

The Italiens was the grandest of the linked avenues that stretched for three miles from the Madeleine in the west to the Bastille in the east. It featured the highest solid stone buildings in Europe and was studded with theatres, cafés, and shopping malls, many of which survive to this day. Without its boulevards, a contemporary remarked, Paris would resemble an eviscerated human body. On the Italiens, politicians, literati, members of the Jockey-Club, 'grisettes' and 'cocottes', also called more graphically and amusingly 'horizontales', all gathered.

The boulevard's gravitational pull emanated from four cafés and two opera houses. The Café de Paris at no. 24, on the north side, had been the unchallenged king of cafés since it opened in 1822. All others paid homage to it, vassals of this grand trendsetter that fascinated the best minds of the capital, the country, and of Europe. To be a regular at the Café de Paris was tantamount to belonging to the exclusive salons of Madame Récamier or Madame de Staël of the era just before. It was the best club on the Pall Mall of Paris. Nestor Roqueplan, Paris's chief impresario, leading light of the Variétés theatre, keen observer of the mores of the capital and of Marie Duplessis, regularly held court here. For him the Café de Paris distilled the intellectual and artistic heart and soul of the capital. His table was ever ready. It was an exclusive haven of style and etiquette in which common words like 'bill' were forbidden—customers asked for their 'menu'—while no-one presumed to summon a waiter ('Pierre, Alphonse, Dominique') by anything other than a discreet gesture. Vulgar abbreviations for food and drink, such as 'une côte nature' or 'une demie' for 'une côtelette au naturel' or 'une demie tasse de café', were frowned upon and corrected by Madame Martin, the owner's wife. The kitchens were out of earshot of the customers and only ever sourced the best produce from the market.[6]

Other regulars at the Paris were the poet Alfred de Musset, Dumas *père*, Eugène Sue, the author of *Le Juif-Errant*, and of course Balzac. Lord Seymour too had his own table here and the British Prime Minister Lord Palmerston never dined anywhere else in Paris. It was also one of Marie Duplessis's favourite cafés. The chronicler of the boulevard, Gustave Claudin, put it none too delicately when he wrote that 'Marie Duplessis, whose star shone brightly at that time, enjoyed intimate relations with the regulars of the Café de Paris'. He admired her singular beauty and recalled that 'she spoke the language of flowers' better than anyone else ever did:

> As long as they could her florists furnished her with white camellias. For three days a month the white camellias were replaced by red ones. She may not have been a follower of Moses, but the colour of her flowers indicated that she too was then crossing the red sea.[7]

Marie Duplessis was at home in the Café de Paris because that is where 'le tout-Paris' converged, when it was not doing so across the rue Taitbout at Tortoni's, the most acclaimed Italian ice cream parlour of Paris, or the Maison Dorée also known as the Maison d'Or ('golden house') in the same block, a legendary venue from the moment it opened in 1840 (Figure 7.3). Its magnificent shell is extant today. This golden magnet too attracted the leading writers and politicians of the day, with its renowned restaurant, among the most richly adorned of the capital, bursting with elaborate sculptures, and a bookshop and 'parfumerie' where rich Parisians could

Figure 7.3 The Maison Dorée at night from a contemporary lithograph by Eugène Lami; its restaurant and salons were a magnet for the city's literati and aristocrats as well as for Marie Duplessis. The legendary ice-cream parlour Tortoni's is attached to the left (west) side of the Dorée.

indulge the then fashionable passion for 'les subtiles odeurs de l'Orient'. Such was the opulence of its gilt-leafed salons and private rooms smothered in silk cushions that contemporaries compared it to Aladdin's cave.

It was a favourite haunt of Paris's Scheherazades, naturally including Alice Ozy and Marie Duplessis, who spent lavishly in its restaurant, as her extant bills from the summer of 1845 amply testify.[8] The irrepressible Lola Montez was a regular. She was notorious for 'her beauty and her consummate impudence... Her gait and carriage were those of a Duchess, but the moment she opened her lips, the illusion vanished... though not devoid of wit, her wit was that of the pot-house, which would not have been tolerated in the smoking room of a club in the small hours.'[9] Montez was in her twenties at the time and was carving out a niche for herself with raunchy performances at the Paris Opéra of the *cachucha*, a Spanish dance rendered popular in Paris by the Austrian ballerina Fanny Elssler, who was involved in a turbulent dispute with the Paris Opéra when she defaulted on her contracts and defected to America instead.

The Café de Paris and the Maison Dorée also boasted lavish private apartments. Lord Seymour, founder of the nearby Jockey-Club, occupied a suite above the Café de Paris, as did the young Richard Wallace, the future founder of the Wallace Collection in London, while the young Duc d'Aumale conducted his liaison with Alice Ozy in her apartment above the Maison Dorée. This was about as public a spot as it was possible to inhabit in Paris: not only did the entire smart set of the capital know her address, but they monitored her comings and goings. To tryst with Aumale in as incognito a fashion as possible, she used to disguise herself as a young man, which was, however, soon known all over the city. There was no escaping the press. Even then there were paparazzi aplenty and, just for good measure, the most brilliant and influential newspaper editor of the age, Hippolyte de Villemessant, editor of *Sylphide*, re-founder of the *Figaro* and inveterate memoirist, occupied rooms directly opposite Ozy's apartment at the Maison Dorée from where he watched her keenly.

This northern corner of the boulevard des Italiens, hemmed in on either side by the rue Taitbout and rue Laffitte, formed the fashionable patrician heart of 1840s Paris. Its arc of chic stretched from the Café de Paris to the Jockey-Club on the adjacent boulevard de Montmartre. Europe's most majestic opera house, after La Scala in Milan, was within a short walking distance of the chief cafés patronized by the city's flaneur elite: the Opéra de Paris at rue Le Peletier rose directly behind the iconic Café Riche in which the biographer of the area, Gustave Claudin, lunched in the same corner for forty years. At no. 13, on the south side of the boulevard, at the corner of the rue Marivaux and the Italiens, across from the Maison Dorée, stood the Café Anglais, a popular brasserie into which flocked the crowds disgorged at the end of shows by the second opera house of the boulevard des Italiens, the Salle Favart, known as 'Théâtre Royal de L'Opéra-Comique' and, popularly, as 'Théâtre-Italien'. According to Jules Janin, the Café Anglais and its cabinet 'le Grand Seize' were long the favoured meeting places of the Paris élite.'[10]

The foyer of the Favart was fifty yards down the cut from the Café Anglais whose upstairs restaurant was keenly frequented by Marie Duplessis and her friends after the opera (see 10.1). Two incidents in this narrative involve Marie Duplessis, the Café Anglais, the Maison Dorée, and the boulevard between them. Standing outside the successor of the Café Anglais today and looking across at the Maison Dorée, glimpsed intermittently through a constant surge of cars, coaches, and vans, it is hard to imagine that in the 1840s this very spot was the magnet for Paris's literati and intelligentsia: Balzac, Gérard de Nerval, Théophile Gautier, Baudelaire, the two Dumas, Jules Janin, Chopin, Liszt, and Nestor Roqueplan all ate, drank and sat here, with or without their mistresses, as did all of Marie Duplessis's lovers, and also, at some point or other, Rossini, Donizetti, and Verdi.

The boulevard as a public space and concept was a creation of the period. In one of her *lettres parisiennes*, dated 25 August 1837, the 'Vicomte Charles de Launay', who was none other than Mme Émile de Girardin, patroness of the arts and chaperone of writers, evokes the glory of the new lights that henceforth graced the boulevards:

> After the railways, what excites the Parisians more than anything, is the new lighting of the boulevards. At night the walk along them is quite wonderful. From the church of the Madeleine to the rue Montmartre, these two alleys of chandeliers, from where surges a white and pure luminosity, create a wonderful effect. And so many people, so many people![11]

The three boulevards ablaze at night were, from west to east, the Madeleine, the Capucines, and the Italiens. Here people strolled while 'les *cabs*', broughams, and hansoms, wove through the crowd at a leisurely pace. An eyewitness described the atmosphere on the boulevard des Italiens as it was when Marie Duplessis lived there:

> At certain times of the day, the *flanerie* homes in on it. Wits and the literary crowd, not always synonymous, meet up here ... On a balmy summer's day,

the boulevard des Italiens flaunts a triple garland of stunning dresses, the latest hat fashions, and a riot of flowers. Tortoni, the Café de Paris, and the Café Riche have put out comfortable seats for the ladies, and benches and temporary tables for lovers of iced punch, cigars and a daily dose of literature. The *'promenade'* affords the richest, the most astounding, most wonderful sight that can be imagined: a majestic tidal river of smart black clothes and silk dresses, flowing by again and again; a world of pretty women and gentlemen who occasionally are handsome but who, more often than not, are ugly and unappealing. Wit, stupidity, and malicious gossip, heavy sentences, politics, and slander clash in multiple cross-fires: news clashes with jokes, puns piggy-back on logic; English whistles above the harmony of the Italiens while the sounds of German cut across the babble of French...Everything you see on the boulevard des Italiens is a smoke screen: those dresses, mostly unpaid for, the bucks...[12]

The 'Revue Parisienne' in the summer issue of the 1843 *Sylphide* recommends Tortoni's as the hub for all the latest information on the capital's fashions, because in this 'fairy tale palace' the *beau monde* likes to cluster. At dusk, the writer remarks, the masses moving on the boulevard assume a mysterious aspect and gradually turn into a a shadow people, until the moment they are suddenly lit up by the bright light of the gas; in an instant the indistinct figures of just a moment earlier are again dressed in colour and vitality.[13] The artificially gas-lit boulevard was one of the glories of Paris during Marie Duplessis's life here, with night as light as day. It must have seemed a perfect companion to the railways encouraging the people of the great city to imagine that they were living at a time of unprecedented progress.

The boulevards were buzzing that spring with rumours about Alice Ozy's affair with the rich young Perrégaux. Alphonsine Plessis knew all about it. Her protector Montguyon was equerry to d'Aumale's elder brother and therefore knew the slightest details of the lives and loves of the court. Ozy's desertion of the Prince for Perrégaux was the most newsworthy social event of the season so far, one moreover in which the boulevard had a stake since Ozy and Aumale had used the Maison Dorée for their trysting. Did Alphonsine meet Perrégaux during her many visits to the theatre and opera? He could hardly be the lover of Alice Ozy without frequenting the two opera houses adjacent to the cafés of the Italiens. Part of the prestige of being the lover of the glittering young woman, who had thrown over a royal prince for him, was to be seen with her. Aumale gallantly removed himself from Paris to avoid the humiliation of facing his rival in public: on 11 March 1842 he left Paris to rejoin his regiment in Algeria commanding troops in the successful skirmishes at Biskra. Alphonsine Plessis could hardly have missed running into her future husband with his new paramour that spring of 1842, as they moved in all the same circles.

No place attracted wealthy and aristocratic Parisians more than Chantilly. In 1842 the races started on Friday 19 May 1842.[14] All eyes were on the new star of the Paris equestrian set, the 28-year old Comte Édouard de Perrégaux who duly appeared with Alice Ozy in his phaeton carriage. He had only just stepped out of it when the horses bolted, plunging towards the lake of the château with carriage and fair passenger in tow. An accident seemed inevitable but in the end Ozy escaped with a fright. It is likely that Marie Duplessis witnessed the event. Not only did all the young bucks of the Jockey-Club converge on the same spaces, in Paris and away from the city too, but her lover of the moment, Montguyon, had a horse, Singleton, racing that day. Among the general consternation the egregious Montguyon found time to bet 'mille louis' that 'Ozy' would be fine and to note, ungallantly, that the scare would have helped her digestion: in other words, apart from soiling herself she would be unharmed.[15]

Little wonder that this was not a lover the young woman from Normandy would tolerate for long. Any barbed jokes at Perrégaux's expense over the incident would soon have evaporated into thin air because, astonishingly, he won the grand prix of the Jockey-Club with his horse Plover. It was the first time he had entered a horse in the race. In the event his take-home total prize money may have been as much as 20,000 francs, the equivalent of almost a quarter of Marie Duplessis's entire estate at her death. Perrégaux's victory at Chantilly was probably the reason why Montguyon's tasteless bet was later remembered at all: far from being doomed, it turned out that Perrégaux's participation had been charmed. It may also have been the first time he actually met Marie Duplessis rather than just crossing her path.

As spring ebbed away, the temperatures continued to climb relentlessly. It promised to be a scorching summer. June still counted as a month of the Paris season but during July chic Parisians dispersed to the fashionable watering holes of Normandy, notably Deauville, Trouville, Cabourg, and also to the ultra-smart Biarritz in the Pyrénées Atlantiques. The exceptional heat of the early summer of 1842 turned the chic districts of Paris into a buckled-up desert even before the traditional sizzler month of August.

8

An old count in Baden-Baden

July 1842

Most on Alphonsine's mind now, and rendered imperative by the glorious weather, was the prospect of that visit to Baden-Baden, or 'Bade' in French, the summer capital of Europe, a small hedonistic German city in which French was the lingua franca. She would feel perfectly at home in it. She and Montguyon had been set for Baden-Baden since February 1842. They needed to be, because the grand hotels of the spa town in the Black Forest filled up months in advance, with some of their suites permanently reserved by the grandest families of Europe and Russia. They must have booked theirs around the time she wrote to her sister.

She required a passport for travelling abroad and had submitted her application. With the kind of support she enjoyed, getting a passport posed few problems. It was issued on 13 July 1842 and was valid for a year. It survives in the Musée de *La Dame aux Camélias* in Gacé. The one-page document obviously does not contain a photograph, but its text and stamps tell an intriguing story. Here is how she is described on her passport:

> Miss Duplessis, Marie, 'rentière', born in Saint-Germain-de-Clairefeuille, Orne. Residing in Paris, rue du Mont-Thabor 28, heading for Baden-Baden. Description: aged 21 years, height 1 metre and 67 centimetres, auburn ['châtains'] hair, medium forehead ['front moyen'], auburn eyebrows, black eyes, handsome nose, small mouth, round chin, oval face, pale complexion.

The endorsements on the back of this document are from the 'Ministère des Affaires étrangères' and the Baden-Baden consulate in Paris. There are also stamps from the police of Baden-Baden, Bordeaux, Bagnères-de-Luchon and, twice, from London, proof of her travels to these places between July 1842 and July 1843. What immediately jumps out from her passport is her new name, 'Mlle Marie Duplessis'. This is the first recorded use of the name by which she has become famous. She altered her name between 28 February 1842, when she signed herself 'Alphonsine' in a letter to her sister, and the time she applied for a passport that spring. Why did she do so? When Romain Vienne teased her about exchanging her 'pretty name' Alphonsine for the much more common one of 'Marie', Marie Duplessis archly replied that she did so because it was the name of the Virgin. 'Have you considered adding "Magdalene"' to it, he joshed, to which her answer was that she might still do so.

At first her choice of 'Duplessis' would seem to suggest a wish to elevate herself to a higher social class, as Duplessis was a well known aristocratic name in France. When Vienne pressed her on this, she referred to the Duplessis manor in Nonant which, she informed him, she would buy one day to become the châtelaine Marie du Plessis. She was teasing him, of course. The real reason for her change of name may be rather more complex. To understand what happened, it is necessary to look again at her mother's death notice, which gives her maiden names as 'Deshayes' and 'femme Duplessis'. It should have read Marie Plessis, which was her married name, but she clearly had started to use 'Duplessis', presumably because she could no longer bear to carry the name of her wretched husband. She may have been 'femme de Plessis' in law, but she called herself 'Duplessis', that is 'du Plessis'. With 'Duplessis' she symbolically divorced her husband and reclaimed her maiden identity, because her father's farm in his home village of Courménil, where she had sheltered, stood in a dip known locally as 'du Plessis'. In other words, by calling herself Marie Duplessis she declared that she was henceforth 'Marie from Plessis in the village of Courménil'.

Her bid to be free found its way into her death record. What must have happened is that Alphonsine Plessis discovered what her mother had done when she applied for her passport. For this she needed to supply her birth certificate with her application. To get it she returned to Nonant, probably around the time she wrote to her sister, in February 1842. She had probably never seen her 'extrait de naissance' before and would therefore have been unaware of the fact that her mother was in fact called 'Marie' on it. Was it her guardian uncle who showed her the death notice of her mother on which she is called 'Marie Duplessis'? Alphonsine, it seems, understood at once her mother's defiant gesture and, out of love for her, she decided to follow suit. But she would go further and assume her dead mother's preferred name, thus becoming another Marie Duplessis. If her mother's self-naming arose from a yearning to shed her married shackles, by her action Alphonsine made her mother live again. In the light of what would happen later regarding mother and daughter, such a gut-wrenching, deeply private, *cri de coeur* by the 18-year-old courtesan seems astonishingly prescient.

She not only altered her name but she also lied about her age. By adding three years to her eighteen—as she had seemingly done earlier when she boosted her age by two years when giving birth in Versailles—she became legally an adult and therefore technically entitled to a passport for travelling abroad. Her name and age both suggest that she and her 'friends' happily forged parts of her birth certificate. The authorities probably chose not to notice this because she was the paramour of some of the most powerful men in the country. As for the description of her as 'rentière', this term was routinely applied in the period to women who lived seemingly independent lives without needing to work. Everyone knew what it meant; there was no need to spell it out. The rest of the information on her passport is remarkably accurate, notably about her appearance, which agrees closely with authenticated portraits of her. As for the stamps in it, the most tantalizing concern her two visits to London; not least because London would provide the stage for a crucial episode in her life. What was she doing in Dickens's London, the city of *Dombey and Son*, and who took her there? Until recently these seemed unanswerable questions.

Wednesday 13 July 1842: This should have been her red letter day as her passport was issued on this day and would set her free to travel. Instead, the day would sear itself into her memory and that of the entire country for a very different reason. What happened was that shortly after noon that day, in the western Parisian suburb of Neuilly-sur-Seine, the 32-year-old Duc d'Orléans, the heir to the French throne, was catapulted out of his carriage when his horses bolted. He died a few hours later. The accident is commemorated by Alfred de Musset in his elegy 'Le Treize Juillet'. It rocked the country because ever since the beheading of Louis XVI in 1793, France had been the most volatile monarchy in Europe; anything regarding the heir to the throne might cause renewed ferment. There was no question of royal aide-de-camps like Montguyon accompanying their paramours to Baden-Baden then. The royal affairs required his full attention, politically and ceremonially. The dead prince would lie in state in Notre-Dame de Paris from 30 July to 3 August, to allow the nation and Paris to show their respect.

For once Montguyon would be earning his keep at the expense of his pleasures. Though it appears that he and Marie Duplessis decided that she would depart for Baden-Baden anyway, as planned, accompanied by two servants.

On Thursday 21 July the three Parisians set off by coach for the spa town. They arrived in Baden-Baden on Friday 22 July. There was as yet no railway station in the town, but the way in on the Rastatt road was much the same as it is today. As the coach turned into the Kaiserallee, it passed on the right the majestic thermal 'Badischer Hof' or 'Cour de Bade'. All hotels were known by both French and German names. Baden-Baden offered its wealthy clientele an exciting choice of accommodation in private houses and hotels. Residences of all sizes could be rented during the summer, as up to 6,000 local owners vanished surrendering their homes to rent. Where, a contemporary observer wondered, did they all go: underground or perch on trees until the end of the summer? One Professor Weih advertised his house at No. 58 Wilhelms Strasse as 'between the Europa and French hotels opposite, and very close, to the promenade and the Trinkhalle. Dining room has a piano and one of the rooms boasts a balcony and superb, wide open, views.'

Among the chief attractions of Baden-Baden were its luxury hotels. They aimed to dazzle the visitors with their lavishness. A contemporary English visitor identified the two 'grandes dames' of Baden-Baden hotels as the Angleterre and the Cour de Bade.[1] They were the best inns 'for married Englishmen', because 'in the former the greatest attention and civility are joined to perfect rectitude and good management which is not surpassed but rivalled by the sister hotel of Baden.' The stress on 'rectitude' might imply that others among the grand inns were somewhat more accommodating when it came to sexual mores; they may have been readier to allow men to bring their mistresses. At both the Angleterre and the Cour de Bade the 'table d'hôte' was 'magnificent' while 'very good elsewhere, and the prices fixed'. Moreover banking facilities were readily available at the Cour de Bade where, 'in rooms looking on the lovely English gardens resides during the season Mr Meyer [whose] London Agency is the firm of Coutts and Co.; at Carlsruhe Mr. J. Kusel has an agreement with him so that the bills are paid indifferently by either when presented, and which will be found to be a very great convenience for my countrymen who reside in Carlsruhe or here.'

The stage Marie Duplessis entered that Friday in July 1842 was set for a summer of luxury and sinful fun. After proceeding beyond the Cour de

Bade for a hundred yards or so, her coach would have emerged onto the straight of the Kaiserallee. What now confronted her was Baden-Baden's latest folly, the neo-classical Trinkhalle (lit. the 'Drinking Hall'), an impudently Corinthian fantasy that had been completed only a few weeks earlier. Across from the Trinkhalle sat the Europäischer Hof while eighty yards further on stood the Hôtel d'Angleterre, an imposing fairy-tale palace much favoured by English and European aristocrats, plutocrats, and artists like the wealthy Liszt.

If the tone of fashionable Baden-Baden was ultimately set by the Englisher Hof and the Badischer Hof, it is also the case that the newly built Europäischer Hof was an instant star in this galaxy of palaces. A French 1842 guide to Baden-Baden noted that in 'l'Hôtel d'Europe, le Zaehringen, la Cour de Bade, l'Hôtel de Russie, l'Hôtel d'Angleterre' visitors could live like princes by renting suites, or merely let a room for three florins, while six florins a day would give them access to everything the town had to offer by way of dining, dancing, concerts, walks. He put the Europäischer Hof at the top of his list because it was brand new (Figure 8.1).

It alone survives in some splendour today, with the same grand central staircase that in the 1840s was graced repeatedly by the light tread of Marie Duplessis, her future lover Franz Liszt, who stayed here a few months after her, Gogol, the Tolstoys, Turgenev, and the British Prime Minister Gladstone, who overlapped here with Marie Duplessis during the last year of her life. Even Empress Elisabeth ('Sissi') of Austria trod these legendary steps leading up from the hotel's resplendent lobby (Figure 8.2).

It is not known which suite Marie Duplessis and her travel companions occupied in July 1842, but it was bound to be at the front facing the Trinkhalle. Just over to the left, as she looked out of her windows, on the gentle slope rising from the Kaiserallee, stood Baden-Baden's palatial Kurhaus, better known as 'Conversation Palace' or 'la Maison de la Conversation'. This stately neo-classical structure, fronted by a portico supported by eight Corinthian columns, echoed by the Trinkhalle, constituted the nerve centre of nineteenth-century Baden-Baden.

The immigration register of 22 July records that a 'Dem. Duplessis mit Bed.[ienten] aus St. Germain [de Clairefeuille, as on her passport]. 3.P[ersonen]' were staying at the Europäischer Hof. Who her two chaperones were is not possible to determine with certainty, although it is likely that one of them was her chambermaid Clotilde, who would still be with her a few years later in her Madeleine apartment. Was the other servant her

Hôtel de l' Europe.
située à la Promenade en face la Trinkhalle et vis à vis de la Maison de Conversation.
hôtel et dépendances 125 Chambres. table d' hôtes à 5 heure

Figure 8.1 The luxury Hôtel de l'Europe (Europäischer Hof) in Baden-Baden, as it was in the 1840s when Marie Duplessis stayed here.

faithful footman Étienne? But he would not have been allowed to share her suite. So it is more likely that she had a second female servant, perhaps the woman who later became her resident cook at the Madeleine.

Marie Duplessis soon discovered that several of Paris's most prominent playboys frequented Baden-Baden at the start of the summer season. At least two of the residents of the Europäischer Hof belonged to her circle in Paris. They were the Plancy brothers, Vicomte and Baron de Plancy, the latter a close friend of Montguyon and one of her alleged lovers. The Plancys had been staying at the Europäischer Hof since 5 July, unaccompanied, it seems, by their mistresses. At least no women are listed as staying with them but that does not mean that there were none. Much of the attraction of the luxury spas of Europe depended on sexual discretion, which is why it was common practice for hotel registers only to record the noble gentlemen, not the unmarried female companions for whose rooms in the same hotels they paid. Another Parisian aristocrat staying at the hotel

Figure 8.2 The legendary staircase in the Hôtel de l'Europe in Baden-Baden. Royalty, writers, and courtesans rubbed shoulders on it. Visitors included 'Sissi' (Queen Elizabeth) of Austria, Tolstoy, and Marie Duplessis.

at that time was the Comte de Saint-Geniès. He was a seasonal swallow in Baden-Baden and may be the same person as the poet and translator Comte Léonce de Saint-Geniès. This was probably the first time he met Marie Duplessis. He evidently took enough of a shine to her to want part of her when in February 1847 he bought her reading accessories at the Madeleine auction of her effects. It turns out that he was not the only person to notice her in Baden-Baden and to get to know her better.

All the Baden-Baden luxury hotels promoted the abundant fare of fun, gambling, and music that was on offer in the town. Marie Duplessis only needed to fling open her windows to catch the murmur of voices and the sounds of music floating up from the Conversation Palace and Trinkhalle. Open-air concerts and serenades started on the terraces in front of the Kurhaus at 3 p.m. and were attended by most of the residents of the palaces on the river Oos. On the dot of five a melodious tune made itself heard. This was the legendary dinner bell of the Hôtel d'Angleterre, the signal, by virtue of its proximity to the Kurhaus, for all boarding guests to return to their hotels for dinner; unless, of course, they desired to linger for dinner at the magnificent restaurant of the Conversation Palace.

After dinner, at 7 p.m., the most important ritual of the Baden-Baden day got under way, the evening promenade up and down the Lichtenthaler Allee, an alley lined by oaks, chestnuts, and elms for a mile and a half along the Oos (see map, Figure 8.3). It stretched from the Schiessbrücke outside the Hôtel d'Angleterre to the former monastic hamlet of Lichtenthal. During long and balmy summer evenings the Lichtenthaler Allee became the parade ground in which to see and to be seen. As the women strolled up and down the alley, they showed off the latest Parisian, English, and Russian fashions, while the men inspected the women. At this dance of taste, lure, and seduction, Marie Duplessis was probably the most accomplished 'artiste' in Baden-Baden, if not in the whole of Europe. How she displayed herself in the Lichtenthaler Allee is not documented but she clearly did so to best effect by a combination of walking, riding, and being driven in a rented carriage. Though primarily meant for walking, the alley was open to riders and cabs too. Indeed, just five days before Marie Duplessis arrived in Baden-Baden, the town's authorities issued a stern notice to decree that, in response to repeated complaints against aggressive riding and speeding cabs, henceforth sections of the alley without pavements could only be traversed by horses and cabs at a slow trot or reduced speed. As she was alone, with Montguyon detained in Paris at least for another week, she was free to enjoy herself, socialize, and imbibe the pleasures of Baden-Baden. Of course she attended all the concerts and balls. She could hardly miss them as few places were closer to the Conversation Palace than her hotel.

We know what was on offer during her stay in Baden-Baden. Thus, the evening of her first Sunday, the Maison de la Conversation hosted a concert which featured extracts from Halévy's opera *Romance de Guido et Ginevra* 'pour cornet à piston' and 'Solo pour cor' by the Czech composer KalliWoda, 'exécuté par A. König, trompette-solo de S. M. le roi de Bavière'.[2] The following Tuesday, again at the Maison de la Conversation, the talented pianist Theodor Döhler gave a concert, which included his own variations on Rossini's *Guillaume Tell*, Irish popular melodies, and motifs from the operas *La Somnambula* and *Lucia di Lammermoor*. That Saturday, 29 July 1842, the conductor Louis Waldteufel, the father of the famous composer of waltzes and polkas, Émile Waldteufel, conducted a potpourri for 'cornet à piston et violin'. In this same venue, in the Salle de Réunion, Liszt had played two years earlier when he performed his own rendition of Rossini's

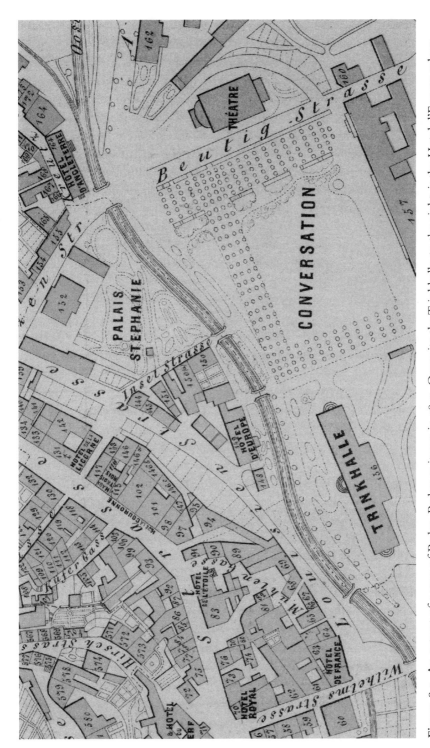

Figure 8.3 An extract of a map of Baden-Baden as it was in 1842. Opposite the Trinkhalle, to the right, is the Hotel d'Europe where Marie Duplessis stayed, with the Hotel d'Angleterre located beyond the Palais Stephanie, at the start of the Allée de Lichenthal.

overture to *Guillaume Tell*, an 'air' from *Lucia*, another from Meyerbeer's *Robert Le Diable*, and his party piece *Grand Galop Chromatique*.

Concerts were not always as popular as the performers might have hoped. One curmudgeonly commentator, well familiar with the season at Baden-Baden, remarked that the town's guests much preferred dancing to concerts, and that the most raucous quadrilles, lively dances by Musard and Strauss, names that were synonymous with the quadrille and waltz, were preferred to ethereal classical music: even the great Liszt, 'poète rêveur du piano', he noted ruefully, failed to fill the house when he performed, while his rival Thalberg, after one look at his audience, fled the town without even playing.

Dancing was indeed the chief fare of Baden-Baden. Such was the spell cast by new risqué dances that two days after Marie Duplessis's arrival, the town's daily newspaper, the *Badeblatt*, advertised the services of the director of the Conversation balls: during the season he would give tuition in the 'Walse, Galopade, Française, Retorte, Mazurka et Boléro, avec des castagnettes'. He guaranteed to teach 'la Walse, le Galop...en 12 leçons. De plus la Mazurka en 16 leçons'. The Conversation or Kurhaus played host to grand formal balls twice a month during the summer. The first of these, a 'Grand Bal Paré' or formal dress ball, happened on Sunday 30 July, after the Waldteufel concert. Marie Duplessis would undoubtedly have shone on this glittering occasion. She was a superb dancer, a fact remarked on time and again by those who knew her well.

The concert programmes at the Conversation attest to a rich mélange of popular and classical music. During the glorious days of July 1842 Baden-Baden hummed with the melodies of Bellini and the harmonies of Donizetti, whose *Lucia di Lammermoor* defined the operatic mood of the time every bit as much as Bellini's *Norma*. The winged arias, duets, and choruses of the two operas had taken Europe by storm; they resonate, undiminished, 180 years later. The 'swan of Catania', as Bellini was known, may have been dead but his music continued to pack the opera houses of Milan, Venice, Vienna, Paris, and London. So did the effervescent genius of Rossini, whose creations matched the riotous polkas that were played all over Europe at this time.[3] Baden-Baden was naturally at the forefront of this rhythmic bacchanalia, which was joined at that moment by the most successful dance of the nineteenth century, the waltz. Polka and waltz broke with tradition by virtue of the intimate physical contact required of the dancing partners. For the first time men and women were glued together as they rocked to the pulsating rhythms of the music or, conjoined, glided along the dance floor. The novel aspect of unmarried couples locked in an embrace as dance partners did worry some. One contemporary observer spelled out the boundless new erotic possibilities:

> Indeed, to hold in one's arms the supple, sinuous waist of a pretty young woman, to feel her bend like a reed yielding under the pressure from one's arms, to brush one's lips against her flowing locks that winds of passion are lifting in a burning rush of pleasure, to hold in fascination her gaze, abstracted while her pulse is racing, a look that almost touches one while burning itself into one's chest, and then to propel ourselves into the dance like two blossoms of the same flower, yes, one may well lose one's mind and footing. Little wonder that the solicitude of a mother or the love of a husband may tremble all over at this.[4]

The polka held such sway that a neologism was born: *polker*, which meant dancing the polka with bacchic abandon. In her *Memoirs*, Céleste Mogador recalls how the Fred Astaire of the Bal Mabille in the 1840s, Brididi, partner of the venue's Ginger Rogers, the tragic 'Pomaré' who lost her baby,[5] called on Mogador one afternoon, all excited, to tell her: 'there is a new dance, the polka: come to see me tonight and we will practise and dance it together.' After practising for five hours they had finally mastered it to perfection: 'we executed a host of figures that made us look like clever dogs: arms, legs, body, head, everything moved at once. One would have thought we were a whirl of telegraph poles and jumping jacks. But it was new and it was thought to be attractive.'[6] Marie Duplessis's facility and grace on the dance floor never failed to impress the men and women who watched her. Still only 18 she outshone all other *polkeuses Parisiennes* of the Baden-Baden dance scene; several years later, when she was already visibly feverish and ill, she could still dazzle onlookers with her dancing prowess. She would have been impossible not to spot during the fourteen days she sojourned in Baden-Baden without her keeper.

Someone who noticed her very much was a rich, 76-year-old count from Paris who was also holidaying in Baden-Baden. He had brought his extended family, ten of them altogether, which was why he rented an entire villa from 'Gärtner Arnold 188' in the Hardtgasse, a short walk from the Angleterre hotel. The name of the wealthy count was Gustav Ernst von Stackelberg, a German diplomat who had been Russian ambassador at the Congress of Vienna. He had retired to Paris and had ten legitimate children with his wife, Countess Caroline of Ludoff. Their matrimonial home in

Paris was at the exclusive address of 7 Chaussée d'Antin, five minutes off the boulevard des Italiens. So sought-after was the address that it was shared by the Belgian embassy, one of the smartest residences in the whole of Paris. By the time he passed Marie Duplessis in the Lichtenthaler Allee, Stackelberg was a living political fossil from a time of turmoil. As one of the architects of the Congress of Vienna, he was notorious now only for his frenzied womanizing. Such was the hoary Lothario's appetite for young women that Parisians nicknamed him 'ravisher of virgins'; for this ageing pike the pool of illicit pleasures of Baden-Baden afforded rich pickings among the shoals of demi-mondaines who darted in and out of its smart hotels and promenades.[7]

Marie Duplessis had of course detected the elderly gentleman who was watching her intently during her daily promenades in the Lichtenthaler. More than most she knew the courting rituals of sex in her circles and would have spotted the prowler. The fact that she was alone had not escaped the old count who would have known full well why her protector was detained in Paris: the death of d'Orléans, his lying in state in Notre-Dame, and the impending state obsequies were on everyone's mind. So Stackelberg must have decided to make a play for the alluring young woman whose name he probably knew well from the boulevard. He did not need to worry about Montguyon: what could a reckless, debt-ridden playboy offer Marie Duplessis that he could not trump many times over with his enormous wealth, except youth and energetic sex? Money and power were his chief assets and these he would put at the service of the eye-catching courtesan, who was making her mark in Baden-Baden as surely as she had in Paris. She may not have been a virgin, but she would still be a terrific trophy.

He made his move while she was walking in the grand Allee. How he broached his proposition to her is not known, but we can be fairly certain that both parties would have played by well-established rules while knowing precisely what this was all about. She would have indicated to him that Monsieur de Montguyon had certain rights over her but that these were not necessarily cast in stone. If deep inside her she laughed at the old man, she would have been in no doubt about the reach and depth of his pockets. Back in the Europaïscher Hof that evening she probably discussed Count Stackelberg's proposal with her two confidants. Although we cannot be sure, it would appear that what he had suggested was that he would put her up in a lavish new apartment in Paris where he would visit occasionally for sex, mostly after the opera or the theatre where she would be expected to share his box. He also wanted her to himself.

There was something else too, something that would play an important part in her own recollections later, and that is the role played by one of the Count's daughters in his pitch for Marie Duplessis. This daughter was cited by Marie Duplessis as the stimulus underlying Stackelberg's propositioning her in the way he did in the Lichtenthaler Allee, and her reason for accepting. But she failed to name the daughter and such is her confusion about timing and detail that two of the daughters need to be considered. One of them was the 21-year-old Hélène de Stackelberg. Six months earlier, in January 1842, she had married the 37-year-old Count Josef Ugarte in the Madeleine church in Paris. She and her husband, who was the Austrian ambassador in nearby Karlsruhe, were staying in Baden-Baden at the same time as the old count. They too had commandeered a private house as they and their retinue numbered fourteen altogether. The other daughter was Marie de Stackelberg, who had died unmarried in Paris two years earlier at the age of 22.

According to Marie Duplessis's later testimony, the old count approached her and pleaded with her to be allowed to become her protector. Not for sexual gratification, but to enjoy her company as a friend. The reason he offered was that she, Marie Duplessis, intensely resembled his deceased daughter, Marie de Stackelberg; he was heart-broken but her company would soothe his pain. At which point she claims to have relented and allowed herself to be wooed and chaperoned by the old man. But this account was derided by Dumas *fils* and others too poured scorn on it, convinced that the old lecher desired the young courtesan for sex and exhibiting. Their incredulity stemmed from Stackelberg's philandering track record. Also, what daughter? they scoffed, mindful of the death of Stackelberg's daughter Marie two years earlier and that of her sister Hélène in February 1843 in nearby Karlsruhe; although Hélène had obviously died *after* the start of the relationship of Marie Duplessis and Stackelberg.

The truth of the matter may be a bit more complex than the death of either daughter. The two young women, Marie and Hélène, may have merged into one in the telling of the story. Marie Duplessis may well have been embarrassed by her liaison with the old count which, in the eyes of all, was predicated on naked material self-interest. To ground it instead in an act of charity and compassion, by casting herself as the guardian angel of a devastated father, made her look good. Perhaps she needed to believe that this was the reason why she let him look after her at all. Also, there may be more than just a grain of truth in this story of grieving father and daughters. Certainly, before long she did indeed find herself comforting old Stackelberg over the loss of a second daughter in the space of two years.

Apart from dancing, concerts, and fashionable walks through the Lichtenthaler Allee, the main activity of Baden-Baden was gambling. While officially everyone was in Baden-Baden for its thermal spas and health-giving reputation, in reality the town in the Black Forest was the Monte Carlo of another era. Here the night was young until the Casino, adjacent to the Kurhaus, flung open its doors after the concerts. It is not known who chaperoned Marie Duplessis into the most elegant gambling den of Europe. Perhaps the two Plancys did, but they could only have done so if someone, such as Montguyon, or perhaps even Stackelberg, provided the funds. Marie Duplessis took to gambling with a passion. Rumours about her profligacy abounded but she was the lucky exception to the rule, because she reportedly won more than she lost.

Would the old count have flaunted her as his new conquest, assuming that she was his already, in front of so many Parisians, with his wife and extended family, including his recently married daughter so close? Probably not. Baden-Baden was too small to afford the anonymity that came with the turf in Paris. Countess Ludoff may not have minded her husband's escapades in the big city, but here, in front of her children, almost all of them older than Marie Duplessis, she could hardly turn a blind eye. What further points that way is the fact that when Marie Duplessis and her two companions cease to be recorded in Baden-Baden on 4 August, Stackelberg stayed on. He was still there on 30 August, nearly seven weeks after his arrival on 9 July. It is tempting to think that he remained there to be close to his daughter Hélene. It is possible that she was already sick, although the record of his sojourns in Baden-Baden suggests that he regularly stayed there for long periods.

In the meantime, Marie Duplessis was probably heading for another resort, perhaps Wiesbaden, Bad Ems, or Spa in the Ardennes. The likely reason why she is not recorded in the other resorts is because after 4 August she was joined by her lover. Montguyon was free by then from his courtier's tasks, as the funeral solemnities for Ferdinand-Philippe d'Orléans were completed on 3 August. Once he joined her, she would no longer be listed separately by the police in the various spa towns they visited. Henceforth her presence in the exclusive summer resorts of Europe could only be guessed at through records relating to her lovers.

9

Partying in Paris and London
with Antinous

1842–1843

When Marie Duplessis returned to Paris for the start of the autumn season of 1842, the short reign of Montguyon was drawing to an end. She would try and stay loyal to the old count who had been busy sorting out her new accommodation while she was touring. On Saturday 15 October 1842 Marie Duplessis left 28 Mont-Thabor, where she had lived for two years, and moved into a new apartment at 22 rue d'Antin, a slim, flat-iron building that juts into the Rue de Port Mahon (Figure 9.1).

For a nomadic orphaned girl, Marie Duplessis was remarkably house-proud, as one of her friends later recorded after visiting her apartment. She adored beautiful objects and was expert at exhibiting them. Her instinctive flair and taste were underpinned by reading about the art and artefacts that adorned her homes. She must have felt like a countess as she took over the keys to her new home.

Stackelberg was generous with his vast fortune, but the glamorous courtesan reneged on her part of their deal almost at once. No sooner was she established at rue d'Antin than a new beau appeared on the scene, the Duc de Guiche. Of course 'le tout-Paris', notably the young men of the Jockey-Club, knew that she and Montguyon had parted company, and that therefore the field was wide open for a successor. They would have been aware also of her liaison with Stackelberg, but the old man was merely an additional challenge. Guiche was a dashing young artillery officer, the scion of a grand aristocratic family, and naturally a member of the Jockey-Club. He was reputedly the most handsome man in Paris, hence his nickname 'Antinous', after the legendary youth who had been the lover of the Roman emperor

Figure 9.1 No. 22 rue d'Antin, a slim, flat-iron building occupied by Marie Duplessis in October 1842, courtesy of her old protector, Count Gustav Ernst von Stackelberg.

Hadrian. 'Antinous' (synonymous with 'pretty lover boy') punned on his real name, which was Antoine X Alfred Agénor de Gramont, Duc de Guiche, eventually Duc de Gramont. He was born four and a half years before Marie Duplessis in the prestigious town of Saint-Germain-en-Laye on the outskirts of Paris, a place that by coincidence Marie Duplessis came to know very well on the arm of another lover, Alexandre Dumas *fils*, and a place that will play a pivotal role in this story.

Romain Vienne barely hid Guiche's identity under the name 'de Tiche Grandon' (for 'de Guiche Gramont'), while his description of the young Guiche closely matches the appearance in an oil painting by Eliseo Sala of the by then middle-aged Agénor de Gramont, with reference particularly to his 'strong moustache and superb dark sideburns' (Figure 9.2).[1]

Her new lover-in-waiting was as suave as he was rich. As he homed in on Marie Duplessis, he was aiming for the sexual nirvana of Paris. He longed to be involved with the most desired, sophisticated, and expensive woman in Paris while all the time someone else, the rich Stackelberg,

Figure 9.2 Agénor, Duc de Guiche Gramont, one of Marie Duplessis's most prestigious lovers.

would pay for her home and keep. He too would shower her with gifts: anything less would have been inconceivable, but the huge cost of daily maintenance was assumed by her old count. Moreover, and much to Montguyon's annoyance, Guiche did not even need to provide her with his own carriage on her daily excursions up the Champs-Élysées to the Arc de Triomphe roundabout. Instead, she used the one Montguyon had given her as a gift while also retaining the black spaniel, another of his presents which, to add insult to injury, was now being walked by Guiche. Montguyon vented his frustration over this to his friend Comte Arthur Beugnot who related it to Plancy, the very Plancy who had stayed in the Europäischer Hof at the same time as Marie Duplessis and whose gossipy memoirs take us right to the heart of this period. When Beugnot suggested that this might constitute sufficient provocation for a duel, Montguyon dismissed the idea out of hand.[2] Fortunately for Marie Duplessis her former lover was sensible, thereby ensuring that her reputation would not be dragged into the deadly quagmire of duels. Her sassy friend Lola Montez would not be so lucky.

Guiche was passionate about riding, women, and Britain, the last his most distinctive characteristic. As a boy he had spent time in both England and Scotland when his family fled France after the July Revolution in 1830. He was confirmed at Holyrood Palace in Edinburgh and eventually married an aristocratic Scots woman by the name of Emma Mackinnon. Guiche's three years of exile in Britain, between the ages of 11 and 14, meant that he was fluent in English. Throughout his life his British connections played an important part. His uncle was the Comte Alfred d'Orsay who was a friend of Disraeli, Bulwer-Lytton, and Dickens, who later corresponded with d'Orsay about the death of Marie Duplessis. So close was the bond between d'Orsay and Dickens that the French nobleman stood as godfather to one of Dickens's children, his son Alfred d'Orsay Tennyson Dickens. Is this the reason why Dickens took a keen interest in Marie Duplessis, because she had been the mistress of d'Orsay's nephew?

The two most mystifying stamps in Marie Duplessis's passport put her in London in February and June of 1843. As she did not speak English she was entirely dependent on whichever protector took her there, twice. That this was indeed Guiche is almost certain. Though how she would explain her London visits to Stackelberg is hard to imagine. One of her two surviving letters to Guiche suggests that they needed to take heed of the old count. The letter is now in the Beinecke Rare Book and Manuscript Library at Yale. Quite how ardent she was about her new lover Guiche is clear from it. At the time of writing they were separated although she seemed set to join him shortly abroad. It is direct and sensuous:

My dear Agénor
Even though it is only a very short time since you left, I nevertheless have a lot of things to tell you. Firstly, my angel, I am very sad I am getting very bored, because I am not seeing you. I don't know yet when I am leaving but I would like it to be soon because, since you left, I'm being bored by the general who is very insistent that I receive him and that I should be with him as in the past. He ought not to have changed his behaviour towards me. We would have been so happy if he had not come and surprised us. Our life was so well organized. But let's talk of the present, my poor angel, and let us not regret the past. I remain in the same position that you left me in. Someone whom you don't know has made me a proposition that I will tell you about. In my next letter, if my life does not bore you too much, I would also like to ask your

advice if I should, or not, leave with Madame Weller. I am very embarrassed because I struggle to understand that woman who is sometimes extremely good to me but at other times changes her manner altogether. So I expect a response from you and friendly advice.

Please write to me quickly and a nice long letter. Tell me everything you are thinking, what you are doing. Tell me too that you love me. I need to believe it. It will be a comfort for your absence, my sweet angel. I am quite sad and love you more tenderly than ever before. I kiss you a thousand times, on your mouth and everywhere else too.

Goodbye, my darling angel, don't forget me too much; think sometimes of her who loves you deeply.

Marie Duplessis
Thursday, Paris

This was an intense love affair. She harboured no illusions about the inevitable absence of love in her liaisons, but hope springs eternal in the human breast and she too longed for a life in which her feelings would not be spurned and in which she could love. The moody 'Madame Weller' of the letter appears to be an English woman, perhaps in the Guiche household, whom Marie Duplessis 'struggles' to understand because of her poor command of French; or perhaps because of her mood swings, or both. Mrs Weller may have been left behind as an English chaperone for Marie Duplessis, with a view to accompanying her on her journey to London to join Guiche. London was destined to play a hugely important role in Marie Duplessis's life and in due course her presence in the British capital would be documented.

As for the 'general', it is hard to see how he could be anyone other than Stackelberg, particularly because Dumas also alludes directly, and independently, to the incident referred to in her letter.[3] Early on in *La Dame aux Camélias*, Dumas recalls how the lady of the camellias had happily obliged her ancient protector for a while. Then, on her return to Paris, 'this girl used to a life of dissipation, balls, even orgies' reverted to her old ways. Anything else would have meant death by boredom (he uses the same word as she does: 'ennui'), never more so now that she looked more stunning than ever. Friends of the old man alerted him to his lover's infidelity, reporting to him that the moment his back was turned 'she received visits and these visits often lasted until the following morning'. In other words, her lovers stayed all night.

Who Stackelberg's dubiously charitable friends were is not recorded but it is a fair guess that they were members of the count's extensive family, concerned about the cost to the family fortune of the septuagenarian's folly. Stackelberg can no longer have harboured any illusions about his trophy courtesan, if he ever did: she would continue as before but at least he would have exclusive rights to her at their box at the opera and, occasionally, be allowed sex. With her charm, beauty, wit and a steely determination never again to be indigent, Marie Duplessis had achieved the apogee of the life of a Parisian demi-mondaine: she had money and security from her old count while enjoying the highlife of the capital, from opera, balls, and dinners in the finest restaurants in town to sex with the city's most sought-after young lions. During the ensuing confrontation with Stackelberg over Guiche, Marie Duplessis at once confessed. She told him candidly to let her go because she could not keep her side of the bargain: 'I have no desire to receive charity from a man whom I am deceiving.' They parted. The old man stayed away for eight days and then reappeared, abjectly pleading with her to take him back on whatever terms she chose. He promised her that he would never again reproach her on anything. And so, Dumas notes in his fictional recreation of Marie Duplessis's life, 'That is how things stood three months after the return of Marguerite, that is in November or December 1842.'[4] Not only does Dumas in his novel broadly confirm the story of the lovers being caught out, but he even gives the right date. He would because he had it from Marie Duplessis herself.

It was in November 1842 that Guiche travelled to London where he appeared at the great Polish refugees' relief ball of Wednesday 16 November, held at the Guildhall by the Corporation of London. According to *The Times* Court Circular, the Duc de Guiche and his father, the Comte de Gramont, featured among the most prominent of the 3,000 invited dignitaries. Guiche could hardly take his mistress with him to London at the time because of his father.[5] Though he may have hoped that she would join him, hence her reference to Madame Weller. At the time the family may not have had much of an inkling about the intensity of their offspring's affair with the louche princess of the demi-monde. The young Guiche was rapidly acquiring a reputation for womanizing. Although barely 23 years old during his affair with the 18-year-old Marie Duplessis, he was already a veteran of a highly publicized relationship with the classical actress Rachel Félix and other notable Parisian women of dubious repute.

Throughout the second half of 1842 and well into the winter of 1842–3, Paris was gripped by a novel that was appearing in the *Journal des Débats*. Such was its appeal that the circulation of this fashionable and highly influential paper increased impressively during its seventeen months of serialization. Marie Duplessis was reading it too. It was more relevant to her life than to that of most Parisians. This 1842 potboiler fast outsold works by the greatest novelists of the age, including Balzac, Dumas, and Hugo. Its title was *Les Mystères de Paris*, its author an early member of the Jockey-Club and regular of the cafés of the boulevard des Italiens, the 38-year-old Eugène Sue. The novel's central figure is an enigmatic young man gifted with superhuman strength: a demon angel by the name of 'Rodolphe', in reality the Grand Duke of Gerolstein. He is classless inasmuch as he is able to blend invisibly into the Parisian underworld. The novel plays on the morbid fascination with the underbelly of a big city, its slums and dimly lit cavernous bars where villains, pimps, and whores gather under the cloak of night.

It is a classic *nostalgie de la boue* novel, steeped in Parent-Duchâtelet's tomes on prostitution in Paris while taking its imaginative bearings from the celebrated *Notre-Dame de Paris* by Victor Hugo. Hugo's novel of a decade earlier features a sinister place called the 'Cour des Miracles', a beggars' ghetto and the slum kingdom of the city. This refuge for outlaws harbours among its denizens the beautiful gypsy girl Esmeralda already mentioned in Chapter 2. She cannot bear to see an innocent man put to death any more than she can stop herself from giving water to the grotesquely disfigured Quasimodo, tied to a wheel and taunted and pelted by a mob. Out of compassion too she marries the luckless poet Pierre Gringoire, who strayed into the Cour des Miracles by accident, to save his life, much to his astonishment and that of the beggars. Hugo's immensely popular novel probably preserved the great Notre-Dame cathedral from demolition, by breathing a life and soul into its crumbling masonry with a plot of love, murder and redemption. The novel concludes with Quasimodo being discovered dead, holding Esmeralda's body in the cellars below the city's infamous gibbet. It was the only way granted him to express his love and gratitude to the young woman who had instinctively seen into his kind heart beyond his hideous exterior.

Hugo's masterpiece spoke to Parisians about their own city through the lens of its notoriously savage past. Sue's *Les Mystères de Paris* similarly engages with its immediate urban environment though it does not carry the sentimental punch of *Notre-Dame de Paris*, because none of its characters engage the imagination the way Hugo's do. *Les Mystères* abounds with scenes of extreme cruelty verging on the grotesque, from extracting a tooth to punish a child to the cold-blooded blinding of a villain. The novel's cast includes bogeymen such as the 'Chourineur', a slaughterer turned murderer, a diabolical killer known as 'the school teacher', two prostitutes called Fleur-de-Marie and the 'Goualeuse', and a young 'grisette' called Rigolette. These struck an instant chord with contemporary readers and Sue became famous overnight.

During the serialization, Sue held Paris in thrall every bit as much as his contemporary Charles Dickens had done London with *Oliver Twist* four years earlier. The novel was provocatively candid in portraying prostitution free from moral guilt, almost brazenly challenging the powers that be to take it to task. If in the character of Rodolphe, Sue unwittingly trailed Edmond Dantès, the avenging hero of Dumas *père's* classic *The Count of Monte Cristo* (1844), in Rigolette and Fleur-de-Marie he set the points for the younger Dumas's *La Dame aux Camélias*. And, more directly, he drew his entire readership into the ambit of slums and 'grisettes' thereby creating a one-city popular democracy in which everyone could thrive.

According to Victor Petrovich de Balabine, a Russian diplomat and avid diarist, in *Les Mystères de Paris* 'the poor saw themselves reflected while the rich found new things in it.'[6] It was a triumph on all fronts and, as Marie Duplessis read about her peers in the city as heroines, she may have felt just a little bit less alone and also reassured about being both a great beauty and simultaneously ostracized. One contemporary noted ruefully that, such was its popularity,

> While it appeared in serial form in the *Débats*, one had to bespeak the paper several hours beforehand, because, unless one subscribed to it, it was impossible to get it from the news-vendors. As for the reading-rooms where it was supposed to be kept, the proprietors frankly laughed in your face if you happened to ask for it, after you had paid your two sous admission. 'Monsieur is joking. We have five copies, and we let them out at ten sous each for half an hour: that's the time it takes to read M. Sue's story. We have one copy here, and if monsieur likes to take his turn he may do so, though he will probably have to wait for three or four hours'.[7]

In December 1842 Paris was plunged into icy fog and blizzards to such an extent that at the start of the week of 5 December the city was paralysed. Marie Duplessis was ensconced in front of the fire in her new apartment in rue d'Antin waiting for her friend Romain Vienne. He was making his way there wading through slushy piles of snow on unmetalled streets without pavements. He took pride in knowing the most famous courtesan of Paris, while never forgetting that she was a most ordinary girl from Nonant. He knew that she freely gave to the poor, not least because she had once needed to beg to survive. When Vienne entered, Marie Duplessis, tended by her maid, was engrossed in the latest instalment of Sue's novel. Perhaps she was, at that very moment, reading the 'Rigolette' chapter, published on Thursday 8 December and occurring one quarter into the 1,300 page rollercoaster novel. She read because she loved books and the boundless worlds opened up by them. Her own life at times must have felt like fiction, with the most recondite luxuries of Paris at her disposal, and all that because she knew how to manipulate men. She had travelled a huge distance from Normandy. It must have seemed like a fairy tale, albeit one with a tawdry veneer. Time and again her friends, mentors, lovers, and chaperones were startled by her quick intelligence and depth of reading, not least because her way of living hardly lent itself to the sedentary leisure demanded of epic novels. By the time she and Guiche were joined together, her routines were known to large swathes of Parisian society.

There was nothing out of the ordinary about them. If anything the pre-dictability of her rituals meant that spectators could watch the comings and goings of the city's most celebrated demi-mondaine if they wished. Mornings barely featured in her day. Instead, she rarely rose before lunch-time. She spent at least an hour at her toilette before setting off in her coupé to the Place de la Concorde, past Crillon's, one of the grandest hotels in Paris and notorious too because outside it the king and Marie-Antoinette had been beheaded fifty years earlier. There followed a leisurely trot up the Champs-Élysees to the Arc de Triomphe, to ensure that she would be rec-ognized by as many people as possible. As one of the fashion trendsetters of the city she needed to be prominently on display. From the Arc de Triomphe she pushed on to the nearby Bois de Boulogne where, in good weather, she would alight from her carriage and walk among its shaded tree-lined alleys for an hour or so. By late afternoon she was retracing her steps into the centre of town.

It was in the Bois that a young woman, accompanied by her little boy, approached her one day and struck up a conversation. Marie Duplessis realized that her *ingénue* interlocutor was unaware of the fact that she was talking to a kept woman. They chatted about her child, and such was Marie's pleasure in her new friend's company that she could not bring herself to reveal her status at first. Perhaps her own little boy came into her mind then. It is hard to see how he could not; maybe he was also the reason why she found it hard to tear herself away from the young mother. But eventually her conscience and fear of compromising the young woman prevailed. She explained who she was and was deeply affected when the young woman protested that it would in no way alter her feelings for her. The friendship may have continued to the graveside of the lady of the camellias.[8]

After resting she changed for the night ahead, either a premiere at the theatre or opera, or else a party, or one of the grand society balls that were the chief pastimes of Paris at this time of the year. The paper *Sylphide*, with its finger on the pulse of Paris's high society and beautiful people, waxes lyrical about winter in Paris: far from the image of 'an old woman crouching beside a fire weighed down by a heavy coat, trembling', winter means 'crowds, noise, balls, pleasures, young blonde heads beaming with pleasure, their hair studded with flowers and diamonds, yes, winter in Paris means all those ivory breasts of young women, lilies in full bloom that undulate and bounce when played by the masterly bow of pleasure.... the sap of winter is all pleasures and balls'.[9]

Romain Vienne caught up with Marie Duplessis one wintry afternoon as she was preparing to go out. She served him tea in her apartment and then entrusted him to her chambermaid while she went to get ready for a night at the opera. When she reappeared from her dressing room, she looked stunning, decked in clothes, diamonds, rubies, and pearls that he estimated at 100,000 francs, a truly colossal amount. She had turned herself into a radiant work of art, with her finery and jewellery serving above all to foreground her natural grace:

> She was deliciously pretty. Her flowing, thick, black hair was magnificently arranged. Her face, oval and regular, ever so slightly pale and melancholy when in a state of calm repose, would suddenly become animated at the sound of a friend's voice and a warm and heart-felt word. She had a child's head. Her mouth, exquisite and sensual, was graced with stunningly white teeth. Her feet and hands were refined to the point that they led one to believe that her fingers might be too long. The expression of her large black eyes, with long eyelashes, was deep and intense, while the softness of her gaze made one dream. There could be nothing more comely than the composition of that luminous open face, whose benign smiles at once inspired sympathy. While her beauty always provoked admiration, her stylish and seductive manners forged friendships.[10]

The inaugural ball of the season was usually hosted by Countess Apponyi at the Austrian embassy and regularly featured the latest Strauss waltzes. The voluble Balabine confided in his diary, freshly returned at 3 a.m. on 9 January, that the ball had been a magnificent occasion, 'quite different from the others:

we danced in two ballrooms to the sound of two orchestras; the foreign guests were in a huge majority, with their sheer numbers overwhelming the indigenous lot.' He then proceeds to describe the various fashions and jewellery on display as well as the personal appearance of the many women who attended, including the hostess of the next great ball, 'Lady Cowley, the British ambassadress, even more ungainly than usual'.[11] The most brilliant ball of the season was traditionally the winter ball of the British Embassy, held every year in January on its premises in the Hôtel de Charost, rue du Faubourg Saint-Honoré.[12] In 1842 the British ambassador was Henry Wellesley, Baron Cowley, the younger brother of Wellington, the victor of Waterloo. He had been in post for only a year. The new Ambassador's and Lady Cowley's initial decision to scale back the size of their receptions, to host more occasions for fewer guests, had been greeted with consternation by the smart Parisian set. Matters were not helped by the fact that the reputation of the British community in Paris was tarnished by excessive drinking: could Lord Cowley rein in the 'prodigious' number of English guests who regularly drank themselves into a stupour at balls in the French capital? Such loutish behaviour by her citizens caused much discomfiture to her Britannic majesty, the French papers remarked gleefully, while offering mock commiseration: as *Sylphide*'s columnist notes, 'the English plead in mitigation that boozing is just an extreme way of consolidating their "spleen"—join us in pitying the poor children of the Thames.'[13]

The Cowleys may have been stung by the charge of a *faux-pas* over their parties and the poor press accorded their countrymen. Hence, in their second year, they flung open their doors and welcomed all of Paris's élite to the great January winter ball on Wednesday 18 January 1843. Festivities opened at 10 p.m., with Lord Cowley partnering the Comtesse d'Apponyi. A grand total of 1,800 invitations had been issued. Such was the crush of people that guests could barely move, even though the embassy's grounds and extensive alleys had all been thrown open and were heaving with flowers and scents.[14] In the rhapsodic words of someone who was there, 'All that elegant Paris, young Paris, famous Paris, noble and aristocratic Paris contains of the most exalted and powerful, had converged on Lord Cowley'. The Guiches and their father Gramont were invited and Marie Duplessis would have shone here too in all her glamour, either as her lover's companion or as the old count's exhibit, if not as both. All through the winter night the bands played Strauss waltzes. She was incomparably graceful on the dance floor, never more so than while dancing the waltz. It may not be a coincidence that she was now discovering Britain on the arm of the Duc de Guiche, first in Paris and shortly afterwards in London. The ball was held a few weeks before she arrived in the British capital for the first time.

If the British Embassy was the prime venue, the balls and parties thrown by the Belgian embassy, in a building next door to old Stackelberg's home at Chaussée d'Antin, ranked next in popularity. Highly esteemed too were those of the Sardinian, Russian (12 Place de Vendôme) and American (23 rue Laffitte) embassies. In addition the feasts laid on by rich individuals such as Madame Belgiojoso, the Comtesse de Latour, or Madame de Pontalba in her brilliant new home next to the British Embassy (today the residence of the American Ambassador), were similarly *de rigueur* for the best set of the city. In the past the most rated balls had been the masked balls of the opera. They had become boisterous affairs of late, noisy and carnivalesque, with crowds spilling over even into the foyers. They really belonged to an age of intrigue and exclusive salons, the era before the revolution of 1789.

But one of the reasons for the enduring popularity of the opera balls was the sheer prestige of opera in the city. In the Paris of the 1840s opera occupied the top of a pyramid of culture, ranking second only to politics in importance. The main papers of the capital discussed at length who should be the new director of the various opera houses and theatres, what their salaries were and should be, and whether or not stars and primadonnas were entitled to the colossal sums they were paid. When the ballerina Fanny Elssler breached her contract with the Paris Opéra, the Minister of the Interior intervened in person to smooth over the ensuing row. In 1842 Paris boasted at least three major opera houses, from the Le Peletier and Favart on either side of the boulevard des Italiens to the Salle Ventadour on rue Méhul, not far from the current Opéra Garnier (inaugurated in 1875), and a few yards away from the Théâtre des Bouffes Parisiens. Of the three major opera houses of the 1840s the Ventadour is the only one still standing from the time of Marie Duplessis, though no longer as a theatre but a branch of the Banque de France (Figure 9.3). In the story of Marie Duplessis it is probably the most important building of all because here some of the grandest Italian operas enjoyed their Paris premieres, including *La traviata*. Right now though, with the festive season heading for the start of a new year, another premiere was scheduled for 3 January 1843, an *opera buffa* by the most acclaimed composer of opera of the age, and one moreover who lived part of the time in Paris. His name was Gaetano Donizetti and the opera was *Don Pasquale*.

Figure 9.3 The famous Ventadour theatre, a favourite venue for presenting Italian opera throughout Marie Duplessis's life in the city.

Although there are no records about Marie Duplessis attending the premiere, it is safe to think that she did and that she would have occupied one of the chief boxes, as was her wont on other documented occasions. Demi-monde etiquette dictated that she sat at the front with, behind her, one of her female chaperones, while her protector Stackelberg sat further back still. It would not have been acceptable for Guiche to share her box. Instead, he was expected to join her later after the old count had taken his leave. The opera starred the favourite tenor of the age, Giovanni Matteo de Candia, who would later be the first Alfredo in *La traviata* on the Paris stage. What would Marie Duplessis have made of the thought that she, under the name of Violetta, would one day soon be sung by one of greatest sopranos of the century, Marietta Piccolomini, with the purest blue-blood of Italy in her veins, while de Candia as Alfredo would hit new heights with a role arising out of her own tragic life?

De Candia sang under the stage name of 'Mario' and was cast in the lyrical part of the romantic Ernesto, the nephew of Don Pasquale, a foolish and wealthy old man, who proposes to disinherit him by marrying a young

woman to produce an alternative heir. The title role was sung on the opening night by another star of nineteenth-century opera, the bass Luigi Lablache,
while the diva Giulia Grisi sang the role of Norina. The production was an
instant hit. If Marie Duplessis was indeed present the opera must have struck
a chord with her, as she sat watching the old money hoarder duped by the
young lovers in cahoots with friends of Don Pasquale's, determined to teach
the old man a lesson. The tricking of a rich old man by young lovers is not
only one of the oldest motifs of comedy but it was also uncannily close to
her own situation, as she and Guiche had cheated on Stackelberg.

Of particular interest to her may well have been the special touch added
by the corpulent Lablache/Pasquale, a detail that moreover involved the
family of one of her closest friends. It is reported by the friend and admirer
of Giuseppe Verdi, Léon Escudier, who wrote about this production of *Don
Pasquale* in January 1843: 'To render his appearance and costume more pic-
turesque and enjoyable, Lablache adorned his buttonhole with an enormous
camellia. At each new performance the marquess of Aguado arranged for
the acclaimed singer to receive the most gorgeous camellia that his gardener could pick in his nurseries.' The marquess, Alexandre Marie Aguado,
was the father of Marie Duplessis's future lover Olympe Aguado, who was
15 at the time of the opera. But the opera-addicted marquess, a Maecenas,
rich as Croesus and friend of Rossini, had died in April 1842, so Escudier
must have been misremembering when he wrote this account twenty years
after the event, in 1863. Perhaps he was conflating Lablanche's camellias
with those of Dumas and Marie Duplessis and freely associated this gesture
with Aguado because of his amorous liaison, three years from now, with
Marie Duplessis?

With the start of the new year, the December fogs and snow dissipated. A
year earlier Marie Duplessis had been full of anticipation about Baden-
Baden. Now, with the city's most desirable lover in tow, she was looking
forward to another trip abroad, this time to London. The last time her
Baden-Baden trip had been rudely curtailed when the heir to the throne
died in a tragic accident. Just as she was poised to travel to London with
Guiche, another death occurred and it too would affect her. What happened
is documented in the death registers of the evangelical parish of Karlsruhe
of 1843. Under 'Hélène Ugarte Stackelberg' the entry records that 'at 11 a.m.,
on 12 February 1843, the Lady Hélène, born Countess of Stackelberg, wife of
Count Josef Ugarte and daughter of Count Gustav Stackelberg and Caroline
Countess of Ludoff, died at the age of 22 years, five months and twenty days

and that she was buried at 3 p.m. on 15 February.'[15] Hélène de Stackelberg died in Karlsruhe because that is where she and her husband lived. Her death rather than that of her sister Marie may be the reason why her father doted on Marie Duplessis with such fervour. In her own later retelling of her first meeting with the old count, Marie Duplessis would stress that he desired to protect her above all because she so reminded him of his recently deceased daughter. But they met six months *before* Hélène died and two years after the untimely death of Marie de Stackelberg. Did the two young Stackelberg women become one in the recollection of Marie Duplessis? Was Hélène de Stackelberg already sick at the time of the meeting between her father and Marie Duplessis in Baden-Baden? We will never know now. There may be a bit of fairy tale embroidery here in Marie Duplessis's mind. The fact is that while the old count was mourning yet another dead daughter, Marie Duplessis eloped to London with the Duc de Guiche.

No trace has been found in the records of either of her first two visits to London in 1843, but it happened after 2 February 1843 because on that day Marie Duplessis settled an invoice in Paris.[16] Guiche's biographer insists that the young man's family spirited him away to London to prise him out of the clutches of Marie Duplessis and that in London he moped about ('se morfondait') in English fogs.[17] Far from moping, though, it seems that he was intent on pursuing his romance with the teenage courtesan by getting her to join him in the desert of anonymity that was London. The city on the Thames could hardly fail to make a huge impression on Marie Duplessis and she would be back in London again sooner perhaps than she had anticipated. Winter arrived late in 1843, but when it did it came with a vengeance.[18] Leaving behind a white Paris, Marie Duplessis fetched up in the wintry London of Dickens's *A Christmas Carol.*

The lovers were probably back in Paris for the Carnival at the end of February. Sadly, it also seems to be the case that when Marie Duplessis returned from London in February 1843, her affair with Guiche was over. She was no match for the powerful opposition to her by his family and Guiche may not have been as committed to her as she would have liked. If they had hoped that London would provide some kind of hideaway from family, they were mistaken. Even in London the long reach of the Anglo-French Guiche–Gramonts was tangible through the d'Orsays. How the two lovers were broken up is not known, but Dumas appears to have based the imagined domestic circumstances of Armand Duval's family on that of Guiche, something that Verdi spotted and openly acknowledged in the opera. It seems fairly clear that the pressure to separate the lovers originated with Guiche's soldier father Antoine IX Héraclius–Agénor de Gramont.

The young Duc de Guiche, beau par excellence, may nevertheless have loved Marie Duplessis rather more than is commonly believed. Although he called his first-born son Agénor after himself, the second boy, born in 1854, was called 'Armand', which is not a Guiche or Gramont family name. It is, however, the name of Dumas's hero in *La Dame aux Camélias*. His next son (b. 1856) is named 'Alfred'. This was one of Guiche's own first names and also that of his uncle the Comte d'Orsay. Nevertheless one may wonder whether this second son's name may not owe something to Armand Duval's alter ego Alfredo in *La traviata*; unless it is the other way round and it is Verdi who is doing the borrowing of names from the Guiche and Gramont families? By the time Guiche's children were born, Marie Duplessis was dead, *La Dame aux Camélias* was a celebrated *roman-à-clef* and play, and *La traviata* was poised to receive its Paris premiere. It is inconceivable that the worldly and much travelled Guiche, ambassador to the Holy See in Rome by 1857, would not have known all about *La Dame aux Camélias* and *La traviata*.

10

A summer idyll on a bend
in the river

1843

The toast of Paris in February and March 1843 was the brilliant pianist
Miss Clara Loveday, whose variations on *Lucia di Lammermoor* and
Beethoven inspired rave reviews. It was her fate to share the 1840s with
the greatest virtuoso pianists ever, Liszt, Thalberg, and Chopin, which is
why she has been eclipsed to some extent today. But as the only major
woman player, she too filled the houses of Europe whenever she performed.
The arts scene in Paris was a fierce, serious business and the Paris Opéra
found itself fighting a battle now on two fronts: their high profile litigation with Fanny Elssler over a broken engagement was followed by a near
riot inside the Le Peletier Opera on 7 February when the house had to
substitute the singer Raguenot for the great tenor Poultier, who had notified them at midnight the day before the show of a desperately sore throat.
A common affliction and presumably rendered more so by the inclement
weather that winter. In spite of the occasional glorious spring day, the
weather stayed resolutely cold and wet. There was no respite as March
turned into April. May was similarly disastrous, with wintry mists and
relentless rain and cold.

Meanwhile, so closely knit were the circles in which Marie Duplessis
and her lovers moved that news of her separation from Guiche would
have been known instantly. With Guiche out of the picture, she soon
found herself wooed by another of Paris's most eligible bachelors, Comte
Édouard de Perrégaux. One night, as she left the opera, a magnificently
appointed coach and horses was waiting for her. The coachman approached
her and offered to drive her home in splendour fit for a queen. At least

that is the received version. If this is indeed what happened, then Perrégaux was wooing Marie Duplessis in almost exactly the same manner as he had Alice Ozy earlier, though it is quite possible that the two accounts are really just one but were later misremembered and transferred from one mistress to another.

Quite when the relationship started is hard to determine exactly, but April or early May 1843 is most likely, because at Chantilly, in late May, Marie Duplessis and Édouard de Perrégaux appeared together. The foul spring weather nearly threw the entire racing season off-balance, and particularly Chantilly, where the biggest derby of the season, the Prix du Jockey-Club, was raced on Sunday 21 May 1843.[1] The paddocks were muddy and by the end of May the track had become a quagmire. Even so, Marie Duplessis looked more glamorous, radiant and happier than ever as she and Perrégaux pulled into the course. As well they both might be because Perrégaux's new horse 'Leporello' was firm favourite to win the derby. And it ought to have won, but it did not, for as the race was building up to its climax, Leporello was so far ahead of the pack that, in a gesture of almost absurd gallantry, its rider, a jockey by the name of Gale, allowed the closest horse to catch up to offer the spectacle of a true contest. His hubris was severely punished when 'Renonce' won the race against the odds. The chivalrous (as it were) jockey was unrepentant afterwards.

Assuming that this was an honest gesture rather than an act of race-fixing for betting purposes, it was a hugely costly deed of dubious sportsmanship. And yet Chantilly had started so well when on 18 May 1843 Perrégaux's horse Slam won the Prix du Commerce. But the following day his horse Plover, the Chantilly derby champion of 1842, developed a limp, perhaps caused by the sheer challenge of racing on tracks that were soaking wet. It was a setback, but the lovers had plans and would not be distracted from their happiness in either Bougival or from their planned foreign travels.

Perrégaux was not unattached when he wooed Marie Duplessis. He who had begged Alize Ozy to throw over her royal lover, now deserted her for another. Not only that, but he fell head over heels in love with his new companion. In the words of an eyewitness, he was so smitten with 'a vertiginous passion' for Marie Duplessis even though she was a courtesan, that it was like first love, perhaps because he grasped instinctively that she was indeed 'a pearl lost in vice'; that whatever her past, she was at heart a kind, generous, and romantic young woman.[2] The narrative of *La Dame aux Camélias* (75–83) suggests that Perrégaux first caught sight of Marie Duplessis

Figure 10.1 A rare photograph of the Café Anglais, opposite the Maison Dorée, on the south side of the boulevard des Italiens, with the passage on the left leading to the Opéra Favart. It was used by Marie Duplessis after operatic shows at the Favart.

in the shop called Susse in place de la Bourse where the Vaudeville theatre then was. Their next encounter, still in 1842, may have been at the Opéra Favart when she was collected by Stackelberg at her box, where she was consuming her favourite *raisins glacés*. On that occasion she walked from the opera to the Café Anglais (Figure 10.1) while Perrégaux darted across to the Maison Dorée from where one could see into the rooms of the Café Anglais.

He was desperately jealous of other lovers and men generally who, like him, would circle around her in the big city: 'in Paris, at every step I could encounter a man who had been the lover of this woman or who would be so the following day.'[3] The safest way to keep her to himself, he decided, was to move her out of Paris altogether and hide away in the country. A wooded hamlet on the left bank of a bend in the Seine, some ten miles west of Paris, came to mind. It was called Bougival. At the time Marie Duplessis and Édouard de Perrégaux prepared to settle there in the summer of 1843 it was a bucolic idyll. A number of landscape artists, attracted by the beauty of the banks of the Seine and its environs, had gathered here and started to spread its reputation. A contemporary account from 1856 notes that

> A small colony of painters [known as the 'paysagistes', i.e. landscape artists] came here during the beautiful season and set up in an inn that they rendered famous, 'l'auberge de M. Souvent', on the waterfront: the artists found here not only shelter but a studio and healthy and plentiful food at what were then very moderate prices. The artists were succeeded by the boatmen and now the railway brings a large number of day trippers to Bougival every Sunday. Its peace and quiet are shattered but the local people are not complaining.[4]

Much the same point was made by the Goncourts who visited here on 28 August 1855, twelve years after Perrégaux and Marie Duplessis. They had come to see the painter Célestin Nanteuil, the 'inventor' of Bougival, and called the village the cradle of the French landscape painters of the modern era: every corner of the river, every willow resonated with echoes of paintings, with 'a number of houses that tell the stories of great passions and the dramatic histories of well-known women . . . at Bougival, as everywhere, business humiliates art and literature'.[5] The Goncourts do not mention the heroine of Dumas's novel, but she may well have been in their minds. By the time they arrived there, Bougival had become the most fashionable place near Paris, with signs alerting tourists to the very spots where particular paintings by François-Louis Français had been created. The engine of this blossoming was the railway which in 1837 first connected Gare Saint-Lazare in Paris to Le Pecq, two miles upriver from Bougival. Local people did not complain because tourists from Paris put their village on the map of commerce and business.

The pioneering colony of painters of the 1830s included now largely forgotten painters such as Auguste Anastasi, Paul Chenavard, François-Louis Français, Paul Huet, as well as renowned artists like Camille Corot and Gustave Courbet.[6] In their wake travelled a second wave of artists. These would eventually spread the name of Bougival throughout the world, as they numbered among them some of the most legendary names in the history of nineteenth-century painting, including Monet, Sisley, and Pissaro. But it was the original bohemians who may have been, at least partly, the reason why Marie Duplessis, who loved art and occasionally patronized painters, agreed to join de Perrégaux in Bougival.

In the novel Dumas warms to his task by evoking the lyricism of the lovers in this gentle and mellow countryside, painting in words what others had done with brushes. He knew the place well indeed, even though he was *not* the Armand Duval character of the novel. Dumas's father ran the most successful theatre of Paris *extra muros* in nearby Saint-Germain-en-Laye, some five miles up the hill from Bougival, the very same place where his son would write *La Dame aux Camélias* four years from now.[7] Also, the elder Dumas was already prospecting around Bougival and Marly-le-Roi for a suitable site for his folly, the miniature château of Monte-Cristo which was completed at Port-Marly near Bougival in 1847, where it stands to this day. Most of the Parisian intelligentsia and of the city's middle and upper classes knew that Bougival also boasted one of the best-known landmarks on the Seine, the 'Machine de Marly', a huge hydraulic system which straddled part of the Seine to the west of Bougival and pumped water all the way up to Versailles. After the Pont du Gard in Provence, the aquaduct of Louveciennes or Marly ranked among the best known in the country.

In *La Dame aux Camélias* Dumas claims that the first port of call of the lovers was an inn that his readers would instantly recognize, the auberge 'Point du Jour' ('daybreak' or 'dawn') run by the widow 'Arnould':

> You probably know this auberge, a hotel during the week and a popular open air dance café ('guinguette') on Sundays. From the garden, which is on the level of an ordinary first floor, one enjoys a wonderful panoramic view. On the left the aquaduct of Marly closes off the horizon, while to the right the view is of an infinity of hills. The river, virtually without current at this point, meanders along like an extended rippled band.

Dumas waxes lyrical over this rakish artists' hideout. Just such a *guinguette* scene on the Seine west of Paris is captured in Renoir's iconic picture of the boatmen at lunch, *Le déjeuner des canotiers 1881*, which features a raised café terrace overlooking the river. Although that picture originated at the Maison Fournaise at Chatou, a couple of miles upriver from Bougival, Renoir's equally celebrated picture *Danse à Bougival* (Figure 10.2) was probably painted, albeit forty years later, in the very same place where Marie Duplessis and Édouard de Perrégaux stayed.

Dumas gives the name of the owner of the auberge where Édouard de Perrégaux and Marie Duplessis stayed as the 'widow Arnould'. The name Arnoult (spelled with a 't') is local to Bougival. The only aubergiste listed in the 1836 census is 'André Arnould', who is the same 'Louis-André Léon Arnoult' who owned the auberge Souvent, which takes its name from another Bougival family of businessmen who intermarried with the Arnoults.[8] Louis-André Léon Arnoult died aged 61 on 23 March 1846,

Figure 10.2 Renoir's *Dance at Bougival* perfectly captures the atmosphere of the *guinguette* culture on the river Seine to the west of Paris when Marie Duplessis eloped here with her lover Édouard de Perrégaux.

leaving his widow Catherine, née Michel (they had married in 1820), in charge of the Auberge Souvent. Hence Dumas's reference to 'widow Arnoult' who certainly was a widow by the time he wrote *La Dame aux Camélias*.

The reason why the inn of *La Dame aux Camélias* has not been traced before is because Dumas confused the Auberge Souvent, at the (eastern)

Paris end of Bougival, the place where Marie Duplessis and Perrégaux stayed, with the Auberge Point du Jour. The latter inn stood downriver, in close proximity to the Bougival bridge, somewhere on the site of 6–10 Quai Sganzin.[9] The Auberge Point du Jour was set up and run by Caroline Souvent, a niece of the Souvents of the artists' auberge. Both inns therefore belonged to members of the Souvent family, hence Dumas's vagueness about which of them his lovers used. The most important point about the Souvents' auberge in the context of the novel's intimate links to real life is that Dumas was once again faithfully recording what he had heard or knew to be the case. The honest mistake over which of the two Souvent-owned inns the lovers stayed in consolidates my argument that in real life the Bougival scenes of *La Dame aux Camélias* reflect the experiences not of Dumas and Marie Duplessis but her time there with Perrégaux. The mismatch of the two inns only firms up the documentary authenticity of the narrative.

The Auberge Souvent, endlessly modified and much grander, topped by a hat-like loft, still stands today.[10] The cabaret inn of the 1830s was packed with art work, a precursor of the renowned La Colombe d'Or in Saint-Paul-de-Vence, a restaurant whose walls were adorned with paintings and frescoes by artists in lieu of payment for food. As late as the 1890s the Souvent house was noteworthy for this:

> One of the last of these hotels and restaurants, perhaps the oldest of all of them, is the Souvent house, today called the Hôtel de l'Union, in which painters have decorated the walls, which poets have praised in their works, and the sight of which prompts us to return to the past.... Still young, but already drawing their inspiration from nature, Corot, Français, Ternaute, Hérault, Meissonier, and many others took up residence during the summer at Souvent's planting their easels in a countryside ignored by the bourgeoisie. The Souvent, at the time a very modest auberge, offered artists hospitality at very modest prices... [When Bougival became fashionable with the Parisian bourgeoisie the artists left and] rustic simplicity yielded to bourgeois elegance. The Auberge Souvent became a hotel, the cabaret a restaurant, the dining room a salon, the arbour a proper garden.... Of the host of painters who laboured here the Souvent house, albeit completely transformed, alone now bears witness.[11]

The author continues with a description of the interior of the former Auberge Souvent house and mentions a number of art works that were still in place in 1890, including a Corot showing the Seine at Bougival near the 'machine'.[12] The spot on the river that Perrégaux and Marie Duplessis had picked for their rural trysting set the points for the most celebrated of all drink and dance venues ever on the Seine, the legendary 'Grenouillière' on the Île de Croissy right opposite Bougival and painted time and again by Claude Monet, Camille Pissaro, Alfred Sisley, and Berthe Morisot. The 'Grenouillière' opened in 1852, opposite the Hôtel de l'Union, but is indubitably descended from the burgeoning river romance that germinated in the 1830s and throughout the 1840s.

After lunch at the auberge, Marie Duplessis, Perrégaux, and her chaperone went out on the river at the suggestion of their hostess.[13] The two islands that almost converge near the quayside at Bougival render the river currents so gentle here that the Seine at Bougival resembles a lake; hence the punting and river joustings more frequently associated with Midi places like Sète. For a rich young man like Perrégaux, the privacy of Bougival allowed him to to enjoy the companionship of his lover in a pastoral on the edge of the metropolis, to which they could resort at any moment if boredom caught up with them or if they needed to attend to urgent business. By coach and carriage they were less than two hours from Arc-de-Triomphe, which could also be reached on foot in little over six hours.

As the lovers idled away that first afternoon in Bougival, Perrégaux spotted on the bank of the river a white, two-storey cottage, with a lawn in front and woodland behind it. Marie caught Perrégaux staring at it and exclaimed that it was lovely indeed, at which point the chaperone offered to get Stackelberg to rent it for them. Perrégaux was shocked by her cynical pragmatism. The thought of getting the old man to pay for someone else's love nest was too much even for this particular rake who, however, accepted quite happily that the old count paid for his love's home in rue d'Antin. Anxious not to embarrass Perrégaux but determined to fulfil his desire for the house, Marie hit on the idea of asking her protector to rent the house for her while, for a modest sum, Perrégaux would lease a small apartment from the widow Arnoult in the Auberge Souvent nearby. He could then live with her in the house but also be based elsewhere. She would explain to the count that she needed to be away from Paris for a while to recover her health. As he would only ever visit during the day, and not unannounced, they could enjoy their new home and privacy to the full.

The following day Marie Duplessis returned to Bougival accompanied by Stackelberg. She took him to the house that they had spotted and persuaded the old man to rent it for her on the spot. He was, it seems, not entirely displeased with this move because it removed her to a place far enough from the lions of Paris for him to nurture the illusion that she would be all, or at least mostly, his while cooped up in Bougival. The reason she gave him for this flight from Paris—'why, when you so love being in Paris?', he had asked—was her health. It had never been good at the best of times, but now she wanted a rest and time to recover. He was hardly taken in by this, but for a while would be spared the open cuckolding that she routinely inflicted on him in Paris. Apart from Stackelberg's scheduled visits, she and Perrégaux had the run of the house and gardens most of the time. Marie Duplessis's confidant Vienne was unaware of the fact that the old count had been coaxed into paying for the lovers' nest. He had assumed that Perrégaux had footed the bill for it presumably because, as a gentleman, he would not accept such an unworthy arrangement. Vienne's information comes from Marie Duplessis and she almost certainly was being economical with the truth, to say the least, anxious not to show herself in too much of a bad light.

Both Perrégaux and Stackelberg would discover, during their first month in Bougival, that in her cottage Marie Duplessis insisted on entertaining her friends and companions from Paris at a riotous rate, with not a day passing when she did not have at least ten visitors. Nevertheless, she and Perrégaux did eventually settle into a routine of eating, sleeping, walking on the banks of the river, sitting in their garden on moonlit nights to smell the flowers, and enjoying each other sexually. The younger Dumas deploys all his considerable gifts to imbue this part of the lovers' relationship with magic, an act of considerable imaginative generosity as strictly speaking this had nothing to do with him: 'We opened the windows which gave onto the garden and watched as summer joyously frolicked among the flowers it caused to open under the shade of trees.'[14] He drew of course on his own intimate knowledge of Marie Duplessis and much of what he recorded in his book about the Bougival times of his lover would have come directly from her; to that extent his record is as authentic as it could be.

Marie Duplessis's first passport was due to expire on 12 July 1843. She must have set about renewing it well before that date. Although only two of her passports survive, it is almost certain that she held passports for most of the years between 13 July 1842 and her death in February 1847, though not continuously: her last passport was issued, for a year, on 25 January 1846, proving thereby that she did not necessarily renew them automatically. As Perrégaux was so possessive of her, he would presumably relish the chance to replicate the intimacy of Bougival in some of the most sought-after

places in Europe where they would be together constantly. That much is
clear. What is baffling is that their first port-of-call abroad seems to have
been London where her passport was stamped in June 1843. She had been
there only a few months earlier with Guiche, so why would she and
Perrégaux in turn head for London now? Was Perrégaux keen to lay the
ghost of his great rival, or had the two of them hatched a plot to get married
in the British capital? We will never know but, though an incontrovertible
fact, their visit to London is both unexpected and mysterious.[15]

From London they may have proceeded to Baden-Baden, according to
Vienne, although no record of either of them survives in the *Badeblatt* records.
There were several other resorts that ranked almost as highly as Baden-
Baden, but the lovers probably returned to Bougival instead, if only to enjoy
the pastoral existence for as much of the summer as they could. Furthermore,
Stackelberg might not tolerate her antics forever. Once, it seems, he turned
up unannounced just when Marie Duplessis was hosting a particularly wild
party of bright young things. He was mortified and his humiliation was all
too apparent. Whether she despised him or not, she needed his money and
that might dry up at any moment. As it is, her hold over him was such that
she need not have worried about these arrangements.

If the lovers were back in Bougival in June, Marie Duplessis was almost
certainly at the Comédie-Française, also known as the Théâtre-Français, in
the heart of Paris on Tuesday 25 July 1843, because that day a comedy called
Les Demoiselles de Saint-Cyr by Alexandre Dumas *père* premiered here. Our
information derives from the elder Dumas himself. It is highly unlikely that
he would be mistaken on the incident that follows as it concerned his son's
most important claim to fame, literary and other. Also, and above all, the
production coincided with the elder Dumas's 41st birthday. It was undoubtedly meant to be just that, a birthday celebration at the great theatre of
Molière, as a thanksgiving to a writer whom his contemporaries ranked
above Victor Hugo and alongside Balzac. Dumas father and son were close
notwithstanding the elder Dumas's eccentric and hands-off attitude to
fatherhood. The younger Dumas used to joke 'My father is a big child, who
was born to me when I was quite small.'[16] Few in Paris would have dis-
sented. During the interval of *Les Demoiselles de Saint-Cyr* Dumas *père* was
strolling along the corridor on the ground floor of the theatre, when he felt
his coat pulled from behind. He turned round and there was his son
Alexandre who had stepped out of one of the boxes. 'You are not alone?',
Dumas senior asked, to which his son replied 'the more the reason', and

then said 'Close your eyes and put your head through the door here. Please don't worry; nothing unpleasant will happen.' Dumas *père* obliged. In his own words, here is what happened next:

> Indeed, I had no sooner shut my eyes and passed my head inside the doorway than I felt on my lips the pressure of two trembling lips, feverish, burning. I opened my eyes. A gorgeous young woman, of twenty or twenty-two years, stood next to Alexandre, and she it was who had given me this somewhat unfilial kiss.

At the time the younger Dumas was 20, his father claimed, but in fact he was a few days off his nineteenth birthday, as he was born on 27 July 1824 and was therefore six months younger than Marie Duplessis. Dumas *père* recognized Marie from having spotted her a few times in the best seats at the theatre. The following exchange now took place, as he gently disengaged from her:

DUMAS: So it is you, my beautiful child?
MARIE: Yes, and it seems that you have to be taken by force.
DUMAS: Do please say that loudly! Perhaps people will start to believe it.
MARIE: Oh, I know that you are not renowned for timidity. Why then are you playing hard to get with me?! I have twice written suggesting that we meet at the Opera Ball.
DUMAS: In front of the big clock at 2 in the morning?[17]
MARIE: There you are: so you did receive my letters!
DUMAS: Undoubtedly, yes...
MARIE: Why then did you not come?
DUMAS: I assumed they were addressed to Alexandre....
MARIE: Come on, why did you not join me?
DUMAS: Because between the hours of one and two in the morning, there are to be found in front of the opera's clock only witty young blades aged between 20 and 30, or else middle-aged fools between 40 and 50. As I am forty years old, I would naturally fall into that latter category in the eyes of observers; and that would be humiliating.
MARIE: I don't follow.
DUMAS: Let me explain. When a pretty young woman like you proposes to tryst with a man my age, it can only be because he can be of use to her. So tell me, what can I do for you?[18]

She smiled, not so much because she was caught out, but because now they were truly attuned and could negotiate. The younger Dumas offered to put the real proposition behind all this to his father later. Dumas *père* recorded in this same document that this was the only time that he kissed Marie Duplessis.

He was at pains to stress this for, probably, a very good reason, because rumour in Paris had it that his son had in fact first met Marie Duplessis at his father's home: if so, it could only be because she was one of his father's countless mistresses and that he simply passed her on to his son. That he made a habit of handing on cast-off mistresses was recorded for posterity by the mordant Horace de Vieil-Castel, who reported, allegedly verbatim, an argument overheard on the boulevard between the two Dumas men. The younger Dumas complained 'I always end up shagging [French "baiser"] your discarded mistresses while having to wear in your new boots', to which his father retorted 'So what! That just proves that you have a big prick [French "verge"] and small feet'. Clearly a far cry from the sanitized fare offered up by Dumas *père* for public consumption in his account above. The argot makes it sound so much more authentic, while also indirectly suggesting that, if Dumas *père* had been Marie Duplessis's lover, he would not have been remotely concerned to hide this from anyone. The fact that she tried to get to the father through the son would seem to confirm the truth of Dumas *père*'s later recollection, which was published in 1855 in a series of essays called *Les Mohicans de Paris*, twelve years after this encounter at the Comédie-Française. So what was it that Marie Duplessis wanted from the elder Dumas, who was indeed 41 then and already enjoyed a huge reputation in Paris? It turns out that she wanted to become an actress, as the son explained to the father a few days later:

> It was a capricious whim: she wanted to become an actress. They all fantasise about that but in the theatre, you know, one has to work, study, rehearse. It is hard and dedicated work, a major decision. It is much easier to rise at 2 in the afternoon, to get dressed, drive out for a tour in the Bois de Boulogne, return for dinner in the Café de Paris or Aux Frères Provençaux, and proceed from there to a box at the Palais-Royal, the Vaudeville, or the Gymnase; to dine after the theatre and to return home, or indeed to someone else's home, at 3 in the morning than labour like Mlle Mars. Anyway, the rookie actress has found herself an Englishman and is no longer interested in her vocation.[19]

The 'Englishman' might have been the character we know as 'Tony', the owner of the most exclusive Paris stables at 102, Champs-Élysées. He knew her, they corresponded with each other, and he bought some of her effects when they were auctioned after her death. But the timing is wrong for Tony. Rather, Dumas's 'Englishman' may refer to another English-speaking French aristocrat, none other than Édouard de Perrégaux.

That Marie Duplessis yearned to be an actress does not come as a surprise since many actresses—Lola Montez and Mogador come to mind—also worked as courtesans, but with the added cachet of being 'artistes'. But there may have been a more pressing reason for Marie Duplessis's desire to become an actress at that moment: her new rival Alice Ozy was on the stage. Her approach to Dumas may be linked directly to her new love. Marie Duplessis was not only trying to imitate Ozy in her profession but was also copying her way of securing roles. It was at just this time that Alice Ozy was expecting to be cast in the part of Rosine in a vaudeville by Théophile Gautier, *Voyage en Espagne*. It would open at the Variétés towards the end of September 1843. Alice Ozy must have felt somewhat insecure about her prospects and so took the not uncommon step to call on Gautier in person to enlist his support. At the time 'Théo', as he was commonly known, lived at 18 rue de Byron off the Champs-Élysées. She got the role but her part of the bargain was, as we saw, to model naked for Gautier. Alice Ozy came closest to being Marie Duplessis's competitor and was, perhaps, the only woman of whom she would be jealous. Ozy counted among her lovers not only the emperor Napoleon III and princelings, but the greatest French novelist of the nineteenth century, Victor Hugo and his son. Like Marie Duplessis, Ozy too was drawn by Vincent Vidal.

Dumas *père*'s account of his meeting with Marie Duplessis at the Comédie-Française not only shines a spotlight on a particular day and moment in her life, but it also places his son's acquaintance with Marie Duplessis squarely in late July 1843. Clearly they had met before then, as the dialogue indicates. There is no doubt about the occasion: the elder Dumas would not have made a mistake about the birthday premiere, a date moreover consolidated by his giving the (almost) correct ages for both his son and himself. He *did* meet Marie Duplessis on 25 July 1843 and she *was* chaperoned by his son. Dumas *père* was on the verge of global fame at that moment: *Les Trois Mousqetaires* would be published the following year, and *Le Comte de Monte Cristo* would be serialized between 1844 and 1846. Dumas was deeply involved in the Paris theatre scene and had even considered running the Comédie-Française jointly with Victor Hugo, at a time when the premier theatre in the country was struggling financially. In 1846 he took over a theatre in Saint-Germain-en-Laye and turned it into a chic venue for Paris's intelligentsia; which is why the theatre is named after him today.

The elder Dumas's piece demonstrates that his son and Marie Duplessis knew each other for over a year before they became lovers. This fact is alluded to repeatedly in *La Dame aux Camélias* when Armand reminds Marguerite more than once of their earlier fleeting acquaintance. As the younger Dumas did not belong to the Jockey-Club, which was out of his league, it was she who must have taken the initiative, obviously because she was keen to get a foothold on the Paris stage. Getting to the father through the son may have been somewhat manipulative, but there seems to have been more to it too: clearly the two 19-year-olds liked each other well enough to stay in touch through the course of at least two more lovers. No-one ever owned Marie Duplessis, as the younger Dumas found out to his cost. By the time Dumas *fils* and she did embark on a fully-fledged relationship, the elder Dumas had become a living legend, thanks to *The Three Musketeers* and *Monte Cristo*.

In August 1843 Alice Ozy and Perrégaux were still linked, though they were no longer in a relationship. The connection is a public one in that in August of 1843 Perrégaux and Ozy were the two joint parties named in a law-suit brought by a jeweller called Marlé. At the same time, by 26 August, Perrégaux had left Paris because that day he checked into the opulent Hôtel de Flandre in Spa where, in 1845, Jules Janin and Liszt also stayed.[20] The only remaining part of it is still visible sitting opposite the church, at no. 1 of rue Xhrouet and on the corner of the place Achille Salée. Its façade faces into the Square so it must once have been a grand hotel that covered the entire space of the place Achille Salée, with separate buildings going round a central courtyard. This was clearly a space for the rich and famous. Above all it was discreet. The Spa police register only cites his name. It is very likely though that he was accompanied by Marie Duplessis. That he would travel alone to the pleasure haunts of Europe is inconceivable. It is a reasonable assumption that Marie Duplessis, with a new passport, and Perrégaux stayed as lovers in Spa at a time when his former love, Alice Ozy, was rehearsing her part in the Gautier play. This is also the view of Guy Peeters who, in 'Les séjours spadois de la dame aux camélias', suggests that 'although she [Marie Duplessis] is never mentioned in the official Liste des Étrangers she came to Spa before and after her affair with the younger Dumas':

Ought one to be surprised by the absence of a reference in the Liste des Étrangers? Not at all. When Alexandre Dumas père resided in the Hôtel de l'Orange, from 22 to 23 September 1857, the Hungarian actress Lilla Bulyovski, his travel companion, occupied the adjacent room. She does not feature in the official list either. Probably because the hotel owners of the nineteenth century, like today's, were routinely happy to record one name only when several travellers presented themselves—out of discretion and sense of decorum—if they were not an official couple... We may therefore surmise that in 1843 Marie Duplessis (aged 19) accompanied the Comte Édouard de Perrégaux to the Hôtel de Flandre (Liste des Étrangers no. 18 of 26 August 1843—Hôtel de Flandre, le Comte de Perrégaux, rentier à Paris, 1)[21]

It has long been known, because of an addressed letter, that by December 1843 at the latest, Perrégaux and Marie Duplessis were deeply involved. Moreover, another relevant, and earlier, letter by Marie Duplessis to Perrégaux, dated 23 October 1843, was discovered by the author of this book.

It is unlikely that the two lovebirds attended the premiere on 21 September of Gautier's *Voyage en Espagne* on their return to the capital. Alice Ozy's reviews as Rosine were mixed and her neighbour, de Villemessant of the *Sylphide*, commented that beauty did not confer a licence to play poorly. The reviewer of the *Journal des Théâtres* was more charitable: 'Mlle Ozy' made the most of a poor part and, in his view, deserved her plaudits. What she needed above all, he suggested, were parts worthy of her talent.[22] If Perrégaux's habit of falling in love with attractive young women had already made the news in Paris, his reputation for loyalty may have been less secure. He had badly hurt Alice Ozy—and that after taking her away from one of the royal princes. This latter, Aumale, hankered after her but to no avail: his suggestion that he and she might try again after a decent interval, if she left Perrégaux, ceased to be relevant when she in turn was deserted. When Aumale married in 1844 he offered to pay Ozy a hefty sum for the return of his love letters. With haughty disdain she sent them back for free. But she would not quite give up on Perrégaux; or perhaps, more likely from what we know about these events, he could not entirely let go of her.

In the meantime Marie Duplessis and Perrégaux, back in Paris after a summer mostly spent in Bougival, sat in the best boxes at the opera and theatre, though always with appropriate decorum as befitted a woman kept by a rich old man: she would sit at the front with her female chaperone while the old count sat at the back when he was present; when absent, Perrégaux would openly commandeer her. More compelling reasons further enjoined them to tread carefully: the beady-eyed Duchesse de Raguse, young Perrégaux's aunt, was a force to be reckoned with and would not stand by idly while one of her two nephews seemed determined to waste his patrimony on actresses and courtesans now that both the young men's parents had gone. The fact that Marie Duplessis was kept by a disreputable old lecher was somewhat reassuring: at least her nephew would not squander a fortune on her living quarters and the daily requirements of a rich luxury-loving woman whose clothes alone cost a fortune. Family heirlooms were a different matter, and the Duchess would do her best to recover whatever her profligate nephew had gifted to his paramour. With a measure of wisdom and foresight, Perrégaux senior had, as we saw, set up a trust to restrain exorbitant spending of the kind that Édouard de Perrégaux was prone to: once he had exhausted his own resources, he was forced to live off an allowance controlled by the family lawyers.

The first letter to survive from the constant flow of notes between Marie Duplessis and Perrégaux concerns jewellery. It is undated but was probably written in June or July 1843. It seems that an order at the jeweller's Breton took rather longer to execute than she had hoped. Above all, there was a pressing reason to expedite matters, as she needed both jewellery and, it turns out, a new passport to travel abroad. This letter is imperious and, unlike the next one, uses the formal *vous*. Although not dated, her address is given at the bottom: she would be there at least until 11 March 1844. Here is the letter:

> My dear Édouard, please be so good as to give my papers to the bearer of this note. I urgently need them. Would you be so kind as to ask Mr Breton not to make me wait any longer for my jewels: because, as you know, I mean to leave as soon as possible and I cannot do so without them as I need them to settle my affairs. As you cannot be in, please be so good as to reply and I will send for them tonight.
>
> Since you are not accompanying me to Italy, I don't quite see why you have told so many people that you would be joining me there later. Do you really intend to hurt me? You have all along been well aware of the fact that this could damage me in the future: are you really trying to render it sad and unhappy for me? I forgive you for this with all my heart, but please do not forget the subject of my letter.
>
> All yours,
> Marie,
> 22 rue d'Antin[23]

The papers she is pressing him to convey to her messenger can only have been her new passport (French 'papiers' usually means 'identity papers'), which he clearly procured for her, presumably by using his many contacts. If this is indeed her second passport, it would date this letter to the summer of 1843. She required it urgently to travel to Italy and would leave very shortly after receiving the jewels she ordered. It is clear from the letter that she would not be accompanied by Perrégaux on this trip south; moreover, she was irritated by the rumours that he was spreading about joining her later.

No record has surfaced of the future 'traviata' in Italy. Until such time that her second passport, with its stamps, turns up, we will not know for certain where she went, let alone who she was with. Italy was not renowned at the time for its spas though Rome, Florence, and Venice were already popular tourist destinations. But mere tourism would hardly be the main reason for her trip to Italy. Its purpose was more likely to be connected to the man she was meant to accompany rather than anything to do with her, much though as a lover of Italian opera she may well have wanted to visit the land of music and lemons in bloom, as Goethe had called it. A foreign trip like this could not be hidden from her protector Stackelberg, but by now the old man was probably resigned to his protégée's promiscuity. Guiche is out of the picture even though he was an international figure whose diplomatic career took him to Turin and eventually to Vienna by way of Rome. Given his family's objections to Marie Duplessis he may not have wanted to cross them so soon after the split between him and her; the more so since the whole of Paris knew about her latest romance with Perrégaux. It would be hugely satisfying were it to emerge that Marie Duplessis did travel to Italy at this time and that she visited Venice. If she did, she would undoubtedly have been taken to La Fenice, a rival house in those days of La Scala in Milan. We will never know but it is an intriguing reverie to imagine her in the very spot where *La traviata* would be first performed a mere ten years later.

Her next letter was also posted to Perrégaux and connects again to her jewellery. It too is undated but was probably written in the autumn of 1843:

> Your letter reached me at 5 o'clock. I cannot possibly meet you, dear Édouard, at Mr Breton's. As Mr Redel will be in a great rush, I am bound to miss him so that my errand would be pointless. Next time, dear Édouard, give me half an hour's notice. I hope to see you soon. I kiss your eyes a thousand times.[24]

It is not entirely clear what is involved here. It appears that Perrégaux wrote her a note asking to meet her at the jeweller Breton's around 5 p.m., pre-sumably for her to try on a gift he had purchased. But she only received his note at 5 p.m. and therefore could not make it. If only he had given her half an hour's notice, she would then have been ready for him. Mr Redel appears to have been a busy craftsman or designer who was servicing Breton for pieces made to order and measure. Marie Duplessis could not possibly wear jewellery unless it was made specially for her: the thought of being spotted at the opera with diadems or necklaces that might grace another brow was unthinkable. She was using the intimate address of 'tu' in the context of this sumptuous gift, while at the same time gently prompting Perrégaux about the etiquette of communicating with her.

In the autumn of 1843 Marie Duplessis's life as courtesan was as busy as it was complicated, whether or not she travelled to Italy that summer with a man who was neither her protector Stackelberg nor one of her declared lovers. Her affairs inevitably became a juggling act, as she needed to retain her protector for his money while at the same time seeking out the excitement and the company of young men. And all this time, we know from her actress friend Judith Bernat, she was hoping for happiness. Perhaps Édouard de Perrégaux would be the one after all? As her life involved much coming and going at night, she increasingly needed somewhere more discreet to stay in Paris. Her official title of 'rentière' fooled no-one, but the constant nocturnal *va-et-vient* of men and lavish parties required accommodation in a place where neighbours would not start to talk or call upon the authorities, and where rich men would not necessarily be recognized. She was looking to move and her old protector would yet again fund her relocation. Before long an ideal place came up. In the meantime Marie Duplessis may have been involved now with two, if not three, men. One of them was Perrégaux.

He was out of town when, at 5 a.m. on Monday 23 October 1843, she wrote the following letter which sat for many years unnoticed in an archive at the University of Virginia. It survives because Édouard de Perrégaux had kept it inserted in his own copy of *La Dame aux Camélias*:

Dearest heart,
You have been gone for a century, it seems. I have written to you twice but you haven't answered my letters. If you harbour just a little bit of affection for me, don't forget me for so long. Would you like to know what I am doing? I often go to the theatre and I see very few people. I love you with all my heart. Dearest one let me have some news. Love me well and please send me some venison; I mean a deer. Tell me how my very own stallion is doing. I want to receive long letters from you often. If not, I might scratch out your eyes and God knows if this time I will spare them. Farewell beloved 'bibi'. In spite of my anger I kiss you deeply, always, and with all my heart.
Marie[25]

Her words 'my very own stallion' have led to suggestions that she may here be writing to her supplier of horses for her carriage, the already mentioned English horse merchant 'Tony' from the Champs-Élysées. In other words, she would be enquiring after a stallion she was stabling in his popular establishment. But the only horse Marie Duplessis ever owned was the one that pulled her brougham; stallions were never used for light coupés. If she is not writing to a horse supplier, to whom *is* she writing?

Her use of 'bibi' does not help much with identifying the addressee as it is a fairly generic, if undoubtedly intimate, form of address in French, not unlike modern 'baby' in English; unless she uses B.B. as an abbreviation, in the same way she does 'A.D.' for Alexandre Dumas. But none of her known lovers had the initials B.B. There is no doubt that the letter is authentic and by her. Its upper left corner displays, albeit faintly and in tiny lettering, an 'M' and 'D' surmounted by a coronet of roses, perhaps because her real first name was 'Rose Alphonsine Plessis'. According to Jules Blois, who rediscovered

Figure 10.3 A tureen with countess Marie Duplessis's crest on it.

some of her other letters to Perrégaux, one of them is on pink paper and carries this same crest:

> The paper is pink. It is folded over to form a triangle and sealed with red wax, in that uniform seal which she never forgets to use, and with those two letters M.D. topped by a marquis's crown.[26]

A marquis's crown is 'a circlet (or coronet) mounted with four pearl florets alternating with four pearl clovers', the same coronet that adorns her crockery in the Gacé museum (Figure 10.3), suggesting that she acquired it shortly after she changed her name to Duplessis.

Rather than alluding to a horse, she is referring to her 'stud' Perrégaux. Almost all her lovers were obsessed with horses; members of the Jockey-Club invariably were. The 'stallion' of the letter is Perrégaux, her acknowledged lover at the time, and the letter is clearly to him. She is complimenting him about his prowess in bed. Her coquettish threat to scratch out his eyes clinches the question of the addressee, as she repeatedly refers to Perrégaux's 'eyes' in other letters to him; as in 'your letter reaches me at 5 o'clock...I kiss your eyes a thousand times', or in this letter in which she refers to one of her girlfriends:

> I am so cross, my dear Édouard, that I did not receive your letter an hour sooner! Zélia wrote to me to invite me to spend the evening with her. I promised I would as I had nothing better to do. If you like, we can dine together tomorrow. Please let me know if you can. While waiting, sweet little brother, I kiss your blue eyes a thousand times and am all yours in my heart.
> Marie[27]

The promised kisses on his eyes have multiplied exponentially in a letter dated Saturday 2 December 1843:

> Darling Ned,
> Tonight at the Variétés they are putting on a special performance for the benefit of Bouffé. It will start with Le Dîner de Madelon, Le Père Turlululu, Phèdre by Audry, Les Armes de Richelieu, Le Solitaire, a melodrama by Audry, Le Gamin de Paris, and a few numbers by the Sylphide troupe of dancers, in short a delightful evening; you would do me a huge favour if you could secure me a box. Kindly reply to me, my beloved friend. I kiss your eyes a thousand million times, if you only you will let me.
> Marie.[28]

Hugues Bouffé's début at the Variétés that night marked the greatest theatrical event of the week. Long queues had formed by 4 p.m. and one reviewer ('Début de Bouffé') noted that Nestor Roqueplan's poaching of Bouffé for his theatre from the less well funded Gymnase was a triumph: the great actor blended effortlessly into a new troupe quite different from his old familiars at the Gymnase. The break had been announced officially towards the middle of November and all of Paris learnt as well of the huge transfer fee of 100,000 francs paid to Bouffé. On the menu that night were reviews by the names of *Roquefinette*, *Le Gamin de Paris*, and *Jacquot*. Marie Duplessis may have had her shows slightly muddled. Not that it matters and in any case the most important thing were not the shows but the fact that she would be present. In the words of one observer, 'the auditorium had entirely sold out in advance and showed off the richest and best people of society', the same elite group who toured the winter balls of the metropolis.[29] Marie Duplessis undoubtedly attended; not to do so would have been a dreadful snub to her standing as the recently anointed queen of Parisian demi-mondaines. She may have harboured another reason for wanting to see the show from a prime spot, because her rival Alice Ozy played the part of Jeanneton in *Jacquot*, one of the shows that she omits to mention in her letter to Perrégaux. He may not have relished the idea of watching his recent lover perform in full view of her replacement.

The letter of Saturday 2 December 1843 proves that Perrégaux and Marie Duplessis were very much in touch at this time and that she felt free to call on him at short notice, again using the familiar 'tu', although she occasionally used both 'tu' and 'vous', as in another letter about the theatre when she arranged to meet him in a box at the Vaudeville:

> It would give me great pleasure, dear Édouard, if you ['vous'] wanted to come and see me tonight [Théâtre de Vaudeville, loge no. 27]. Impossible for me to dine with you ['toi'] tonight as I am quite unwell.
>
> With a thousand kisses,
> Marie.[30]

That she occupied Box 27 at the Vaudeville is a piquant detail, but more intriguing is her unwillingness to meet him for dinner while being happy instead to see him at the theatre. Her manipulative switch to 'toi' in the course of this note, to cajole him to accede to her request, is characteristic of her need to keep her various lovers apart by granting different favours at different times. This entailed a string of white lies and excuses. She reputedly joked that it was all those 'lies' that accounted for her flawless white teeth. One such lie, quite similar to the one served up to Perrégaux here, would eventually cause a break-up with a lover who could not accept what were effectively the rules of this game. That lover was the young Dumas. But Marie Duplessis was constantly under pressure from different men, and it was not possible for her to reject any rich suitors outright as she never knew who would pay the rent, if her old count died suddenly or else left her to her own devices.

Marie Duplessis's liaison with Édouard de Perrégaux as her chief lover continued into 1844, although other admirers were weaving in and out of her life and bed too during this period. It is not known what broke up Perrégaux and Marie Duplessis but it is a fact that in April 1844 Perrégaux tried to re-enlist in the army and in the same grade as before, a grade he had resigned in 1841 for 'reasons beyond my control'.[31] By requesting to rejoin his regiment, he wanted to get away from Paris and from Marie Duplessis. In this he failed and in June 1844 he was still living in Paris, at 25 rue de la Ville-l'Evêque, not far from the Madeleine. By then Marie Duplessis had moved on.

What caused the rift between them? For once Dumas's *La Dame aux Camélias* cannot possibly be right though he is hinting at what must have been the cause of their separation. The Bougival scenes in Dumas imply that the rupture between the lovers was caused ultimately by Armand's father appearing to break them up, to safeguard the honour of his family and particularly his daughter's future. Taken literally, this constitutes pure fantasy as Édouard de Perrégaux's parents were both dead by 1843 and he had a brother, not a sister. Even if the Armand Duval of the novel was at least partly based on Dumas, the elder Dumas would hardly have bothered to prise his son away from a courtesan; and the younger Dumas did not have a sister either. What may well have happened instead in real life, is that Marie Duplessis surrendered to a combination of pressures from Perrégaux's family and Stackelberg's threatening to stop supporting her unless she left Perrégaux. Dumas may not quite have known the true reason for the lovers' separation, even though his sources were both Marie Duplessis and, probably, Perrégaux too. Vienne on the other hand depended on Marie Duplessis for whatever knowledge he possessed about the lovers and, crucially, on friends back home in the Orne, not to mention his own mother. For Nonant enters into this and perhaps not unexpectedly as suddenly Marie Duplessis's birth certificate became an issue. When two strangers from Paris turned up in the autumn of 1843 to ask questions about a former native of Nonant, word naturally spread, the more so since the two took lodgings at the very same Hôtel de la Poste where the subject of their enquiries had stayed two years earlier.

The outsiders arrived in Nonant between the summer of 1843 and March 1844. One of them was the Perrégaux family solicitor, whom Vienne's mother nicknamed 'Old Blue-Glasses Sideburns', because of his eccentric blue glasses and huge sideburns; the other may have been either Delisle or Carlier, trusted servants of the Perrégaux–Raguse families. Whatever the villagers thought of Marie Duplessis's chosen life, of which by now they were well aware, none of them apparently turned on her. Her former teacher from Saint-Germain-de-Clairefeuille, Sister Françoise Huzet, bore eloquent witness to her sweet character as did others who were consulted. The mairie released a copy of her birth certificate which showed that in the autumn of 1843 she was still only 19 and therefore technically a minor in law.

This must have reassured the lawyer and his employers. What they dreaded most was that Édouard de Perrégaux might marry Marie Duplessis in a fit of besotted love. As we saw, she had lied about her age on her passport applications. For now the Perrregaux family could rest easy: the elopement to London had mercifully not resulted in a union that the family would have had to disown, at whatever cost. In the end the two men got nowhere but the pressure was building on Perrégaux now while at the same time Marie Duplessis was probably becoming increasingly concerned about her future. Perrégaux's Achilles heel was not so much his impetuous romantic character as a chronic inability to manage his finances. In a mere two years he had squandered a vast fortune by reckless womanizing. It was not, Vienne remarked, as if Comte Robert de Saint-Yves, Perrégaux's alias in his memoir, were a callow young man who knew nothing about women. On the contrary, he was a man in his early thirties—in fact Perrégaux was 28 in 1843—with a string of affairs behind him by the time he became involved with the two most costly women in Paris, Alice Ozy and Marie Duplessis. (Dumas blamed Ozy for walking off with a large part of Perrégaux's inheritance.)

Marie Duplessis certainly did not need keeping because Stackelberg underwrote most of her daily living expenses while Perrégaux showered her with gifts and heirlooms. He was far from spineless but in the end he buckled under the pressure from his family over his mistress. In his submission to the Ministry of Defence he notes that it was his debts that lay at the root of his failure to follow through on his career in the army and that he had let himself and his family down. The exact date of his final parting from Marie Duplessis is not known, but it must have been in the course of the first three months of 1844. His relationship with her may have been her only happy one, because he loved her and she probably loved him. Her reward for the separation and for moving back to Paris was, it seems, an even more lavish place to live; and one that would be far more discreet.

On New Year's Day 1844 torrential downpours turned the streets of Paris into an unsightly sea of black umbrellas in muddy streets. It was the day of the year when the city's leading courtesans habitually received gifts from their admirers, while new ones left their calling cards and presents in the hope of attracting attention and favour. For the next two and a half years Marie Duplessis would reign in the metropolis as the uncontested queen of courtesans. She had become a celebrity, virtual royalty in a world that was less shadowy than is generally alleged, and she would conduct her reign from a brilliant new home next to the Cité Vindé, a recent block of buildings running up the boulevard de la Madeleine (the old rue Basse-du-Rempart) from the corner of the rue Duphot. It was one of the smartest among the new shopping malls that were starting to sprout in the richer parts of Paris at just that time.

The shops spilled over the eastern end of Cité Vindé into 11 boulevard de la Madeleine. Here were the exclusive premises of 'Modes Golberg', the property of Madame Duhay de Golberg, spelled 'Golsberg' in the photographic sketch from the period reproduced in Chapter 11 (Figure 11.2). The boutique of Clémence Pratt was next door in the Vindé itself, at mezzanine level. It sat above the chic 'Bazar Provençal', which was much sought after in the wake of the new health food fads in Paris. In the Bazar, owned by one J. Aymès from Marseilles, discerning customers could enjoy a true taste of the south, including excellent olive oils, nougats, calissons d'Aix, and chocolates from Marie Duplessis's favourite Pyrenean spa town of Bagnères-de-Luchon. A piece in the *Sylphide* of June 1846 notes that the shop's instantly recognizable emblem was an olive tree, 'a symbol of peace', a version of *mens sana in corpore sano*. The Vindé acted as a magnet to the city's fashionable set, attracting above all those who longed to be seen in all the latest finery. It was named after the recently deceased rich politician and philanthropist Viscount Charles-Gilbert Morel de Vindé. His main Paris residence until his death in 1842 had been 11 boulevard de la Madeleine. While the Vindé shops and boutiques were bustling with smart crowds during the day, they were deserted in the evenings. When a mezzanine apartment underneath the Golberg shop became vacant, Romain Vienne, who knew Mr Golberg, may have tipped Marie the wink; or else the information about the free apartment came from Madame Pratt whose own living quarters, at 13 boulevard de la Madeleine, directly butted onto the empty apartment underneath the Golbergs.

The large and lusty Clémence Pratt had become one of Paris's leading hat designers whose latest creations were keenly watched and reported by the city's top fashion magazines. At the time of the reign of Marie Duplessis, Pratt was 'la modiste à la mode' and was featured regularly in the 'Modes' chronicle of the *Sylphide*; her new hats were routinely exhibited in the most fashionable resorts of the time such as Deauville and Baden-Baden.[32] The 'Revue des Magasins' praised her 'rare talent' for fitting her customers with hats that moulded themselves around their faces to perfection: 'the shape of the hats seemed to have been designed expressly to bring out the best in each woman's features: not a trivial feat because one may be very pretty, sport a gorgeous hat, and still look shoddily covered. What is needed is a discriminating eye for human features...the clientele of Madame Pratt appreciates this gift which is essential for creating elegance.'[33] In 1844 Clémence Pratt was around 40 years old and the mother of a 12 or 13-year-old daughter, a curious fact only known because of the very rare first edition of *La Dame aux Camélias*. She regularly, it seems, accompanied her mother to the theatre. This would not be significant in itself were it not for the fact that Clémence Pratt was a retired prostitute, who was convicted of immorality towards minors in the years following Marie Duplessis's death, perhaps even because she used her daughter to cover up her true activities.[34] In his survey of the bills of the lady of the camellias, the bibliophile collector Lucien Graux reports that one of the invoices in his compilation refers to Madame Pratt's dubious reputation. The document concerns unpaid bills by Marie Duplessis which, it seems, are dealt with by Pratt:

> The hat designer C.Pratt, Cité Vindé, of the mezzanine of boulevard de la Madeleine, 13, directly next door to the customer whose bills are overdue for payment [i.e. Marie Duplessis]...the fact is—a slip of paper with blue pencil writing on it, in an unknown hand, spells it out plainly, in our file—that Mme Pratt is not an honest woman...rumour is rife that she is a procuress. We will be careful not to pass judgement on this.[35]

Pratt invoiced Marie Duplessis for 500 francs altogether for sixteen hats. She constantly plied her with hats, a new one roughly every five days. We know that Marie Duplessis was indeed the recipient of multiple hats from Pratt, but one may well wonder too whether these invoices, under the guise of hats, were not in fact for other services rendered?

By all accounts Madame Pratt was a dead ringer for Chaucer's Wife of Bath. It is alleged that she used her contacts and former clients from among the upper classes of the capital to set up in business and make a success of it. Only two years earlier she was still based at 12 rue Saint-Sauveur, a narrow medieval street north of Les Halles, and listed as working in 'fab. broderies', that is embroidery and fashionable materials. The Parisian world of designs, fashion, and millinery was almost as full of young women doubling as good time girls as the world of the theatre, as the case of Marie Duplessis demonstrates better than any other from the time. It is quite possible that from her shop in Saint-Sauveur Madame Pratt employed fashion and sex workers in equal measure, until such time as she moved to new premises in the recently opened Cité Vindé where she reinvented herself as a hat designer.

She obviously would have known about Marie Duplessis's life and her various lovers. When, as seems likely, the young woman turned up in her shop one day from nearby rue d'Antin, Madame Pratt must have realized that money, perhaps a fortune, could be made from running Paris's most celebrated courtesan. It may have been her after all, rather than Vienne, who alerted Marie Duplessis to the flat at 11 boulevard de la Madeleine. Not only that, but she may well have approached the young Normande and put it to her that she could act as a respectable chaperone, in reality of course a procuress, in public places and also by looking after her if she moved next door. For a fee she could act as a dragon at the gates.[36] Most of the sophisticated set of Paris knew full well who Madame Pratt was, what she had been and that she doubled as designer and procuress; and even, occasionally with eager young men, as a twilight prostitute. In the novel Dumas calls her 'Prudence Duvernoy' while at the same time being remarkably explicit about where she lived and what she did. He probably escaped a lawsuit because too many people knew that he was telling the truth. Madame Pratt could hardly deny it, the more so since she knew Dumas *fils* very well and may in fact have serviced his friend Déjazet, the son of the actress Virginie Déjazet, during his first night in Marie Duplessis's apartment

When Marie Duplessis learnt that the mezzanine apartment ('entresol') underneath the show rooms of Madame Golberg, whose living quarters were higher up the same staircase, had become free to rent, she must have jumped at the opportunity.[37] An entire floor could be hers and it would

be completely safe from prying eyes at night when she needed to entertain and party. She would not disturb anyone and no-one in turn could
interfere with her business. Above her would be an empty shop at night
and beneath her the porter's lodgings, occupied at the time by one Pierre
Privé. Also, adjacent on the east side of her proposed new residence, at
9 boulevard de la Madeleine, were the exclusive stables and riding school
('*Ecole et cercle d'equitation*') of Stephen Drake, a fact that can only have
added to the attraction of the move, given her love of horses. The apartment
at no. 11 was just what she needed, which is why she persuaded her protector Stackelberg to secure it for her. This he did, although in the latter
stages of her stay there it was not he who was paying her rent to the
owner but Perrégaux.[38]

11

Sin and luxury at 11 boulevard de la Madeleine

1844–1847

When Marie Duplessis took up residence in her grand new home (Figure 11.1), she not only moved house but also became a truly kept woman, with Clémence Pratt as her 'manager'. Henceforth the two women became close business partners even if Pratt's greed stood in the way of true friendship. Their *modus operandi* was that young men who desired a more intimate acquaintance with Marie Duplessis would try and catch the eye of Madame Pratt at the opera in the first instance. Pratt's cover was her teenage daughter. Her innocent presence was clearly deemed shocking enough for Dumas to remove it from all editions of the novel subsequent to the first, but the girl was undoubtedly privy to the assignations at the opera and obviously shared her mother's home at 13 boulevard de la Madeleine. Here young men would wait their turn before being taken by the procuress to her neighbour's flat next door.

11 boulevard de la Madeleine was the place of some of Marie Duplessis's most notorious love affairs, including those with Dumas and Liszt. The precise date of her move is not known, but it was probably around February 1844, because by 11 March 1844 she was being invoiced at her Madeleine address by the house of Lacoste of 37 rue Neuve-Saint-Augustin. Lacoste's bill stipulates that their customer inhabits the mezzanine 'entresol' floor of her building. This would seem conclusive proof that by then she had moved to 11 boulevard de la Madeleine, unless we assume that she also lived in mezzanine quarters in d'Antin, an unlikely coincidence. The invoice from Lacoste can only mean that she had moved by 11 March and that she commissioned them to furnish her new premises, because they had done so well

Figure 11.1 The five windows of Marie Duplessis's last and most famous home, the mezzanine apartment at 11 boulevard de la Madeleine: the left-hand window was her boudoir's, the three middle ones belonged to her salon, while the right-hand one was that of the maid's room. The caryatids are a dubious twentieth-century homage to the block's most famous resident.

with her previous home. She seems similarly to have kept faith with her hairdresser Denise Eugène from the rue Neuve-Saint-Augustin who, during the period from July to October 1844, was instructed by Marie Duplessis to send daily 'a skilful young man to do her hair, at the cost of forty "sous" per visit'.[1]

A photographic sketch of the outside of 11 boulevard de la Madeleine appeared in *L'Illustration: Journal Universel* of 1845, when the paper ran a series of drawings of all the major boulevards between place de la Madeleine and the Bastille. It shows the south side of the boulevard de la Madeleine as it looked when she lived there (Figure 11.2). The outer shell of the building has not changed all that much in the intervening years, while the Cité Vindé to the west of it has been completely rebuilt.

The Madeleine apartment is the most important place in Marie Duplessis's life and she died in it. Here she received Stackelberg, Perrégaux, Liszt, Dumas, Aguado, and others who paid her court as well as friends like

Figure 11.2 The south side of the boulevard de la Madeleine as it was in 1845 when Marie Duplessis lived here. Clearly visible above her apartment is the store of 'Modes Golberg', owned by her neighbour Madame Duhay de Golberg. To her right (east, and to the left of the picture), just visible to the naked eye, are the exclusive stables of Stephen Drake; to her left (west) are the luxury shops of Cité Vindé.

Romain Vienne, Judith Bernat, and Lola Montez. In it she also occasionally hosted parties. Mme Golberg and her husband did not seem to mind the kinds of goings-on in the mezzanine apartment at night. True, there were strangers on the stairs at all hours and they were not always on their best behaviour as they caroused into the early hours of the morning with the young mistress. Sometimes parties would return after the opera and dinner at one of the cafés on the boulevard des Italiens. It would routinely be after 1 o'clock in the morning before they even started. The apartment is one of the most celebrated interiors of 1840s Paris, because of Marie's notoriety and the detailed 1847 Auction Catalogue which itemizes its fixtures and furnishings room by room. Several visitors left detailed eyewitness accounts of it. These include her lover Dumas, a young lawyer by the name of Lumière, instructed by his locksmith client to collect monies that were owing to him by the mistress of the Madeleine, Romain Vienne, who visited here repeatedly, and the Variétés (and Comédie-Française) actress Judith Bernat, who was taken on a guided tour by the mistress of the house.

Dumas in particular records minute details of the apartment in the rare first 1848 edition of *La Dame aux Camélias*, published by Alexandre Cadot, who later bid for one of Marie Duplessis's most prized possessions. Only a handful of copies of the first edition survive in the Bibliothèque Nationale and the library of the Comédie-Française. It differs substantially from all subsequent editions, particularly with regard to intimate details about the apartment. All modern French editions of the novel, and the excellent English translation by David Coward, are unfortunately based on the revised third edition of 1852. For Dumas the apartment was hugely important sentimentally, which is why in his memoir novel he went out of his way to evoke the atmosphere of this ultimate temple of pleasure and luxury in Paris, sitting in full view no less of the Madeleine church, the capital's chief temple dedicated to the Mary Magdalene who was cleansed by Christ.[2] He freeze-frames the apartment in the 1848 edition of the novel, just as he had done already in a brilliant elegy written immediately after her death. It is called 'Péchés de Jeunesse'. In it he retraces past visits to the apartment, room by room, starting on 'that well-known staircase' that led up to it from the boulevard de la Madeleine. For Dumas, the personality of Marie Duplessis was inextricably linked to this particular home and her many cherished possessions. Tantalizingly one of the most celebrated pictures of her, the so-called 'Olivier' portrait, was painted in one of the rooms at 11 boulevard de la Madeleine, as we shall see.

The apartment was reached by steps that skirted the porter's lodge. It consisted of six rooms and stretched across the entire mezzanine floor of number 11. Its front gave onto the boulevard de la Madeleine and the grand Madeleine church itself, while at the back it overlooked a courtyard. Each room is named separately in the 1847 Auction Catalogue. It so happens that the seven-page inventory by the 'tapissier' overseeing the refurbishment of the apartment for her survives in a private collection that was last seen in 1929. It seems that Stackelberg commissioned the fashionable Maison Grandvoinnet, his neighbours at 11 Chaussée d'Antin, a local Harrods that carried everything, from silks to clocks, wall papers, and mirrors, to furnish his protégée's new living quarters. The total cost of the overhaul was around 20,000 francs in 1844 which, very tentatively, would come to around €165,000 in today's money, although some commentators would put it much higher than that.[3] The true figure may lie anywhere between €165,000 and €400,000.

The first room of the apartment was a spacious 'Antichambre', which contained a mahogany table and chests of drawers as well as six cherry-wood dining chairs. The walls were clad in latticework of gilded wood, which supported a variety of plants climbing out of rosewood tubs. The overall impression was of a harmonious ensemble of fresh and cheerful colours, according to Henry Lumière who entered here by appointment to collect money that the mistress of the house owed. Straight ahead, through a door, was the dining room while to the left a door led into the salon, the main room of the house that ran almost the length of the apartment on the boulevard side. To the left of the salon, at the bottom western end of the apartment, was a small room where Clotilde the chambermaid slept. The catalogue says 'à gauche du salon', meaning to the left as one entered, while the refurbishment inventory refers to it as 'chambre d'amie', that is a spare room or guest bedroom.

The green motif of the antechamber continued into the *salle à manger*, or dining room, which overlooked the courtyard. This was hardly ever visible though because the room was used almost exclusively at night when its hand-made green, damascene curtains sealed off the outside world. The walls were clad in rich cordwain, panels of gilded and embossed leather hangings that were the ultimate in luxury decoration. The sculpted oak dining room table was surrounded by twelve chairs, covered in green velvet, while two silver and vermeil sideboards graced the room which also har-boured an oak bookcase. There was in addition a grandfather clock, which

Dumas heard striking the hour when he lay in bed next to Marie Duplessis at night.

The dining room connected to her bedroom at the far end, and to the salon on the left. The salon was the most public room in the apartment and included the three central windows (called 'trois croisées' in the Auction Catalogue) out of the five that gave onto the boulevard (Figure 11.1). It boasted a magnificent fireplace. The colour scheme interleaved white and gold with cherry which was picked up by the hues and tones of her rose-wood furniture. Much thought and design had gone into this. All her treasured possessions from rue d'Antin had probably accompanied her to her new home, but there must have been some new ones too.[4] Three pieces in particular invariably attracted attention. One was a superb gold and bronze clock 'the size of a child', in Dumas's words, which sat on the mantelpiece where it was surrounded by elaborate pieces of china. The second was the true centrepiece of the room, a stunning turquoise chandelier of twenty-four lights, studded with carved pieces of 'vieux Saxe' (i.e. Dresden) china, featuring flowers and birds. And finally, there was her rosewood Pleyel piano. The greatest pianist of all time, Liszt, played on this very instrument on several occasions. He notably, and of course to perfection, performed Weber's *Invitation à la Valse*, which was not only one his great party pieces—it is technically hugely challenging—but also happened to be Marie Duplessis's favourite piece of music. Her attempts to play it even passably were invariably doomed, and Dumas recalls how on their first night she tried again before finally, in desperation, flinging the sheet music across the room.

It is in this very salon that she was painted by Olivier between the spring of 1844 and the autumn of 1846 (Figure 11.3). It has not been possible to identify with certainty this painter. All writers on the portrait confidentially refer to him but none identifies him or gives his first name. The *Almanach Général de la France* 1842 lists an 'Olivier peintre, artiste' at 5 Quai Voltaire, now, and then too, an exclusive address facing the Louvre across the Pont du Carrousel. Olivier was probably a high society painter and had been commissioned for that reason. No other portrait captures her melancholy expression so well, or better conveys a sense of her wistful personality. In the image she appears as a cross between the Esmeralda of Hugo's *Notre-Dame de Paris* and a Bellini Madonna, wearing sleeve-length white gloves and lace ringlets.[5] A Velasquez-style lace mantilla covers part of her hair, those magnificent ringlets for which she was well-known, and is artfully wrapped around her shoulders and arms. She looks intensely sad

Marie DUPLESSIS, tableau d'Olivier.
Collection de Mme Alexandre Dumas.

Figure 11.3 The Olivier portrait of Marie Duplessis, painted in the salon at 11 boulevard de la Madeleine. According to her lover Dumas *fils*, it is the most faithful and expressive of all her portraits.

and resigned. Olivier's image is a powerful tribute to his sitter. In essence he presciently drew Verdi's Violetta as much as he did Marie Duplessis. She did not live to hear *La traviata*, but she saw perhaps the next best representation of her in this profoundly compassionate image. By matching her innermost self and outer appearance, Olivier had drawn her soul just as Verdi would do in his music.

This is the most important portrait of Marie Duplessis: not only did contemporaries vouch for its true likeness, but it was painted in the famous
Madeleine apartment. Several details of the picture place it firmly in its
salon, the most obvious place in which to receive guests and, as in this case,
model for one of them.

The most striking clue perhaps is the large amphora urn sitting on the
tassle-brocaded table behind a small jewellery box. The two are described
together in the auction catalogue as 'a very beautiful rosewood chest
mounted on feet, with rich gilded bronze ornaments and plaques of fine
porcelain decorated in a turquoise blue background with pastoral scenes'
('très beau coffre sur son pied en bois rose, avec riches ornements en bronze
doré et plaques en porcelaine tendre, décors fond bleu turquoise à médaillons, sujets pastoraux'), which is followed immediately by the description of
two vases, one of china and one of 'Saxe', both 'mounted in gilded bronze
and moulded gold' ('monture en bronze doré or moulu'). An imposing
mirror hangs on the wall. Its elaborately carved and undoubtedly gilded
bottom left frame and glass are glimpsed on her left above the vase. This is
without doubt 'the mirror in a carved wooden and gilded frame' ('glace dans
son cadre en bois sculpté et doré') of the sale catalogue.[6] Another clue, and
perhaps the clincher, would be the piano stool ('tabouret de piano en pallisan-
dre') that can be glimpsed to the left of the picture and which is listed as part
of the salon furniture. Finally, there is the broad vertical slat of the casement
window on the left of the picture. These 'croisées' or 'muntins' can be clearly
seen in an old photograph of 11 boulevard de la Madeleine and also in the
contemporary drawing of its outside (Figure 11.2).

The fact that the backdrop of the Olivier aquarelle shows specific details
of the furniture in the Madeleine apartment consolidates the picture's
authenticity, which was moreover attested after her death by its first two
owners, who had both known her very well. They were her horsey friend
Tony and the younger Dumas. It seems that she had presented the Olivier
portrait to the loyal Tony as a gift. Or so Gérard de Contades claims in his
authoritative 1887 essay on the extant portraits of her, for which he consulted several people who had known her, including Dumas *fils* and the
painter Charles Chaplin.[7] Five years later, independently of the Contades
essays, an ageing buck of the period, Alfred de Montjoyeux, another member of the Jockey-Club,[8] recalled in the 'supplément littéraire' of an 1892
issue of the *Lanterne* paper that Stackelberg had commissioned the portrait
only to see it disappear from her flat almost immediately when she presented it as a gift to another admirer:

For his many hours of leisure he wanted a portrait of his Susanna [alluding to the young Susanna in the *Marriage of Figaro* who is desired by Count Almaviva] and commissioned it in the workshop of the then fashionable painter Olivier. No sooner was it hung in her apartment than it was taken down again and carried to the home of her young lover, who was at that moment taking his love for her on a tour of Britain. On his return he rushed back into the arms of his beloved.

At that point, according to Montjoyeux, the old count appeared and the young lover, 'Duval', had to hide behind the curtains while Marie Duplessis was berated by the count for the absence of the portrait. It ends with her instructing her factotum Clotilde to retrieve it from 'Duval' who is probably Perrégaux in real life.

There is an entire narrative here surrounding the Olivier picture, but the most important thing is that it is genuine. That Stackelberg commissioned it is likely, the more so as he probably also ordered the one painted by Édouard Vienot, because Vienot, 'portrait painter', lived at 62 rue de la Chaussée d'Antin, close to the count's home.[9] After Tony's death his widow passed the Olivier portrait to Marie's former lover, the younger Dumas. He still owned it in 1887 when it graced one of the state rooms of his residence at 98 avenue Villiers.[10] Dumas was adamant that Olivier's watercolour was the truest likeness of Marie Duplessis; he should know. Dumas owned both the signed Vienot and Olivier pictures and kindly showed them to Contades whose 1887 essay on the portraits of Marie Duplessis is as influential today as it was then. The Olivier image spoke like no other to Dumas because he knew the exact spot in the apartment where she posed for the painter; and for him Marie Duplessis and the apartment were inextricably linked, which is why in *Péchés de Jeunesse* and in the first edition of *La Dame aux Camélias* he wrote about it in such detail, as if hoping to recreate her magic through the space she inhabited. The delphic Mona Lisa look of Vienot's portrait (Figure 11.4) and the dreamy, soulful vulnerability of the Olivier complement each other. Between them they capture the human face of the music of *La traviata*. The rose in her hair consolidates the authenticity of the image, echoing the crest on her letter head and her flowery name of Rose Alphonsine, both acquired long before she ever became the lady of the camellias.

In an important article about her, one L. Deschaumes, 'a friend and biographer of La Dame aux Camélias', who knew Madame Alexandre Dumas and saw both the Olivier picture and Édouard Vienot portraits together in her residence at Champflour, compared them in the following words:

> In the Vienot painting Marie Duplessis is depicted in a white silk ball gown, with bare shoulders and her hair done with lightly waved coils round her head

Figure 11.4 The best-known portrait of Marie Duplessis, the one which most eloquently conveys her enigmatic character. The painter was the society artist Édouard Vienot who signed the painting.

and long ringlets framing her face. The Olivier portrait of her is much better executed and has kept its exquisite freshness. The young woman is painted standing next to a table adorned with a large vase of flowers. She is dressed in a black velvet gown gathered at the waist in tiny pleats, which grow into heavy flowing folds. The heart-shaped bodice has a boldly plunging neckline following the line of her breasts and just revealing their shape. Her face expresses a charming sadness emanating from large and very soft brown eyes set in whites of an extraordinary bluish shade. A black lace mantilla with a red camellia pinned on one side has been tossed, Spanish style, onto hair divided into slightly bouffant coils which almost completely cover her ears. Alexandre Dumas thought this portrait a very good likeness. It is the one which I believe will become the model sought after by souvenir hunters and the defining image of La Dame aux Camélias.[11]

The description proves that the original Olivier portrait, reproduced here in black and white from an 1890s copy, was in colour, hence the reference to the red camellia and to the the whites of her 'brown eyes' which boasted a 'bluish shade'.

Beyond the salon lay Marie Duplessis's boudoir. In the novel Dumas notes how he and his friend 'Gaston' (Déjazet) passed from the 'salon' into the 'boudoir' and there found another man leaning against the mantelpiece while she was seated at the piano.[12] It was the room in the apartment that she cherished above all others. It overflowed with yellow silk and boasted circular couches ('divans') for reclining. Among its many luxuries was a 'love seat' armchair whose fabric was unusually worn, 'proving that it was the mistress's favourite and that she passed much of her time on it at her fireside'. The boudoir looked down onto the boulevard de la Madeleine. It was near this window that she spent much of her time as she lay dying.

If the boudoir was what would now be termed her den, it also formed an antechamber in a labyrinth of vice. The catalogue calls it 'Boudoir, formant Cabinet de toilette', confirming that her boudoir and dressing room were contiguous, as one would expect them to be. At the far end of the boudoir a door led into her cabinet de toilette, which intervened between the boudoir and her bedroom at the back. Cabinet de toilette and its English translation of 'dressing room' are both accurate and are also euphemisms. The reason why she fled into her 'cabinet de toilette' when racked by a coughing fit was because this was where pitchers of fresh water were kept. The 'boudoir-cabinet' would later attract intense interest at the auction, not only because it was the cabinet de toilette of a legendary courtesan, but because a number of her lovers left behind initialled toiletry gifts thus providing tantalizing clues about her clients. On display were Scheherazade's treasures, a forbidden cave ablaze with gold and silver trinkets by Casimir Aucoc, Paris's premier provider of luxury accessories for personal grooming (his former premises, at 6 rue de la Paix, today fittingly house Tiffany & Co), and Charles Odiot, the city's chief gold and silversmith, a Cellini of the 1840s whose renowned shop was situated at 26 boulevard de la Madeleine, a stone's throw away from her boudoir.

One piece of furniture in her cabinet de toilette was described as 'I grande toilette formant commode, aussi en palissandre, garnie d'une glace'. This may have sold under another name at the auction itself; the perhaps euphemistic 'toilette en palissandre et la garniture en porcelaine' would seem a possible candidate. The 'toilette formant commode' was literally her toilet and almost certainly corresponds to the 'grande glace sur bidet' that she bought at the exclusive Parisian shop of Klein's.[13] It was one of the few items for which she paid herself, clearly out of a sense of personal modesty and decorum. The catalogue also lists a 'bain de siège', a bathtub exactly like the one featured by the journalist Edmond Texier in a chapter entitled 'Les Grisettes et les Lorettes': he portrays a risqué illustrated scene of a young woman in her bath, with her chambermaid sitting on the side of the tub ready to assist in her ablutions; next to them stands a hatchet-faced 'ancienne', a veteran of the sex industry.[14] The cameo could have been sketched at 11 boulevard de la Madeleine, starrring Marie, Clotilde, and Madame Pratt.

The fact is that her boudoir doubled as dressing room and bathroom as well as toilet, effectively an en suite bathroom to her bedroom. Parisian apartments in the 1840s did not have water closets as we know them. Chamber pots were used almost universally and were emptied routinely by the servants, in this case Clotilde. The fact that Marie Duplessis used a seated toilet (modern English 'commode' describes it exactly) in a luxurious décor itself reflects on the sophistication of her living quarters, as does the presence in it of a bidet. In the end though, even the elaborate lavatory provisions in her apartment were ultimately discreet versions of chamberpots. Perhaps her bath and toilet were deemed to be too provocative to be sold to strange men, or perhaps no-one quite dared bid for them openly; unless they were smuggled through the sale under other names.

Marie Duplessis's bedroom was entered from her cabinet de toilette at one end and her *salle à manger* at the other. Its two windows, flanked by thick dark red curtains overlooked the courtyard at the back of the building. The walls and door of the room were clad in the same deep red silk. At the far end ('au fond de la pièce'), that is facing the door into the *salle à manger* and running from east to west, was the centrepiece of the entire apartment: slightly raised above the floor on a podium stood a richly carved, canopied four-poster bed, each leg adorned by caryatids representing fawns and bacchants. Perching on the four capitals were ewers featuring intertwining vines. The bed struck young Lumière as 'a sanctuary of red silk', surrounded by delicious red netting and with a coverlet made of the finest lace imaginable. The younger Dumas similarly thought that this inner sanctum was dressed for a goddess, with its refined beauty evoking a place of worship.

The entire bedroom was a temple to the famous eighteenth-century 'Boulle' style, characterized by its inventive and exquisite marquetry. A Boulle dresser occupied the space between the two windows and was artfully filled with various pieces of china while above it hung a drawing, undoubtedly of her, by Vidal. A Boulle wardrobe with mirrors graced the room with more vases of the most fragile china. Some of these boasted the renowned name of Sèvres Clodion while several other pieces in the apartment originated with the legendary cabinetmaker Jean-Henri Riesener and the master craftsman, Pierre Gauthier, whose bronzes ranked among the most sought-after in France. Along the side of the room was a comfortable couch in front of a sumptuous dressing table covered with elaborate pieces of lace work and personal ornaments. Over it hung another of her Venetian mirrors, this one too in a carved and gilded frame. The room enjoyed a fine fireplace and was lit by two magnificent chandeliers, the work perhaps of Pierre Gauthier. This was the bedroom of a queen, a Marie-Antoinette of the night, but royalty nevertheless.

Marie Duplessis probably first heard Liszt play in February 1844, shortly before her move into the Madeleine apartment. He returned to Paris in April when he played to a packed Salle Ventadour. The concert was the talk of the town. A contemporary, Le Vicomte Charles de Launay alias Delphine de Girardin, noted that 'bevies of fair women' had turned out to watch Liszt's peerless performance; and not only Parisians, but the international crème de la crème had converged on the Salle Ventadour to watch the darling of music-loving audiences.[15] He was the unchallenged wizard of the keyboard.

Did Perrégaux meet his estranged lover at the concert and was this why he tried to rejoin his regiment? She would undoubtedly not have gone alone. In fact, she did not meet Liszt on this occasion nor, it seems, a few days later when, on 26 April 1844, she probably heard him again at a party hosted by Madame d'O——.[16] Liszt gave a brilliant virtuoso rendition of Weber's *Invitation à la Valse*: was this the first time she heard it, and was Liszt the reason why she was so eager to learn this hugely complex piece, which only the greatest pianists of any age, such as Yvonne Lefébure, could ever master? The idea of Marie Duplessis trying to perform it is touching in her innocent belief that she could try anything. No wonder she was seen flinging the score across the room in frustration; many amateurs have done so since.

It may have been during one of the two Liszt nights of April 1844 that she was approached by someone whom she had met during her first stay in Baden-Baden in 1842, Liszt's friend, the rich and flamboyant Felix, Fürst von Lichnowsky (1814–48), adventurer, duellist, mercenary, and lover of music. Vienne almost certainly disguised his identity under the alias of 'Prince Paul'. At the time of his meeting with Marie Duplessis Lichnowsky occupied a luxury suite in the exclusive Hotel Meurice in the rue de Rivoli, the favourite residence of aristocrats and stars and a hop from her apartment in the Madeleine.[17] He had earlier watched her in Baden-Baden and now made his move. It was probably he who presented her with a superb piano bought from Pleyel's, on the corner of the rue Drouot and the boulevard de Montmartre, with the Jockey-Club occupying the upper floors of its prestigious premises.[18] As she had just recently changed homes, he may have bought her the Pleyel as a house-warming gift.

As the piano moved into 11 boulevard de la Madeleine in April 1844, not long after the mistress of the house, so probably did Lichnowsky into Marie Duplessis's bed. Did he also deliver the great pianist to her house? Her friend Romain Vienne thought so: 'Very close to Liszt, the illustrious pianist, he brought him twice to her apartment where he had him play and try out the piano, after giving a lesson to Marie.'[19] But Vienne may inadvertently be conflating her affairs with Liszt and Lichnowsky because Jules Janin, who was present when Liszt first met Marie Duplessis, places their first encounter a year and a half later than this. Marie Duplessis's presumed new friend Lichnowsky would achieve posthumous fame in Georg Weerth's satirical novel about him, *Leben und Thaten des berühmten Ritters Schnapphahnski*, a parody of both Lichnowsky and the entire shiftless aristocracy of the time. He was as restless as he was rich, and shortly after their original trysting he carried Marie Duplessis off to Baden-Baden. He is duly recorded in the *Badeblatt* on 10 May 1844 as 'Linovsky (the French spelling of Lichnowsky) from Brussels' because he had probably travelled from there by way of Spa. In Baden-Baden he stayed in the Hôtel d'Angleterre. No mention is made of anyone else with him, but it is likely that he was accompanied by Marie Duplessis and perhaps her faithful maid Clotilde. He was still in Baden-Baden on 29 May 1844 but had left by 1 June.

Quite where they moved on to after that is not recorded: it could have been any of Wiesbaden, Bad Ems, or Homburg.[20] Lichnowsky, unlike most of her lovers, did not belong to the Jockey-Club and was not immersed in horse racing of some kind or other: for any other of the Paris lions to miss the derby at Chantilly would have been almost unthinkable. Marie Duplessis and Lichnowsky were away for, probably, much of the summer although they could not afford to overlap anywhere with her protector's family. The Stackelberg clan did not gather in Baden-Baden until 10 July 1844 when they arrived at the Europaïscher Hof. They were still here on 31 July, during which time Marie Duplessis could play to her heart's content in other European pleasure capitals. She and Stackelberg must have agreed beforehand that they would not run into each other in the casino towns of Europe.

The previous summer at Bougival could hardly have been more differ-ent from the places where she found herself now. As a Prussian officer and mercenary, Lichnowsky was one of her few foreign lovers. He knew Paris well, having been initiated there into the Masonic society in 1842, and he evidently spoke French. He had recently turned 30 and loved the com-pany of artists, partly perhaps through his friendship with Liszt. While he and Marie Duplessis were playing the casinos of Europe and wining and dining in the most exclusive spa towns, a certain family in Baden-Baden arranged to move from one residence to another, something which the police records of the time carefully recorded. There could hardly be any-thing more self-evidently banal than a move from one address to another in this spa town where guests moved routinely. What renders this move of Wednesday 17 July 1844 of acute interest to the story of Marie Duplessis is the fact that the people were called the 'Dlles Yarboroughs, Angleterre'. They moved into the royal shoemaker's villa, house no. 394, between the Hôtels de la Ville de Nancy and Strasbourg. They had obviously arrived at some earlier point as they were now moving on to other accommodation. Remarkably, they stayed on in Baden-Baden uninterruptedly until Friday 13 September 1844.

Does this prolonged sojourn suggest that the Yarborough girls, or one of them, were trying to recover from some illness in Baden-Baden? As they lingered there for so long, it is likely that their paths crossed that of the Stackelbergs at some point. Did the two families talk? If they did, they would soon have discovered that they had more in common than they could ever have imagined. It was probably known in Baden-Baden that the old count had lost two daughters in the full flower of life, one of them dying in nearby Karlsruhe, and that visiting her grave was perhaps the reason why her father returned to there. Baden-Baden was a small town and it is likely that the Yarboroughs also heard rumours that the count was keep-ing a young demi-monde woman as a sentimental substitute for his lost daughter, the wife of the ambassador d'Ugarte who himself undoubtedly overlapped with the Yarboroughs and Stackelbergs too. What may have happened in Baden-Baden in the summer of 1844, unbeknown to Marie Duplessis, was that the seeds were sown of an event that would a year from now flood her with sorrow and joy in equal measure. Quite who the Dlles

Yarboroughs were exactly is not entirely clear, but they can surely only be the Anderson Worsley Copley family, who boasted Yarborough as their most illustrious title.[21] By calling them 'Dlles Yarboroughs' the police record would seem to suggest that this was a group of Yarborough women rather than just a mother and daughter, who would probably have preferred to stay in a hotel rather than rent a house. Unless, that is, one of them was too ill to stay in a public place. Perhaps the move to a house was after all a move out of a hotel, for privacy and comfort because of the illness of one member of the party.

The reason for thinking this is because Lady Copley, née Anderson Yarborough, had a daughter who died tragically young in either 1844 or early 1845. To date neither her birth certificate nor her place of death has been found, but we know that she died around the age of 15. In view of this I believe that the Dlles Yarborough were Lady Copley and her daughter, perhaps chaperoned by further women from the Yarborough family. Lady Copley Anderson was an early global citizen and she was well read, as her family library at Sprotbrough shows, an evangelically minded aristocrat who thought of others before remembering herself. It is likely that she heard enough during this summer in Baden-Baden to begin to suspect that the count's courtesan was one of the daughters of her beloved friend who all those years ago had died in Montreux. At the time she had not followed up on a promise she had made, perhaps because she was young, carefree, and happy as she would marry shortly afterwards. Now she may have been struggling with a dying child and therefore was once more prevented from delivering on her promise while being forcefully reminded of an unredeemed pledge.

In the meantime, as summer drew to a close and rich Parisians converged once again on their city in September, Marie Duplessis and Lichnowsky were approaching the end of their relationship. They had greedily devoured each other but now it was time to part. Their separation may have been expedited by the illness of his father back home in Germany. It seems that Lichnowsky returned in time to join his parent who died on 1 January 1845.

12

Alexandre Dumas *fils*, Lola Montez, and Olympe Aguado

1844–1845

Another young man now reappeared on her scene, Alexandre Dumas *fils* (Figure 12.1). In the course of 1844 he had followed his father to Saint-Germain-en-Laye, where the two of them lived in the villa 'Médicis' in the rue de Médicis.[1] One day he rode into town with his friend Eugène Déjazet to dine and to see a play. His account in *La Dame aux Camélias* of his tryst that September night with Marie Duplessis is close to the truth, as he himself confirms in 'Note A' (1898), his posthumously published autobiographical account of the genesis of the novel and play.[2] He already knew her by then and the novel repeatedly alludes to this earlier meeting. In his 'Note' Dumas cites the Variétés theatre on boulevard Montmartre as the place of their decisive encounter, but in the novel Armand and Marguerite meet at the Favart opera house (Opéra-Comique), from where she walked to the nearby Café Anglais on the boulevard des Italiens. As this was probably where her affair with Perrégaux started it is further proof, if any were needed, that the Armand Duval of the novel is based more on Perrégaux than on Dumas.

There is also the possibility that Dumas and Marie Duplessis met at the Vaudeville, the theatre where *La Dame aux Camélias* eventually premiered and where Marie Duplessis did indeed book a box for a night in September 1844. The collector Lucien Graux quotes a letter by her from around 30 August 1844 to the 'distributeur des faveurs d'un théâtre, le Vaudeville':

My dear Monsieur Amant,
May I yet again have a box? I hardly dare ask you for one of the top ones. You would just tell me to go to the devil. But if you could be one such devil, well then, you would do me this favour. Otherwise a good central box of the next

Figure 12.1 Alexandre Dumas *fils*, author of *La Dame aux Camélias*, at the time of his love affair with Marie Duplessis.

best ones. Has Laure Cogniot arranged for a top box to be requested for herself? If not, I pray you arrange one for her. As for me, do please, I beg you, remember to arrange one for me at once. I would be very grateful.

It is the least you can do for me. I called on you but did not find you in.

With my friendship and best thanks.
M Duplessy [*sic*][3]

Was this the night she met Dumas in the company of Déjazet? The fare that evening consisted of a manic harem farce ('folie-vaudeville à grand spectacle') called *Les Marocaines* by Claireville. The last show Marie Duplessis ever saw in December 1846 was scripted by him.

In the end though Dumas's later recollection of the start of his affair with Marie Duplessis is the most plausible, even if his account may not be entirely reliable:

> We had entered the Variétés theatre where we had seats in the orchestra stalls. The ground-level box to the left of the stalls [literally 'to the right of the actor'] was occupied by Marie Duplessis. She was alone or, at least, one could only see her between a bunch of flowers and a box of chocolates. She alternated between smelling the one while munching the others, barely listening while constantly scanning the audience with her opera glasses, exchanging smiles and looks with three or four of our neighbours. From time to time she would lean back into her box to chat briefly with someone who could not be seen. This was none other than the old Russian count S[tackelberg] ... who would later serve me as the model for the Duc de Mauriac. ... My future heroine Marie was making all sorts of telegraphic gestures to a fat woman who occcupied the front box on the first floor of the other side of the stalls from her. This gossip had a blotchy complexion, wore flashy clothes, and was restlessly fidgeting about. She was flanked in her box by an inane-looking young woman, nervous and anaemic, probably a new protégée whom she was proposing to launch into prostitution. The fat woman was one Clémence Pr.t [Pratt], a milliner whose apartment at the time was in the boulevard de la Madeleine, Cité Vindé, in the house next to Marie Duplessis on the mezzanine floor.[4]

By the time he wrote this, Dumas had apparently forgotten that in the 1848 first edition of his novel he had identified the young woman, or rather teenage girl in the box, as Pratt's daughter. Looking back now, Dumas remembered that Pratt had played Prudence Duvernoy, that is herself, at the Théâtre de Montmartre (today's Théâtre de l'Atelier) when they produced *La Dame aux Camélias* in 1859: 'She was perfectly mediocre in the role; try as she might, her recollections and brazenness did nothing for her, which only shows how, under certain circumstances, art is always superior to nature.' He also records that not long before her death Pratt was sentenced for prostituting minors; she was no longer alive when Dumas wrote his autobiographical notes for the third edition of his collected plays.

Young Eugène Déjazet, who knew Pratt, sought her out in her box that night to convey to her the young Dumas's interest in Marie Duplessis. They agreed that the two young men would make their way to Pratt's home; then, if the old count did not see her home to her door, Marie Duplessis would receive the youths. Dumas vouched for the fact that the rest of the evening passed off more or less as he reported it in the novel, that the novel's first act was exactly as it had been lived, 'absolument *vécu*'. Marie Duplessis was in a flirtatious mood: she already knew him from their earlier tryst when she had tried to woo his father. Over dinner, which was served by the chambermaid Clotilde ('Julie' in Vienne, 'Julie Duprat' in the novel), Marie Duplessis was shaken by a racking fit of coughing. Excusing herself, she rose and left the room to recover in her 'cabinet de toilette'. Dumas followed her, leaving Déjazet with Pratt. On entering the cabinet Dumas spotted that she was coughing over a bowl of water leaving behind a filigree of red marble, blood. Only later did he fully realize what this meant. She may not quite have grasped the significance of it either as their conversation soon reverted to levity and dalliance.

This scene of dining and coughing and the unplanned tête-à-tête between Dumas and Marie Duplessis corresponds roughly to the first two scenes of *La traviata*, the joyous party scene with Alfredo's drinking song, 'Libiamo nei lieti calici' (Let us drink from the joyous cups) and Violetta's fainting fit, which leaves her alone with Alfredo and elicits from him the aria 'Un dì felice eterea' (One happy day ethereal), in which he declares his love for Violetta. It constitutes one of the most romantic moments in nineteenth-century opera. The reality behind it was more mundane, but not any less interesting for that. It was certainly raw and raunchy compared to the opera but also tender. While Marguerite and Armand in the novel were agreeing terms to become lovers, Déjazet and Pratt enjoyed vigorous sex in the dining room. Pratt's hair was dishevelled when the other two returned to the dining room and her dressing gown was open, a scene worthy of the risqué brothel drawings of George Grosz. As the two young men walked out into the early hours of the morning, Déjazet was still in thrall to his delicious encounter, telling his friend: 'You may not believe it, but she is still terrific at it, that buxom Duvernoy.'[5] While Pratt was the next-door neighbour and Clotilde, Marie's chambermaid, lived with her, her footman Étienne would have attended to everything to do with her brougham. He did not reside on the premises. Did he have a 'chambre de bonne', those notorious cubbyholes in the lofts of French apartment blocks? He certainly knew her home well but it would have been inconceivable for him to live in her rooms: the whole point of her space was that it was feminine, for male visitors to immerse themselves in the delights of a sophisticated erotic world of women.

In the months following the scene in the boudoir, Dumas would no more enjoy exclusive rights to Marie Duplessis than any of her other lovers. Not only would he have to share her with the old count, whom he heartily disliked, and other lovers too, but he would always be the poorest among them, as he was eventually forced to acknowledge. She let him into her bed probably because his father ranked as the most celebrated, if not necessarily the best, writer in the city, vastly influential on both the literary and theatrical scenes. Of course the younger Dumas was talented in his own right, charming and, as the future was to prove, magnanimous.

He also took her to see his father at Port–Marly, where the elder Dumas was building his extravagant Villa Monte-Cristo, and to Saint-Germain-en-Laye where he lived with his father while the latter was simultaneously overseeing the local theatre and the construction of Monte-Cristo. Later Dumas recalled how he and Marie Duplessis often walked the majestic sweep of the 2 km Grande Terrasse of Saint-Germain, a stunning creation by Louis XIV's favourite architect André Le Nôtre, designer of the parks and gardens of Versailles. The sun king himself was born in a pavilion at the southern extremity of the Terrasse, on premises that survive today as a luxury hotel proudly announcing its historic pedigree. Because of its royal affiliation, the Grand Terrasse had become one of the most sought-after playgrounds of wealthy Parisians, a version of Baden-Baden's Lichtenthal Allee on the outer periphery of Paris; and particularly so in the 1840s, when the railways turned this elegant spot into a virtual suburb of the city.

The richest men, young and old, and the prettiest women, including the city courtesans, converged on an exclusive set of stables and riding school that stood fifty yards or so up from the Louis XIV pavilion, on the site of today's floral roundabout (Figure 12.2). This was the Ravelet establishment where horses could be hired for a leisurely stroll through the extensive forests, a popular pastime of Paris's elite. Ravelet's speciality though was a form of 1840s Parisian rodeo. He regularly bought up the most unruly horses from the local garrison at Saint-Germain and let them out as a challenge to the young bucks of Paris. Marie Duplessis was in her element on the Grande Terrasse. Many years later Dumas *fils* recalled how she loved riding these contrary horses at full speed, presumably charging down the terrasse before entering the woodlands where no-one would see her.[6] She who had grown up in the heart of horse-breeding country could always use her riding skills to good effect to charm men, whether they belonged to the Jockey-Club or were, like Dumas, just amateur horse lovers. The Grande Terrasse also offered a legendary opportunity for walking and for admiring the valley of the Seine from high above Marly-le-Roi and Bougival. Across the sweep of vineyards rolling down to the Seine, Parisians could catch a glimpse of the windmills of Montmartre in the far distance;

Figure 12.2 The Grande Terrasse at Saint-Germain-en-Laye, a place loved by Marie Duplessis, who came here to indulge her passion for riding through the extensive forests of Saint-Germain. It was in this very spot that Dumas decided to write *La Dame aux Camélias*.

today the buildings of Défense and Sacré-Coeur compete for the skyline from the Terrasse.

As we saw, a persistent rumour at the time had it that the younger Dumas first met Marie Duplessis at his father's home in Saint-Germain-en-Laye. This is not impossible but unlikely. Rather, the 42-year-old author now became truly acquainted with her, as his son brought her home to meet him. One cannot rule out the possibility that the two men shared her sexual favours over the next eleven months.

As Marie Duplessis joined Dumas on the Grande Terrasse, to view and to be seen in turn, she may more than once have gazed down into the valley below, towards the Île de la Loge and Bougival where, little over a year earlier, she had let herself dream about becoming the respectable wife of a young nobleman. Perrégaux had loved her to distraction and they used to pass themselves off as a married couple. That much is clear from an invoice for horse provender that was posted to her on 24 October 1844 by one L. Peigné. It was for the princely sum of 324 francs, rolling into one bill the two most recent debts, the earlier one incurred when she was with Perrégaux. The scale of the expense is not unusual: horses were more expensive to feed than men and women. Rather, what is interesting is that Peigné seemed to think that he was servicing 'Madame la comtesse "Deperégaud" '.[7]

When, on 25 November 1844, the Duke of Aumale married his cousin Princess Marie-Caroline of Salerno, Marie Duplessis may have mused about the mysterious shaping powers of destiny. Aumale's heart had been broken by Alice Ozy when she left him for Perrégaux only for her to be abandoned in turn by Perrégaux for Marie Duplessis. At that very moment Perrégaux was living not far away from the Madeleine, under strict instructions by his family and aunt to stay away from his siren courtesan. Here Marie Duplessis was now with a young author who could not possibly afford her but who had somehow succeeded in reaching something else in her, a part of her being that she had never quite rationalizaed, her love of reading. If she discovered the magic of literature through Morny in the first instance, Dumas was her first literary lover. In the eyes of posterity he has inevitably been overshadowed by his prodigious father. But the younger Dumas's own gifts were precocious and remarkable too. If his work could never match the sheer scale of his father's output, his novel about the young woman at his side as well as the play and his poem about her testify to a considerable talent. This it must have been that kept her tied to him for quite as long as it did. It is occasionally alleged that if Marie Duplessis had not died young her only future in middle age would have been one of misery and destitution. But all the signs point in the opposite direction: that she would have overcome her past and the loss of beauty and would have found a life elsewhere. Marie Duplessis was genuinely fascinated by men and women of culture, literature, dancing, acting, or music.

In the meantime no crush of other lovers could apparently dent the old count's devotion to his protégée, for on 18 December 1844, Dumas notwithstanding, he bought Marie Duplessis another lavish gift, a glorious 'ring with a diamond weighing 20 grains to the value of 4.560 fr etc.'[8] The ring was probably a Christmas present and shows that the old man would not give up. This accords with Dumas's account of his first night with Marie Duplessis when she sat in her box at the theatre discreetly chaperoned by Stackelberg behind her, almost hidden from public view, though openly walking her out of the theatre at the end of the show.

The count's loyalty did not stop her from partying without him. On a snow-bound night in December 1844, Marie Duplessis's friend Romain Vienne was making his way home through the boulevard de la Madeleine. As he passed in front of her apartment, he noticed that it was ablaze with light and the sound of festivities, probably in anticipation of Christmas. He rang the bell. It was the only time he attended a party at Marie Duplessis's: he was not wealthy or famous enough to be a regular guest and Marie may in any case not have wanted rumours about her soirées to reach her home village in Normandy. Some of these gatherings were high-class evening entertainments, while others were somewhat different. Marie Duplessis answered the door. She seemed delighted to see Vienne and planted a camellia in his buttonhole. The apartment's internal doors were all flung wide open; the scene was operatic with chat and music. On the piano some-one was playing a popular tune from an 1832 opera called *Pré-aux-Clercs*. Seeing the two old acquaintances, one of the guests, the cabaret 'artiste' Lola Montez (Figure 12.3), somewhat the worse for drink, sidled up to them with: 'My, my, you two little sweethearts, has someone died? An inheritance gone wrong? You are about as cheerful as two undertakers! How come, Marie, that you kept this little treasure a secret?'

Sensing Vienne's gaucheness, Montez challenged him to take on a woman like her: surely he must want to? She sat him down, planted her foot on his armchair, hitched up her skirt and demanded that, as a man of the world, he pull up her garters. A flustered Vienne obliged and for his pains she affec-tionately scuffed him. At that point Marie Duplessis rushed up to rescue him. She was mortified, Vienne reports, but tried to laugh it off, apologizing for her raucous friend. While the buttoned-up provincial guest beat a hasty retreat, Lola Montez was heard laughing uproariously.

Dumas was probably present at the party in Marie Duplessis's apartment along with his friend Déjazet and, one suspects, other 'artistes' from the beau monde. He must have known Vienne even though he never refers to him while Vienne and Perrégaux met at her funeral and at least once more after that. Vienne was never her lover but he is a more interesting and enigmatic character than he is sometimes given credit for. By turning himself into a Boswell figure, belatedly chronicling parts of her life, and by allegedly boast-ing about his familiarity with her, he is sometimes cast in the role of an objectionable courtier. Her undoubted trust in him should, however, count in his favour, and so ought the fact that he became the executor of her estate. Vienne was not so much a fop as an occasionally prissy, self-righteous

Figure 12.3 Lola Montez, future Countess of Landsfeld, a friend of Marie Duplessis's, as raucous and loud as Marie was restrained and stylish.

character who tried to safeguard his young friend's best interests according to his own lights.

On New Year's Day 1845 Marie Duplessis received a truly *recherché* gift that was bound to arouse her curiosity. It consisted of twelve large oranges each wrapped in a bill of 1,000 francs, enough to pay the rent of her fabulous apartment for nearly a year. Naturally she was impressed by what turned out to be the most generous gift of the day. She held court all evening on 1 January, like a patrician Roman hostess receiving homage from her *clientes*. Men would call and leave their cards. If they were lucky they would be granted an audience. But the mysterious stranger of the oranges did not appear, which intrigued her. Instead, he waited for her birthday which, he had learnt, fell on 15 January. It coincided with one of the coldest spells that winter. Even the attaché to the Russian embassy, Balabine, who was used to deep winters, commented on the glacial curse that had invaded the great city and would ravage its poor who had no means to protect themselves as they were huddling on top of one another in garrets and under leaky eaves, immured in wet and cold spaces, without fire, lacking all means to procure it, countless families…suffering death in this Babylon of luxury and pleasures. The cold was accompanied by thick fogs that wrapped themselves around Paris like an impenetrable and mysterious shroud.[9]

Marie Duplessis was queen of the Babylon of pleasure, although she, more than most, knew all about the cold and desolation from her childhood in Normandy. That must have seemed a distant memory on this birthday in January 1845 when she turned 21. Her new admirer and lover, his imaginative present notwithstanding, was a veritable oaf whose only gift was his fortune. His name is lost to posterity but not his character. He was reputedly boorish, loud, and bumptious, a provincial butt of jokes for cultured Parisians, who enjoyed poking cruel fun at outsiders, never more so than when they were richer than themselves. His wealth would only hone their malice, particularly because Marie Duplessis's embarrassment at his vulgarity knew no bounds. She indulged his attentions for a while: he had after all paid a small fortune for her. He probably partnered her at the two great charity benefit events of the winter season, the ball at the Opéra Comique on 22 February 1845 and the annual ball at the Variétés, both put on for the welfare of the players and singers. His expansive wallet would have qualified him admirably for this.

One night at the opera, during an intermission in the last performance of the season in Meyerbeer's *Huguenots*, he started to roar with laughter while joshing with some young men. Marie Duplessis rose and left.[10] And that was it. She palmed him off on another young demi-mondaine (he did not seem to mind), while she presumably returned into the arms of Dumas. As long as Dumas lived at his father's in Saint-Germain she was reasonably free in Paris, the more so since all her lovers needed to accept a measure of sharing her with her 'owner', Stackelberg. At a powerful moment in *La Dame aux Camélias*, Marguerite lectures Armand on the sheer rigour of her business arrangement with her keeper: her credibility as a courtesan depended on her keeping to the terms of arrangements that could not be openly flouted, however much covert bypassing of them there might be.

On 11 March 1845 an event involving Marie Duplessis's friend Lola Montez rocked the capital. Two journalists, Rosemond de Beauvallon of the *Globe* and Alexandre Dujarrier of *La Presse*, fought a duel. They had clashed four days earlier over a gambling debt during a dinner hosted by the actress Mlle Anaïs Liévenne, of the Vaudeville, at the restaurant Les Frères Provençaux, owned by the same Collot who may have been Marie Duplessis's first keeper. One of them, Lola Montez's lover Dujarrier, was killed. He went 'like a lamb to the slaughter rather than being branded a coward', in the words of the art dealer Richard Wallace, who noted moreover that, unlike his opponent de Beauvallon of the rival *Le Globe*, Dujarrier knew nothing about fencing or shooting but could not face the dishonour that an accommodation would have entailed. Montez was distraught. At the trial of Dujarrier's killer in Rouen, she gave evidence using the witness stand to flaunt her looks.[11] Wallace was there and so was the whole of Paris's elite. Wallace stood next to a young man who was pumping him for information about Montez. His name, it turned out, was Gustave Flaubert, the future author of *Madame Bovary*.[12] Although she had in no way been implicated in the duel, the ensuing prolonged trial rendered Lola Montez's presence in Paris intolerable. So she left for pastures new. She and Marie Duplessis would not meet again until the steeplechase in Croix de Berny in April 1846.[13]

In the meantime Marie Duplessis did not want for distractions or the relentless attentions of men. For a while now a young lion had been keenly interested in her. He was the progeny of a rich immigrant who had made a fortune in banking and by collecting art. His father had died in April 1842, at around the same time as the father of Édouard de Perrégaux. Both young men had come into fortunes at roughly the same time. They were both destined to be Marie Duplessis's lovers and both, like Dumas, seem to have genuinely loved her. His name was Comte Olympe ('Olimpio') Aguado (Figure 12.4), son of the banker Alejandro Aguado, owner of the Châteaux Margaux vineyard and art lover who, at his death, left his three sons his art collection and an estimated 60 million francs.

In the spring of 1845 Olympe Aguado had only just turned 18. After his opera-loving father's death three years earlier he found himself so rich that there seemed no bounds to his aspirations. For him the proverbial sky to reach for was the most coveted woman in Paris. When he started courting Marie Duplessis it was the first time that she was wooed by someone who was younger than herself. His huge wealth and his evident devotion may well have tempted her to flee the tutelage of Stackelberg, even though the latter was hardly demanding. In any case, it seems that she and Aguado were involved by the spring of 1845 and that he carried her off to the playgrounds of Europe that summer.

Vienne calls him 'Gaston de Morenas' and is adamant that the two lovers stayed in Baden-Baden. The record does not support this even though the celebrated spa town was one of the places Aguado had visited earlier when he was duly listed in the *Badeblatt*. There is another reason for thinking that

Figure 12.4 Olympe Aguado, a rich heir, would become one of France's pioneering photographers. He was in love with Marie Duplessis, comforted her in her dying days, and protected her from creditors.

they did not go to Baden-Baden: Stackelberg stayed there every year while his now widowed son-in-law lived in nearby Karlsruhe. The old man's patience may have been tested to the limits before, but it is inconceivable that he would have colluded with her openly flouting her liaison with Aguado in the spa town. Vienne's account notwithstanding, it is probable therefore that Marie Duplessis did not visit Baden-Baden in the summer of 1845. Not only was Stackelberg there, but so, and of course unbeknown to her, were the Anderson Yarboroughs, who were once again staying in Baden-Baden. This time the two families seem to have talked, with remarkable consequences.

Where was Dumas all this time, while Marie Duplessis and young Aguado were touring Europe? Perhaps helping out his father in the theatre in Saint-Germain, while hoping to make enough money to own Marie Duplessis for good? It was during this period in 1845 that, one afternoon, Olympe Aguado was approached at a sumptuous party in the Faubourg Saint-Honoré by several aristocratic society hostesses. They wanted to enlist his complicity for a scheme to test Marie Duplessis's legendary generosity, which seemed too good to be true. They proposed to invite her to a stage-managed fund-raising event: she would not know that its true purpose was to watch her behaviour when solicited for money towards a good cause. Aguado considered this for a moment, then replied: 'she is extraordinarily generous to the poor and is bound to attend any fund-raising event for them.'

The duchesses, pruriently curious about the woman who was mesmerizing their husbands, each offered the princely sum of 500 to 1,000 francs as a levy for the Paris orphanage for girls. Marie Duplessis duly appeared at their party, dressed with impeccable modesty as befitted the occasion. By her sheer presence and conversation she charmed the very people who sought to patronize her and who had hoped to catch her out.[14] She gave generously to the collection and stood up well to the scrutiny of the assembled duchesses. She had not chosen to join them. Indeed, she had tried to send her gift of money without turning up in person because she knew full well that she could never be accepted in those circles.

A few days after this event an elderly woman appeared on Marie Duplessis's door step: she was asking for money to tide her over for a brief period. Marie knew that her visitor had to be either a decent, impoverished lady, who knew her reputation for charity, or else she was a huckster. She gave her the benefit of the doubt, as she did invariably, and a hundred francs, five times more than her unannounced visitor had requested. The woman only accepted twenty. The following day the caller returned and presented Marie Duplessis with a brand new twenty-franc bill and a little sealed box. She asked to be allowed to keep the bill that Marie had given her. Also, could she please not open the box until her visitor had left? Finally, could she kiss Marie? The young courtesan was profoundly moved. By now she had guessed that her visitor was a grand Parisian hostess in disguise. After she had left, Marie opened the box. It contained two pieces of paper: one was a thousand franc bill, the other a note saying 'for your poor, with thanks.' The episode of the testing of Marie Duplessis, though cynical, suspicious, and voyeuristic in origin, has a strangely biblical feel to it. By submitting herself to the ordeal of aristocratic female scrutiny this nineteenth-century Mary Magdalene raised 23,000 francs for the orphanage, more than she owed at the time of her death. The donation was passed on anonymously.

On 4 August 1845, the Comte d'Ugarte, described in the Baden-Baden police records as 'ambassadeur d'Autriche, av.[ec]. f.[amille] et d[omestiques]. . . . 10p.[ersonnes]' arrived at the Hôtel d'Angleterre. He was the widower of Hélène de Stackelberg, returning to Baden-Baden accompanied by his family and servants, a total of ten people who needed to be accommodated in the hotel. The following day another family arrived in the same hotel: 'Anderson a[vec]. Fam[ille]. et dom[estiques]. Angleterre, 6p.[ersonnes]. These can only be the Anderson–Yarborough–Copley family who would now reside in the same hotel as d'Ugarte. The previous year they had overlapped with Stackelberg in the Europaïscher Hof; now they did with members of the same family again, in the Angleterre. In the past the Yarborough women had stayed throughout the summer, perhaps for reasons connected to the health of one of the family's children. This time everything was different. It is likely that the Copleys' daughter had died by the time the Andersons returned to Baden-Baden in 1845. It is equally probable that this time, in the intimacy of the hotel, the two families talked at length. Now the dots were, perhaps, joined up as they discovered that they were united in grief over the loss of young women: the old Count's daughter had been d'Ugarte's wife while the Count's young mistress, Marie Duplessis, was the daughter of a woman whom the teenage Lady Anderson had adored, the same Lady Anderson Copley who was herself now bereaved.

On 12 August 1845, at the Variétés theatre, Judith Bernat, well-known for her talent and also, given the attitudes of the time, for her Jewishness, opened in the role of Régine in a comedy by Eugène Bourgeois called *Madame Panache*. She was among Marie Duplessis's favourite actresses and the Variétés theatre, under its shrewd director Nestor Roqueplan, ranked among the foremost in Paris, second only to the Théâtre-Français also known as the Comédie-Française. The Variétés was keenly patronized by Marie Duplessis alongside the Vaudeville, Gymnase and the Ambigu-Comique, although the three great opera houses were always her preferred venues, not least because they possessed grand auditoria in which she could display her regalia to best effect. It is likely that Marie Duplessis repeatedly saw Judith Bernat play; her premieres were much sought-after. Before long the two women would meet face to face.

It so happens that this particular premiere coincided with the unveiling in Bonn of the 'Beethoven Denkmal', a memorial occasion orchestrated by Liszt, who had donated a huge sum towards the monument. Liszt's triumph was somewhat marred by an unseemly fracas that ensued when he inadvertently left out the French from his thanksgiving toast. The scene degenerated

into farce when a less than sober, apparently uninvited, and certainly uninhibited Lola Montez jumped on the tables, knocking over champagne bottles and glasses while pirouetting and adding her voice to the melée.[15] The
Bonn city fathers blamed Liszt for her behaviour, undoubtedly aware of the
rumours that these two were having an affair.

From Bonn, Liszt headed to Paris where he and Marie Duplessis at last
met. That she should be in the city during August is almost unthinkable, but
she was nevertheless demonstrably in Paris that month because on 23 August
1845 she settled a substantial bill at the Maison Dorée to which she moreover returned on 27 August, when she ordered and paid *carte de nuit*, that is,
probably, late dinner after the theatre or opera.[16] Her relationship with
Dumas was coming to an end. It may well be at this time that she wrote the
following letter to him, the only one from her to him to survive:

> Dear Adet, why haven't you been in touch and why don't you talk *candidly* to
> me? I believe that you ought to treat me as a friend. I am looking forward
> therefore to a word from you and I kiss you very tenderly, as a mistress or as
> friend, whichever you prefer. In any case, I will always be devoted to you.[17]

She was partying at the Maison Dorée again on 30 August and on 17
September. Her sole reason for staying in Paris in August would be a new
lover. It would have to be somebody very special. By now Aguado and she
had parted. Perhaps he was too young to interest her, or perhaps his puppy
love unnerved her. As for Dumas *fils*, it so happens that the very night she
went to the Maison Dorée, Saturday 30 August 1845, he waited outside her
apartment to see her but was not admitted. At midnight he wrote her a
letter, which has survived. It is a fascinating document because two slightly
different versions of it are extant and they throw an interesting light on the
way this story has been transmitted to us. Here is the real-life letter:

> My dear Marie,
> I am not rich enough to love you the way I would want to nor poor enough
> to be loved the way you would want it. Let us therefore forget, both of us—
> you a name that must be almost indifferent to you—me a happiness that is
> becoming impossible for me.
>
> It is pointess telling you how sad I am because you know already how much
> I love you. Farewell therefore. You have too much heart not to understand the
> reason for my letter, and too great a spirit not to forgive me for it.
>
> With a thousand memories
> A.D.[18]

By signing off with 'A.D.', Dumas is alluding one last time to their shared intimacy as she teasingly called him 'A.D.' or 'Adet'. What he does not say here, perhaps because it had always been part of their tacit understanding, is that he left her because another man had appeared in her life, someone whom Dumas knew about, because she had told him about him and because he had seen him going up to her apartment and spending the night there that Saturday. Armand Duval's letter in *La Dame aux Camélias* spells this out and gives the true reason for the breakup:

My dear Marguerite,
I hope that you have recovered from your indisposition of yesterday. I appeared at eleven o'clock last night to ask how you were, and I was told that you were not home yet. M. de G…was more fortunate than me because he appeared a few moments later, and at four in the morning he was still with you.

Forgive me for the few tiresome hours I caused you to endure with me and rest assured that I will never forget the happy times that I owe you. I would have fully wanted to hear more news about you today, but I have to return home to my father.

Farewell, my dear Marguerite. *I am not rich enough to love you the way I would want to, nor poor enough to be loved the way you would want it. Let us therefore forget, both of us—you a name that must be almost indifferent to you—me a happiness that is becoming impossible for me.*

I am returning your key, which I have never used but which you may need if you are often ill the way you were yesterday.[19]

The note of sarcasm in the last sentence, almost taunting her with her bogus excuse for not seeing him, fits with the flavour of a book in which, perhaps from guilt, the author repeatedly takes sides against himself. *La Dame aux Camélias* was written very soon after the events it fictionalizes; the italicized lines (my italics) in the letter are cited verbatim from Dumas *fils*'s own letter to her. The letter in the novel is more peevish than Dumas's to Marie Duplessis. It is also far more revealing about his anxieties about wealth and moreover tells us that he sat outside her apartment all night waiting for the unidentified M. de G. to emerge. Who this was is not known. He features in both novel and play. It is tempting to see the Duc de Guiche/Gramont in him as he never quite erased Marie Duplessis from his mind. But there is a more obvious candidate, someone who, unlike Guiche, had not left Paris: Édouard de Perrégaux. That he did return to her at some point between the end of August 1845 and February 1846 is not in doubt; the only real question is when exactly this happened.

What Marie Duplessis replied to Dumas we will never know.What could she say anyway since Perrégaux held out prospects for her that Dumas could never match, particularly that coveted title already used by at least one of her suppliers to address her even before she was formally a countess. This was Jonas Rothschild, the Viennese coachmaker of 4 *bis* rue Notre-Dame-de-Grace who, on 14 October 1845, invoiced Marie Duplessis by the name of 'De Blessy' for a large sum after extensive refurbishing of her carriage. Indeed the scale of the work he carried out on her instructions was so elaborate and expensive that the invoice constitutes proof of a liaison with a rich man, whoever he might be. She probably wanted her carriage back in mint condition because the greatest artistic event of the Paris autumn season was imminent, the première on Thursday 16 October 1845 of Verdi's opera *Nabucco*. Premières of major operas were events that 'le tout-Paris' could not afford to miss. They attracted snobs, music lovers, and the rich of all social strata. Boxes were rented by the year and served as settings for refined dinners and social trysts. They were prime occasions for displaying one's wealth and sexual conquests.

For posterity almost everything relating to Marie Duplessis carries a poignant charge because of *La traviata*. We inevitably 'hear' her story through its heart-rending music. Few moments in her life may be more tantalizing than the night when the future 'traviata' sat in the audience of the Paris premiere of *Nabucco*. How could Marie Duplessis have grasped the idea that an opera intimately based on her own life would one day outsing all other operas and soar with the imagined music of her own soul. Even if *Nabucco* is a colossal work in the way Verdi's *Aida* would be later, neither opera can compete with the deliquescent melodies of *La traviata*. If ever life and art coalesced in a dynamic harmony, it was in the convergence of the generosity of Marie Duplessis, the imagination of Dumas, the incomparable ear for language of Piave, and the musical genius of Verdi, which all combined forces to produce *La traviata*.

When *Nabucco* opened at the Salle Ventadour, at the time the Paris home of the Théâtre des Italiens, its huge reputation preceded it. At its world premiere at the Teatro alla Scala in Milan on 9 March 1842, *Nabucco* had propelled Verdi to instant stardom. By the end of the season the whole of Italy was singing *Va pensiero*, the most rousing chorus yet in Italian opera. Here it is, the Chorus of the Hebrew Slaves, in the unforgettable poetry of Temistocle Solera. These are the very words that apparently swayed Verdi into tackling the libretto after vowing never to compose again, because of the fiasco of *Un giorno di regno* in the aftermath of the death of his wife and children. He had flung the libretto of *Nabucco* on the table on returning home from his encounter with the director of La Scala when these verses caught his eye. A few months later they were sung throughout Europe and the world. The hour, the man, and the music had all come:

Va, pensiero, sull'ali dorate;	Fly, thought, on wings of gold;
va, ti posa sui clivi, sui colli,	go settle upon the slopes and the hills,
ove olezzano tepide e molli	where, soft and mild, the sweet airs
l'aure dolci del suolo natal! Del	of our native land smell fragrant! Greet
Giordano le rive saluta,	the banks of the Jordan
di Sionne le torri atterrate...	and Zion's toppled towers...
O, mia patria, sì bella e perduta!	Oh, my country, so beautiful and lost!
O, membranza, sì cara e fatal!	Oh, remembrance, so dear and so fatal!
Arpa d'or dei fatidici vati,	Golden harp of the prophetic seers,
perché muta dal salice pendi?	why dost thou hang mute upon the willow?
Le memorie nel petto raccendi,	Rekindle our bosom's memories,
ci favella del tempo che fu! O simile	and speak to us of times gone by! Mindful
di Sòlima ai fati	of the fate of Jerusalem,
traggi un suono di crudo lamento,	give forth a sound of crude lamentation,
o t'ispiri il Signore un concento	or may the Lord inspire you a harmony of voices
che ne infonda al patire virtù.	which may instil virtue to suffering.

Va pensiero instantly became the anthem of the Risorgimento. In Paris *Nabucco* was predictably a huge triumph. As at La Scala three years earlier, the Chorus of the Hebrew Slaves had to be given as an encore, and Parisian audiences were just as smitten with it as their Italian counterparts. Paris was now eagerly awaiting a visit by Verdi himself. No-one could be in any doubt that the legendary figures of Italian opera who had made Paris their first or second homes, Rossini, Bellini, and Donizetti among them, had found their match, if not master. The expressive and dramatic power of *Nabucco* ranged perhaps above even *Norma* and *Lucia di Lammermoor*. Time would tell, and it did.

It would seem inconceivable for Marie Duplessis to miss *Nabucco* when the whole of Paris was expected to be there, in the hope perhaps of seeing the maestro himself who surely needed the approbation of the undisputed world capital of opera. The French newspapers were unanimous in their view that Verdi needed to be fêted in Paris before he could really be the greatest opera composer of the age: his wary aloofness could not possibly be disdain! If only Verdi had appeared for this premiere. Then he and the real 'traviata' might at least once have walked past each other in the corridors of the Ventadour: she the queen of the audience, he the maestro taking curtain call after curtain call. Alas, he was not there and she too may have been missing on this occasion, as the timing could hardly have been worse for her.

The reason is that she was probably expected to be home in the Orne the following day because on that day, Friday 17 October 1847, her elder sister Delphine Adèle married Louis Constant Paquet in the church of Saint-Germain-de-Clairefeuille. Delphine was a 23-year-old laundry woman while her 25-year-old husband Paquet was a weaver. Romain Vienne, who is confused about the date (he gives it as 1841), reports that Marie Duplessis left a purse for her sister as a gift. Whereas Paquet signs his name clumsily, his new wife writes out 'Delphine Plessis' in an elegant cursive hand, consolidating the idea that the two Plessis girls' primary education at Infant School, run by the nuns of Sées, was reasonably sound. Marie Duplessis is not listed as a witness in the register, perhaps because she did not after all attend.[20] It is not known how often Marie returned to the Orne but it is unlikely to have been more than once a year or so, if that. In one of her letters she alludes to a visit but what could she do there other than remind her relatives by her refined presence how far she had left them behind. It is surely significant that in her hour of greatest need she was wholly abandoned by her family, a fact commented on by various people at the time. Nor did she send for them, as far as we know, even though they knew that she was very sick because she had stayed in the Orne as late as May 1846 when her declining health must have been evident to all her family.

13

The pianist, the baroness, and the actress

October 1845–February 1846

Just over a week after *Nabucco*, Saturday 25 October 1845 marked the premiere of the elder Dumas's new play, *Les Trois Mousquetaires, Vingt Ans Après*.[1] Father and son were both there. Years later the younger Dumas wrongly recollected this date as the day when he and Marie Duplessis finally parted company:

> The first representation of *Mousquetaires* happened at the Ambigu...I remember the date exactly because that day I fell out ['je me brouillai'] with Marie Duplessis, who would become *La Dame aux Camélias*. I fell out with her because I could not arrange a 'loge de galerie'. I had a box with...I was young and with me in the box sat Maquet and his family, who were there simply as spectators of the piece.[2]

Auguste Maquet had dramatized Dumas's sequel *Vingt Ans Après* and was touched when Dumas *père* summoned him to join him for the applause on the stage afterwards. This was a big premiere, because it was a Dumas premiere and because the three musketeers had by now become the stuff of legend.

Marie Duplessis and Dumas had already separated at this stage, but now they appear to have quarrelled also because he would not procure her an exclusive box. Perhaps he was too embarrassed to do so, because of the young woman who shared the box with him on this night (Anaïs Liévenne from the Vaudeville troupe?), or maybe he dreaded the thought that on his father's big night he and she would be eclipsed by Marie Duplessis. The word he used for 'quarrel' here he would also use in the poem he wrote immediately after her death, *Péchés de Jeunesse*: 'We were estranged, and why?

I can't remember. / Over nothing: the mere suspicion of another love.' She may have been piqued at being left out of this spectacle, not least because she traded on enjoying exceptional connections.

By letting her down, as he did in her eyes, Dumas unwittingly played a role in bringing her together with her next lover, Franz Liszt. The genius pianist reached Paris that Saturday and headed straight for the home of Jules Janin. He knew both Janin and his wife and the two men had already collaborated earlier that summer on a cantata.[3] Janin was Paris's leading critic and Arts reviewer for forty years, and he contributed a regular column ('feuilleton') for the *Journal des Débats* characteristically signing off as JJ. When, around lunchtime, Liszt arrived, Janin noticed that he was still suffering from the after-effects of the jaundice he had contracted earlier. He brought Janin the *Cantate* he had composed in Bonn for the Beethoven celebrations. Janin would now translate the German prose into French verse, with Liszt to hand in the same room.[4] The *Cantate* needed to be ready for performance by the start of the following week, which is why Janin, whose wife was away, worked all out on his assignment. He probably read the extensive coverage of the *Mousquetaires* in the press on Sunday. He rose early on Monday 27 October to continue working on Liszt's *Cantate*, even before writing his almost daily letter to his wife who was due back on Thursday. He had wanted to take her to the Dumas show on her return, but now decided that he would see it that day together with Liszt. They had worked hard and this would be their way of relaxing and celebrating a mission accomplished. It was also work, and Janin would eventually write a long and detailed review of the 'play'—it was really rather more a chronicle of scenes—in the *Journal des Débats* of 2 and 3 November 1845.

With its huge auditorium of 1,900 places, the Ambigu-Comique ranked among the most exciting of Paris's theatres, jutting out rakishly into the boulevard Saint-Martin (Figure 13.1). It was demolished in 1966. Thanks to this act of unconscionable vandalism, an atrocity squats on the site of the illustrious theatre today. Gone therefore is one of the best documented spaces associated with the lady of the camellias, the foyer of the Ambigu-Comique. It was there, during the interval before the third act, that Liszt and Marie Duplessis not only met but initiated their liaison. There are several slightly variant versions of the event. The most authoritative is Jules Janin's, who was present and indeed partly instrumental in what happened. He is usually a reliable witness and a keen aesthetic observer of Marie Duplessis.[5]

What happened is that the two men had wandered into the foyer, presumably to stretch their legs after enduring the ordeal of the Ambigu's

Figure 13.1 The Ambigu-Comique theatre. Liszt's relationship with Marie Duplessis started in the theatre's foyer during the interval of a play by Dumas *père*.

infernal stalls, veritable torture instruments ('chevalets') according to another reviewer, 'Fiorentino', who had also endured Dumas's interminable epic (it would subsequently be shortened).[6]

Liszt and Janin had just sat down on a bench in the badly lit, smelly foyer. A noisy crowd was milling about, talking about shows and potato chips ('on causait de tout, de l'art dramatique et des pommes de terre frites'). Marie Duplessis stepped into this scene like a radiant apparition. As she entered the foyer itself, she gently lifted her skirt as she might have done on a muddy boulevard, so as not to dirty her dainty fabrics. She was 'as graceful as an invisible perfume', Janin thought. With just the slightest touch of haughtiness, holding her head high, she crossed the foyer and joined Liszt and Janin. Turning to Liszt she told him that she had heard him play a while ago (in February and April 1844) and that he had caused her to dream. Liszt was instantly smitten, seduced by the sound of her voice and her cultured conversation. All along she spoke to him with a certain aloofness, as if she were a duchess. By now the threesome had been joined by the young woman's female companion, undoubtedly Clémence Pratt. When the gongs summoned the audience back for the third act, the foursome stayed put in the foyer. As she had moved closer to the fire, with just a hint of coquettishness, the two men admired the sheer delicacy and flair of her appearance. She was a breathing work of art and looked every inch as if she were to the manor born. Liszt was a great artist and he loved women. It was clear to Janin how this would end: she was irresistible and he adored beauty. They talked throughout the third act while bringing Janin into the conversation occasionally too, out of courtesy. In the end he returned to his seat in the stalls while Marie Duplessis remained with Liszt. The 34-year-old musician and the 21-year-old courtesan probably trysted in her apartment that night of 27 October 1845, after dining at the Maison Dorée or the Café de Paris.

By not finding her a suitable box for the premiere the younger Dumas had opened the door for Liszt. Years later he was quite happy for the Janin piece to be reproduced as a prefatory sketch of Marie Duplessis in his novel. He had forgotten that Liszt and she met at his father's play and that it had been partly his doing that they met. The simple truth is that Janin had misremembered and given the Gymnase rather than the Ambigu-Comique as the name of the theatre. Where on this night were Perrégaux and Stackelberg? Marie Duplessis had been upset because she did not get her chosen box for the premiere on Saturday. If she chose to appear on Monday it can only be because there was a particular reason for doing so rather than merely a desire to see the latest Dumas play. Did she know that Liszt would be present? For the two of them to meet the way they did seems too much of a coincidence. Perhaps Liszt's great friend and her former lover Lichnowsky alerted her to Liszt's coming to Paris and suggested that the two of them ought to meet. We can be reasonably confident that she knew that Liszt would be there and for that reason she decked herself out in all her finery to make his acquaintance.

Liszt and Marie Duplessis now became lovers and would continue their affair when he returned to Paris in November 1845. Liszt idolized her. She was, he would later claim, the first woman he had ever truly loved.

> She was so graceful, high-spirited, and full of a childlike abandon...She was all heart and possessed a wonderfully spirited temperament. She was unique among women in her walk of life. Dumas has understood her very well. He did not need to do much to recreate her in his novel. She was undoubtedly the most perfect incarnation ever of womanhood.[7]

Their affair was necessarily short-lived because Liszt was forever travelling, although he was still in Paris on 30 October when he was spotted in the salle Érard at a matinée premiere of César Franck's oratorio *Ruth*.[8] Not even the most assiduous popstars of today could have a programme more charged than his. He played all the major cities of Europe at once. The only constant thing in his life was restless motion, on boats, in coaches, and soon on trains, not to mention his sheer nervous expense of energy on the keyboard.

How often did he play on Lichnowsky's piano just for her? How could she not adore his God-given gift as he effortlessy coaxed almost unimaginable beauty from her Pleyel piano? As for the man behind the genius, Liszt was not so much an inveterate womanizer as a man who was ceaselessly mobbed by women and who rarely declined their favours. His stunning aquiline features, strong and masculine, in conjunction with his genius, conspired to turn him into one of the nineteenth century's great Don Juans (Figure 13.2). He gave Marie Duplessis a picture of himself which was later

Figure 13.2 Franz Liszt, the greatest pianist of the age, at the time of his involvement with Marie Duplessis

sold at the auction of her effects in February 1847. When he left Paris
towards the end of November she wrote to him, pleading with him to take
her along: she assured him that she would not be a burden:

> I will not live much longer. I am a peculiar young woman. I cannot possibly
> value a life that is the only one that I know how to live while loathing it at the
> same time. Take me, carry me away to wherever you fancy. I will not get in
> your way. I sleep all day; in the evening you will let me attend shows and at
> night you will do with me whatever you want.[9]

Liszt had promised to take her with him to Constantinople, 'because it
was the only realistic journey that I could propose to her', meaning that
only there could he openly appear with a courtesan lover in tow. In the
end nothing came of it. Liszt felt guilty about this in the years to come,
later recalling 'that proposed journey to Constantinople filled her with
joy; it is one of those stages avoided with great sorrow, and I have always
regretted it.'[10] By the time Liszt arrived in Constantinople in 1847 Marie
Duplessis was dead.

If in her letter to Liszt, Marie Duplessis expressed revulsion at the kind
of life she led, Providence offered her a way out within weeks of Liszt's
departure. It was in early December 1845 when a woman presented herself
at 11 boulevard de la Madeleine and asked to speak to the mistress of the
house.[11] Her French was heavily accented; she was unmistakably English.
When she was admitted, she explained, without much ado, that she had
been sent by a noble English woman who resided in the rue du Faubourg
Saint-Honoré. The British Embassy was at that address. Marie Duplessis
knew the buildings and gardens well: they stood within ten minutes' walk
from the Madeleine and she had partied there on more than one occasion.
It is not impossible that the address given that day was in fact the British
Embassy itself, as the sender of the note is not listed as owning a property
in Paris at this time; she may have stayed at the embassy courtesy of the
ambassador.

The English messenger explained that a Lady Anderson had sent her,
the same lady who had known Marie Duplessis's mother many years earlier. She now desired at last to fulfil a promise that she had made long
ago to Marie Deshayes about her two orphaned little girls. During a
recent journey through Normandy, on her way back to Britain, she had
by 'providential chance' found out Marie Duplessis's address. She knew
about her sister's recent marriage, and she knew too about Marie Duplessis's

profession, which did not in any way change her mind about loving Marie Duplessis as much as she had loved her mother. The baroness had recently lost her only child, a beautiful daughter, not yet 15 years old, and was still in mourning. She would cease to grieve if Marie Duplessis joined her as her ward. She would love her as a daughter, at once settle a fortune on her large enough to take care of all of her immediate needs and, two years from now, would adopt her as her sole heir.

Marie Duplessis listened to this in amazement. It had been seventeen years since she had last seen her mother. What happened next affected her more deeply than anything yet. The English woman now produced a picture that she wanted Marie Duplessis to have. It was one of the two Chamonix ones of her mother from around 1829, the very one that is today displayed all over the Orne, including the panel outside the church of her home village of Saint-Germain-de-Clairefeuille. The baroness would keep one of the pictures while giving the other one to Marie Duplessis who must have been shaken to the core of her being as she gazed at that adored face from long ago (Figure 13.3). In that soulful expression her mother's sorrow is there for all to see. She had longed for this image to be seen by her two little girls, to give them hope and to share her love. Now at last her portrait was home.

Marie Deshayes could never have imagined that it would take seventeen years for one of her daughters at last to see her picture, nor could she have grasped her younger daughter's predicament. She would have been thrilled by Marie Duplessis's beauty and shocked by the fact that she had abused her natural assets to become a prostitute. Marie Duplessis may well have felt the depth of her betrayal of her mother's innocence. If her mother could see her now, in that luxurious gilded cage where everything spoke of sin and degeneracy, might she not want to disown her? The hurt of looking at that image, knowing that it was drawn for Delphine and herself to assuage their longing for the woman in the picture, was perhaps offset partly by the knowledge that at least she could now clutch it to her heart for the rest of her life. When her English guest had finished she suggested that Marie Duplessis consider what she had said and then contact her mistress.

As her visitor was leaving, the most urgent thought on Marie's mind must have been the picture of her mother: while not doubting its authenticity, she craved to have it confirmed. As she sat in her boudoir, with its window over the boulevard, Marie Duplessis was trying to take in the sheer scale of the news about her mother. The past, not the present, mattered above all

Figure 13.3 Marie Deshayes, the mother of Marie Duplessis, in a drawing commissioned by her employers in Chamonix. This picture was given to Marie by Lady Anderson in memory of her mother.

else. Everything was different now as she pondered her future and her past. More than anything she needed to share the news of her mother. That she wrote to Delphine we need not doubt, but above all she needed irrefutable proof of the miniature. The only person in the whole of Paris who could vouch for its likeness was her friend Romain Vienne.

He was summoned the day after. Her message simply read 'Greetings and an invitation to come and chat with me tomorrow night. Marie'. He was mildly intrigued by the more than usually laconic tone of her message, and duly turned up the following day. She had ordered in a dinner from her favourite supplier, Voisin of the rue Saint-Honoré. She could barely disguise her impatience, he noticed, when he arrived. He had dined already, so she sat him down 'for a long talk' while he smoked a cigar. Suddenly she rose, stepped over to the mantelpiece, and picked up a small miniature. She passed it to him with 'I would be grateful for your opinion on this portrait: what do you think?' Vienne took one look at it and exclaimed 'No doubt about it, what a resemblance! It is a portrait of Marie Deshayes, your mother; she looks a little bit younger in this, but it is her. Explain this to me quickly.'[12]

At first Marie Duplessis was too overcome to reply, but then told him about the events of the last forty-eight hours. She also explained to him that she could not possibly accept the English woman's offer of respectability, however generous. It was precisely the baroness's courage and sacrifice, she stressed, that made her realize that she could not yield. If she did, Lady Charlotte would quickly become ostracized in her own circles whatever her expectations to the contrary. Of that Marie Duplessis was certain, as she explained to Vienne while also probably wondering whether she could ever fit in with the lives of the English upper classes. She possessed a smattering of English phrases at best. It was all too much for her, the more so since consumption already held her in its fatal grip. She was too tired to move on to pastures new and out of her niche in the Madeleine. There was another reason why she was not willing to leave Paris at that moment: the presence in her life again of Édouard de Perrégaux.

Shortly after her interview with Vienne an anxious Marie Duplessis made her way to meet the lady in question. The woman she encountered on this autumn day was 35 years old. Nothing is known about her appearance, but Lady Charlotte Anderson Yarborough Copley was undoubtedly a passionate woman. On the day she met Marie Duplessis, so many years after promising her dying mother to look after her and her sister, she was grieving for the daughter she herself had so recently lost. The girl had not even reached the age of 15 and had died by December 1845. The absence of the Copleys from the 1841 England census—the three that followed, 1851, 1861, 1871, all list them at Sprotbrough—suggests that they lived abroad in the 1840s. At the time they were in either Paris or Montreux/ Geneva. It is likely that the Copleys' daughter was born abroad and that she also died abroad.

The timing of the death of her daughter matters because it was in its wake that the baroness remembered her painful and neglected promise of many years ago. Her own terrible loss galvanized her into action. Now she understood the pain that had racked Marie Duplessis's mother fifteen years earlier, which is why at this late hour she had decided to make good her promise. It may well have been Stackelberg's 'adoption' of Marie Duplessis, on the grounds that she so resembled his dead daughter, the wife of the very man the Andersons had probably recently encountered in a hotel in Baden-Baden, that launched a similar train of thought in the baroness's mind. If the old count was able to do so, why could not she too? And whereas for him Marie Duplessis would always be a sexual partner first and ersatz-daughter second, the baroness could truly act as Marie Duplessis's fairy godmother. Not only would it soothe her conscience over her past failure to seek out two little girls in the grip of a brutish father, but Marie Duplessis might restore to her much of what she too had lost when Marie Deshayes died. The baroness and the courtesan, who was not quite fourteen years her junior, wept together, never more so than when the English woman remarked on how much Marie Duplessis resembled her own lost daughter. When Lady Anderson spoke about Marie Deshayes, the young demi-mondaine must have been comforted to learn, after all this time and for certain, that her adored mother died surrounded by people who loved her, who had sheltered her and who had admitted her into their family in spite of her humble position.

Many years after these events, the last will of Joseph Copley, who died in 1883, seven years after his wife Charlotte Anderson, testifies to the striking regard and care the Copleys had for their servants.[13] In the case of their servant Marie Deshayes, they had grasped her inner nobility and had remained loyal to her memory all these years, enough to seek Marie Duplessis out now. Did the baroness mention that she had run into both Stackelberg and d'Ugarte in Baden-Baden? Her messenger suggested that it was a chance encounter in Normandy, perhaps during a visit to the studs of the Orne, that first revealed Marie Duplessis's real identity to the baroness and brought her to Paris. Does this rule out an encounter in Baden-Baden with the Stackelbergs as the source of the Copleys' information about Marie? Not really, as the two may well complement each other.

How long the two women talked is not recorded but they agreed to meet again, and they did, even though Marie Duplessis had firmly, if tearfully, rejected the offer made to her. She was so stunned by Lady Anderson's proposal that when she left the Faubourg Saint-Honoré she felt the need to get out of Paris. So she rode her freshly burnished coupé to the Bois de Boulogne. She was still in turmoil that night at the theatre, irritated by the attentions paid her and the ambient noise, to the point where she locked the door of her box. At home that night she tossed and turned, but sleep eluded her all night. The thoughts that were racing through her head are not hard to imagine. Incredible as it was, it seemed that the things that she had coveted most in her life, a title, nobility and respect, were all within her grasp.

What was offered her was nothing less than a life of wealth and respect, with homes on Lake Geneva, London, and the wonderful manor of Sprotbrough Hall in Yorkshire. Marie Duplessis would achieve what Emma Hamilton never could, because the young woman in Paris was possessed of an innate dignity, class, and generosity that Nelson's lover might never have understood. One may wonder whether Marie Duplessis could have been saved if she had followed the Andersons to Geneva and Yorkshire. The answer is almost certainly 'no'. Her dreadful disease killed regardless of class or virtue. She may well have suspected as much, although she fought her illness almost to the end with countless visits by various doctors and a string of prescriptions, a number of which survive and make for tragic reading in the more fortunate age of antibiotics.

And what of Lady Anderson? She was clearly as charmed by Marie Duplessis as everyone else and was now left to grieve all over again: for her own dead child and for the lost young courtesan of the Madeleine who could have become her life's companion. With hindsight we know that she would only ever have enjoyed Marie Duplessis's company for a short time at best, but that might have been enough as a consolation. Did the great-hearted baroness know quite how sick Marie Duplessis already was? At no point, as she lay dying, did Marie Duplessis turn to her English friend who had dreamt in vain about becoming her new mother. If she had, there can be little doubt that Lady Anderson would have rushed to her bedside. Was it pride, respect, or shame, or all three, that stopped Marie Duplessis from contacting the one person whose love for her was probably unconditional? We will never know. Nor do we know whether Lady Anderson ever visited the grave in Montmartre, or what she thought of the novel and the opera based on the life of the woman she now wanted to mother, trying to carry out Marie Duplessis's mother's injunction seventeen years too late. If she ever did see *La traviata* it is hard to imagine anyone more likely to be moved to floods of tears.

What we do know is that Charlotte Anderson made a will in November 1846, twenty-nine years before she died. Why she would do so then is not at all clear. Had she waited, in vain, for Marie Duplessis to change her mind? She was back in England when the will was drafted and may not even have known quite how ill her young friend was at that very moment. The baroness died in her London home at 13 Carlton House terrace in 1875. She outlived Marie Duplessis by twenty-eight years. In the intervening years she would have had many opportunities to see the opera in London. In the library at Sprotbrough the Copleys owned an impressive collection of French books, among them a copy of the 1852 edition of Dumas's *La Dame aux Camélias*, which included Janin's twelve-page essay 'Mademoiselle Duplessis'. Five volumes of the French dramatist and librettist Eugène Scribe's *Oeuvres* sat next to Dumas's memoir.

The bulk of the family's French books were to be found in rooms used by Lady Charlotte such as her bedroom and sitting room. One glance at some of the titles indicates quite how keenly interested she was in the theatre. Why else would she be reading the *Répertoire du théâtre de M Scribe et Poirson*, *Répertoire du Gymnase Dramatique*, *Théâtre de Victor Hugo*, and *Théâtre de Molière*? Taken in conjunction with her owning an 1852 edition of the novel, this might suggest that she too saw the now legendary production of *La Dame aux Camélias* at the Vaudeville in Paris in 1852. It was this event that may ultimately have planted the seed of *La traviata* in Verdi's mind. More mundanely (though this was not how it was seen at the time), it made the reputation of the actress Eugénie Doche, who shot to stardom in playing a woman she had herself seen at the theatre and who, in turn, had watched her play.[14]

One of the many sorrowful aspects of the story of Marie Duplessis is that she was mourned by so many for so long because she died very young. Most of her contemporaries outlived her, which is why many now underwent the eerie experience of seeing one of their own turned into fiction and myth while they were still only in their twenties or early thirties. If Lady Anderson did see the play and acquired her copy of the novel afterwards, she might have been grief-stricken to learn that Marie Duplessis had been doomed even as she spoke to her. She would have discovered too how much she suffered and how her generous nature apparently refused to surrender to the world of vice that she inhabited. In that there might have been a crumb of comfort for the baroness: if she ever had the slightest doubt about Marie Duplessis's moral character, the novel paid homage to her just as surely as Verdi would a year after the first long run of *La Dame aux Camélias*.

Among Lady Charlotte's possessions that were sold at auction in 1925 were a number of paintings in oil and watercolour. They included a 'lady's head on panel' which hung in the 'Housekeeper's Room' at Sprotbrough.[15] Could this be the twin of the one that she presented to Marie Duplessis in December 1845? She had kept both pictures of Marie Deshayes from 1829 until then, and we may be sure that she also held on to the remaining one to honour the memory of her friend, or rather now her *two* friends. The Sprotbrough Auction Catalogue does not record who bought what and the pictures were not identified any more than they were when Marie Duplessis's estate was sold off.[16] Today far more remains of Marie Duplessis's apartment than of the grand manor just outside Doncaster that might have been hers. Looking up from the Trans Pennine Trail towpath by the river Don, one can still catch a glimpse of the former balustraded viewing area, which lay directly in front of the old Hall, long since demolished. Nowadays the village is best known for its association with the Second World War flying ace Douglas Bader, who grew up in the village parsonage. The fact that Sir Walter Scott set *Ivanhoe* (1820) in the area and may have finished it there may suggest that the Copleys of the Hall knew Scott and, perhaps through him, also Lady Compton of Clarens-Châtelard.

Marie Duplessis's love and social life were singularly hectic that autumn of 1845. She had separated from Dumas, probably resumed some kind of affair with Perrégaux, became involved with Liszt, held on to Stackelberg and struggled with the turbulent effect of seeing her mother as she was more or less the last time she held her when she was a 4-year-old. Throughout all this time she continued to indulge her passion for revelling, particularly the opera and theatre. One night shortly before Christmas 1845 she attended a performance at the Variétés theatre. Her favourite actress Judith Bernat, her junior by three years, was starring. She had been brought to the Variétés by its mercurial director, Nestor Roqueplan. He was someone whom Marie Duplessis not only knew but to whom she may have had reason to be grateful because he had once fed her on the Pont-Neuf. Moreover, his brother Camille, it seems, painted Marie Duplessis at the theatre, although the authenticity of this picture has been questioned (Figure 13.4).

On this particular winter's evening Judith Bernat was playing the role of Florine in *L'abbé Galant* by Laurencin and Clairville when, suddenly, she collapsed in mid-performance.[17] Bernat later blamed 'brain fever' for her fainting fit. As she lay convalescing at home, a young woman delivered glorious bunches of flowers to her apartment daily. All Judith knew about the woman was what her servant told her, that she was young and very

Figure 13.4 An early painting attributed to Camille Roqueplan of, probably, Marie Duplessis, at the theatre or opera.

beautiful. Intrigued she asked her servant to pass on a note to the stranger begging her to reveal herself. The letter that came back read:

> Mademoiselle,
> The admiration I feel for your talent made me most anxious about your health, and I am very glad indeed to hear that you are better and that I may soon have the pleasure of applauding you again. Forgive me, however for having hidden my name. I was afraid that if you knew it you would refuse to accept my flowers. And now I fear, lest learning it, you should decline to receive them any longer.
>
> Your devoted and unworthy admirer,
> Marie Duplessis[18]

There may have been another reason why Marie Duplessis felt an affinity with 'Mlle Judith', as she was often called. Rumours had recently been spreading about the actress's sexual immorality in an attempt to blacken her reputation. In the end Judith sued for defamation and won.

The bond between the two young women was possibly deeper than shared concerns over their good names. In any case, they had in common an important lover, the Duc de Morny. The same man who had elevated Marie Duplessis to demi-monde royalty was now courting the 18-year-old Judith. In her own words,

> The Duc de Morny, who was one of the habitués of the Variétés, used often to come to my dressing-room to compliment me on my acting, and he never failed to remonstrate with me in a friendly way for my good-nature. 'Look here, Judith', he would say 'Are you not ashamed to sing under such embarrassing circumstances? I know what a great talent you have and how well you can speak. Do give up playing and singing in such silly parts and try to get into the Française [Comédie-Française] company. I'll do all I can to help you.' He had a great deal of influence at the time and his recommendation was very useful to me.... His wit, his handsome features, elegant get-up, and dandified manners made him the admiration of the aristocracy. He was the very acme of fashion.... Morny still continued to show the greatest confidence in my future career and often used to say to me 'You are lucky to have such a gift of elocution!' And one day he asked me if I would give him some lessons on how to speak in public.[19]

Four years on from his relationship with Marie Duplessis, the 34-year-old duke was as interested as ever in spirited young women. The Deputy for Clermont-Ferrand was a master at elocution. It had been at his behest that the girl from the Orne was taught to speak in the polished ways of high-class courtesans. Judith's memoir is discreet about the duke's advances and his womanizing, alluding only to his widely publicized liaison with the Countess Le Hon. It is safe to assume that Morny eventually had his 'elocution' lessons from Judith because a few months later, in 1846, she did indeed join the prestigious Comédie-Française. Did Judith know about Morny's earlier relationship with Marie Duplessis? She would only have done so if he told her and even then she may not have been aware of its full extent.

Judith replied to Marie Duplessis's letter of December 1845 by inviting her into her home. The two young women instantly became fast friends. Of course it was Marie Duplessis's beauty and 'most extraordinary charm' that immediately struck Bernat. She must have seen her visitor on many occasions at the theatre, but never this close up. Not only was she refined-looking and comely, but 'her face was of an angelic oval shape, her large dark eyes were full of seductive melancholy, her complexion was dazzling, and her hair, that resembled masses of black silk, was perfectly magnificent'. Moreover, for a creature of the 'galanterie', she was, unexpectedly, profoundly intellectual. Her conversation was captivating, Bernat acknowledged, and her tastes in art were impeccable. She moved in all the right circles and was in a position to refer to Dumas and Liszt as 'friends'.

When Judith was better, she in turn visited Marie Duplessis in her apartment in the Madeleine. By doing so she put her respectability on the line, but this did not deter her. She knew all about being an outsider, if not an outcast, because she was Jewish. Paris and the arts may have been unusually tolerant at the time, but as a bright young child at school Judith had been refused a prize she had won fairly because of her Jewishness. The memory and humiliation rankled with her years later. She would not now be denied Marie Duplessis's gracious presence. As her hostess gave her a guided tour of her home and its many treasures, its Louis XV furniture, couches covered in Beauvais tapestry, rosewood tables, vases by Clodion, and much else, all of which she knew and appreciated like a proper connoisseur, Judith sensed more than ever that her friend was an exceptional person.

As they talked, Marie Duplessis acknowledged to Bernat that her way of life had turned her into a social pariah, the kind of woman whose mere presence might stain the honour of any decent young woman who was seen with her. It was, she confessed, the threat of poverty that had turned her into a courtesan; and once she had tasted a life of luxury, wealth, and glorious clothes she could not bear to go back:

> A workman's wages would never have got me the luxury for which I had an irresistible craving. But in spite of all the appearances against me, I swear to you that I am neither covetous nor utterly degraded. I wanted to know the refined pleasures of a cultivated taste, the joy of living in educated and elegant society. I always chose my lovers for myself. And I have loved—oh, yes, I have loved deeply, but no-one has ever returned my love, and that is the real horror of my life.[20]

Once she told one of her protectors that she had fallen in love with him and wished that they could set up home together. He pulled back, incredulous at the thought that she might be serious about her feelings. Marie Duplessis remarked ruefully, 'I realized that my former misdeeds condemned me irrevocably and that a woman who has once fallen can never rise again, no matter how sincere her repentance.' She told Judith how the old count Stackelberg had approached her one day and how she had agreed to become his substitute daughter, even pledging a chastity that she knew full well she could not observe in the long run:

> For some time I lived without lovers. I hoped to rehabilitate myself. I even dreamt that I might perhaps meet with some young man who would understand my repentance and make me his permanent companion. Oh, my God, how I would have loved him! With what tenderness, with what joy I would have filled his life. But no one came to me except adventurers attracted by the money I had at my disposal. Young men who might have won my heart scorned my ideas of marriage, made sport of my good resolutions and flung my past in my face. I realized that my former misdeeds condemned me irrevocably, and that a woman who has once fallen can never rise again, no matter how sincere her repentance. Then in my despair I went back to the ways that are killing me.[21]

Worryingly, Judith Bernat also noticed that Marie Duplessis coughed repeatedly during their chats. Reminiscing about her friend years later, Judith recalled how Marie Duplessis saved her from marrying a 'bounder' who had charmed her but who was soliciting sexual favours from Marie Duplessis all the time he was proposing to the star of the Variétés. It was thanks to Marie Duplessis that she did not walk into a hollow marriage, a further reason for being grateful to the young woman whom she had known briefly in 1846. When Judith returned to the Variétés for *Le Lansquenet* by Dumanoir on 8 January 1846 her new friend was probably in the audience, loyally sharing her glamour with Bernat while keeping a discreet distance.

14

A registry wedding in London
21 February 1846

Throughout December 1845 and into January 1846 the weather in Paris was unduly mild and the papers wondered whether spring had now replaced winter.[1] Not for long, it turned out, as spring would make up for winter with unseasonal icy temperatures. Marie Duplessis too may have felt a premature vernal call when, on 25 January 1846, she acquired a year's passport made out in the name of 'Mademoiselle Plessis (Alphonsine), rentière, native de Nonant (Orne), demeurant à Paris, boulevard de la Madeleine, 11, allant à Londres'. Like her earlier passport, this one also enabled her to travel abroad beyond the destination given specifically on her passport. She needed it urgently because she and Édouard de Perrégaux were not only reunited but had decided to marry: he no longer possessed a fortune to squander but he still had his name and title and these he desired to bestow on her. It was all he had left, all he could and wanted to give, knowing how much she longed for the social recognition it would confer. It is not known how the two found each other again but they only ever lived a few hundred yards apart in Paris and would inevitably encounter each other at the multiple premieres in the city. The 'vast desert that is Paris', in the words of *La traviata*, as far as Marie Duplessis was concerned, contracted to a few thousand people who ran both the city and the country. They all frequented the same parties, embassy balls, opening nights of plays and operas, and rubbed shoulders with people of the same ruling and moneyed class.

Whatever happened with regard to their finding each other again, on Saturday 21 February 1846 Édouard de Perrégaux married Marie Duplessis at the Kensington Register Office in London. The wedding licence gives their names as Alphonsine Plessis, 22, and his as Edward (*sic*) de Perrégaux, 29 (he was in fact 31), adding his title of 'count'. She is called 'spinster' while he is 'bachelor'. She gave her father's name as 'Jean' and his status as 'gentleman', both far from the truth.[2] They boarded at 37 Brompton Row (now 'Road'), in a smart Dutch-gabled building a short walk from where Harrods stands today (the luxury store did not yet exist at the time). The marriage was perfectly legal although it was not valid in France, at least not as far as Perrégaux's inheritance and estate were concerned. Quite how worried his family were nevertheless about this allegedly invalid marriage will become clear later. As for Marie Duplessis, she was probably well aware of the rights that the ceremony conferred on her: why else would she request a copy of her marriage certificate six months from now, if not to have proof of her legitimate married status?[3]

Whether or not it is true that Marie Duplessis (henceforth Comtesse Marie Duplessis, with the right moreover to style herself Comtesse Édouard de Perrégaux), and her husband separated soon after their return to Paris, she immediately commissioned various artisans to adorn her crockery and cabriolet with her new coat of arms. It is tempting to wonder whether the whole London episode with Perrégaux was a charade, initiated by Marie Duplessis in the full knowledge that they could have no future together given the hostility towards her of powerful forces in his family. Édouard de Perrégaux was weak when it came to women, but that he loved Marie Duplessis, and selflessly, is clear from the way he mourned her and by his securing a place for her in eternity, literally as we will see. One can only imagine what Stackelberg made of her elevation but he too seems to have taken it on the chin inasmuch as he continued to underwrite her expenses. Or perhaps not quite, because after Marie's death, her husband produced incontrovertible proof that he had been paying the rent of her Madeleine apartment (for how long is not clear), that it was he who had bought her a number of her most exquisite jewels as well as the thoroughbred that she used to ride. We know this because Perrégaux wanted to claim them back from her estate after her death: he may have been generous to a fault towards Marie but did not see why he should fund her heirs.[4]

The fledgling countess was radiant at her next recorded public appearance, at the Opéra-Comique, Salle Favart, on Friday 27 March 1846 (Figure 14.1). The occasion was a benefit night for Gustave-Hippolyte Roger, the house's young new tenor. The stars who appeared included the singer Déjazet and the actor Bouffé as well as the dancer Carlotta Grisi. In 1841 she had been the first ever Giselle in Théophile Gautier's classical ballet of that name.[5] Marie was accompanied by a young man who seemed proud to show her

Théâtre Royal de l'Opéra Comique.

Figure 14.1 The Salle Favart, much patronized by Marie Duplessis and her set.

off as his, while she seemed keener than ever to be noticed on this occasion. The couple flamboyantly entered their grand front-of-theatre box after almost everyone was seated, including Paris's prince of reviewers Jules Janin, who recorded what he witnessed on this night. He notes that she was holding a bunch of flowers. Her companion can only have been Édouard de Perrégaux.

What no-one in the audience knew yet was that on this chilly night at the Favart opera the couple in the exclusive box were the almost brand-new Count and Countess de Perrégaux. She was wearing the glamorous clothes of haute couture, a white dress covered by a scarlet coat, 'sparkling in all the splendour of her conquests, her head gloriously covered and her beautiful hair mingling with diamonds and flowers, a breathing tableau animated by studied grace'. Janin watched her as much as he did the show that he was meant to review. What struck him in addition to her almost matchless beauty was how bored ('ennui' was one of her favourite words) she appeared to be, as she repeatedly scanned the orchestra stalls with her opera glasses, shying away, as he thought, from gazing too long at the handsome respectable Parisian women whose class she could never match. Boredom had settled over the couple in their expensive box, the cost of which would have fed a family for six months, according to Janin. To the poor waif from Normandy all that wealth had ceased to have any meaning. Musing on the glorious creature looking down on him without, he noted ruefully, recognizing him, Janin could not know that her disenchantment may have stemmed from the fact that she and Perrégaux were probably at odds that night at the opera.

No sooner was the opera part of the night's offering over than she rose, eager to be gone. Three more hours of the night's entertainment remained, but she was determined to leave. Janin stood close to her and helped her with her coat while her companion was paying the box lady. When he wanted change back she told the poor woman to keep it with a gracious smile. As she descended the grand staircase she seemed set on parting from her companion at the door of the theatre. There was about her, Janin thought, an aura of profound loneliness. All people ever talked of was her beauty, her triumphs, her exquisite taste and sense of fashion, while ignoring the debts, lost fortunes, the betrayals of the world of demi-mondaines: 'surrounding this young woman, carried off so prematurely by death, was undoubtedly a certain moral character, an irresistible decency. She lived apart, even in the world apart that she inhabited, in a region calmer and more serene.'[6]

That she was heading for stormy waters he could not possibly doubt, as rumours about her sickness were rife in the capital. And how long could a girl like Marie Duplessis last at the best of times? If not phthisis then syphilis was bound to catch up with her sooner or later. Janin, reviewer, chronicler, librettist collaborator of Liszt, never quite appreciated how extraordinary it was that the young woman whom he had known would become the heroine of *La traviata*, whose premiere was held in the Salle Ventadour (Figure 14.2). While he and his contemporaries were well aware of the astonishing hold of the grave in Montmartre over the popular imagination, they never really grasped the scale of the translation from the 23-year-old woman to myth. Or, if they did, it was primarily with reference to Dumas's novel rather than *La traviata*.

Was it after this fraught night at the opera that the couple decided to part? It seems that Perrégaux pleaded with her to be released from the commitment he had made in London and that he followed this up with a letter further explaining his reasons for wishing to do so. In response she told him face to face that he should consider himself free of any obligation towards her, and then repeated this message in a short note replying to his letter.

Figure 14.2 The auditorium of the Salle Ventadour, in a lithograph by Eugène Lami (*c.*1843), familiar to Marie Duplessis; the Paris premieres of *Nabucco* and *La traviata* were staged here.

Here is what she said in a terse, somewhat weary, note dating from around late March or early April 1846:

> My dear Édouard,
> In everything you write to me, I can only see a single thing to which you want me to respond, and here it is: You wish me to say in writing that you are free to do whatever you want. I told you so myself the day before yesterday, and I am repeating it to you and am signing it.
> Marie Duplessis[7]

The tone of the letter is not exactly contemptuous but impatient and exasperated. She knew that he was weak and indecisive, that he would be frightened of the family's lawyers and his aunt and that he would probably be crawling back to her for more anyway soon enough. Hence perhaps the lofty confidence of her letter, which would turn out to be tragically short-lived. It was one of Marie Duplessis's private tragedies that the only person who truly loved her, to the point where he was prepared to sacrifice his reputation as well as his fortune for her, was also the one she would hurt most deeply, and punish at a time when there was no more opportunity to make up for it afterwards.

The world of debt referred to by Janin in his vision of her at the opera would catch up with Marie Duplessis presently. Throughout her career as the chief 'lorette' of Paris, debt always lurked just round the corner before closing in on her in her dying moments. Had her creditors seen her at the opera—none of them, one imagines, would have contemplated paying those prices for the opera—they might have justifiably felt aggrieved by such profligacy with their money. Take the lingerie lady, a widow by the name of Fournier, whose suit to recover thousands of francs owing to her had finally come to court on Wednesday 1 April 1846. On this occasion, Marie Duplessis, 'rentière', was accompanied by a 'Mr X', who may have been Stackelberg; unless the break with Perrégaux happened a few days later than is suggested above and that it was him. When asked about her marital status she stalled at first and, not without some cheek, suggested that her private status was irrelevant. The president of the court demurred, reprimanded her, and insisted that she answer the question. She replied that she was 'demoiselle'. It would seem from this that her union to Perrégaux was not generally known even though she was at the time flaunting her new status as countess with a coat-of-arms.[8] The court sentenced her to settle her debt, which she would again fail to do. Hence she was summoned back to court on 17 July but on that occasion she did not appear; she was in Baden-Baden and was therefore represented by her 'avocat'.

She seems to have shrugged off her April court appearance as a minor nuisance. On Sunday 19 April 1846 it was business as usual when, in pouring rain, the steeplechase was run at La Croix-de-Berny just outside Paris. The English were represented in force and, according to the French papers, had evidently brought their weather with them. On this occasion they were the unchallenged masters of the races. The lions of the Jockey-Club put in an appearance as did their companions. Marie Duplessis had arrived in her coupé after participating in the traditional procession of the carriages on the Esplanade des Invalides in Paris. Here she was spotted by, among others, Charles Duhays from the same Duhays family who had helped her mother escape from the Orne. On this ceremonial occasion her carriage was drawn by four white horses. What struck Duhays most though was how pale and distressed she looked.

The same white horses took her to Croix-de-Berny where the courtesans' coaches were much admired and courted. A contemporary noted that:

> In spite of the pounding rain and the cold, there were plenty of spectators. The elite of Paris's silly vulgarity had turned out and the most fashionable kept

women represented the feminine world. Mlle Lola Montez displayed here her alluring curves on top of a highly strung steed, while Mlle Marie D... reclined voluptuously deep inside an elegant carriage. A crush of gentlemen—in the new meaning of the word—mobbed the carriage doors of these ladies; uses of 'tu' and 'toi' were flying about from mouth to mouth. Mlle Liévenne [by now she was the mistress of Dumas *fils*] stayed smiling and calm like virtue itself under the barrage of gallantries, while Mlle Maria, the pretty polka dancer half hid at the bottom of her pistachio coupé, underneath the delicate lace of her veil, as if she were ashamed to find herself in such disreputable company.[9]

The demi-mondaines were holding court at the side of the racetrack. Curiously, the reporter of this scene refrains from giving Marie Duplessis's name. There would seem to be little reason for such coyness since most of the other women were fully identified. But in this case it would have been obvious to anyone reading these society pages why he did so because she was, and was not, the comtesse de Perrrégaux. By calling her 'Marie D...', which could be Duplesssis or de Perrégaux, he advertised that 'le tout-Paris' knew about their London marriage. At Berny, Marie Duplessis would not be denied her coat of arms, something that must have been galling to some among the aristocracy and mildly amusing to others, not least for the discomfort it caused the Perrégaux–Raguses. Then again her natural tact and sense of propriety, and perhaps too her feelings for Perrégaux, stopped her from ever using the Perrégaux title.

It seems that at this late stage yet another man became her lover. He was someone she had known all her life, the local lord of the manor from down the hill at Exmes (where she had been the victim of the old shoemaker Plantier's sexual abuse): Vicomte Théodoric Narbonne Pelet, an important member of the Jockey-Club and one of the most powerful men of the Orne. The Vicomte and Duhays probably met through the club, perhaps as recently as the races at Croix-de-Berny in April. The viscount's Paris residence was at 22 rue de Varenne, which led straight into the Esplanade des Invalides where Duhays spotted Marie Duplessis in the ceremonious procession. Had she perhaps come from his Paris home that very morning? It is highly likely that Duhays and Narbonne knew each other through the stud at Haras du Pin. Romain Vienne too knew the viscount well but he makes no mention of her late stay in his own backyard, which is, it seems, where she now headed in the course of May 1846. If a certain reserve about Marie Duplessis and the local aristocracy caused Vienne to be more than usually reticent about details of Narbonne's affair with her, he did not shy away from including him in his book.

On the contrary, he was very clear that Perrrégaux was succeeded in Marie Duplessis's affections by 'le vicomte de La Roche-Albert, un Vendéen pur sang'. The reference to a 'thorough-bred Vendéen', referring to a region in the west of France, is a canard. Instead the clues are, probably, in the stud language ('thoroughbred'), which might point to Haras-du-Pin—it literally borders on the estate of Narbonne—and in 'La Roche-Albert' (Narbonne was the châtelain of 'La Roche-Nonant'), with moreover a rhyme, in French, between the fictional 'Albert' and 'Cochères', the real name of the hamlet which houses the Narbonnes' estate outside Exmes. Today a panel outside Haras-du-Pin notes that Narbonne, one of the wealthiest men in France, sheltered Marie Duplessis as she was ailing, offering her what he could by way of comfort, rest, and fresh air, mostly through riding which she adored and at which, we know from Dumas, she excelled.[10] While passing over her 'hospitality' at Narbonne's with silent tact, Vienne does record that in the spring of 1846 she visited her guardian Louis Mesnil and also her sister Delphine in a house that still stands at the intersection of the Nonant to Rouen road with the path that then as now led into Saint-Germain-de-Clairefeuille a couple of hundred yards away.[11]

Marie Duplessis sojourned in the Orne for three weeks. She must have been acutely conscious of the fact that she would not see her family again, that her visit at the château a mere three miles away from her previous home was also a leave-taking. She was so young and yet so very grown-up by the time she faced a fate that most people are allowed to defer into the far-off future.

15

A summer sunset in the spas of Europe

1846

On 29 May 1846 Marie Duplessis was back in Paris because that day she placed orders with the house of Révillon for various coats, including ermine, sable, lynx, and a fur boa. She always wore furs, even in summer. A few days later she took a final delivery of ass's milk, which she had been prescribed. She would now travel abroad one last time and spend much of the summer in the spa pleasure grounds. She had been invited, by whom is not known, to the grand opening of the northern railway that linked Paris to Brussels and would prepare for it with a stay in nearby Spa. It was from here that, on Friday 12 June 1846, she wrote to her loyal friend Tony, the guardian of her horses:

[Dear Tony]

I beg of you not to be cross with me, my dear friend, for my slowness in writing and hope that you will not therefore surmise that I have forgotten you or that you do not matter to me. I am delighted about your friendship, but you know that among my many faults laziness is not the least. You will understand that long rambles through the countryside only further lessen my appetite for writing; and far from accusing me, you will need to thank me for the effort just now to overcome the sleepiness that is oppressing me.

Goodbye, Tony, I will stop here as I would only bore you otherwise. Farewell once more and a thousand best wishes,

Marie Duplessis

PS: a thousand thanks for being so indulgent towards me. Please, dear, do not sell my coupé. I shall soon have the pleasure of seeing you; at least I hope so. M.D.[1]

Her reference to the sale of her carriage suggests that she owed money to Tony as well, perhaps not surprisingly given the sheer cost of maintaining her horses, one of the main expenditures borne by anyone living at the time. Her creditors had started to circle, perhaps because rumours about her sickness were spreading in Paris. They could not know that her estate would dwarf her debts by four to one, something not even its auctioneers had anticipated. She had obviously seen Tony before leaving Paris in order to park her carriage at his place where her horse would be fed as well. She had promised to write the moment she reached Spa, but had been unable to do so. Her letter, reassuring about her affection for him, suggests that Tony was in love with her. It is not impossible that she cleared a part of her debt with him by sex. She had done so all her life and why not in this case too?

She and her servant, probably her chambermaid Clotilde, were firmly entrenched in Spa by the time the Royal Train set out on its inaugural journey from Lille to Paris on Sunday 14 June 1846. On board were the French princes, the Dukes de Nemours and Montpensier, and the King and Queen of Belgium. So was Théophile Gautier, who corresponded with his mother about the journey.[2] That evening, with Belgian and French royalty in attendance, a lavish reception was hosted by the city of Brussels in the splendidly decorated station of the Northern Railroad. After the banquet the floors were cleared for a ball, to commence at 2 a.m. Marie Duplessis was present and in her element on the dance floor, basking in an aura of glamour. In spite of her sickness, perhaps because of it, she danced with abandon. She was chaperoned by a Teutonic-looking young man whom Janin described as a cross between German and English. She soon deserted him to dance instead with a well-known Parisian society painter. The rhythm of her waltz was perfect and so was her posture. To onlookers she seemed equally attuned to the inner cadence of the music and its audible measure, hardly at all touching the dance floor with her light foot, simultaneously animated and at rest, her eyes fastened on those of her dancing partner. Other dancers surrounded them, hoping perhaps to be touched by her gorgeous hair that echoed the motions of the fast waltz, or to be grazed by her robe, which was, we are told, lightly scented.

A few days later, on the night of Friday 19 June at the grand ball in Spa, she again displayed her waltzing prowess, one of the last times in her life. When she was not dancing she was partying manically, or else tearing on horseback through the Allée des Sept-Heures (Turner had recently painted it), easily taking on even the most challenging obstacles that might be erected.[3] At other times she could be found dreamily resting in the shade of the alley's trees, reading.[4] She was a bundle of nervous energy, trying to squeeze as much vitality out of the summer of 1846 as her slight frame could support. Who paid for this last pleasure trawl through Europe is not known. The police records of Spa and Baden-Baden are silent on this subject, but those of Bad Ems may contain a clue, just, to the identity of her most recent conquest and protector, if Janin's description of him can be trusted. It should be easy enough to discover who else stayed in these three places at the same time as her and thus, by a process of elimination, match her to a likely candidate. Unfortunately though none of the obvious names can be traced in the records of the time.

From frenzied exertions in Spa, Marie Duplessis progressed to Baden-Baden. She was there by 26 June when she, or rather her room at the Europaïscher Hof, no. 79—there were 125 rooms altogether—was invoiced by the owner of the hotel. She may still have been here on 17 July when the court in Paris was informed that Marie Duplessis could not attend her summons because she was in Baden-Baden at that very moment. Tantalizing though the 26 June 1846 invoice by M. F.-X. [François-Xavier] Maier is, it relates only to candles and chocolates and says nothing about who really settled the bill or the identity of the not so mysterious occupant of room 79.[5] Marie Duplessis stayed in Baden-Baden for three, perhaps four, weeks, longer than usual. Every year the crest of the Parisian wave hit Baden-Baden at the start of July, and with it came the fashion journalists who eagerly covered the Baden-Baden scene as here the latest Paris fashions were on display. Interestingly, the house of Golberg, Marie Duplessis's own neighbour, found particular favour with the Parisian papers this season. Is it too fanciful to imagine that some of this was down to Marie Duplessis, who may have been exhibiting some of Madame Golberg's latest designs, perhaps in return for getting to wear them free of charge?

Careful scrutiny of the *Badeblatt* for this period may, very tentatively, point to one person as her protector during this trip, someone who has never before been associated with Marie Duplessis, the Comte Alexis de Saint-Priest. He arrived at the Badischer Hof on Thursday 25 June 1846 and is recorded as 'pair de France, avec d.[ame], Paris', that is a peer of the realm of France accompanied by a woman who was not his wife. The fact that he stayed in a hotel fifty yards away from hers hardly matters, the more so since both were owned by the same family (the Maiers). Alexis de Saint-Priest

Figure 15.1 Formerly the 'Englischer Hof' in Bad Ems, the last place in which Marie Duplessis stayed during her final tour of Europe's spas. From here she wrote a poignant letter to her husband begging for forgiveness.

was a much travelled career diplomat, journalist, and literary amateur. His chief claim to fame today is that he beat Balzac to a seat at the Académie Française.

From Baden-Baden she proceeded, it seems, to Wiesbaden and then on to nearby Bad Ems, where she stayed at the Englischer Hof (Figure 15.1), a luxury hotel dating from 1825 and patronized by her lover Liszt in 1840.[6] It ranked as one of the grandest among the elegant palaces that flanked the Römerstrasse in the nineteenth century, facing towards the park and the river Lahn. In its time it played host to kings, princelings, generals, and artists, like its ancient neighbour across the road, Die Vier Türme, and its peers Der Russischer Hof, Europaïscher Hof, Darmstädter Hof, and Die Vier Jahreszeiten. Today the Englischer Hof is the Malberg Klinik for rehabilitation.

Less than a ten-minute stroll east from the hotel, through the meticu-lously planned alleys and gardens that divide the Römerstrasse from the Lahn, rose then as now the magnificent Kursaal, the heart of Ems (Figure 15.2). Since its recent completion in 1839 by the master builder

Figure 15.2 The legendary Kursaal in Bad Ems. Marie Duplessis knew it well and may have danced for the last time in this room.

Johann Gottfried Gutensohn, the Italianate Kursaal with its columns of Lahn marble and inlaid ceiling, had been a magnet for artists and performers.

Not only Liszt but his future son-in-law Richard Wagner, the great soprano Jenny Lind, the composer Jacques Offenbach, and countless others passed through here. The luxurious indulgence of the 1840s in Europe is today perfectly captured in this pristinely preserved, palatial interior. The Kursaal was the social and artistic pulse of the town, the place where men and women gathered to chat and conduct assignations, after spending time in the thermal baths and showing off their wealth or newest fashions during the evening promenade. In the 1840s this stretched between the Kursaal and Marie Duplessis's hotel, the Englischer Hof. Visitors would take pleasure trips up or down the Lahn, while the surrounding countryside boasted challenging walks through the hills. King William of Prussia and his chancellor Bismarck and the Tsar and Tsarina of Russia may have been the spa town's most eminent visitors, but multitudes of others among the rich and powerful also gathered here as they did in the other spa towns.

Page 157 of the *Emser Kurliste* of the 'resident and passing foreigners' of 29 June to 1 July records as a new arrival in the Englischer Hof during this period a 'Miss Duplessis with servant from Paris' ('Mad. Duplessis m. Bed. a. Paris.'). The numbers on the register reveal that she and her servant woman ('Bediente') were visitors no. 1727 and no. 1728. Numbers were used only for new arrivals. We therefore know that there were only two of them: Marie Duplesssis and, probably, Clotilde. Both Marie Duplessis and servant and also one 'Weddelw', who arrived on the same day, are still listed in the *Kurliste* of 14 July, which covers the period 10–13 July, but they are no longer on the Thursday 16 July list. Weddelw for some reason does not feature among the Englischer Hof entries on the lists of 10–13 July and 16 July, but he is definitely still in the hotel according to the 'Alphabetical List' of 16 July, even though by then Marie Duplessis had left. He is listed on 18 July 1846 at the Englischer Hof and again on 21 July, which means that he remained in Ems after she had gone. It may be worth pausing over 'Hr. [Mr] Weddelw'. Should that be Weddel or Waddell, W[illiam?]). He is recorded as 1729, the number after Marie Duplessis, in Bad Ems's Englisher Hof. So is 'Hr. Williamson', also from England. Both Weddelw and Williamson are 'Rentners' from 'England'. Was either, 'Weddelw' in particular, the Teutonic, German-English beau who partnered her at the ball in Spa? Janin calls him 'Anglo-Allemand'. Food for thought. Someone was undoubtedly picking up her bills in Bad Ems, even though she pretended to be there alone.

It was from the Englischer Hof in Bad Ems that, on pink paper, Marie Duplessis wrote an ardent letter to Perrégaux, imploring his forgiveness:

> Forgive me, my dear Édouard, I beg you on both knees. If you love me enough for that, only two words, your forgiveness and your friendship. Write to me poste restante in Ems, Duchy of Nassau. I am alone here and I am very sick. So, dear Édouard, quickly my pardon. Goodbye.
>
> Marie Duplessis[7]

Did she need his pardon for misleading him about their marriage, for decking herself out as a countess, or was it because she had sexually betrayed him and regretted it? Had he written to reproach her over something and was this late summer letter her response? She was at pains to stress that she was alone and sick. We will never know for certain what prompted her to write other than a craving for security and comfort from a loving person. A connection to her marriage may be the most plausible reason, particularly since she had requested a copy of the licence from London around this time. By the time she received it, towards the end of August (it is dated 19 August 1846), she was back in her apartment in the Madeleine. It is not clear what she intended to do with it, whether to show it to the authorities as proof of her right to display her coat-of-arms or whether she hoped to use it against the Perrégaux family if they stepped too close. Is it possible that Perrégaux tried to deny that the marriage was ever contracted? We know two things for certain about the copy of the licence: she let the Perrégaux-Raguses know that she owned it and she hid it very well, because they failed to find it when they searched her apartment after her death.

16

Agony and death of a maiden

October 1846–3 February 1847

On 18 September 1846 Paris buzzed with the latest theatrical sensation, *Hamlet*, which was being staged at Alexandre Dumas *père*'s theatre in Saint-Germain-en-Laye, in a verse translation by the young poet Paul Meurice. The younger Dumas invited Théophile Gautier to accompany him to the premiere. The two men departed on the new railway from Saint-Lazare where they were joined by a posse of Paris's finest reviewers, including Jules Janin. The *Courrier de Paris* of 21 September noted that there were some 600 invited guests and that the evening, an artistic triumph, finished with a feast. By happenstance the opening night of the Saint-Germain *Hamlet* coincided with the first visit to Marie Duplessis's bedside by the renowned Dr Manec of the Salpetrière Hospital. Over the next eight weeks he would return 38 times. He was one of several doctors who attended her during this period, which included 177 calls from Dr Davaine, with constant visits on her behalf to pharmacies.[1]

Sometimes her doctors turned up in pairs and prescribed various cocktails of homeopathic drugs that she would take or inhale. The best her physicians could hope to achieve was to mitigate the pain and create the illusion of treatment. Earlier she had used her near neighbour, the society quack Dr Koreff of 68 rue Basse-du-Rempart, who would shortly be charged with allegations of serious lapses in his patient care. He may have been a charlatan, but Liszt and others rallied to his defence and Koreff was eventually acquitted.[2] Marie Duplessis needed the best doctors and she got them, because she was famous and well connected and someone somewhere always picked up the bill; this time probably young Olympe Aguado, who was her good Samaritan in these protracted months of dying. She was not yet totally confined to her bed. Autumn chills permitting, she still escaped

to the Bois de Boulogne whenever she could to walk in one of her favourite bowers.

One particular young man was invited along on one of these trips to the
Bois. He was half-English, half-French, and his name was Charles Joshua
Chaplin (1825–91). He had been commissioned to draw Marie Duplessis by
one of her lovers, Pierre de Castellane, who was her exact contemporary
from a grand noble family in Provence.[3] She was Chaplin's first portrait,
which is why he nervously brought along two recent works of his to show
her. They were copies of masterpieces from the Louvre. As he unveiled his
credentials, she burst out laughing: he had painted madonnas, unaware of
the irony of this with regard to the 'madonna' of 11 boulevard de la
Madeleine. When he arrived, she had only just risen from her bed and was
not made up. Even so she agreed to be drawn by him.[4] The result is the
well-known 'Comédie-Française' picture, a disarmingly vulnerable image
(Figure 16.1). It is reproduced in the rare 1848 first edition of *La Dame aux
Camélias* currently held in the library of the Comédie-Française.

Chaplin's second picture of her, which he signed, is known exclusively
through an intermediary version of it by the heliographer Adolphe-Pierre
Riffaut, who worked for the magazine *l'Artiste* between 1840 and 1853. The
Riffaut sketch, an early instance of photorealism, was engraved by Marie
Duclos. In the light of Riffaut's pedigree, we can be almost certain that the
image loyally replicates the pose and melancholy expression of Chaplin's
original (Figure 16.2). Versions of it featured in later nineteenth-century
editions of Dumas's novel.

Marie Duplessis rewarded Chaplin handsomely for his labours. When he
balked at the amount of money she was pressing on him, she reassured him
that the person who commissioned the drawing could easily afford it. She
also, it seems, granted him more than one session. As the first one was drawing to a close, she suggested that he accompany her to the Bois de Boulogne
as the weather was gorgeous that afternoon. He agreed. By the time they
stepped into the boulevard, spectators had gathered outside around her
coupé. As soon as her footman had parked her carriage on the other side of
the road, word spread that she would take off for the Bois de Boulogne
shortly. A crowd swiftly formed, avatars of the celebrity spotters of the next
two centuries. Chaplin was astonished and could hardly believe his good,
and undoubtedly envied, fortune as he rode up the Champs-Élysées with
the most desirable woman in Paris at the time.[5] Her outing to the Bois de
Boulogne with the young Chaplin was probably one of the last in her

Marie Duplessis
(La dame aux Camélias)
16 janvier 1824 – 20 février 1847.

Figure 16.1 The first of several drawings of Marie Duplessis by the young artist Charles Chaplin, who knew her during the last months of her life.

beloved cabriolet which the loyal Tony had evidently managed to safeguard from her creditors.

Perhaps there was more to her friendship with Chaplin. In a gossipy feuilleton of 24 December 1846, the theatrical magazine *L'Argus* turned its attention to the city's favourite courtesan. It noted that the 'brilliant', 'gorgeous', 'regal', 'intuitive', 'generous' Marie Duplessis was given to a thousand 'caprices'. One of them was a crush on 'a young painter with some modest talent' and an even more self-effacing character. She had apparently been struck by his intriguing features and melancholy expression, which is why

Figure 16.2 A copy of another Chaplin drawing, sketched by Riffaut and engraved by Marie Duclos.

Marie wrote him a most gracious letter inviting him to her home to paint her. She added a postscript explaining that, due to particular circumstance, she needed to schedule the sketching sessions after midnight. To a mind less innocent than that of the young painter, an invitation with such a postscript would have made clear the intentions of Marie Duplessis. But our painter was blessed with that very timidity that attracts women . . . During three sessions, in the thick of the intoxicating atmosphere of her boudoir, in the presence of his goddess, alone with Marie, whose eyes were sparkling with their most provocative allure, he remained cold, unaffected, slavishly copying all these treasures, projecting them onto his canvas without guessing the ardent desires of his model. Marie Duplessis was baffled by this inane impassivity and was repeatedly tempted to smash the painter's palette. When the portrait was finished, she told him in a tone of imperceptible mockery 'These are indeed my features, it is really me! And yet I have to reproach you mildly because I think that, with a little bit of good will and in the circumstances in which you found yourself, you should have done more than just a good copy; you could have done the original even better! What do you think?'

The joke lies in the use of French 'croquer', which can mean to sketch her or to eat her, a sexual pun that English 'do/done' renders adequately. How much of any of this conversation actually happened is impossible to ascertain. Clearly stories about Marie Duplessis and Chaplin were circulating in Paris in the autumn of 1846. That Chaplin was the painter in question is beyond doubt, because he *was* painting her just then, he was young, and his innocence about her and her way of life is well attested to by his gaffe concerning the Louvre madonnas. The chemistry between him and Marie Duplessis was there for all to see, and that he adored her we need not doubt.

He painted her repeatedly. The unattributed water colour of her in the Comédie-Française archives may be a third Chaplin picture (see frontispiece of this book). Of all the pictures of her, this exquisite medallion is arguably the most beautiful. There is no question about the identity of the sitter. Her winsome expression and her perfectly aligned features convey her appeal better than any other image. As her contemporaries were keen to remark, there were many more obviously attractive women in Paris, but none who knew to bewitch as well as Marie Duplessis. Nothing is known about the provenance of the picture, but the fact that it found its way into the Comédie-Française collection of Édouard Pasteur may suggest that its source is the same as the other Chaplin in the collection, namely the auction of Chaplin's estate. However, because the miniature bears a distinct resemblance to the Olivier picture, Olivier cannot be ruled out as the artist.

Chaplin may also have painted a fourth picture of her, the one showing her in a bathrobe (Figure 16.3).[6] The painting is part of the legend of the lady of the camellias because it was known to exist in 1847 but disappeared after the auction, when her family rolled up the canvas and carried it away. Sketches of it, drawn from memory, circulated in various publications throughout the nineteenth century until 1960 when, during a national French radio auction, the painting suddenly reappeared and was sold by a descendant of Marie's sister Delphine; it was acquired by an anonymous buyer.[7] It was photographed and attributed, very tentatively, to the painter Vincent Vidal. He did indeed paint her—two portraits by him are mentioned at the 1847 Madeleine auction and Janin describes them—but this

Figure 16.3 The 'bathrobe Madonna' picture of Marie Duplessis, probably Chaplin's third drawing of her.

one does not look remotely like any other Vidal. It does however bear a striking resemblance, in one particular detail, to Chaplin's last painting of her, the death bed one of 3 February 1847: her hands, oddly long, are the same in both drawings, and her expression in the bathrobe picture moreover strongly resembles that in his first picture of her. And, yes, he does seem to have used the Madonna as a model in the bathrobe picture.

There is probably a fifth, and last, drawing of her by Chaplin, one that he held onto all his life until he was separated from it by his death, forty-four years after hers. It lies in all likelihood behind the most devastating of all images of her.

As late as November 1846 Marie Duplessis managed to charm her way out of tight corners. It was at this time that one of her creditors resorted to the offices of a young lawyer by the name of Henry Lumière. His account of his visit to 11 boulevard de la Madeleine is of interest today primarily because he later recorded in detail his impressions of his encounter with the

mistress of the house and, above all, the appearance of her rooms and furnishings. Lumière at first invited her for an interview to his firm's offices.
She replied almost at once:

> Sir—You will be aware that the sick enjoy sad privileges. I am very ill at the
> moment and therefore need to invoke these with your kind permission. May
> I request that you kindly inconvenience yourself and come to me to discuss
> the matter in question? Please accept my kind regards. Marie Duplessis

So Lumière made his way to the Madeleine. On arrival he was instructed
by her maid to wait in the bedroom while madame was dealing with
some other business in the 'salon'. Lumière had just finished admiring
her bed with its pink silk sheets and sumptuous, exquisitely folded curtains, when a door opened and 'the goddess of this exquisite temple of
voluptuousness appeared'. She was no longer, he noted, quite the radiant
beauty that had so inflamed passions and inspired such poetic rhapsodies,
because the disease was beginning to leave its mark on her. Even so,
Lumière declared, 'such was her exquisite presence that enough of her
youth remained intact to charm effortlessly and to be unforgettable'. He
was almost too embarrassed to broach the vulgar matter of debt with her:
doing so seemed wholly out of place, he later recalled, in that setting. She
responded to his errand by explaining that she had fallen behind on some
debts because of her illness. If only he could hold off a short while, all her
creditors would soon be repaid. Lumière at once gave way and promised to
stall his clients for as long as she needed. Such was her charisma, he con-
ceded. Shortly afterwards he read in a newspaper column by Jules Janin
that she had died.

On 18 October 1846 the younger Dumas wrote to Marie Duplessis from
Madrid. He was accompanying his irrepressible father who would duly
publish an account of their journey, as was his wont. Dumas had heard that
she was sick:

> Moutier recently arrived in Madrid and told me that, when he left Paris, you
> were sick. Will you kindly allow me to add my name to those who are sorry
> to see you suffer?
>   Within eight days of you receiving this letter, I will be in Algiers. If, in the
> poste restante, I find a word in my name that forgives me for a mistake I made
> about a year ago, I will return to France less sad, if I am forgiven. And I would
> be utterly happy if you were recovered.
>
> Affectionately,
> A.D.[8]

She did not reply. But she was not entirely abandoned by her friends in these crepuscular days of 1846. Several among them called on her including her loyal countryman Romain Vienne. His mother had died in Paris on 11 October 1846. Perhaps, at the suggestion of her son, she had come to be treated in one of the capital's hospitals, the Salpetrière, as there would be no other reason for her to leave her native Orne. Vienne had looked after her as best he could. Maybe it was his mother's passing that prompted him to visit Marie Duplessis in the Madeleine. He did so on 20 October 1846, as he very precisely points out. The date stuck in his mind because it was so close to the day his mother died.

When he arrived in the apartment, he found that Marie was unwell but he did not realize how very ill she was. They had been talking for a while when she did something wholly out of character. It happened when he brought up the subject of her marriage or 'union' to Perrégaux, which everyone knew about by then because of her coat of arms. She bristled with hostility to Perrégaux to the point where she, who seemed incapable of saying anything bad about anyone, tore into the one man who had given her most. He had obviously hurt and offended her profoundly. When she proceeded to reveal intimate details about their relationship, Vienne stopped her in her tracks, in case she ended up regretting it. Clearly the forgiveness she had implored from Perrégaux when she was stranded alone in Bad Ems had not been forthcoming. Did her bitterness stem from the fact that just when she needed him most he had returned to Alice Ozy?[9] Or worse, had Perrégaux, in a moment of madness, cast up Marie Duplessis's life as a courtesan at her, as Armand does in *La Dame aux Camélias* and Alfredo in *La traviata*? Whatever he had done, it seems that throughout her final illness he called again and again, but she resolutely refused to see him. If she wanted to hurt him, she succeeded, not just for the duration of her illness but for the months immediately after her death and indeed probably for the rest of his life.

As ever Vienne was an indulgent interlocutor. He told her about his mother and that he was heading home to assist his father with settling his mother's affairs: he would be away for nearly four months.[10] He undertook to see Marie Duplessis's sister and pass on Marie's wishes regarding her surrender of her share in a local field that the sisters had inherited. As he left the apartment he promised to call in when he was back from the Orne.

In the course of the last two months of 1846 Marie Duplessis was visited repeatedly by her young friend Olympe Aguado, generous to a fault and determined to protect her from indigence as much as he could. He did not ask for anything in return. Not that she could grant sexual favours any longer anyway. She spent most of her days now in her boudoir. Here she had access to the clean water that she needed constantly, as she was coughing up blood ever more frequently. Also, the window of her boudoir opened on the boulevard. Her favourite armchair, the only item of furniture in the apartment to show any wear and tear, sat in the window, with the fire blazing continuously in the hearth; an invoice for her fuel, which was kept in the cellar of the building, survives among the bills that the bibliophile Lucien Graux, an enthusiast of the story of the lady of the camellias, inspected. She presumably tried to read to pass the time. When she was stronger she had devoured Sue's *Mystères de Paris*, because it was effectively a fashion accessory and because of the novel's topicality, more so for her than for most.

Now, between October and December 1846, another book was being serialized in the *Constitutionnel* and read by the whole of Paris, Balzac's *La Cousine Bette*, probably the greatest, most scandalous and most riveting novel to be published in nineteenth-century France. No work of fiction had up to that point dared to be so explicit about sex, greed, and pregnancies, and the sheer scale of men's and women's subjugations to their animal drives. Even today the novel stuns by its savage and unforgiving view of humanity. If Marie Duplessis did read the serialized extracts, the evolving novel must have seemed like a parable of her own life. This was the world of predatory trading of sex for money and power that she knew. The novel positively revels in exposing the raw physicality that underpins the genteel rituals of courtship. Marie Duplessis might have been startled by the brilliant sketch of Valérie Marneffe, the ruthless young woman who prostitutes herself from poverty and greed and then relishes the sway her sexuality confers on her. In due course the thwarted spinster Bette, the brains behind a monstrous plot to destroy her innocent rival, becomes Valérie's procuress. The teaming up in the novel of older and younger women to run sex as a business echoes the situation of Marie Duplessis and Clémence Pratt. Not that Pratt and Bette were comparable, but the novel has its finger on the pulse of the seedy side of Paris better than any other. Its action moreover plays in locations that would have been very familiar to Marie Duplessis, thereby adding to the sense of immediacy that forms such a powerful part of the novel's appeal.

During these closing months of the year, her old count too called on Marie Duplessis to take his leave. For him the spectre of death ought to have been a familiar ghost. He had already lived far beyond the median life expectancy of the period. Long life for him had meant outliving several of his children. Having lost two of his daughters in their early twenties, he now stood to lose another beloved young woman, and she was not yet 23 years old. It seems that he sat in a chair talking to her and weeping. What else could he do? She did not like it when he visited, because of the shameful history between them and because he made the spectre of death all too real. Another of her former lovers called repeatedly in the autumn of 1846, Agénor de Guiche Gramont. He had been one of her most exalted companions and she must have been pleased and grateful, the more so since he was at this period spending a lot of time in London.[11]

Even at this late stage, Marie Duplessis experienced moments of defiance. Until the end of the year she was still able to drag herself out occasionally to the Maison Dorée and she still drank champagne: one of her last shopping lists of medication also includes an order for more champagne. She would party as long as she could, and perhaps beyond. All of fashionable Paris knew that she was dying. Those who did not would know for certain by the end of December, because during the last week of the year, if not on the very last day, Marie Duplessis dragged herself out to the theatre one last time. The show was *La Poudre-coton: Revue de l'année 1846*, by Dumanoir and Claireville at the baroque theatre of Palais-Royal, a five-act gallimaufry, with an interval and shorter shows before and after.[12] Performances started at 7 p.m. and were running intermittently during the second half of December.

The doormen had to carry her into her box. She chose to be seen in spite of her haggard appearance. Perhaps she craved the compassion of those same audiences who once doted on her and who had licensed her reign as demi-mondaine. Or maybe she just needed to immerse herself one last time in the social world of playing, laughter, human cheer and solidarity. When she returned home to her apartment she probably guessed that she would never leave it again alive. Her world henceforth contracted to her chambermaid Clotilde, her footman Étienne, and the concierge of the building, Mr Privé. Clémence Pratt was quickly fading from view now that their business arrangement was well and truly over; although not quite, because Pratt would pop up one more time when, to the amazement of Paris, she briefly played herself in a revival of *La Dame aux Camélias* in Montmartre.[13] The only people who persisted in calling now at 11 boulevard de la Madeleine were Marie Duplessis's creditors, who faced the prospect of losing everything she owed them. Aguado did his best to fend them off. If only this future brilliant pioneer of photography had pursued his trade a few years earlier: Marie Duplessis and her splendiferous apartment would undoubtedly have been among his first subjects.

The last few days of Marie Duplessis's life in a wintry Madeleine would be as terrible as Keats's had been in Piazza di Spagna twenty-six years earlier. Worse, because she had no Joseph Severn to hold her, to soothe her fears, to tell her that she was loved and precious, that her kind heart would never be forgotten. No mother, father, sister, close friend, or lover was present to comfort her. This young uneducated woman had come from nowhere and conquered Paris. She had been formidably gifted and knew all there was to know about the world she lived in. But no-one could help her now. And how could she have found solace anyway, when she was so young, confronting the senseless waste of her life. Verdi understood that more than anyone because he had witnessed the cruel randomness of life and death a few years earlier. He understood perfectly, which is why he grants Violetta her heart-wrenching aria 'Grand Dio! Morir sì giovane / io che penato ho tanto' ('O God, to die so young when I have suffered so much').

As the end drew near, Marie, coughing and permanently sweat-drenched, requested that her bed be moved into her boudoir. She wanted to see the Madeleine church and the boulevard; the silence and solitude of her bedroom on the inner courtyard had become unbearable. Gazing at the austere temple church she knew that her funeral service would be held there. Perhaps, knowing how much it meant to her, friends like Aguado had reassured her that she would be buried as a countess. In previous years the first day of the new year and her birthday on 15 January had been joyous and exciting occasions. Suitors had called and sent gifts and lavish birthday presents. On this birthday, if her chambermaid can be believed, the bailiffs tried to seize her remaining possessions. Fortunately Aguado was there that day and saw them off with a huge bribe, although her belongings were formally impounded and set aside, it seems, to satisfy her creditors. If this is true, then she was no longer in charge of her life in any way other than still having the most basic right to stay put until she was dead. In the meantime, the men and women of the city partied all night at the same venues in the very part of town where she now lay. January and February, the height of the social season, may have been even more frenzied than usual this year because Ash Wednesday, the start of Lent, fell early, on 17 February. The metropolis had only six weeks to revel, and party it did.

Looking out today through the window of her boudoir at what were once the rue de la Ferme-des-Mathurins (today's rue Vignon) and the rue Godot, almost directly opposite, it is hard not to feel some of her anguish in that very same space. No-one will ever know how frightened she was, what passed through her mind in those final days. Almost certainly she clutched her mother's medallion as she lay waiting, an act of solace that may be the source of a rumour that spread through Paris after her death, namely that her mother appeared at her bedside in her final moments to comfort her doomed daughter. Perhaps some of her friends wanted to believe this, to soothe their consciences about forsaking her in her hour of greatest need. Unless she was after all visited by Lady Anderson as she lay dying and that this was why her mother was thought to have turned up at her bedside? Vienne makes no mention of this and neither did Clotilde when she talked about her mistress's dying.

On 1 February she began to drift in and out of consciousness. She still, apparently, recognized young Aguado as he wept at her bedside. Most of the time Clotilde sat with her. A delirious Marie Duplessis hung on for three days, fighting off the coma that was gradually taking hold of her. The closest we have to an eyewitness account of those last hours comes from Théophile Gautier. In a stirring obituary, written three weeks after her death, he includes an account of her final hours which is almost certainly true to the facts. As he passed her still richly caparisoned bed in the thick of the auction a few days after her death, he was struck by the incongruity of its delicate pinks, cushions, and elaborate carvings and the dreadful scene that, 'we had been told', had lately been played out on it:

> She was afraid of death, this beautiful young woman, because death means ugliness and oblivion. Over three days, feeling herself slip over the edge of the abyss into which we are all destined to fall, she clung desperately to the hand of her maid. That warm hand in her icy one seemed to her a last hold on life. She never wanted to let go. Only once did she do so and that was when the pale angel of death came to claim her. It was the final revolt of youth recoiling from annihilation. She rose up straight to flee, cried out three times, and then fell back dead into her winding sheets.

The detail of her rising one last time, desperate to escape the clutches of death, is powerfully echoed by Verdi in *La traviata*.

Marie Duplessis died around 3 a.m. on Wednesday 3 February 1847, a little over two weeks after her twenty-third birthday. Her chambermaid seems at once to have sent for her husband Perrégaux, who at the time lived at 12 rue de la Victoire, some twenty minutes away; unless he had been alerted earlier. It is possible that he joined her in her dying moments even though there is no account to confirm that.[14] But he did call frequently enough to know how far she had deteriorated. He may have been at her bedside within an hour of her death and it may have been he who reportedly knelt in front of her bed and prayed and wept. What is certain is that two retainers of the Perrégaux–Raguse family either accompanied him or were sent as soon as news of her death reached them. They at once shamelessly began to rifle through her possessions, her papers and letters, stuffing everything they found into a large bag. The scavengers clearly belonged to the Raguse–Perrégaux clan; perhaps they were the family agents Delisle and Carlier. They were overheard talking about an 'English' piece of paper which could only be the 1846 Kensington marriage licence. Clotilde eagerly assisted them in their search, but it turned out to be fruitless. Marie Duplessis had wisely not trusted her maid enough to share with her where she kept this most important document. She clearly suspected that after her death Clotilde would look to anyone who could grease her palm in return for what she could offer from her mistress.

Marie Duplessis's young artist friend Chaplin called that morning to draw her. He had obviously been invited by one of Marie Duplessis's lovers, if not by her husband because he knew that she had died. Or perhaps the gallant Aguado had wanted her to be drawn by Chaplin; the two men were almost exact contemporaries and may have known each other. However Chaplin came to be there in the course of Wednesday 3 February, he would have been devastated by the sight of his dead friend.[15] His immediate impulse was, it seems, to commemorate her, which is why he drew her exactly as she was, perhaps wishing to reveal to the world her full tragic humanity. This sketch of the dead lady of the camellias has not been found, but we know that it existed because among Chaplin's effects at his death in 1891 it was described as a red chalk drawing ('sanguine'): it was lot no. 60, *La mort de La Dame aux Camélias*, in the *Catalogue de la vente* of his estate.[16]

As with Chaplin's earlier portrait copied by Riffaut, he may also have allowed this one to be replicated for illustrated editions of *La Dame aux Camélias* after 1865. His picture very probably survives in the engraving by d'H. Linton, said to be after a drawing by Alphonse de Neuville. The image first appeared among Neuville's 1865 illustrations of *La Dame aux Camélias*. What immediately brings Chaplin to mind as the painter behind the engraving is not only the recognizable presence in it of Marie Duplessis, but the details of her bedding and, in the far left corner, the ornate signature post of a Boulle bed, obviously the canopied Boulle bed in which she died. The figure on the bed and the bed itself jointly suggest that the picture was drawn by someone who was there. As with the Riffaut–Duclos copy of Chaplin's 1846 portrait, so here too it seems safe to assume that the Linton and Neuville image faithfully renders what Chaplin drew on the morning of Wednesday 3 February 1847 (Figure 16.4).

The Boulle bed was the only major item of furniture and fittings missing from the auction. Instead, under 'Chambre à coucher, donnant sur la cour', there features a much more modest '1 couchette en palissandre sculpté', along with a full set of bedding. Nevertheless, in his obituary of 28 February Gautier stated categorically that he saw the Boulle bed: 'the bed, hallowed by death, displayed under red silks and lace curtains its rosewood sculptures, its cushions and pillows still damp from the death sweat—such a bed was never meant for the moans and pains of dying'. In his celebrated 1852 preface to *La Dame aux Camélias*, Jules Janin similarly noted that 'every piece of furniture in this luxurious apartment was still in its place; the bed on which she had died looked barely touched while at the bottom of the bed a stool [perhaps the one in the Olivier picture?] preserved the imprint of the knees of the man who had closed her eyes'.[17] What happened to her Boulle bed is not recorded, but it is possible that a certain decorum prevailed at the auction and that the bed was sold outside of the auction proper.

Although she died heavily in debt, she did not breathe her last in a derelict, stripped-down home. It is tempting to presuppose that in her final days she decided to move from her luxury courtesan's bed into the much humbler bed that would find its way into the auction catalogue. This is certainly possible as she spent much of her final days in prayer and repentance. Perhaps she did not want to be found in the bed in which she had committed so many sins. One cannot rule out that she wanted the bed to be moved out of her home, the more so since she spent most of her last days on a couch in her boudoir. But the Chaplin image suggests otherwise: the bed in which he drew her is unmistakably a Boulle bed with one of its distinctive ewers clearly visible on the left of the picture. The drawing depicts an emaciated Marie Duplessis on a lavishly bedecked bed: a ravaged victim of tuberculosis, with her mouth open as if gasping for one final breath of air to fill her wasted lungs, set already in the rictus of rigor mortis. The figure resembles Marie well enough, with her slim bust and surprisingly long fingers, a curious detail of her appearance commented on by several people who knew

Figure 16.4 A famous picture of Marie Duplessis on her deathbed, attributed to Linton and Neuville, but probably copying Chaplin's fourth and last drawing of her.

her. Her once glorious hair looks frazzled while her nose is etched sharply in profile, cruelly relieved by the receding grimace of her face.

The day after she died, on Thursday 4 February 1847, Romain Vienne called at 8 p.m. He had left his card at the porter's lodge the previous Tuesday evening, announcing his intention to visit on Thursday night. No-one, it seems, had thought to tell him that his friend had already sunk into a coma. Perhaps he had missed the porter because all hands were required upstairs by the dying woman? A more likely explanation is that Marie Duplessis's chambermaid had not wanted the precise Vienne any-where near her mistress as she was hoping to extract more money from her death: after all Clotilde would now lose her employment, which had been gainful, exciting, and had come with a room in one of the choicest parts of the capital. She could easily have notified Vienne, who lived a ten-minute hop away at 5 rue Favart, next to the Opéra-Comique off the Boulevard des Italiens. But she disliked Vienne. He attributed this to his steadfast refusal to tip her, on the grounds that he had never availed himself of her assistant procuress's labours. She was eminently bribable, he noted, but that came with the territory. Above all he was madame's executor, so she needed to be on her guard. He was bound to disapprove of her allowing anyone near the possessions of Marie Duplessis before he had had a chance to assess them. In fact, he would be too late anyway because by the time he arrived at her home her creditors' agents had already confiscated her belongings.

As he climbed the few steps to the mezzanine apartment that Thursday evening, Vienne was still unaware of the fact that Marie had died. Clotilde opened the door and, in a matter-of-fact manner, as he noted reprovingly, imparted to him the news. He was stunned as she guided him through the dining room into Marie's bedroom, which was all decked in black and fitfully lit by candles. She was laid out in an oak coffin, which was perched on trestles along the windows. 'Knowing that you would come and thinking that you would want to see her one last time, we did not seal the coffin', Clotilde told him, referring to instructions apparently given by the bailiff acting for the creditors. A young priest, kneeling, was discreetly praying at the fireside.[18] Vienne was overwhelmed by grief as Clotilde lifted the lid of the coffin and folded back the winding sheet, to let him see her face one last time:

> I gently lifted her head, with both my hands; her body was already stiff. I ran my fingers over her forehead and temples, then parted her lips and her eyes, which were half-closed. Her hair looked untidy, so I separated it into two strands and tresses, which I arranged alongside her body, tucked under her arms. I held her two icy hands in mine, which were hot and feverish. I examined her hands in the minutest detail, with such intensity that Julie [Clotilde] involuntarily shuddered. The priest rose to see what I was doing. The two of them, motionless and silent, watched me, surprised, horrified. I asked Julie to fetch me a pair of scissors while I continued with my examination.

While Vienne waited for Clotilde to return he felt a rush of blood to the head. Fearing a stroke, he fled to her sitting room where he collapsed in an armchair. When Clotilde brought the scissors he requested that she cut a lock from Marie's forehead for keepsake: he himself could not face seeing Marie again. Clotilde did as instructed after which the coffin was sealed.

Liszt was touring Russia when he heard the news that his lover had died. Grieving, and guiltily remembering his unfulfilled promise to take her with him to Constantinople, he wrote to his mistress Marie d'Agoult: 'Now she is dead, I do not know what mysterious antique elegy echoes in my heart at her memory' ('maintenant la voilà morte, je ne sais quelle étrange corde d'élégie antique vibre dans mon coeur à son souvenir'). Hers, he declared, had been the sweetest nature, pure and serene, unsullied by the corruption of her shadowy world. He had loved her passionately and she had touched his artistic soul: 'I had for her a solemn and elegiac attachment, which inspired me to poetry and to music' ('Je m'étais pris pour elle d'un attachement sombre et élégiaque, lequel m'avait remis en veine de poésie et de musique'). Marie Duplessis never heard this testimonial to her sweet and innocent nature. If she had known that she had meant that much to the genius of Liszt, it might have comforted her even in those dreadful final days in the Madeleine. As it was, Liszt would keep faith with her beyond this immediate response in a daring and pointed musical offering, if not in two.

17

Two winter funerals in Montmartre

February 1847

French law required that the body should be buried by the end of the week and so the day after Vienne's visit, Friday morning 5 February 1847, the future dame aux camélias left her apartment for the last time. Her coffin, smothered in white camellias, was taken across the boulevard to the Madeleine church for the funeral service. It was followed by Clotilde, her footman Étienne, Romain Vienne, and the concierge of no. 11, Mr Privé. Vienne and Privé signed the church register after formally identifying the body. Then they joined the 150-strong congregation that had gathered in the church.

Her husband Édouard de Perrégaux had arrived too late to see her in her coffin and could not therefore vouch in law for the identity of the body. Quite how affected he was by this would shortly become evident. To compound his hurt, the ecclesiastical authorities refused to accept that she was married to him. Not long ago he had wanted her to deny their union, but now he longed for her to be his. It may have been some comfort for him, as he knelt in the front pew, that the cushions bore the arms of Comtesse Marie Duplessis, even though the funeral service was officially held for 'Alphonsine Plessis', the name recorded on her death certificate and on her tomb. Such was the fate of the real life 'traviata' as she lay in state in the grand temple named after female sinners. She was beyond hurt by the church's petty repudiation of her aristocratic prefix and chosen first name. Moreover she would soon be honoured under names that no-one could have anticipated: 'Marguerite', 'Camille', 'Violetta', and above all 'la traviata', a name whose glorious Italian vowels and the transcendent music associated with them disguise the fact that it means 'fallen woman', literally 'the woman led astray'.

The Madeleine service cost an impressive 1,354 francs. Either Perrégaux or Stackelberg was paying for what must have been a grand occasion that included her countess's kneeling cushions, a sea of camellias, and a sumptuously decked coffin. As was the custom for deaths in the Madeleine, Marie Duplessis would be buried in her local cemetery, the 'Cimetière du Nord' also known as 'de la Barrière Blanche', now the famous 'Cimetière de Montmartre'. When the cortège embarked on its sombre way outside the Madeleine, a number of onlookers gathered, among them the greatest living English novelist, Charles Dickens. He was writing *Dombey and Son* at the time, a novel with a saintly heroine, Florence Dombey, the spurned but unflinchingly loyal daughter of a hard and unforgiving father. One might have thought that the creator of Florence would be sympathetic to the plight and desolation of Marie Duplessis, even more so now that she was cruelly put back in her social place. He after all harboured intense resentment about his own ignominy when his father languished in the debtors' prison. Not so: rather, Dickens confided in his friend, the Comte d'Orsay, that he thought the fuss made over Marie Duplessis smacked of hysteria. Most Parisians disagreed. Marie Duplessis had been one of theirs, a glamorous fixture in the capital's burgeoning celebrity culture. Much of her life had been lived through public exhibitions of herself. Her fabulous clothes, jewels and impeccable taste had turned her into an icon. Here now was their last chance to catch her, to see who would accompany her coffin, to be part of her final appearance, to witness this moment in history. Her fascination lasted to the end. Her life of assignations had been an open secret. Now the crowd could see for itself.

First behind the hearse walked Édouard de Perrégaux, with Romain Vienne at his side, followed at a short distance by several others who had shared her life and occasionally her bed too. They included the loyal Olympe Aguado, old Stackelberg, Agénor de Guiche Gramont, who had hurried back specially from London to attend her funeral, Édouard Delessert, another lover, future explorer, and son of the powerful banker and préfet of the Paris police Gabriel Delessert, the Vicomte Théodoric Narbonne Pelet, her 'horsey' friend Tony, and Comte Alfred de Montjoyeux, another member of the Jockey-Club, author of a revealing account of her life in the 1892 *Lanterne* and friend of several of her lovers.

The two most conspicuous absentees were Charles de Morny and the younger Dumas, who had not yet returned to Paris after his travels in Spain. Morny was busy forging an ambitious political career. As chairman of the recently created Central Railways, and with his sights probably set on the presidency of the first ever French republic with full male suffrage, he could ill afford to be seen paying homage to a courtesan, let alone run the risk of having his paternity of her baby exposed. His relationship with Marie Duplessis had been the most secret of her many affairs, while also being the most creative: he had after all turned her into the most cultured, refined, and sought-after demi-mondaine of nineteenth-century Paris. Their baby son might have sealed their bond but his premature death stopped the relationship in its tracks. Nevertheless he would prove his affection for her one more time five years from now, as we will see, and thus play a crucial part in her afterlife as a legend.

As the cortège wound its way north to the cemetery from the Madeleine, Perrégaux broke down repeatedly. The melancholy procession passed her home one last time before turning up left towards the rue de Clichy. Half an hour later it reached the gates and lodge of the cemetery at the bottom of the Montmartre promontory, which at the time was not yet linked to place Clichy by the pont Caulaincourt. Once inside they turned right and headed north to a section directly below today's rue Joseph-de-Maistre on the ridge of Montmartre, with the avenue Halévy as its southern border. This is an almost exclusively Jewish part of the cemetery. Many graves remind today's visitor of the horrors of recent history, with death dates evoking faraway camps rendered infamous for all time. But some Jewish graves here are much earlier, dating from just the period when Marie Duplessis was laid to rest in this section. It seems that the authorities had decided that her courtesan's remains would spend five years in this unconsecrated, non-Christian part of the cemetery before being moved into a mass grave. The Jewish Judith Bernat's solidarity with Marie Duplessis could not have been more fitting: here in extremis was the proof of how much she and Marie Duplessis ultimately shared as outcasts.

At the graveside a brief funeral service was held over the coffin. Then the mourners blessed it before it was lowered into the earth. Perrégaux was first in line. He nearly lost all self-control when the priest passed him the holy water sprinkler. He was steadied by Vienne who then handed the 'goupillon' to the next mourner. One by one they filed past and blessed the young woman's remains. While this was going on Vienne noticed that a number of grieving women had turned up to pay their last respects to his friend. Although he does not say so, we may assume that among them was her actress friend Judith Bernat; also perhaps her innocent nameless interlocutor from the Bois de Boulogne, her maid, the mysterious visitor who had contributed so generously to her fundraising, and other young women whom she had helped in their hour of need, if the records can be believed.

Far from forgetting Marie Duplessis, Judith Bernat would eventually play the part of Marguerite Gautier in the provinces; in Paris the role was reserved for Eugénie Doche whom she knew well.[1] In Bernat's own words:

> If Madame Doche may be said to have created the *rôle* of the Dame aux Camélias, I was the first to interpret it in the provinces. It was not without difficulty that I procured the necessary authorization, for people are always more prudish in the country than in Paris. The piece had been the rage on the boulevards of the capital for a year before the embargo on it was removed in the rest of France. Fortunately, however, the authorities thought that my position as a member of the Comédie-Française would act as a salve to consciences easily shocked, and they removed their veto in my favour.[2]

Perrégaux remained inconsolable throughout the burial, so much so that the others at the graveside left him alone and kept a respectful distance as he made his way out of the cemetery. They did not know that he had formed a bizarre plan there and then. More than anything he wanted to see Marie again. She had banned him from visiting her during her last days on earth. It is hard to imagine that she could have known how deeply affected he would be by this. The once aimless playboy who had buckled under pressure from his family twice, who had cravenly deserted his wife at their behest, was guilt-ridden. She was gone, forever lost, yet now he would prove his love to her.

And he knew exactly how he intended to achieve this: by applying for a reburial for which the law required formal identification. To prove to the world, and himself, how much he cared, he would move her into a perpetual grave in the heart of the Christian section of the cemetery. These were rarely granted but Perrégaux, the child of a family of Parisian bankers, knew people. And so, on Friday 12 February 1847, for the fee of 526 francs, a week after the funeral in Montmartre, a licence for reburial was issued by the Préfecture de Paris to 'Édouard, comte Perrégaux'. It granted a plot of '2 mètres' in the cemetery 'to create there the individual grave, in perpetuity, of Mademoiselle Alphonsine Plessis who died on 3 February 1847' ('pour y fonder la sépulture particulière et perpétuelle de Mademoiselle Alphonsine

Plessis, morte le 3 février 1847').[3] The reburial would take place on 16 February.

Dumas *fils* arrived back in Paris on Wednesday 10 February 1847 and at once rushed up to the cemetery in Montmartre. As he reports in the novel, what he saw was 'a plot of flowers that would never have been taken for a grave, were it not for a piece of white marble, an upright headstone with a name on it. An iron trellis ran round the grave which was covered in white camellias'. As he stood dumbfounded by the speed with which death had claimed her, he noticed that the camellias on her tomb were fresh. At that point the head gardener came up and told him that Perrégaux, the man 'who wept so much the first time he came', was paying for him to replace each camellia as it faded. Dumas learnt that Perrégaux had since left Paris to seek out the dead woman's sister, to discuss moving Marie Duplessis into a more fitting grave. This is plausible enough, because Perrégaux knew Nonant and the area around it from his earlier visits. But it seems that he missed Delphine and her husband Paquet, because when they arrived in Paris they were unaware of any plans to move Marie Duplessis.

Dumas had been almost as affected by Marie's fate as Perrégaux. His first response on hearing news of her death was to write a haunting elegy about days and nights spent together in her apartment at 11 boulevard de la Madeleine. This poem, *Péchés de jeunesse*, is dedicated to his friend Théophile Gautier. After learning from the cemetery's gardener about Perrégaux's grief, and perhaps too about his quixotic plan, Dumas decided to seek him out. He may have been drawn to him by the sheer melodrama of what Perrégaux was proposing to do. In Dumas's novel the two men meet because at the auction of Marie's possessions the narrator (Dumas) buys a copy of the scandalous novel *Manon Lescaut* inscribed to 'Armand' (Perrégaux), which he subsequently decides to return to the dedicatee after learning of his intense grief and breakdown. The version of their encounter in *La Dame aux Camélias* is entirely fantastical, although the choice of novel was fitting inasmuch as it was Marie Duplessis's favourite. The real-life meeting between the two men ultimately resulted in one of the most remarkable allusive literary works of the nineteenth century, with Dumas's *La Dame aux Camélias* a barely disguised account of the loves and lives of Marie Duplessis and Édouard de Perrégaux, not of Dumas's own affair with her. According to Dumas, Perrégaux was in a state of feverish distress when they met, barely able to exist from day to day. Now the two became a team.

Less than a week intervened between Dumas's return on Wednesday and the reinterment the following Tuesday. De Perrégaux was probably in Normandy then, but Dumas knew where to find him in Paris when he was back. They had friends in common, not least among them Théophile Gautier, whose intimate acquaintance, Alice Ozy, was again Perrégaux's lover. Or so it appears from a letter she wrote to Gautier in March 1847, only a few weeks after the funeral of Marie Duplessis in Montmartre, in which she refers to Perrégaux as 'mon cher comte'. If Perrégaux did indeed go to Normandy, he was back in Paris on Friday 12 February when the perpetual concession was granted to him. It was probably during the weekend of 14 February that Dumas and Perrégaux, his senior by eleven years, met and talked, endlessly, as he reports in La Dame aux Camélias, about the woman they had both loved. Dumas had probably not yet considered writing anything about Marie apart from the elegy, but now he became privy to an affair with her that had been on a vastly different scale from his in every way. It had been the key relationship in Marie's life, made her respectable, and conferred a much coveted social elevation on her. Dumas had never been in the league of the Perrégauxs, and this was almost certainly the first time he learnt details of the marriage from the very person who was there, although he probably knew about the months at Bougival already. He must have been spellbound and before long he knew exactly how he would transmit this story to the world. It says much for both men that they could not let go of a woman they had bought and loved at the same time. Their unquestioning commitment to her memory would launch three very different tributes to her.

The two men did not share their plans for a reburial with any of the previous mourners, for on the day of the ceremony only the two of them made their way to Montmartre. Of all the days of the year 16 February 1847 happened to be Shrove Tuesday, the last day of carnival, which is traditionally marked by festive extravagance. Marie Duplessis might have appreciated the irony of Paris heaving with crowds of masked revellers the day she was buried for the second time. Some of them were making their way down the Butte de Montmartre as Dumas and Perrégaux entered the cemetery. The grim mood of the occasion was compounded by the relentless squalls of icy rain that lashed the capital all day. Five men eventually gathered for the act of reinterment: Perrégaux, Dumas fils, two gravediggers, and a haughty official of the état civil. They met up at the front lodge and then visited the site of her proposed new resting place, barely three minutes' walk away from the main entrance in the new southern part of the cemetery. After that they hurried across to the old section for the exhumation.

Perrégaux was about to have his wish granted, to gaze on his dead wife's face one last time. Less than a year earlier they had married in London and before that they had enjoyed carefree days of 'honeymoon' bliss in Bougival. He alone had come to know the real Marie Duplessis as she briefly reverted to being the country girl she had once been, but this time with money and comfort. Perrégaux's desire to see her face in these extreme circumstances was partly self-indulgence by a spoiled young man, but he was clearly also determined that she would not rest in some forsaken unmarked grave in years to come. If he had not done right by her when she was alive, he would do so now that she was dead.

The dreadful weather meant that the gravediggers were working in a quagmire. At last they reached the coffin and brushed off the stones that had been deposited on it, as was the custom in this Jewish section of the cemetery. They lifted it out and proceeded to unscrew the oak top. One can only imagine Marie's two lovers' trepidation as the cover came off. Immediately 'a fetid smell escaped from it in spite of the aromatic plants with which the corpse had been covered.' Shockingly, her winding sheet had already been gnawed away at one end so that one of her feet stuck out obscenely. The gravediggers rolled back the blanket to uncover her face for formal identification. Staring out at the onlookers was a grisly parody of the woman they had known: her eyes and lips had disappeared, her jaw had locked, and her cheeks had turned green. Perrégaux reeled but was able to confirm that she was indeed Alphonsine Plessis. The coffin was swiftly resealed. There then followed a disconsolate trek behind a lumbering tumbril to the avenue Saint-Charles and her new grave, which the records identify as 'n° 12, 4ᵉ ligne, 15ᵉ Division'.

Was she buried in the ground here with a funerary monument, or does the sarcophagus, which sits on top of the grave, contain her mortal remains? The former has always seemed more plausible, but it is impossible to be sure. It is unlikely that the sarcophagus could have arrived so soon after commission, or that the text on it would have been put on in the few days intervening between the granting of the concession on a Friday and the reinterment the following Tuesday. On both marble side panels it says ICI REPOSE / ALPHONSINE PLESSIS, / NÉE LE 15 JANVIER 1824, / DÉCÉDÉE LE 3 FÉVRIER 1847, / DE PROFUNDIS (Figure 17.1). Underneath, on the limestone base, are carved the almost faded words 'Concession à perpétuité N° 83,

Figure 17.1 The sarcophagus grave in Montmartre, Marie Duplessis's final resting place.

Année 1847'. The main text is probably taken from the headstone of her first grave, but a striking emblem was now added to the front of her new tomb. It takes the shape of an artfully conjoined 'AP', an arabesque for 'Alphonsine Plessis' or 'Alphonsine Perrégaux', or both. The Plessis and Perrégaux names would be intermingled forever.

As soon as Marie was buried, the supervisor urged Dumas to take his friend home; which he did. If Dumas is to believed, Perrégaux suffered a nervous breakdown in the aftermath of this experience. This may be why he did not appear at the auction of her effects that started just over a week later. What he could not have known at the time was that Dumas would turn his account of his relationship into a novel. Did he grant permission to Dumas to do so? The answer would probably have to be affirmative. We know that Perrégaux owned a copy of the novel and there is no record of him ever protesting about it or indeed the play that followed. His story was a safe secret, because all but a handful of readers in the know would suspect that the hero of the novel, Armand Duval, was Alexandre Dumas *fils*.

The day after the reinterment, Romain Vienne, now executor of her estate, turned up to visit the original grave in Montmartre. He had Marie Duplessis's sister and her husband in tow, after arranging for both of them to visit Paris to attend the upcoming auction. He was going to show the grave to her sister. On the way to the cemetery they stopped off at a stone-mason's to pick a suitable gravestone for Marie Duplessis. When they arrived at the lodge of the cemetery they discovered to their dismay that she had been moved. According to the supervisor, 'the mortal remains of the person you talk of, sir, were exhumed and now rest in the grave that you can see over there, twenty feet to the left.'[4]

Vienne was understandably outraged. He had met and supported Perrégaux at the first funeral and was deeply hurt as well as offended by his stealthy decision to move the body. Vienne may have been a provincial but he was well connected in the capital and knew his way in the corridors of power. He at once threatened to sue on behalf of the family and called on the 'préfet' of the Paris police, whose own son had been one of Marie Duplessis's lovers. Vienne knew this and, shamelessly, presented the father with a copy of a damaging love letter addressed to Marie Duplessis by his son. He let old Delessert destroy it there and then, thus enlisting his support should it be needed. Eventually though, and without recourse to litigation, Perrégaux and Vienne came to an accommodation when the latter realized how grief-stricken Perrégaux was: the transfer of his wife's body had been an act of love and she would be in her new home in perpetuity. It was better that way. Also, Vienne may not have been aware of a possible deal struck between Perrégaux and Delphine. As we saw, he had petitioned the court for the return of some of his gifts to Marie but then had, inexplicably, not pursued his claim so that on 15 February, the day preceding the reburial in Montmartre, the court ruled that his jewels would be auctioned off like the rest of the estate. From this it would appear that Perrégaux and Marie's sister perhaps agreed that he could move his wife and that she would not need to face a court battle over the jewels.

The Montmartre cemetery log, still kept in the same place as 150 years ago, contains an extensive set of notes about the lady of the camellias. Among others it records the following lyric about her:

> The dust floated up
> Heavenward; pebbles sparkled.
> The wind blows less gently now, the swallow is not quite so
>   prompt.
> Under a canopy of leaves a shadow whispered
> O Marie, where are you walking upon wild thyme?[5]

The author's name is not given. Nor is it known who wrote the following lines, which appeared after her death:

> Who does not remember Duplessis, the pretty courtesan,
> Sitting on her bed, her hair flowing,
> Her forehead even whiter than the flower of a liana,
> Her dark-red lips and sparkling eyes,
> Large azure pearls framed by a translucent flow
> And her gorgeous swanlike neck and her provocative breasts.[6]

They were reproduced in his brilliant *Confessions 1830–80* by Arsène Houssaye, director of the Comédie-Française and friend of Théophile Gautier and Charles Baudelaire, who dedicated *Spleen de Paris* to him.[7] Houssaye notes that there are another ten stanzas in the same vein by the anonymous rhymer who was not quite, he remarks, in the league of Musset and who signs himself 'a camellia'. Nevertheless both poems testify to the affection that she inspired even after her death among people who will forever remain anonymous.

18

Auction at 11 boulevard de la Madeleine

February 1847

Marie Duplessis's apartment had been sealed on 5 February to safeguard the interests of her creditors and, if anything was left after they had been compensated, her heirs. Vienne took her sister Delphine and husband there and, in front of them and various other witnesses, including Clotilde, he proceeded to empty her chest of drawers. He made it clear that he was well aware that a large stash of letters had been taken, that this constituted theft, and that as the legal representative of the family he would act accordingly if these were not returned. He then explored the drawers and released a secret compartment. Marie Duplessis had obviously shown it to him but not to anyone else, least of all her chambermaid or Pratt. It contained some 300 letters. Vienne perused these and then burnt all but thirty of them in the hearth, asking that his act be witnessed and minuted. The remaining letters he reserved for himself.

No-one present demurred but posterity has protested vigorously about this alleged act of vandalism, a violation of his duty to history. Vienne claims that he wished to save reputations. He was no Baudelaire, Balzac, or Gautier. At heart he was a conscientious petty bourgeois who happened to be the intimate confidant of a famous courtesan. The thirty letters he chose to keep for himself were lost subsequently in a fire in San Francisco when he worked there as a journalist, along with many others of his most prized possessions; or so he claimed.[1] To be fair to Vienne, he did attempt to have Marie Duplessis's story told by the best, hence his visit to his friend Théophile Gautier within days of her death, to persuade him to become her chronicler. Like the rest of Paris, Vienne had read Gautier's brilliant obituary of Marie Duplessis, details of which, such as the manner of her death, may well have come from Vienne, who cast himself in the role of upright executor. He was determined to trace all of Marie Duplessis's belongings that had already disappeared but in the end clashed over this with Delphine Paquet-Plessis. She was as headstrong as she was foolish and unschooled in the ways of the capital. And she may have been greedy, particularly when it became clear that she stood to inherit a fortune from her sister's estate.

The viewing ('Exposition Publique') of Marie Duplessis's belongings was announced in the Paris press for Tuesday 23 February, 12 noon to 5 p.m.; the auction itself would be held on the premises of her apartment over a period of four days, from Wednesday 24 to Saturday 27 February 1847. It had been exactly three weeks since she died. Several eyewitness accounts survive, as does a sales catalogue itemizing her belongings, room by room, with a detailed list showing who bought what. It was a major event in the Paris social calendar. The boulevard and adjacent streets were congested by the parked carriages of wealthy visitors and bidders. The crush in her spacious apartment was aggravated by the number of society hostesses who had turned up. They were there not necessarily to buy but, as Dumas remarked, to inspect for themselves the 'splendide cloaque' that was her home, and particularly her boudoir, which was salaciously investigated. Dumas attended the auction but he is not listed as a bidder, even though he bought back his parting letter of 30 August 1845 as well as the necklace he had given Marie.

Édouard de Perrégaux did not appear either, but his aunt, the Duchesse de Raguse, did, intent on redeeming some of the gifts, presumably family heirlooms that her nephew had given to his paramour. It is tempting to conclude that the nervous collapse at Marie's second funeral accounted for his absence: how could he bear to revisit her home in the thick din of bidding when all he wanted was to grieve in silence? It is possible that he sent the Duchesse de Raguse, although it is more likely that she was instructed by the family lawyer, 'Blue-specs Rouflaquette', to attend and bid. The lawyer was very much in evidence at this time, among others, apparently tendering a magnanimous offer of 80,000 francs to Delphine, if she renounced all interest in Marie Duplessis's estate, which she declined.[2]

Among the crowd was Marie Duplessis's neighbour Madame de Golberg, who bid and bought while at the same time she was owed 504 francs by Marie at her death.[3] At some point the salon, where the auctioneer presided, became so congested that two of Paris's best-known faces, Richard Wallace and Théophile Gautier, were together pushed back into the bedroom by the

tide of people. Irritated by the sanctimonious tuttings of the respectable
bourgeoises hovering like vultures over Marie's luxurious possessions,
Gautier wondered aloud whether they had any idea how much of a price
the wretched young woman really paid for each item, meaning that she had
reluctantly traded herself to the husbands of these same prurient women:
'Perhaps they would have accepted them on the same terms,' the amused
voice of Richard Wallace replied behind him, as he and Gautier were
squeezed out of the salon.[4]

The millionaire Wallace (Figure 18.1) was a familiar of most of the people
who ran Paris and France as well as the country's artists and writers. In a
memoir called *An Englishman in Paris*, an important document discussed
further in Chapter 19, he claimed that he was 'a frequent visitor to
Compiègne throughout the Second Empire' and that he was 'one of the few
privileged persons who travelled down to Boulogne with Louis-Napoleon,
on Friday 17th of August, 1855', to welcome Queen Victoria to France.[5] He
also knew that other Bonaparte, the Duc de Morny, of whom he offers a
bracingly candid portrait.

Wallace inhabited the centre of the literary and artistic powerhouse of
1840s Paris. He lived above the most famous café of them all and next door
to most of the others, while his [half]-cousin, Lord Seymour 'Arsouille',
founder of the Jockey-Club, occupied a lavish apartment at 1 Taitbout.[6] A
will from the period places Wallace right inside Seymour's rooms in Paris,
while the 1842 Almanach of Paris places the home in which he also lived,
that of the 'Countess of Yarmouth, later the Marchioness of Hertford (wife
of Francis Charles Seymour-Conway, the Third Marquess' (Lisburn), at 2
Laffitte, on the other side of the Maison Dorée.[7] Unless this was the home
in which he spent his early years in Paris before moving into the Seymour
home. A statuette of Seymour graced Wallace's study in his grand mansion
of Hertford House in Manchester Square, London, suggesting that he may
have felt more of an affinity with his relative, founder of the Jockey-Club,
than is commonly assumed.[8] He had known and liked Marie Duplessis and,
it seems, she had reciprocated his affection.

Richard Wallace, who was born Richard Jackson, moved to France when
he was 7 years old. Unlike his relative Lord Seymour, he spoke perfect
English. On his mother Agnes Wallace's side, whose maiden name the illegitimate Richard Jackson proudly adopted in 1842, he may have been descended
from the legendary medieval Scots freedom fighter William Wallace, with
whom the Wallaces of Craigie Castle, Ayrshire, claimed kinship.[9] A clue to

Figure 18.1 Sir Richard Wallace, who knew Dumas *père et fils* and Marie Duplessis.

his Scots parentage is perhaps found in an almost casual remark in his memoir when he recalls that 'It was very touching, in after years, to hear *the lads and lassies* [my italics] refer to the 1st of January, 1871, as the New Year's Day without the New Year's gifts.'[10] Surely only a Scots speaker would ever talk about 'lads and lassies' in this way? Did he pick this up from his mother?

He was remarkably familiar with the novels of Dickens with whom he overlapped in Paris in the 1840s. In fact, they were both spotted at the auction of Marie Duplessis's effects at 11 boulevard de la Madeleine in February 1847. In his memoir, Wallace repeatedly quotes the great comic novelist and almost casually refers to some of his greatest creations, including the intensely irritating Mrs Jellyby, the 'telescopic philanthropist' in *Bleak House* who neglects her own family to indulge in futile charitable pursuits in Africa (Wallace had in mind the writer and politician Lamartine's wife, whom he considered profligate and unsound), and Pumblechook and Wemmick from *Great Expectations*, to mention only three. Wallace shared

Dickens's distaste for humbug and his pen is almost as sharp as the novelist's when offering a sketch of the pompous, over-dressed fop Eugène Sue, another person reputedly present at the auction. He was reported by Dickens to have been bidding, but the published catalogue of the auction suggests otherwise. After the success of *Les Mystères de Paris*, Sue started to take himself very seriously, and as a result was widely thought to lack class and self-knowledge. He was a parvenu and, being Jewish, inevitably an outsider. In the eyes of many of his contemporaries, this rendered his habitual lingering with a cigar on the steps of the Café de Paris, as reported by Wallace, particularly 'egregious'.

Wallace was the richest collector by far at the Madeleine auction, so why is he not personally listed as buying anything? He must have bid through a proxy, but who was his agent on this occasion? The clue may lie in the auction record, the most mystifying aspect of which concerns the huge sums bid by Marie Duplessis's brother-in-law Paquet. How could this humble weaver from the Orne possibly offer 1,250 francs for a piece of rosewood furniture, 1,631 francs for jewellery, and a colossal 8,700 francs for two clocks and two grand chandeliers, including undoubtedly the gorgeous mantelpiece clock, when he and his wife could have no conceivable use for such artefacts in their home?

Vienne inadvertently confirmed that Paquet bid for a mystery client when, many years later, he recalled the possessions that survived in Delphine's home decades after the auction: her sister's *prie-Dieu* ('prayer-desk'), her rosewood couch, the miniature of her mother, and some further trinkets. His memory may not have been entirely accurate as the records of the auction show that Marie Duplessis's *prie-Dieu* was bought for 30 francs by her friend Tony. In essence though, he would seem to confirm that the Paquets only ever held a few modest possessions from the Madeleine auction.

That Paquet was acting for a rich sponsor seems undeniable, but who: Wallace, the Perrégaux–Raguses, or someone else altogether? Whoever it was, Paquet was obviously prompted by someone who wished to remain anonymous while hoping that others would be reluctant to bid against the dead woman's brother-in-law and family representative. The clock and chandelier had been the most stunning pieces in her salon and were the kind of ornament that would attract the attention of a collector.[11] Since Wallace was present but did not bid, he is an obvious candidate. It is impossible to tell from the exhibits in the Wallace Collection in London today whether or not any of Marie Duplessis's pieces feature among them. In any case, it does not by any means contain everything that was ever bought by him or his family. If the items were not acquired for a collector, then it can only have been for a stately home or the kind of grand Parisian apartment owned by the likes of the Seymours, who were related to Wallace, or the Raguses. Marie Duplessis's Pleyel piano on the other hand, once graced by Liszt's magical touch, was bought for 775 francs by one M. Cadot, none other than the publisher of the first 1848 edition of *La Dame aux Camélias*.[12]

Others who attended but who did not leave a trace in the *procès-verbal* of the sale, even though they apparently bid, included Eugène Sue. He must have been gratified to discover that she owned several of his novels. Perhaps this was why he apparently bought the prayer book of the young courtesan, a bid that caused rather a stir, according to Dickens in a letter written in French to his friend d'Orsay.[13] Dickens seems to have turned up as observer here just as he had done at her funeral on 5 February.[14] The predatory anarchy of the auction in the temple of sin would have appealed to him, as he observed this lost life being dissected in public by people fascinated with its more sordid aspects. He hovered at the edges of the auction. Most people in the apartment knew that he was the legendary English novelist, but they did not therefore, in the words of a contemporary, appreciate his cold, disdainful smile as he watched all that fuss and carry-on in the home of a prostitute.[15]

Marie Duplessis's good friend Tony also put in an appearance. He bought several of her pictures and paid the princely sum of 1,800 francs for her horse, while the Comte de Saint-Geniès, who several years earlier had over-lapped with her in Baden-Baden, purchased her pony and hunting dog. The overall value of the auction added up to 89,017 francs, of which some 20,000 francs were disbursed to her debtors, not all of whom, it turned out, were genuine claimants.[16] This left the Paquets rich beyond their dreams even after the auctioneers and everyone else had duly been paid. When they first arrived in Paris on 17 February 1847, they were chaperoned by their countryman Vienne, whom they trusted and whom they keenly retained as their execu-tor. But in the week between their first visit to Montmartre and the start of the auction Delphine and Vienne fell out. Why is not known, although he was quick to blame her headstrong temperament and approaches made to her by other interested parties. Someone, he claimed, was also poisoning her mind against him. Although he does not say so, he meant Clotilde, because he suspected her of hiding some of Marie Duplessis's most valuable personal belongings in a nearby apartment. If Clotilde was indeed the same woman who ten years earlier had worked in the Gacé umbrella factory with Marie Duplessis, she too was most probably from the Orne region of Normandy and might have used this connection as a way of ingratiating herself with the Paquets to dupe them. The fact though that the Paquets were not only bidding for themselves but also for a rich client proves that Clotilde was not alone in trying to do deals with them. In the years that followed Vienne and the Paquets made their peace, and forty years after the auction he visited them in Normandy to alert them to the fact that he was publishing a book about Marie Duplessis.[17]

19

La Dame aux Camélias, by Alexandre Dumas *fils*

1848

Shortly after these events Dumas *fils* wrote the elegy 'M.D.', as a tribute to her and a comfort to himself. Then, in May that year, Dumas and a friend were visiting the elder Dumas in his folly of Monte-Cristo, the miniature château built by him between Saint-Germain-en-Laye and Marly-le-Roi and christened after his celebrated romantic revenge yarn *Le Comte de Monte Cristo*. Here Dumas would hold court and relax after the rigours of staging plays in Saint-Germain. On this occasion his son and a friend stayed late; too late, it turned out, to catch the last train that night from Saint-Germain back to Gare Saint-Lazare in Paris. So they decided to stay overnight and return to Paris the following morning. They took rooms in an inn by the name of Auberge du Cheval Blanc, the only hotel still open in the Grande-Rue at that late hour. It stands today at number 59 in the renamed rue Pologne (Figure 19.1).

The following morning the two young men woke to a glorious May day. It was perfect weather for a canter through the extensive woodlands of Saint-Germain, which is why they strolled to Ravelet's stables on the Grande Terrasse, a short distance from their lodgings. It was probably as they passed the new railway station outside the Château Vieux that Dumas's companion suggested that he double back to Paris to collect fresh garments so that they could stay on and play in Saint-Germain for a few more days to make the most of the weather. While his friend travelled back to the city, Dumas ventured on to the Grande Terrasse. Later he recalled what happened next: 'No sooner was he gone, no sooner did I find myself alone on that terrace where I had so often walked with Marie Duplessis, than I started to think of her

Figure 19.1 The former Auberge du Cheval Blanc in which Dumas *fils* wrote the memoir novel that made Marie Duplessis famous.

and that the idea formed in my mind of writing her story, or rather a story about her.' His very wording, from nearly forty years later, reveals the doubt in his own mind about whether the story told in his *roman* would be true or fictionalized.

It seems that he did not do much riding at Ravelet's that day in May 1847. On his way back to the Cheval Blanc he purchased writing implements and paper and started *La Dame aux Camélias* as soon as he was in his room. When his friend returned that evening, Dumas was in full flow and determined to stay put in Saint-Germain until the book was finished. What better place in which to write, because of the still tangible presence and echo of Marie Duplessis in that very spot, and because the Bougival scenes in the novel took place a few miles away from Saint-Germain, in a bend on the Seine in full view of the Grande Terrasse. Dumas's friend agreed to keep him company and act as amanuensis, to copy out the novel in a clear hand ready to submit to a publisher; on condition that Dumas would let him have his autograph version as a gift, which he did. Unfortunately this precious manuscript does not survive: it was chucked overboard as ballast a few years later when his friend was caught in a storm off the Cape of Good Hope while sailing to India.

La Dame aux Camélias was written over a period of three to four weeks, 'on the edge of a table' in a room in the Cheval Blanc.[1] When it was finished, Dumas took it to the publisher Alexandre Cadot, whose interest in Marie Duplessis and her circle, including Liszt, was such that he had purchased her piano at the auction. Cadot rushed out publication of the novel, in two volumes, that same year. Of the various versions of the story, this little known first edition is the most revealing and important one, because of its sheer wealth of detail about her apartment and by being the least inhibited about its controversial subject matter. The fledgling novelist set out to capture Marie Duplessis's character as authentically as possible. In the novel he explicitly invites those who knew his heroine to bear witness to the truth of the book: 'I thus urge my reader to believe in the truth of this story, in which I have only changed the names of the participants, because they are all, with the exception of the heroine, still alive. Indeed, there are people in Paris who witnessed the facts presented here and who could confirm them if my testimony were deemed to be inadequate.'[2]

Much of it is demonstrably 'documentary', including the bare bones of the plot, which echoes the heroine's life. Her old protector, the count, plays a part and so does her rural escape to Bougival, which is evoked with infectious lyricism. Dumas's account of her apartment, her tubercular coughing fits, the raw sexuality of the world she shares with Prudence Duvernoy, the material cynicism of her environment, are all authentic and make shocking reading. It was one thing to inhabit and share this world discreetly, quite another to broadcast it to the world by flaunting it openly in writing. Even today the frankness about sex of *La Dame aux Camélias*, the calibrations of *vous* and *tu* before and after intercourse, are startling. Little wonder that the book required all the prestige of the Dumas name to get past the censor.

By calling his hero 'Armand Duval', Alexandre Dumas would seem to insist that the two A.D.s are one and the same, that the story of Duval is that of Dumas. At times the real-life character and its fictional alter ego in the novel are indeed indistinguishable, as in the two almost identical versions of the parting letter Dumas and Duval wrote to their real and fictitious lovers Marie and Marguerite. Ironically the fictitious one, which cites the true one mostly verbatim, is probably more faithful to life and more revealing than the

tersely dignified one that Dumas wrote to Marie Duplessis that Saturday
night in August 1845: it is more specific about the author's sexual jealousy
and hurt and even hints at the identity of his rival. In the novel Dumas
locates the apartment at 9 rue d'Antin, a few yards away from the place
where she lived when Dumas first knew her at the time of the encounter
between her and his father at the Comédie-Française in July 1843. While the
apartment is situated in the rue d'Antin, its interior details regarding furnishings and the layout of the rooms closely correspond to the sales catalogue of
11 boulevard de la Madeleine. Dumas could have sited his fictional apartment anywhere in the chic quarters of the city between the present place de
l'Opéra and the place de la Concorde. The fact that he chose a street in
which she had actually lived for sixteen months indicates quite how keen he
was to preserve the link between his narrative and the real events.

   Dumas's boldest move though was to conflate his own relationship with
Marie Duplessis with the life she shared with Édouard de Perrégaux, while
grafting on to his story a father–son dilemma that becomes the cornerstone
in *La traviata*. He did this in spite of the fact that Perrégaux's father died
before his son first became Marie Duplessis's lover while Dumas's father
hardly cared about his son's juvenile 'amours'. Moreover, Perrégaux's sister
Adèle had died at the age of 12 many years earlier, while his elder brother (by
one year) Alexandre de Perrégaux was a career diplomat. At the time of
Perrégaux's involvement with Marie Duplessis there was therefore no sister,
let alone the 'pudica vergina' of the opera whose future marriage prospects
form the altar on which Violetta's happiness must be sacrificed; nor was
there a father. Rather, the monitory father figure of the novel stands for
various members of the Perrégaux clan, including their lawyer and
Perrégaux's aunt, the Duchesse de Raguse.

   The bulk of the romance attributed to Armand Duval and Marguerite,
and particularly the Bougival interlude and the eloping to London, happened to Perrégaux and Marie Duplessis. Dumas discovered the most intimate details of his rival's love life from the man himself in a manner described
at the start of the novel. He goes out of his way to reassure the reader that
almost every detail in the book is true to life; he even goes so far as to claim
that his characters' real-life models would happily vouch for the documentary authenticity of the story. He was too young a novelist in 1847, he
asserted, to be inventing fiction while conceding at the same time that he
attributed to his heroine—for that is what she is in the novel—some 'aven-
tures' that did not really happen.

While much of the fascination with the novel's encoded names has inevitably revolved around the A.D. of Dumas/Duval, it is also worth pausing over the name of the heroine. After all she does not have a name whose initials cross the divide between life and fiction. That Dumas wanted to give the lady of the camellias a flower girl's name is perfectly understandable: the 'm' of 'marguerite' (daisy) has the same initial as the heroine's real life counterpart and 'Marguerite' happens to be a French name too. Quite how felicitious the choice of name turned out to be will become clear in due course when it emerges that the very first prompt for *La traviata* may have come from the name 'Marguerite' above all else.

No-one seems to have commented on the surname Dumas gave to his heroine. Clearly he considered this carefully and in the end came up with 'Gautier'. The only literary Gautier in Paris in the 1840s was Théophile Gautier. The most likely reason why Dumas chose the Gautier name for his demi-mondaine is because he had read his friend Gautier's striking obituary of Marie Duplessis; we know he had, because he says so. It is quoted at the beginning of this book and called for her to be immortalized. Because of his impassioned plea for Marie Duplessis to find a champion to save her from oblivion, Vienne had sought out Gautier within days of her death and asked *him* to write her story. But Gautier had not felt able to help.

Dumas was doing it instead now. Perhaps Gautier's clarion call flooded back into his mind as he pensively strolled down the Grande Terrasse at Saint-Germain-en-Laye that May day in 1847. Moreover a simile from Gautier's piece also seems to have lodged in the echo-chamber of Dumas's memory: Gautier had compared Marie Duplessis's skin to the texture of camellias, an image evidently inspired by her love of that flower. Gautier's 1847 obituary in *La Presse* was the first time ever that Marie Duplessis was compared to camellias prior to Dumas's novel. Marguerite's surname and perhaps the very title of the book constitute a huge tribute to Gautier who would repay the favour handsomely when he reviewed Dumas's play at the Vaudeville.

La Dame aux Camélias was published in July 1848 and rocked Paris. It did so for three reasons: it was exceptionally frank about illicit upper-class sexuality in the capital; it was evidently scandal-mongering 'à clef', that is autobiographical; and, lastly, it carried the Dumas name. That it passed the censor is astonishing. It may have done so for much the same reason that the play would eventually pass muster, through patronage in the highest places and the prestige of the elder Dumas, who was the literary Lord of Misrule of Paris. Only a handful of intimates of Dumas and Perrégaux, including the Raguses, would have known that the young author had drawn primarily on the count's life with Marie Duplessis rather than his own much more modest affair with her. The Bougival scenes are so obviously lifted from Perrégaux's life that the count might well have sued—people did almost as readily then as now—if he had felt that the book betrayed his confidence, and indeed his privacy. The fact that he did not suggests that he took the novel in his stride, perhaps sensing that it set a monument to his late wife even more lasting than the new grave that he had secured for her 'in perpetuity'.

And Dumas knew where to draw the line. Hence his withholding the most significant clue about the true identity of the novel's A.D., the marriage in Kensington. While London is mentioned in the novel, the marriage is not and the lady of the camellias does not die as a countess, as she did in real life. Her claim to nobility, advertised if not flaunted on her carriage after February 1846, was inevitably known to a number of people who were otherwise ignorant about the details of her relationship to Perrégaux. To have introduced the marriage into the novel would have given the game away as that event was an incontrovertible fact. If death certificates from Montreux could be requested by far-flung villages in the Orne, so could marriage licences from the British capital; more easily so. On balance the evidence would seem to suggest that Perrégaux gave Dumas virtual carte blanche with regard to all the details he had told him about his long affair with Marie Duplessis.

There is a further glaring omission from the novel, her baby son. That Dumas knew about the child is clear from interviews with his wife who was emphatic on this issue. By omitting this crucial detail, Dumas ensured that the imaginative focus of his narrative would rest resolutely on the young woman and A.D. A baby would have opened up a Pandora's box about motherhood and related issues that would inevitably have detracted from the novel's drive and its interest in the secret world of Parisian underground sex.

A singularly perceptive account of Dumas's novel occurs in an extraordinary memoir about the Paris of Balzac, Lamartine, Sue, and Dumas *père et fils*. It is a two-volume, largely eyewitness, documentary that starts in 1835 and arches forwards all the way to the end of the Commune in 1871. It touches at length on both Marie Duplessis and *La Dame aux Camélias*. Its testimony is of huge importance, which is why it is essential to establish its authenticity and credibility, given the wilful mystification to which this memoir has been subjected. Its anodyne title is *An Englishman in Paris*. It was published in 1892 and translated into French almost immediately afterwards. Its author enjoyed unparalleled access to the writers, artists, and politicians who shaped the nineteenth-century French metropolis. But ever since 1892 his identity has been shrouded in mystery and mystification. Assertions and counter-assertions abound, with the result that the acknowledged 'editor' of the volume, the journalist Albert Dresden Vandam (1843–1903), was credited in his obituary in the *Times* with being the author. If this were true, the memoir would be an elaborate hoax, a free-wheeling collage of anecdotes from the period, with none of the materials from the 1830s to the 1850s grounded in experience. The detailed account of the Siege of Paris and the Commune, indubitably one of the glories of the narrative, would be a fantasy, fabricated with the sole intention to implicate one man only, Sir Richard Wallace, and all that to throw the reader off the scent of the 'real' author, an anonymous writer furtively pretending to be Wallace.[3]

Nothing could be further from the truth than this master plan of a hugely elaborate charade. Rather, the overwhelming burden of internal evidence from the memoir points to its author indeed being the founder of the Wallace Collection in Hertford House, Manchester Square. It is one of the greatest collections of art and armour in the world and includes works by Canaletto, Delacroix, Fragonard, Gainsborough, Hals, Lawrence, Vernet, Rembrandt, Rubens, Titian, and many others. The Wallace Collection is as integral a part of the artistic landscape of the British metropolis as the Courtauld Gallery, Victoria and Albert Museum, and the two Tates. Historically even the National Gallery repeatedly benefited from Wallace's munificence. The Collection has been in London since 1875 when Wallace moved much of his art out of Paris. He was keen to safeguard the bulk of his invaluable works from the sort of horrors inflicted on some of the French capital's galleries and museums during the Siege of Paris and the Commune a few years earlier, both of which he witnessed at first hand. The scale of Wallace's philanthropy and his selfless commitment to the poor of Paris throughout the bitter four months of siege, from September 1870 to the end of January 1871, are stunning and well documented. He became the city's guardian angel, a Florence Nightingale with money, and was recognized as such by the people on the ground and by the powers-that-be at the time.

When *An Englishman in Paris* first appeared from Chapman and Hall in 1892, the French intelligentsia and their peers in Britain were adamant that

Wallace, who had died two years earlier, was the author. Shortly afterwards the same people retracted their opinion in a snide and singularly lazy piece in the *Figaro* of 31 August 1892, an article which plagiarized a cogent, but misguided, essay on the memoir published in the *Athenaeum* in London shortly before. Wallace himself had guessed that by withholding his name he would inevitably weaken the credibility of his memoir. Writing in the memoir about his role during the Siege of Paris, he comments on his anonymity:

> For private reasons, which I cannot and must not mention, I have decided not to put my name to these jottings, whether they are published before or after my death. I am aware that by doing this I diminish their value; because, although I never played a political or even a social part in France, I am sufficiently well known to inspire the reader with confidence. As it is, he must take it for granted that I was probably the only foreigner whom Frenchmen had agreed not to consider an enemy in disguise.[4]

The narrative voice of *An Englishman in Paris* seduces by its tolerance and understanding. It is a classic that deserves to be ranked alongside Edward Trelawny's evocative account of Byron and Shelley in Pisa while being probably a good deal more reliable. Until the memoir appeared, no-one knew what a resonant writer Wallace was, or quite how accurate, if not finicky, his record keeping had been all along. This most gregarious and charitable of men was also, it seems, in other respects one of the most private of people. He must repeatedly have had recourse to notes taken or copies made of documents, when he lists and itemizes dinner menus with prices or when he recalls specific events in a manner that testifies both to a photographic memory and a hoard of papers. Indeed, some of his Siege of Paris pages are written as a diary in the present tense. Perhaps that is what one might expect from an assiduous art collector who built up one of the greatest private art collections ever assembled.

Had it not been for the mischievous *Athenaeum* piece, Richard Wallace's hand in *An Englishman in Paris* would never have been doubted. The *Athenaeum* essay argues, with a certain perverse panache, that every one of the many clues pointing to Wallace in the long memoir constitutes a sophisticated trap intended to fox readers by making them think Wallace was the author. But the *Athenaeum* contributor's reasoning is not only intrinsically implausible, it is demonstrably wrong in places. Thus, while he is clearly up to date on some parts of the memoir, he is not really familiar enough with its detail, or indeed with the wider history of Wallace's collection. He seems unaware of its temporary removal to the East End of

London while Hertford House was made ready, and thus misses the discreet allusions to this.

If the memoir were not by Wallace, then it would be by someone who studs his very long narrative with details and references that could only ever connect to Wallace. To the *Athenaeum* reviewer, some of the more obvious clues about Wallace's identity, such as his age and his unexpected election to the Jockey-Club, constitute self-evidently clumsy attempts to mislead the reader, but presumably only those readers who happened to know when Wallace was born and who knew about his membership of the Jockey-Club? The clincher for the *Athenaeum* is Wallace's alleged solecisms as in his use of 'the particle before the surname of people when neither Christian name nor title is expressed', as in 'de Morny', 'de Persigny,' and, more amazing still, in plural form as 'the de Caulaincourts', and worst of all, the repeated misspelling of Dijon as 'Dyon', a gaffe according to the reviewer that proves that this could not be an authentic document.[5] He is exercised further by the inclusion in the two volumes of stories that had been published earlier, as for example the Balzac anecdote about suing the *Almanach* (1.44–5). But these are always reported and never passed off as the author's own experiences. Rather, his long footnote on Marie Duplessis's early life in Normandy shows quite how scrupulous he was about his sources and also the extent to which he was guided by an urge to inform and share:

> The following is virtually a summary of an article by Count G. de Contades, in a French bibliographical periodical, *Le Livre* (Dec. 10, 1885), and shows how near Alexandre Dumas was to the truth. I have given it at great length. My excuse for so doing is the extraordinary popularity of Dumas's play with all classes of playgoers. As a consequence, there is not a single modern play, with the exception of those of Shakespeare, the genesis of which has been so much commented upon. It is no exaggeration to say that most educated playgoers, not to mention professional students of the drama, have at some time or other expressed a wish to know something more of the real Marguerite Gautier's parentage and antecedents than is shown by Dumas, either in his play or in his novel, or than what they could gather from the partly apocryphal details given by her contemporaries.

As for the charge by the anonymous author of the *Athenaeum* piece that none of Wallace's friends remembered him meeting Balzac, Musset, or Sue, it is instead hard to see how he could possibly avoid them. After all, his two Paris addresses were 1 rue Taitbout (1837), above the Café de Paris and next door to the block Tortoni-Maison Dorée, and 2 rue Laffitte (1842), on the other side of the Maison Dorée. Balzac, Musset and

Sue were regulars in these cafés and restaurants. Wallace could hardly not run into them, and the rest of *le chic Paris* for that matter, simply by stepping out of either of his two residences.

The notion of an elaborate conspiracy to foist upon Wallace a memoir that he never wrote is as implausible as the idea that Shakespeare's plays were farmed off on a yokel from Stratford-upon-Avon because serious and important aristocrats, the real authors, could not be seen to be indulging in the writing of plays. As with the case of Shakespeare, so here too the clues in the memoir point almost irrefutably to Wallace. There are several more trails that the author of the *Athenaeum* piece overlooked, although he would have dismissed them as further red herrings. Actually, Wallace might as well have signed his name on the flyleaf for all the hints he drops. If there is a mystery about the memoir, it is why Wallace littered it with oblique references to himself while not ultimately putting his name to it. The accuracy and attention to detail to the point almost of pedantry, as when he reproduces the menus that were on offer in Paris's most exclusive restaurants before and during the Siege, all point to a hoarder's and secret diarist's mindset.

The most obvious clues about Wallace involve specific details of age, the Jockey-Club, the Commune, his intimate lifelong involvement with painting, from the 1830s right through the ensuing decades, and striking links between works of art discussed at length in the memoir and the presence of some of the self-same masterpieces and painters in the Wallace Collection to this day. The anonymous author twice offers up his age in the memoir, when he claims that he was 27 at the time of the Dujarrier duel (1.143), and again when he asserts that he was six years older than Marie Duplessis (1.161), both of which agree on 1818 as the year of his birth, the year Richard Wallace was born. His membership of the Jockey-Club, conferred on him in the depths of winter during the darkest days of the siege of the city, would seem to provide incontrovertible proof of Wallace's identity. According to the author's laconic note, 'In January [1871] I was elected a member of the Jockey-Club, but I had dined there once before by special invitation' (2.325). Perhaps he had done so at the invitation of his half-cousin and neighbour off the boulevard des Italiens, Lord Seymour, founder of the Jockey-Club and its first president? Sure enough, the 1871 membership records of the Jockey-Club note that on 14 January 1871 Sir Richard Wallace was elected 'spontaneously' a member of the Jockey-Club and that the same Wallace was shortly after honoured also by the directors of the 'Musée de Paris'.

That such independent, corroborative evidence should be credited, as it presumably must if common sense prevails, constitutes in the eyes of the *Figaro* (13 September 1892) proof of the unsurpassed naivety of the British public. Surely, its writer expostulates, the reference to the Jockey-Club is an all too transparent ruse, a sleight-of-hand to make us think of Wallace! In the Kafkaesque world of the *Athenaeum* and its French understudy, the *Figaro*, proof positive at once translates into its opposite. Theirs is a paranoid world of cunning ploys and delusions in which nothing is what it seems. They singularly fail to engage with the memoir's detailed account of the Siege of Paris, the harsh prelude to the blood-soaked Commune that succeeded it.

The Siege of Paris lasted from September 1870 to the end of January 1871, with the latter stages coinciding with a bitterly cold winter. Wallace could easily have slipped out of the city and across the Channel to the safety of England. Instead he chose to stay, suffer with the Parisians, and use his vast fortune to help wherever he could. He participated in the attempted 'airbridge' to provision Paris through the use of balloons; one of the balloons that flew out of the city, 'Ballon No. 66', was the 'Richard-Wallace'. But it was his English ambulance which turned him into the city's single most effective benefactor at this time of extreme crisis. In his own understated words, 'I was during the siege overburdened with business, on the nature of which I need not dwell here', while the *Journal des Débats* of 18 January 1871 refers to 'the inexhaustible generosity' of Richard Wallace for creating the *ambulance anglaise*, staffed by English surgeons to look after the wounded of the Siege at 16 rue d'Aguesseau, in a magnificent property that still stands and which was probably owned by Wallace.[6] In addition to his ambulance service he offered the enormous sum of 100,000 francs towards the relief of the poor, who had suffered from the shelling of the city. He referred to them as his 'pensioners'. He was the most charitable millionaire in the capital, truly a man for all seasons whose fortune had been made in the art world. His love of art and his taste as connoisseur were unmatched, as was his popularity, it seems, with artists.

Fittingly it was art that probably saved him when he stumbled into the thick of an angry mob that was both hungry and loathed the thought of outsiders or foreigners. He was on his way to visit a sick English groom when he aroused the suspicion of a curmudgeonly concierge. He was marched off to a nearby military post where he was exonerated the moment he produced his identity card. The officer in charge told him:

> 'I know your name very well.... I have seen your portrait at my relatives' establishment'—he named a celebrated picture-dealer in the Rue de la Paix— 'and I ought to have recognized you at once, for it is a very striking likeness, but it is so dark here.' Then he turned to his men and the crowd: 'I will answer for this gentleman. I wish we had a thousand or so of foreign spies like him in Paris. France has no better friend than he.'[7]

The thread that more than anything else holds together the memoir is a lifelong love of art. In his early years in Paris Wallace was friends with a louche group of artists and writers based in 1830s Saint-Germain-des-Près, known as the Childebertians. Almost everything we know about the 'Childebertians' comes from this memoir. They were a raucous, anarchic colony of painters and bohemians who, in the 1830s, lived in an infamous, pre-Haussmann slum tenement known as 'La Childebert' in Saint-Germain-des-Près. Wallace was in his twenties when he consorted with them. With his keen eye for art he instantly spotted the talent of a number of them, and with a memory honed by countless bids at auction he years later recalled the impressive prices fetched the various Childebert artists (I.11). His account of the 'nose' cartoon, one particular Childebertian's master work, the talk of 1830s Paris for weeks on end, plunges us right into the social and artistic heart of the Paris of the time. So does his reporting of the deliberate flooding of La Childebert by a frustrated tenant who finally rebelled against the female Scrooge who owned the building and refused to protect it with a proper roof (I.17–18). The water-carriers of Paris played a key role in the rebellion of La Childebert as, until the late 1830s, water in Paris was provided by special carriers who assured a constant water supply to the city's houses and tenements with their carts, a detail that Wallace stresses, mindful perhaps of the fact that one of his most enduring contributions to the city's long-term hygiene and welfare would, many year later, be the Wallace water 'colonnes' that at last dispensed clean water to the capital's citizens and still do so today.

Wallace's closest friend among painters in Paris was Delacroix, many of whose works now grace the walls of the Wallace Collection. The eighth chapter of *An Englishman in Paris*, on Delacroix, Vernet, and Alexandre-Gabriel Decamps, is nothing short of a fascinating preview of the Wallace Collection. He was as close to Delacroix as he was to Dumas *père*: 'I knew Eugène Delacroix better than any of the others in the marvellous constellation of painters of the period, and our friendship lasted until the day of his death, in December 1863,' Wallace writes.[8] He prides himself on the fact that he was one of the few friends whose presence Delacroix 'tolerated whilst at work'. He notes that those paintings that were rejected by the public became Delacroix's favourites 'with which he would not part, subsequently, at any price, as in the case of his *Marino Faliero*', a point made too by others who knew Delacroix.[9]

Today *Marino Faliero* hangs proudly in the Wallace Collection, one of its most cherished treasures. It was acquired by Lord Hertford, the father of Richard Wallace in 1868 and between 1872 and 1875 Richard Wallace allowed it to be exhibited in the Bethnal Green Museum, the temporary home of the Wallace collection while Hertford House was being refurbished as a major art gallery. The Wallace Collection also features a number of paintings by Decamps, who was another friend of the author and features alongside Delacroix and Horace Vernet, several of whose paintings similarly belong to the Wallace Collection. Referring to the entry on horseback into Paris of one of the fire-brand leaders of the Commune, the author of the memoir remarks that 'The whole reminded me irresistibly of Decamps's picture *La Patrouille Turque*', a picture which happens to be one of no fewer than twenty-eight Decamps in the Wallace Collection.[10] Elsewhere the memoir refers to Ary Scheffer's portrait of Béranger when, again, the Wallace Collection holds six Scheffers.[11]

The Commune and its pitiless crushing took an appalling toll on Paris's population and destroyed emblematic civic buildings such as the Hôtel de Ville, which contained most of the *état civil* records for Paris. Wallace inevitably felt that the heart of his collection would be safer in London and therefore proceeded to move the bulk of it across the Channel. While the grand mansion in Manchester Square was prepared, the Collection was exhibited at the Bethnal Green Museum. *The Times* of 22 June 1872 features a brilliant survey of the art on offer. In a passage not picked up by the memoirist's detractors in the *Athenaeum* or *Figaro*, Wallace notes almost casually that in 1883 (he means 1873) 'I had occasion... to go frequently, and for several weeks running, to one of the poorest quarters of London. I often made the journey on foot, for I am ashamed to say that, until then, the East End of London was far more unknown to me than many an obscure town in France, Italy, Germany and Spain' (Wallace went to the East End to oversee the installing of his Collection in its temporary home in Bethnal Green) (2.286).

The tone and style of Wallace's *An Englishman in Paris* bring the streets and small change of Paris to life with the zest of Dickens, the unsentimentality of

Thackeray, and the moral fibre of George Eliot. He brings to his task a photographic memory, underpinned by detailed notes that he made at the time
and a readiness to use published accounts of the period such as Claudin's,
when it suited him to do so.[12] Wallace's temperament was eclectic, his mind
that of an avid note-taker, a collector exercised by minutiae. Few of his
cameos are more entertaining than his account of Balzac's nocturnal strolls
along the boulevards warding off arrest by the police with an almanach
giving the correct time of sunrise for each day.[13] The point was that Balzac
was 'réfractaire' regarding his military service, an arrestable offence, but the
law only allowed arrests during daylight hours. Wallace here follows
Claudin's memoir while adding to it the story of one Ouvrard, who did just
what Balzac did but who was caught out. He subsequently sued the *almanach*
for misleading him about the time of sunrise and won.

Wallace's best friend in Paris was the elder Dumas. Above all other men,
Dumas *père* was the one that Wallace liked best for his madcap generosity, his
freewheeling spirit, and irresistible *joie de vivre*. Dumas, as portrayed by
Wallace, was Falstaff without the malice and low cunning, a bear of a man,
a brilliant amateur chef, a great and hopelessly promiscuous lover of women,
wine, and food, with never a thought or anxiety about anyone's motives.
This was why he never had any money while rarely wanting for anything
either.

Wallace knew both Dumas and also Marie Duplessis. His evocation of
her and the younger Dumas's *La Dame aux Camélias* was written many years
after her death, though Dumas *fils* survived the publication of the memoir
by three years. It constitutes a further tribute to Marie Duplessis's essentially
sweet nature, without being overly sentimental about her. Wallace acknowledges that she chose a life of louche glamour and wealth over honest,
poorly paid work, pearls and 'priceless jewels' over 'a cambric cap and a
calico gown'.

He is making a point that Marie Duplessis had herself made to her friend
Judith, and one that George Bernard Shaw would pursue in his play *Mrs
Warren's Profession*, published the year after the Wallace memoir and immediately banned by the censor, just like the play *La Dame aux Camélias*. Trying
to justify her past and her choice of the oldest profession in the world—Mrs
Warren runs a chain of brothels, which brought her a fortune and allowed
her to send her daughter 'Vivie' to Cambridge—Mrs Warren compares her
long and prosperous life to that of one of her more respectable half-sisters.
One of them 'worked in a white-lead factory, twelve hours a day for nine

shillings a week, until she died of lead poisoning', while the other married a labourer 'and kept his room and the three children neat and tidy on eighteen shillings a week, until he took to drink. That was worth being respectable for, wasn't it?' she asks Vivie, a rhetorical question to justify a life in lucrative, high-class prostitution, after earlier slaving away as a waitress in Waterloo Station for meagre rewards.

The two Plessis sisters inevitably come to mind: on the one hand Delphine, marooned in the girls' rural backyard of Normandy, married to a farmhand, and unforgivably called an 'ugly duckling' by a Parisian in her hearing as she appeared in her sister's home after her death; on the other hand the brilliant cosmopolitan Marie Duplessis, pampered, beautiful, and adored by the leading lights of the capital. Marie was well aware of the choice she had made, and was candid about the contrast between her life and one of honest work and relative indigence when talking to Judith.

All Wallace's virtues as narrator are in evidence in his account of the Marie Duplessis he knew: his magnanimity, his analytical intelligence, and a style that rarely fails to produce the *mot juste*. His intimacy with Dumas *père* is particularly important here because it complements and consolidates other accounts of the father's pride in his son's success with *La Dame aux Camélias*. Wallace's acquaintance with Marie Duplessis and his friendship with Dumas equipped him uniquely to comment on the young woman and on how she was perceived by the inner circle of the family who first turned her life into a legend. The recollection of the lady of the camellias by this exceptional eyewitness is given here in full:

I frequently met her [Marie Duplessis] in the society of some of my friends between '43 and '47, the year of her death . . . The world at large, and especially the English . . . have taxed him [Dumas *fils*] with having chosen an unworthy subject, and, by idealizing it, taught a lesson of vice instead of virtue; they have taken it for granted that Alphonsine Plessis was no better than her kind. She was much better than that, though probably not sufficiently good to take a house-maid's place . . . to see her marvellously beautiful face, her matchless graceful figure set off by a cambric cap and a calico gown, instead of having the first enhanced by the gleam of priceless jewels in her hair and the second wrapped in soft laces and velvets and satins; but, for all that, she was not the common courtesan . . . [who] would have descended to her grave forgotten, but for the misplaced enthusiasm of a poetical young man, who was himself corrupted by the atmosphere in which he was born and lived afterwards.

The sober fact is that Dumas *fils* did not idealize anything at all, and, least of all, Alphonsine Plessis's character. Though very young at the time of her death, he was then already much more of a philosopher than a poet. He had not seen half as much of Alphonsine Duplessis [*sic*] during her life as is commonly supposed, and the first idea of the novel was probably suggested to him, not by his acquaintance with her, but by the sensation her death caused among the Paris public, the female part of which, almost without distinction,[14] went to look at her apartment, to appraise her jewels and dresses, etc. 'They would probably like to have had them on the same terms,' said a terrible cynic.' The remark must have struck young Dumas, in whose hearing it was said, or who, at any rate, had it reported to him; for if we carefully look at *all* his earlier plays, we find the spirit of that remark largely pervading them.

Alphonsine Plessis had probably learned even less in her girlhood than Lola Montez, but she had a natural tact, and an instinctive refinement which no education could have enhanced. She never made grammatical mistakes, no coarse expression ever passed her lips. Lola Montez could not make friends; Alphonsine Plessis could not make enemies. She never became riotous like the other, not even boisterous; for amidst the most animated scenes she was haunted by the sure knowledge that she would die young, and life, but for that knowledge, would have been very sweet to her. Amidst these scenes, she would often sit and chat to me: she liked me, because I never paid her many compliments, although I was but six years older [Richard Wallace was born on 21 June 1818] than the most courted woman of her time. The story of her being provided for by a foreign nobleman because she was so like his deceased daughter, was not a piece of fiction on Dumas's part; it was a positive fact. Alphonsine Plessis, after this provision was made for her, might have led the most retired existence; she might, like so many demi-mondaines have done since, bought herself a country-house, re-entered 'the paths of respectability,' have had a pew in the parish church, been in constant communication with the vicar, prolonged her life by several years, and died in the odour of sanctity: but, notwithstanding her desperate desire to live, her very nature revolted at such self-exile.

When Alexandre Dumas read the 'Dame aux Camélias' to his father, the latter wept like a baby, but his tears did not drown the critical faculty. 'At the beginning of the third act,' he said afterwards, 'I was wondering how Alexandre would get his Marguerite back to town without lowering her in the estimation of the spectator. Because, if such a woman as he depicted was to remain true to nature, to her nature, and consequently able to stand the test of psychological analysis, she could not have borne more than two or three months of such retirement.... Honestly speaking, it wanted my son's cleverness to make a piece out of Alphonsine Plessis's life. True, he was fortunate in that she died, which left him free to ascribe that death to any cause but the right one, namely, consumption.... Still, my son has been true to Nature; but he has taken an episode showing her at her best. He was not bound to let the public know that the frequent recurrence of these love episodes, but always with a different partner, constitutes a disease...for which it is impossible to find a cure. Messalina, Catherine II, and thousands of women have suffered from it. When they happen to be born in such exalted stations as these two, they buy men; when they happen to be born in a lowly station and are attractive, they sell themselves; when they are ugly and repulsive they sink to the lowest depths of degradation, or end in the padded cells of a madhouse, where no man dares come near them. Nine times out of ten the malady is hereditary...'

There were few of us who, during Alphonsine Plessis's lifetime, were so interested in her as to have gone to the length of such a psychological analysis of her pedigree. Nevertheless, most men were agreed that she was no ordinary girl. Her candour about her early want of education increased the interest. 'Twenty or twenty-five years ago,' said Dr. Véron, one day, after Alphonsine Plessis had left the dinner table, 'a woman of her refinement would not have been phenomenal in her position, because at that period the grisette, promoted to the rank of femme entretenue, had not made her appearance. The expression "femme entretenue" was not even known. Men chose their companions, outside marriage, from a different class; they were generally women of education and often of good family who had made a faux pas, and, as such, forfeited the society and countenance of their equals who had not stumbled in that way, at any rate not in the sight of the world. I confess, Alphonsine Plessis interests me very much. She is, first of all, the best-dressed woman in Paris; secondly, she neither flaunts nor hides her vices; thirdly, she is not always talking or hinting about money; in short, she is a wonderful courtesan.'

The result of all this admiration was very favourable to Alexandre Dumas *fils* when he brought out his book about eighteen months after her death. It was in every one's hands, and the press kept whetting the curiosity of those who had not read it as yet with personal anecdotes about the heroine. In addition to this, the title was a very taking one, and, moreover, absolutely new; for, though it was obvious enough from Alphonsine Plessis's habit of wearing white camellias the greater part of the year, no one had ever thought of applying it to her while she was alive; hence, the credit of its invention belongs decidedly to Dumas *fils*.[15]

With its artful conflation of fact and fiction, Dumas's novel had Paris guessing with a certain frisson at who was who in the story. At times its narrative sounds notes as urgent and intense as the most incandescent love story in the English language, *Wuthering Heights*, which was published the year Marie Duplessis died and which therefore precedes the publication of *La Dame aux Camélias* by barely a year. In Emily Brontë's classic, as in Dumas's novel, the heroine's coffin is also opened, though seventeen years after her death. Talking to Nelly Dean, Heathcliff remarks:

'I'll tell you what I did yesterday! I got the sexton, who was digging Linton's grave, to remove the earth off her coffin lid, and I opened it. I thought, once, I would have stayed there, when I saw her face again. It is hers yet. He had hard work to stir me, but he said it would change, if the air blew on it, and so I struck one side of the coffin loose, and covered it up—not Linton's side, damn him! I wish he'd been soldered in lead—and I bribed the sexton to pull it away, when I'm laid there, and slide mine out too. I'll have it made so, and then, by the time Linton gets to us, he'll not know which is which!'

'You were very wicked, Mr. Heathcliff!' I exclaimed, 'were you not ashamed to disturb the dead?'

'I disturbed nobody, Nelly,' he replied, 'and I gave some ease to myself. I shall be a great deal more comfortable now; and you'll have a better chance of keeping me underground, when I get there. Disturbed her? No! she has disturbed me, night and day, through eighteen years, incessantly, remorselessly, till yesternight; and yesternight, I was tranquil. I dreamt I was sleeping the last sleep by that sleeper, with my heart stopped and my cheek frozen against hers.'

La Dame aux Camélias never quite hits the lyrical stratosphere of *Wuthering Heights*, a novel written moreover by a woman, a shocking fact that was not known to Emily Brontë's original readers. Even so, both works were deemed to be offensive by their contemporaries: the Yorkshire novel for its reckless passions and lack of religion, epitomized in Catherine Earnshaw's symbiosis with an amoral, swarthy, and wild creature from nowhere; *La Dame aux Camélias* because it dared suffuse the sordid world of prostitution with an aura of tenderness. While the Parisian intelligentsia read the younger Dumas's novel, so too, we may be sure, did her former lovers. Some of them must have leafed through the work with trepidation, while being grateful in many ways to Dumas for pretending that this was all about him. The Duc de Guiche Gramont need not worry any more than the father of her baby, Charles de Morny. Although Dumas knew his secret, he had kept it safe, at least as far as the book was concerned.

20

La Dame aux Camélias at
the Vaudeville
February 1852

The novel's runaway success prompted Dumas to broaden the appeal of his story even further by turning it into a play in 1849. He wrote it in a week, with Act 2 completed in a single afternoon, thus replicating the inspired impetus of the novel. Even so the drama was very nearly still-born in spite of initial moving responses to it by his father and Virginie Déjazet, the mother of the very friend who had shared that first night at 11 boulevard de la Madeleine with him. No theatre could be found to produce it and so, at the end of the year, Dumas, despairing of finding a home for his play, put it in a drawer. It was 1 January 1850. In the autobiographical 'Note A' about *La Dame aux Camélias* he remembered:

> The first day of the year always left me melancholy and the custom that makes the living catch up with one another on that day invariably reminded me of those who were no longer there. At that time I did not yet have my own dead; the only person I knew in the cemetery was Marie Duplessis, my heroine, whose grave I imagined to be utterly deserted (she had died in 1847). I therefore set out to pay a kind of superstitious visit to her grave. In fact I was looking for a pretext to cry. I seemed to have no future...I was drifting both as a writer and person. So I set out, as it were to seek guidance from all the dead who know the road ahead and it was with that poor girl, at the bottom of her forgotten and lonely tomb, that I shared my anxieties.

On that rainy January morning, in a spot where many thousands have paused since, Dumas communed with the spirit of the young woman whose life and death had already rendered him famous and who would soon make him rich. It seems that he may not have been back in the

Montmartre cemetery since February 1847. He does not comment on his visits beyond this one.

From Montmartre he returned straight to his apartment at 34 rue Taitbout, pulled the curtains, lit a number of candles and once more settled down with his manuscript. In addition to a number of corrections, he modified the third scene of Act V when, with reference to the presents that arrive, as they always did for Marie Duplessis, Marguerite sighs 'Ah yes, today is the first of January!... So much has happened since last year. A year ago, at this time, we were dining, singing...' Dumas had just finished his redrafting and was in tears when he heard a knock at the door. His friend Henry Mirault, to whom Dumas dedicated several books, was calling and asked Dumas to read the play to him. Dumas obliged and together they wept over the fate of the doomed heroine. In the drama Dumas reshaped his work mostly by toning down its raucous sexuality and by making the story sing, literally. The songs and piano pieces of the novel now became real so that the advertised full title of the play was *La Dame aux Camélias: pièce en cinque actes, mêlée de chant*, as much 'revue' therefore as drama. When the play finally opened, an orchestra performed the music under the baton of the 'chef d'orchestre', Édouard Montaubry. Dumas found him superb and commented that he

> caused the dinner party to sparkle with an energetic dance (*ronde*), original, graceful, and with skill and deep feeling returned, in the last act, at the moment of Marguerite's death, to this gay motif, like a lasting memory of the life of abandon that was expiring.[1]

The 'ronde' of the party corresponds to the celebrated drinking song or brindisi of *La traviata*. It almost certainly inspired it. What renders the play's dance music especially significant is that its 'ronde' is used structurally in the same way as Alfredo's aria 'Di quell'amor' is in *La traviata*, both being repeated as Marguerite/Violetta lies dying.

When the play finally found a director willing to take it on, it was banned for being immoral and shocking even before it hit the boards, in spite of the fact that some of the most powerful men in the country had signed a petition to grant it a licence. Dumas's barbed account of how the play finally came to be staged, after a first refusal, and then a second refusal *after* its initial successful run in 1852, lambasts the philistinism and arbitrary nature of the process. It mattered whom you knew, and the two Dumas and their friends in the theatre, notably M. Bouffé of the Vaudeville (Figure 20.1), 'le gros Bouffé' (to distinguish him from the actor Bouffé), were on intimate

Figure 20.1 A rare photograph of the Vaudeville theatre where *La Dame aux Camélias* premiered in 1852 and where Verdi and his companion Strepponi saw it.

terms with most of the makers and shakers of the city. Among them were two of Marie Duplessis's lovers, Montguyon and Morny. First of all, Bouffé approached

> M. Fernand de Montguyon, M. Fernand de Montguyon was a friend of M. de Morny, M. de Morny was friends with Prince Louis-Napoléon [de Morny's half-brother], and Prince Louis was president of the Republic....M. de Montguyon called on de Morny to explain the theatre's dilemma after which M. de Morny, accompanied by M. de Montguyon, made the time to view one of the rehearsals of the play to see for himself the value of our work before pleading for it to the Prince. He did not find it nearly as offensive as had been alleged.[2]

Morny urged Dumas to secure the support of other literary figures, who obliged. Jules Janin was one of them. Even so they failed. Then, in

December 1851, a new government came to power on the back of a veritable *coup d'état*. One of its two main drivers, a signatory of the 1851 petition for *La Dame aux Camélias*, became the Minister of the Interior and immediately licensed it for performance. He was none other than the Duc de Morny, who would later briefly serve at the helm of the country alongside his half-brother Napoleon III. This is why Dumas dedicated the play to Morny. His tribute is quoted here in parallel English and French versions for reasons that will become clear presently. Choosing his words carefully, he wrote:

A MONSIEUR LE COMTE DE MORNY
Monsieur le Comte,

Voulez-vous accepter la dédicace de cette pièce, dont le succès vous revient de droit? Elle doit d'avoir vu le jour à votre protection, que vous m'avez offerte au mois d'octobre dernier, et qui ne s'est ni arrêteé ni ralenti quand vous avez eu l'occasion et le pouvoir de la montrer. C'est un fait assez rare dans l'histoire des protections pour que je le consigne ici avec l'expression de toute ma reconnaissance.

Agréez, monsieur le comte, l'assurance de ma considération la plus distinguée.
A. Dumas *Fils*

A MONSIEUR LE COMTE DE MORNY
Monsieur le Comte,

Would you be so gracious as to accept the dedication of this piece which owes its success to you? It saw the light of day thanks to your protection, which you offered me in October last year [when de Morny signed the petition for the play] and which has not ceased or weakened when you had the opportunity and the power to exercise it. This is a fairly rare occurrence in the history of protection which is why I note it here with my deepest gratitude.

Please accept, monsieur le comte, the pledge of my highest esteem.
A. Dumas *Fils*

Is there a hint in the wording here that Dumas may be thanking the count for more than just his support in getting his play staged? The sentence 'Elle doit d'avoir vu le jour à votre protection', literally 'She', meaning 'it' (the play) or 'she' (Marie Duplessis) 'owes its/her very existence to you', is ambiguous enough to allude to the real-life story behind it. Whether or not Dumas was communicating here with Morny in code, the duke's intervention launched the story of his former lover and mother of their baby onto the Paris stage. He was called Pygmalion earlier in this book because he took in hand an unformed country girl and moulded her into a model of feminine sexual royalty. Now he had set the points for his 'fair lady' to be immortalized. Théophile Gautier's pitch in 1848 for Marie Duplessis to be reborn in art was coming to fruition sooner than he dared hope. In retrospect signing the licence for *La Dame aux Camélias* to be performed in the theatre would prove to be Morny's single most important act in his life, at least as far as posterity is concerned. By licensing *La Dame aux Camélias* he also unwittingly launched *La traviata*.

Rumour in Paris at the time had it that there was more to Morny's granting that coveted licence to Dumas, that one of the most persuasive voices in support of Dumas's play belonged to the young woman who would be the first ever Marguerite Gautier, Eugénie Doche, probably Morny's mistress at the time just like Marie Duplessis a few years earlier. Doche did not lag far behind Marie Duplessis with regard to lovers, although she was always first and foremost a 'comédienne'. She was primarily affiliated to the Vaudeville in her early years. In the winter of 1851 she was languishing in London, struggling with problems with her voice that threatened to terminate her career. She was feeling very low when her friend Charles Fechter, a French actor born in London, called on her. He wanted her to read a manuscript he had brought with him, in fact a draft of Dumas's play *La Dame aux Camélias*. Paris's leading actresses and theatre managers had turned it down, he informed her: they thought it was too much like *Manon Lescaut* or Henri Murger's recently published *Vie de Bohème*, and they were wary of its alleged immorality. Fechter disagreed and started to read the play to Doche. In the words of one of her chroniclers, 'during the first act Madame Doche was having a riotous time; during the third she wept, and during the last ordered her luggage to be got ready'.[3]

The following day, after hotfooting it back to Paris, she hurried into the Vaudeville theatre. Its actor manager Bouffé told her that, as lady of the camellias, she would be on only every second day. Dumas's drama would alternate with another play starring Virginie Déjazet. The Vaudeville were hoping that she would create a stir by playing 'un nègre amoureux' in a long forgotten transvestite farce called *Ouistiti*, which is slang for marmoset. Bouffé desperately needed a hit to keep his theatre afloat. Bouffé's pessimism about the prospects for *La Dame aux Camélias* was abetted apparently by the younger Dumas's nonchalance about the rehearsals.

The censor's axe fell after the company had started rehearsing but the play was reprieved by a last-minute intervention, apparently, by Madame Doche with Napoleon III himself. Dumas *fils* hastily returned from Brussels where, in disgust at the censor, he had fled to join his father, in time to be present on 2 February. The studio dress rehearsal the night before, in front of an invited audience, had prompted the response that the play was dangerous and cynical, but that Duval *père* was admirable. Fechter, the first ever Armand Duval, and Doche as Marguerite were put out and felt that they had been wrongly overshadowed by the 'pompous pontificator':

> The 2 February, a complete turnabout. The auditorium was packed with an uncertain crowd, boisterous, but vibrant. What a premiere! What a battle! The 'pompous pontificator' returned to his rightful place in the background while the soul of the crowd went out to the lovers. There were floods of tears and a storm of applause. Madame Doche walked as if in a dream, her head exalted, her nerves very tense. She found, as she fell at Armand's feet, an action she had vainly attempted to carry out in the previous two days: she fainted for good as the curtain came down! Trying to catch her, Fechter tore 6,000 francs' worth of lacework. Who cares though? The two of them were transported into the Elysian fields; they experienced that extraordinary triumph of actors who shed their terrestrial persona only to put on an ideal one.[4]

For Doche the immediate aftermath spelled adulation, flowers, and rhapsodic tributes. Thirty-five years later, at the age of 66, she kept a shrine to the 1852 *La Dame aux Camélias*, preserving all the letters and press cuttings referring to it. A poem addressed to her and purporting to be by 'Marie Duplessis' thanked her for her performance:

> Your talent, Doche, gifted me an apotheosis,
> It turns out I lived on in gentle hearts,
> That five years after the tomb closed over me,
> I would once more bewitch Paris.
> I can hear them from the bottom of my re-opened grave,
> Those cadences that my fate inspires in you every night.
> In the beauteous traits of your face mine is shown
> As if in a mirror.[5]

Whoever the author of the poem was, they could hardly have guessed that someone else in the audience of the play, Giuseppe Verdi, had much the same thought, but with a different art form in mind. Marie Duplessis deserved to live on in ways that lay beyond the reach of words, in the most emotionally powerful medium of all, music. Doche would encounter this work in the course of her 69 years. In fact not long before she received a pedigree journalist, Adolphe Brisson (who would write about her in a series of sketches called *Portraits Intimes*), she was visited by a brilliant young singer who was already reaching for the stars. This was the 26-year old Australian soprano Nellie Melba, who at that very moment, in 1887, was preparing to sing Violetta in *La traviata* and had come to seek guidance on the role she had undertaken.

What Doche made of the opera is not recorded, but from her opening remarks to Brisson, when he called on her in her apartment on the Champs-Élysées, it is clear that she knew that the momentum had shifted from the stage to the opera. Before her visitor left, she granted him a tour of the many mementoes of her long career during which she played Marguerite Gautier 617 times. Only Sarah Bernhardt (Figure 20.3) appeared in more performances but, understandably perhaps, Doche was not entirely happy with Bernhardt's interpretations of the role. Taking pride of place in Doche's collection was a framed drawing of her as Marguerite Gautier by the English painter Richard Buckner. It showed her at the play's premiere, 'her head with her hair in plaits like the Virgin, studded with diamonds, was ravishing, and so was her waist. She had vowed never to wear crinoline but instead wore a very generous and wide dress supported by pleats' (Figure 20.2).[6]

Doche had been an inspired casting for Marie Duplessis. Buckner's exquisitely attired Doche, complete with jewellery, may be the closest we will ever get to what Marie Duplessis looked like on one of her nights out. This particular wardrobe may have been taken from life. The two young women not only shared good looks, but they were also both accomplished dancers: Marie Duplessis excelled at waltzing while Doche shone at the polka.[7] The result was one of the most triumphal runs in the history of nineteenth-century French theatre.

For Dumas *fils* the opening night of *La Dame aux Camélias* trumped even the pleasure he took in the novel's success. He telegraphed his father in Brussels with the words 'A triumph, so resounding that I imagined I was present at the première of one of your works' ('Grand succès, si grand que j'ai cru assister à la première représentation d'un de tes ouvrages'), to which Dumas *père* replied proudly 'My best work is you, my child' ('Mon meilleur ouvrage, c'est toi, mon enfant').[8] In his 1867 preface the younger Dumas recalled that Doche 'so perfectly incarnated the role that her name is forever inseparable from the title of the piece... just by seeing the actress enter the stage, the audience was ready to forgive the heroine everything'. Over four pages he thanked the cast individually as well as Bouffé, the director of the theatre, and the musicians and conductor. Far from being blasé about the play's fate, as some had surmised, he was clearly deeply affected by its triumph.

Figure 20.2 Eugénie Doche as Marguerite Gautier in *La Dame aux Camélias*, a role that made her famous, by Richard Buckner.

So too was the man who had first suggested that Marie Duplessis should be commemorated. In *La Presse* of 9 February 1852, Théophile Gautier reprinted most of his obituary of Marie Duplessis of four years earlier. At the time he had deplored the fact that no great figurative artist was to hand to immortalize the young courtesan from the Madeleine; now he felt vindicated:

Our expression of regret was apparently heard by the young writer, brimming with courage, whose name was greeted with enthusiasm in the thick of a shower of bunches of flowers, thrown spontaneously and torn by women from their bosoms drenched with tears. He did not carve a pure and cold portrayal in the whiteness of Pentelic marble but a figure who moves and breathes, who loves and who suffers, who has true tears in her eyes and real blood in her veins. Marie Duplessis at last has the statue that we demanded for her. The poet has fulfilled the task of the sculptor and instead of her body we have her soul, to which Madame Doche lends her charming figure.

Figure 20.3 Sarah Bernhardt, the greatest lady of the camellias after Doche. Her portrayal of the role so moved Dumas that he presented her with his parting letter to Marie Duplessis.

Now you know the lady of the camellias. That name was bestowed on her because her delicate nervous constitution rendered her allergic to the scent of any flower.[9] *All is true.* Don't feel sorry for your tears: they are not flowing over a fictional grave.

Gautier's reassurance, that *La Dame aux Camélias* is a true story, again makes the important point about the play and novel, that they are both directly grounded in recent history. Did Gautier know that *All is true* was the 'true' title of Shakespeare's last and collaborative play, *Henry VIII*, another work keen to advertise to its audience that it dramatizes a true story?

Not everyone agreed about the production's merits. The inseparable Edmond and Jules de Goncourt, connoisseurs of the demi-monde, men of the world and sexual predators, felt that Doche 'deployed in this role everything she possessed... of diamonds and clothes', though not much by way of acting. Even her dress sense, they thought, let her down at times: 'We protest in the name of the [exquisite] taste of Marie Duplessis', they wrote in *L'Éclair* of 1852. Shortly afterwards they were at it again, this time excoriating the countless women who thronged to the Vaudeville to see *La Dame aux Camélias*: they all imagine that it is the story of their own lives, the Goncourts expostulated, they believe that they resemble Marie Duplessis because they too sell the flower of their youth. Alas, the brothers conclude, no amount of jewels, cashmere, lace, or ruining twenty fortunes, could turn them into the real-life heroine of the play, because 'Marie Duplessis possessed a heart and soul while you are venal and lubricious whores'.

It was not only women who converged on the Vaudeville. Men who expected to loathe Dumas's play also flocked to see it to loathe it. One such humbug was Horace de Vieil-Castel. He caught up with the play a week after its première and left a scathing account of it:

> Last night [Tuesday 10 February 1852] I saw a play by Alexandre Dumas at the Vaudeville. Our theatres are subject to censorship to ensure respect for morals, public decorum [*pudeur*], and good manners. *La Dame aux Camélias*, the play by Alexandre Dumas *fils*, constitutes an insult to everything that censorship ought to make one respect. This piece shames the times in which it is written, the government that tolerates it, and the public that applauds it. Every night the Vaudeville is sold out, the carriages crowd one another on the place de la Bourse [the site of the theatre at the time: see Figure 20.1]. The most decorous women are perfectly happy to be seen in the Vaudeville's boxes at this spectacle. *La Dame aux Camélias* has all the makings of a public scandal.
>
> Over five long acts, *La Dame aux Camélias*, really 'The Kept Woman', wheels out to a civilised audience the shameful details of the life of a prostitute. Nothing is missing from the picture: neither her chaperone procuress, nor the knights-errant of 'baccarat', nor the cynical phrasings, nor various scenes lifted from the most abject places. The entire piece reeks of vice and debauchery. All the characters in it are degenerates; even the ones the author intends us to empathize with are worthless. *La Dame aux Camélias* does indeed represent true love, and how! here she is, twisting her body in a paid bed under the caresses of a paying lover before doing the same a few hours later under the kisses of a lover of the heart, taking the money of the rich man to feed the pleasure of the poor one. There follows a scene of a father demanding that his son return to him, and who, to inspire in him disgust of his mistress, persuades her to revert to her old profession...

Finally the girl of pleasure dies, rehabilitated, in the arms of her lover and friends, after paying fulsome homage to religion!...the whole finally crowned by this funeral oration over her grave: *Much will be forgiven her because she loved much.*

Not much point in analysing such depravity: it's a disgrace, but the spectacle of the audience is even more so.

One particular numbskull—he is conned and cozened in the play—is a caricature of a well known real person. His name in the drama is Monsieur le Comte de Gervilliers: language and demeanour all fit. Would you know, the real Comte de Gervilliers, ruined by the very Mme Doche who plays the lady of the camellias, turns up every night at this mud-slinging spectacle. He stoically watches the ham on stage mock him to the general applause of the audience.[10]

De Vieil-Castel's bilious diatribe reacts to the boldness and sexual candour of the play and also, perhaps, to its trumpeting of the carefree luxuries enjoyed by the young men and women of the age. This did not necessarily sit well with older members of the audience and the wider Parisian society, many of whom, like the 51-year-old de Vieil-Castel, had grown up in the aftermath of revolution, war, and the defeat of 1815. The story of *La Dame aux Camélias* would have seemed to them a self-indulgent pot-pourri of frivolous antics, stripped of all moral fibre, familial duty, and a suitably decorous response to recent history.

Throughout the winter and spring of 1852 Parisians continued to flock to *La Dame aux Camélias* in their thousands. The story of Marie Duplessis was better known than ever now. Eugénie Doche portrayed Marie Duplessis as a tragic and open-hearted heroine, more idealized on the stage than she ever was in the novel. How much Doche's lover of the moment, Morny, told her about Marie Duplessis whom he had so adored, is not known—if he told her anything at all, for Doche may have been unaware of a relationship that in 1852 lay nearly twelve years in the past. The reviews of 'la touchante histoire de Marie Duplessis', according to the *Revue Dramatique* of 1852, which praised Doche and Fechter's Armand, consolidated the play's success and put it on the map. If it has since then been a staple of the French theatre scene, this is due at least in part to the immense popularity of *La traviata*, which would provide an inexhaustible life-support for the play that launched it all. When *La Dame aux Camélias* eventually finished its run in Paris in May 1852, after one hundred performances, it must have seemed to many of the men and women who had known Marie Duplessis that her story would now gradually fade and, before long, be completely forgotten. How many of the contemporary plays popular in Paris in 1852 are still regularly performed today? None, is a fair guess, with the sole exception of *La Dame aux Camélias*. Not only was *La traviata* waiting in the wings to revitalize the story even before it had run out of steam, but the grave in Montmartre started to attract a constant stream of visitors.

One wonders whether Verdi and his female companion went there too during their stay in Paris in 1852, as they may well have been aware of the fact that the premiere of the play was scheduled for the fifth anniversary of Marie Duplessis's death. Even if they did not necessarily attend the premiere of *La Dame aux Camélias*, they almost certainly saw the play before returning to Italy. At the time Verdi was a handsome man of 38 and his companion a statuesque 36-year-old woman. Parisian music lovers would at once have recognized her, as she used to sing in the capital's opera houses and had recently been coaching in the city. Her name was Giuseppina Strepponi, known as 'Peppina' (Chapter 21, Figure 21.2). Although her days as diva were now well and truly over, she had been praised by Berlioz in 1846 when she first moved to Paris where she lived in the rue de la Victoire, not far from the boulevard des Italiens. At the time she frequented some of the exclusive salons familiar to Marie Duplessis and her lovers.

By 1852 Verdi and Strepponi had been lovers for several years. They were staying in Paris in February 1852 to escape from the buzzing gossip about their relationship in Verdi's provincial home town of Busseto in the province of Parma, and above all to negotiate with the Paris Opéra (Le Peletier) for a production of a grand new work that would eventually become *Les Vêpres Siciliennes*. Exactly when Verdi and Strepponi saw *La Dame aux Camélias* is not clear although the premiere cannot be ruled out since they had been in the city since December 1851. The Verdi corrrespondence and archives are silent about the event itself in spite of its eventual momentous repercussions. The couple may have been attracted to the play by its scandalous reputation. Not only does *La Dame aux Camélias* condone sexual relations outside marriage, by infusing the central affair of a courtesan and her lover with pathos, tenderness, and sex, but the guilty parties in it represent ancient paternalistic values. The cosmopolitan anonymity of Paris allowed the composer and Strepponi to walk the streets together uninhibited. They could dine tête-à-tête in the great cafés of the boulevard des Italiens where no-one thought to cast a stone. The nonchalance of the French capital about individuals allowed Verdi and Strepponi to appear together as a couple at this most improper of plays. The two Italian visitors knew enough people in the *beau monde* of Paris to be invited to this Dumas *pièce-à-clef* by several of them. The thrill of the guessing game can hardly be underestimated. In the auditorium people might be rubbing shoulders with some of the very characters featured on the stage. De Vieil-Castel said as much. The Dumas name could moreover be trusted to deliver the 'in-crowd' of the city, ranging from poets and novelists to its most influential journalists and leading members, male and female, of the upper bougeoisie and aristocracy.

The audience during the early performances of the play probably sensed that they were present at an historic occasion. After all, the censor had had his arm twisted by ministers to license a scurrilous play about sex, perhaps for the first time. A few members of the audience might have tutted in whispered tones that they knew why he had relented. Dumas, Perrégaux, Guiche, Montguyon, and probably others too, were aware of the hidden narrative that had led to the premiere of 2 February 1852, which had been carefully timed to coincide, almost to the day, with the fifth anniversary of Marie Duplessis's death. But none could have imagined that the human interest and daring subject matter of *La Dame aux Camélias*, ultimately a somewhat trifling work in the galaxy of great French dramatic classics, would in due course launch one of the greatest and most enduring works of the nineteenth-century artistic imagination.

His biographer Mary-Jane Phillips-Matz notes that 'Verdi himself was said to have told Filomena Maria Verdi, the maestro's adopted daughter, that he began to compose the music for what would later become *La traviata* immediately after seeing the play, without either a scenario or a libretto. She, in turn, passed this information on to her son, who repeated it to his children, the present heirs.'[11] If this is true, it means that Verdi heard the *tinta* of *La traviata* in his head during *La Dame aux Camélias*, the *tinta* being the distinctive musical colour that confers unity of mood upon a piece.[12] In *La traviata* this includes its uses of the key of F Major and of the waltz, commonly called 'valzer' in the context of Italian opera, a lively dance for couples in 3/4 time, conjoined with the most sonorous use of strings in Italian opera.[13] If the haunting music of *La traviata* did surge spontaneously to the surface from the depths of Verdi's inner musical soul even before the libretto, we may be certain that he could never again let it go. He would instantly have recognized it as some of the greatest operatic music since Mozart.

Filomena Verdi's account of the composer's epiphany at the Vaudeville is inevitably anecdotal. Its credibility is nevertheless enhanced considerably by the survival of an extraordinary sheet of music from *La traviata*, demonstrating that a key scene from the opera was imagined and composed before the libretto was available. This consists of a sketch of Act I of *La traviata* in which Violetta is called 'Margherita', as she was in the novel, the play, and also in the early drafts of the libretto; Alfredo does not as yet have a name but is referred to as 'tenore'. The melody of the brindisi ('Libiamo nei lieti calici') is there, though in the key of C major rather than the definitive B flat major of the final score, and so is a draft of the most expressive soprano aria 'Ah fors'è lui' ('Maybe he is the one'), when the heroine wonders whether Alfredo may after all be the love she has been longing for all those years, the one man who will love her for herself and honour her. The fact that the aria features in this pre-libretto draft conveys a sense of the urgency of Verdi's desire to capture the romantic innocence of Violetta. According to one Verdi expert, 'what emerges most clearly from a comparison of sketch [of 'Ah fors'è lui'] with finished product is that search for simplicity and directness of expression which is the hallmark of the opera as a whole. The number of bars is the same in each case; but the final realization is purged of all superfluity.'[14]

A consolidating contemporary testimony about the close links between the Vaudeville performance of *La Dame aux Camélias* and *La traviata* is provided by a friend and champion of Verdi's in Paris, the music critic Léon Escudier. When the opera finally opened in Paris in December 1856, he wrote in the prestigious journal *France Musicale*:

> Verdi, leaving aside for a moment his great heroes and dramatic pomp, desired to plumb the depths of a drama of intimacy. He once attended a production of *La Dame aux Camélias* and was struck by the subject matter. He felt the chords of his lyre humming at the prospect of engaging with his dramatic heroine's joy, shame, and repentance. On his return to Busseto he sketched the outline of *La traviata*; twenty days later libretto and music were ready for production. (14 December 1856)

Escudier does not get it quite right because the incubation period of *La traviata* and particularly the collaboration of Verdi and Piave and their dealings with La Fenice (Venice's famed opera house) are well documented and took much longer than 'twenty days'. But he did know Verdi well and there were evidently parts of the opera that were composed long before the libretto was to hand. Indeed, it is likely that Escudier misremembers something that Verdi told him, namely that the *schizzi e abbozzi autografi* were indeed completed in a very short time after the Dumas premiere at the

Vaudeville. Unless we assume that Verdi's adopted daughter and his friend were independently making things up, the burden of evidence suggests that Verdi not only saw the play in February 1852 but set about plotting musical motifs and scenes almost immediately afterwards.

We will never know for certain why Verdi and his lover attended a performance of the Dumas play. Perhaps Strepponi suggested it. She had after all overlapped in Paris with Marie Duplessis during the last year of her life. It is quite possible that she saw the young courtesan at the theatre or opera. She would have been well aware of the furore caused by *La Dame aux Camélias* when it was published in 1848 and so would Verdi, who spent much of that year in Paris. Whether or not Verdi was aware of the lady of the camellias before the premiere of 1852, it is highly likely that it was the play and the stellar performance by Eugénie Doche that sowed the seed for *La traviata*.

Less than a year before the première of *La Dame aux Camélias* at the Vaudeville, in March 1851, Verdi had basked in the glory of *Rigoletto*. Now, even as he sat through Dumas's play and its musical numbers, Verdi was gestating *Il trovatore*, the premiere of which preceded *La traviata* by just two months. At the Vaudeville, the composer of *Rigoletto*, the most sensational Italian opera to date, probably grasped instinctively that the emotional magnetism of Dumas's story could be enhanced tenfold by the visceral power of music. His lyrical and dramatic gifts were at their most honed at this time. In addition to the epic *Nabucco* and the almost equally grand *I Lombardi*, he now counted to his credit *Macbeth* (1847), *Luisa Miller* (1849, based on a play by Friedrich Schiller), and *Rigoletto* (1851)—the last two among the most melodious operas since the heydays of Bellini and Donizetti. But all three were also powerful musical dramas, as febrile and dynamic as the plays of Shakespeare and Schiller.

With *Nabucco* Verdi had propelled himself into the limelight of nineteenth-century Europe. There were political reasons for the opera's resounding success, notably the longing for a united country by the people of Italy who were as yet bonded only by their language (and even that was fragmented into different dialects) and a shared hatred of the Austro-Hungarian yoke. Above all the triumph of *Nabucco* stemmed from the fact that no-one, not even the Donizetti of *Lucia di Lammermoor*, had ever composed a more rousing chorus than *Va pensiero sull'ale dorate*. In the end though it was *Luisa Miller* and the ebullient, stunningly bold *Rigoletto* that broadcast to the world that Verdi's melodies could be as mellifluous, complex, and expressive as

Mozart's. No other composer could have imagined the dulcet *bel canto* arias, duets and fragrant choruses of *Luisa Miller*. Luisa's diaphanous cabaletta 'La tomba è un letto sparso di fiori' ('the grave is a bed decked with flowers') is the purest piece of lyrical soprano music in Verdi—he marked it *delicatissimo* on the score—before Gilda's aria 'Caro nome' in *Rigoletto*, while the valzer in *Luisa Miller* anticipates the quintessential rhythm of *La traviata*.[15]

Unlike *La traviata*, the Dumas play and novel allow considerable scope to the various young men who woo the courtesan, including, in the novel, the narrator, who relates the story of Armand Duval and Marguerite Gautier. Dumas's reason for having a narrator at all probably has its roots in the novel's complex relationship to real life. After all Dumas does not tell primarily the tale of his own affair with Marie Duplessis, although that does enter the book and colours the narrative, but the story of her relationship with Perrégaux. *La Dame aux Camélias* is not a multi-layered, prismatic narrative in the Flaubertian or Jamesian sense, where the story self-consciously acknowledges its essential artifice and unreliability, but is instead a creature of its documentary origins. The play inevitably dispenses with a narrator, but its cast of primary and secondary characters is considerably larger than the one in *La traviata*. In the opera the action centres squarely on the heroine, with Alfredo and his father refracting her predicament at various points: the entire opera gravitates around its heroine.

Nothing much in *La Dame aux Camélias*, one imagines, could impress the maestro who had already composed grand operas that towered far above Dumas's play. Nevertheless he was clearly affected by the story of *La Dame aux Camélias* which, like *La traviata*, explores the sacrifice of a young woman on the altar of a bourgeoisie concerned primarily with legitimacy and passing on its patrimony through the generations. Fathers play important roles in both *Luisa Miller* and *Rigoletto* just as they do in *La Dame aux Camélias* and *La traviata*. Verdi's relationship with his own father Carlo was notoriously fraught and marred by what, to an outsider, might well appear petty squabbles over money. Carlo Verdi had recently been seriously ill, which could only add to Verdi's distress and feelings of guilt at just this time.[16] So many different strands from Verdi's own life and operas intersected at that time with the imaginative motifs of *La Dame aux Camélias* that, in retrospect, *La traviata* assumes all the force of a work whose destiny appears to have been written in the stars. Not only did the idea for the opera probably originate in the composer's mind during a Vaudeville performance of Dumas's play, but at least two of its key musical numbers seem to have taken shape the night he saw it. There may have been more; if so, no corroborative trace is left. It is tempting to imagine that, in addition to 'Libiamo nei lieiti calici' and 'Forse è lui', Verdi had also already 'heard' the preludes Acts 1 and 3, the two intimately linked orchestral pieces that in their plangent music distil the quintessence of the opera.

21

Verdi and the Barezzis

The genesis of *La traviata*: 1823–1852

Verdi and Strepponi eventually left Paris for their new home of Sant'Agata, in the Emilia-Romagna region of northern Italy, northwest of Parma. Here they arrived on 18 March 1852. Sant'Agata was three miles from Busseto and not far either from his native hamlet of Roncole. The estate stretched all the way up to the Po river and was surrounded by wide open fields that included small farms producing crops, as well as mosquito-infested swamps and pools. Verdi had bought it in 1848 and moved his parents here in 1849. But the main reason for the purchase was that he could not share his life with his new companion Peppina in his house in narrow-minded Busseto. Sant'Agata on the other hand was a profoundly private place, sheltered from wagging tongues and church. Verdi rose daily at 5 a.m. to tour his domain and ensure that his 'contadini' were working the fields. He was reputedly a tough but fair taskmaster and granted their cottages to elderly retiring workers. To this day his house is inhabited by descendants of the Carrara-Verdi family, but a number of rooms are open to the public. These include adjacent bedrooms of Giuseppe Verdi and Giuseppina Strepponi on the ground floor. The rooms are largely undisturbed apart from the electricity that now illuminates them. A shelf of Strepponi's books, in different languages, bears witness to the scale of her reading and breadth of interests. Also on show are the two pianos on which Verdi played, the desk at which he sat at night, his preferred time for composing, his top hats, his luggage, and furniture from the hotel room in which he died in Milan. The bedrooms were on the ground floor: in Verdi's house the servants lived upstairs, probably to afford the master and his companion and guests maximum protection against the heat which in the summer can easily hit 40 degrees Celsius. Verdi extended the house to his own designs, including the pond in the garden, which curves in the shape of a treble clef and which the Verdis used for punting. At the back of the house were a wine press and a garage with the maestro's carriages, which included the ones he used for travelling across Europe, among them a coupé for town use, not unlike the one owned by Marie Duplessis.

By March 1852 Verdi might have been expected to rest on his laurels just a little bit, to bask in the fame that *Nabucco* had brought him and to savour the recent triumphs of *Rigoletto*. In a disarming letter to him, written during the final stages of preparing for the production of *La traviata* and on the eve of his resounding triumph in Rome with *Il trovatore* (19 January 1853), Strepponi urged him to do just that, suggesting:

> if you did not have the contract for the opera, we could—either at Sant'Agata or in some other deserted place—enjoy our peaceful life! enjoy our pleasures, so simple and so delightful for us! Sometimes I am afraid that the love of money will reawaken in you and condemn you to yet many more years of work! My dear Wizard [*Mago*], you would make a big mistake! Don't you see? We have lived a great part of our lives and you would be absolutely mad if, instead of enjoying the fruit of your glorious and honoured works in peace, you should sweat to accumulate money and make happy those who—in the sad word *Death*—see the moment when their infamous expectations are realized, in the sinful word *Inheritance*!
>
> We will not have children (since God perhaps is punishing me for my sins in not granting me any legitimate joy before I die!) Well then, not having any children by me, I hope you will not make me sad by having any by another woman.[1]

Little could 'Peppina' have imagined that over forty years later her beloved Verdi would still be writing operas, his last one, *Falstaff*, premiering in February 1893. Verdi could never stand still, however much he would constantly gripe about his workload, referring to the sixteen years up to *Un ballo in maschera* (1859) as his 'anni di galera', years of hard labour. Throughout his life he was on the move between his gentleman farmer's estates in Emilia Romagna and the far-flung opera houses of Europe, from the Teatro San Carlo in Naples to the Teatro Apollo in Rome, the Pergola in Florence, the Fenice in Venice, the Staatsoper in Vienna and the grand houses of Paris and London. In the years before the arrival of the railways in the 1840s, his peregrinations constituted epic journeys by boat and coach. During this nomadic existence he did much of his composing in hotel rooms and suites, large enough to accommodate the pianos he inevitably required. His long periods on the road and his need to be kept posted by impresarios, librettists, publishers, and directors of the major opera venues, and of course his friends and his companion Peppina, entailed a lengthy and continuous correspondence, much of which he copied out for his own records and which survives in the so-called *Copialettere*.

It so happens that the maestro's correspondence from the period of *La traviata* is more often concerned with business matters, or casting, or practicalities such as his requirements in a particular hotel than with the extraordinary music he was composing. He may grumble about the lack of light and the fog of London, and he may report tersely to friends, agents, and publishers, on the successes or failures of his works. But one of the rare glimpses of the truly private Verdi occurs in his much cited reply to his father-in-law Barezzi of 21 January 1852, written from Paris shortly before the premiere of *La Dame aux Camélias*. It contains the only extant evidence of a temporary rift between them. To understand the importance of this letter, it is necessary to know more about Verdi's relationship with Barezzi, perhaps the most important in his life, and its links to the genesis of *La traviata*.

Antonio Barezzi was a local businessman and music lover who had spotted Verdi's genius and funded his private music lessons in Milan after the fledgling composer had been rejected by the Conservatorio of Milan. The panel who examined him had found his technique at the *cembalo* (piano) deficient while one member allegedly predicted that Italy's greatest musician would 'turn out to be a mediocrity'. Barezzi's faith in Verdi never wavered and the two men stayed the closest of friends throughout their lives. When Antonio Barezzi lay dying in July 1867, Verdi returned to the *salone* of the Casa Barezzi in Busseto that summer to play on its piano one last time for his beloved father-in-law. The tune was 'Va pensiero' from *Nabucco*. It had overnight turned Verdi into the brightest star in a lustrous firmament in which already shone Rossini, Donizetti, Bellini, and Meyerbeer, not to mention Mozart. The melody had confirmed Verdi's genius at a time when he and Barezzi were in a state of abject despair because of the death of Verdi's wife. In more ways than one the famous chorus had saved them both. In this extremity, Verdi may have been urging Barezzi to let his own spirit soar and fly home with the 'pensiero' of the Hebrew slaves or, like Violetta's soul, to break free of the body and rejoin its place in heaven among the angels, to echo Germont's words from *La traviata*. The dying Barezzi lay in the room next to the 'salone' when his former protégé played. 'Il mio Verdi, il mio Verdi', he is said to have uttered when he heard 'Va pensiero'. These words were reputedly the last ones Antonio Barezzi ever spoke. After his death Verdi wrote to his friend Clara Maffei: 'You know that I owe him everything, everything, everything; and to him alone.'[2]

The young Verdi was barely 10 years old, the son of an ambitious inn-keeper from Roncole, when he was invited by Barezzi to join his Bussetan philharmonic orchestra. Soon afterwards Verdi started to perform in the palatial *salone* of the Barezzi home in Via Roma. Its windows opened on the Rocca di Busseto, which today houses the small town's tourist office and, since 1868, a miniature opera house, the Teatro Verdi. One of the greatest opera tenors ever, Carlo Bergonzi, was a regular visitor to Busseto where his son still manages the hotel 'I Due Foscari' near the Teatro Verdi. Bergonzi was known occasionally to launch into impromptu conducting from one of the theatre's boxes. He had also, on many occasions, sung in this very space and he produced *Luisa Miller* in the Piazza Verdi in full view of the Barezzi house. His RCA Classics 1967 rendition of 'Un dì felice' in Act 1 of *La travi-ata*, opposite Montserrat Caballe, broke new ground for its flawless lyrical line, unmatched legatos, and the crystalline purity of his vowels.

Verdi himself never graced the theatre in Busseto with a visit and relented only to the point where he allowed them to name it after him. He and the people of the town had long been at odds over their treatment of Strepponi. But today Busseto is virtually a monument to its most illustrious son whose statue has him seated in the main square, facing away from the rocca to gaze out to far-off horizons. A far cry from 1820 when arcaded Busseto would have seemed almost metropolitan compared to the featureless hamlet of neighbouring Roncole and the Verdis' home known as 'old inn' (Osteria Vecchia). As a child he slept above the horses' stables to keep warm during the damp and icy winters of the marshy Po valley. One night a wandering fiddler by the name of Bagasset played in Roncole. Verdi was enthralled. Such was his passion for music that his parents—Verdi was well educated early on at a time when this was rare in Italy—bought him a second-hand spinet, a small, harpsichord-like keyboard. It was restored for free by a local craftsman because the little boy was so eager to master the instrument. Verdi proudly held on to it for the rest of his life, as he did to the note left in it by the craftsman who had recognized his precocious talent.[3]

A flame had been lit that would one day blaze its way across the world in some of the greatest romantic and dramatic musical masterpieces of the last two hundred years. Verdi soon played the organ in the church of San Michele Arcangelo opposite the family inn. The organ on which the little boy practised in the early 1820s is still in the same place in San Michele and is once again in regular use, restored with funds provided by Franco Zeffirelli, the director of one of the greatest films of *La traviata*. It was here that Verdi encountered the local Roncole priest, Don Giacomo Masini. The roots of Verdi's uncompromising anticlericalism have been traced to his loathing of this priest who one day manhandled the 7-year-old Verdi at the altar for inattentiveness while serving Mass. As he fell the little boy cursed Don Masini with 'May God strike you with lightning!' Eight years later the priest was indeed killed by lightning in a nearby church; so were several other people, including a cousin of Verdi's. Even then, it seems, Verdi could not forgive the person who had humiliated him in public. As he and others reached the scene of the tragedy, a church called La Madonna dei Prati, he saw, in his own words 'that miserable priest, sitting where he had been when the lightning struck, as he was taking snuff: his thumb was still pressed against his nostril, as if it were glued there. His blackened face was terrifying.'[4]

Verdi never looked back after *Nabucco* but went from strength to strength, composing a number of major works until, six years later, he was once more the toast of all of Italy with his opera *Macbeth*. It was the first of his three Shakespearian operas—the others are *Otello* and *Falstaff*—and premiered triumphantly at the Pergola theatre in Florence in 1847. The composer dedicated its score to Barezzi, noting that it was his favourite among all his operas and one worthy to be presented to his benefactor: 'The heart offers it; may the heart accept it, and may it be a witness to the eternal memory, the gratitude, and the love felt for you by your affectionate G. Verdi.'[5] On receiving this gift, Barezzi wept. In his reply to Verdi he assured him that

> your recognition of me will always remain engraved in my heart. Deign to receive in exchange the hot tears of love that I shed for you, the only tribute that I can offer you. Love me, O my adored son of my heart, as I love you; and receive a thousand kisses. Addio! Your Antonio Barezzi.

It may not be entirely fanciful to hear in these words an anticipation of the climactic 'Amami Alfredo' in *La traviata*. *Macbeth*, for which Francesco Maria Piave, the future librettist of *La traviata*, had written the text, elicited from the poet Giuseppe Giusti the remark that Verdi was destined for success. He added, 'if you will trust someone who loves both art and you, do not lose the chance to express with your music that sweet sadness in which you have shown you can achieve so much. You know that the tragic chord is the one that resounds most in our soul...'[6] Giusti was complimenting Verdi on both his powerful sense of melodrama and the political sway granted him by his genius, which had been in evidence ever since *Nabucco*.

However, Barezzi's 1847 *Macbeth* letter had started with a puzzling reference to something that was troubling him: 'Dearest son-in-law, if my heart were not unfortunately immensely troubled, I would have died at the consolation of reading your very dear letter of the twenty-fifth of the month.' What so upset Barezzi may have been the blossoming relationship between Verdi and Peppina. She was boarding in the same hotel as the composer in Florence when Barezzi and his son turned up for the premiere of *Macbeth*, and was mistaken for his 'wife'. This would have been Barezzi's first intimation of his daughter's successor in Verdi's affection. It is unlikely that she visited Verdi in his grand new home, the Palazzo Orlandi (also known as Cavalli or Dordoni), an imposing town house in Busseto that he had acquired in 1845 from the former mayor and which stands to this day less than a hundred yards from the Barezzi home in the Via Roma. It was here that Verdi composed *Luisa Miller* and *Rigoletto*.[7] Although Verdi continued to refer to Barezzi as his father-in-law, Verdi had in fact been a widower for nearly seven years at the time of *Macbeth*.

By hiring the young Verdi as his daughter Margherita's music teacher years earlier, Barezzi, perhaps intentionally, had played Prospero to his Miranda, because Giuseppe and Margherita fell in love and decided to get married. The bond between the budding maestro and the Maecenas of Busseto must have seemed very secure. Verdi and Margherita Barezzi married on 4 May 1836, when he was not yet 23. They had two children, a boy and a girl. Both died in their infancy, neither of them reaching the age of 2. By 22 October 1839 the Verdis had lost both their offspring. Then, on 18 June 1840, at the age of 26, Margherita Verdi-Barezzi died of encephalitis in Milan where she and her husband were living while he was working on a new opera, *Un giorno di regno*, for La Scala (Figure 21.1).

Barezzi had joined the couple when his daughter's health deteriorated. It was he who held her in her final moments. In his diary he wrote:

From a dreadful disease...there died in Milan at noon on the Feast of Corpus Domini, in her father's arms, my beloved daughter Margherita in the very flower of her youth and at the peak of her fortune because [she was] the faithful companion of the excellent young man Giuseppe Verdi, maestro di musica. I beg for peace for her pure soul, even as I weep over this tragic loss.[8]

Figure 21.1 Margherita Barezzi, the young wife of Verdi, who died of encephalitis at the age of 26.

Margherita died surrounded by the two people whom she loved most, her husband and father. If she and Verdi had been inconsolable at the deaths of their children, at least they had each other then for mutual comfort. Now, a mere eight months after the death of their baby boy, she too had gone. Recalling the moment the body of his wife, still only 26, was carried out of the house for the funeral service at the basicila of Sant'Ambrogio, an anguished Verdi wrote: 'A third coffin goes out of my house. I was alone! Alone!'[9]

This cataclysmic event in Verdi's life came at a time when he was a little-known new composer struggling to provide for his young family. All that was left to him now were the deep bond with his father-in-law, the desperate memories of his children and wife, and his musical gifts, of which he must have been aware but which the world had as yet not validated, apart from the relative success of his first opera, *Oberto*. The opera he completed for La Scala, *Un giorno di regno*, in a state of deep distress, failed to impress the audience, who were mostly unaware of Verdi's tragic loss. He never forgave them for the poor reception they accorded it even, and perhaps particularly, during his exultant progress in the years that followed the spectacular success of *Nabucco* eighteen months later. Nearly twenty years on he recalled how profoundly he had been hurt by the audience's cruel reaction to the work of 'a poor, sick young man... heartsick and torn by a horrible misfortune'.[10]

At the time of his wife's death Verdi was only 26 years old. He could not, and would not, stay single for the rest of his days. When *Macbeth* opened seven years later, his life's companion, Giuseppina Strepponi (Figure 21.2), was firmly part of his life. Perhaps one of the reasons for dedicating the score to Barezzi was because Verdi felt guilty about this inevitable break with their shared tragic past. While he was not answerable to anyone about his private life, the times were very different from today, and particularly so in provincial Italy where the writ of the Church, an institution that Verdi loathed, held sway. His decision to move Peppina into his house at Sant'Agata in 1851 caused consternation and then outrage at such defiance of public morality, the more so since Peppina's reputation was less than wholesome. It was widely known that she had given birth to illegitimate children by different fathers. So had many singers and actresses of the period, who were vulnerable to sexual exploitation during the companies' tours when they were lodged with their male singer and acting companions in close proximity and often far away from home. They were bohemians and shared everything, including the beds of fellow performers and impresarios.

Obviously the person most affected by rumours about Verdi was his father-in-law Barezzi. The *Macbeth* letter in 1847 may have been prompted by the presence of Peppina; the letter of 21 January 1852 certainly was, even though Barezzi may have pretended, to judge from Verdi's long reply, that it primarily concerned matters relating to the managing of Verdi's estate. As before, Verdi addresses his revered patron in affectionate terms, but then cuts to the chase after the slightly injured 'Dearest Father-in-law, After such a long wait, I did not expect to get from you such a cold letter... If this letter were not signed "Antonio Barezzi", which means my benefactor, I would have answered very sharply, or I should not have answered at all.' After several more or less emollient paragraphs touching, among other things, on

Figure 21.2 Giuseppina Strepponi as Violetta from *La traviata*, wearing a camellia and holding the score of *Nabucco* in which she herself sang.

Barezzi's son Giovannino and Verdi's professed trust in him with regard to the estate at Sant'Agata, Verdi turns to the real issue at stake:

> And since we are now revealing things, I have no difficulty whatever in raising the curtain that hides the mysteries shut behind my four walls, and telling you about my private life. I have nothing to hide. In my house there lives a free, independent lady, a lover—like me—of the solitary life, with means that cover her every need. Neither I nor she owes any explanation for our actions to anyone at all; but on the other hand, who knows what relationship exists between us? What business connections? What ties? What rights I have over her, and she over me? Who knows whether she is or is not my wife?[11]

Verdi is defiant and defensive in equal measure here. He is after all writing to his dearest friend, without whom he might never have been anything other than a grafting 'contadino' on a swampy landholding in the Po valley. The two letters of 1847 and 1852 would seem to suggest that during the five years leading up to *La traviata* Verdi and his father-in-law wrestled with the composer's relationship with Peppina. That Verdi was ruminating on the idea of *La traviata* at the time of his January 1852 exchange with his father-in-law may be suggested by the letter he had written nine months earlier, on 9 April 1851, to Salvatore Cammarano, the Neapolitan librettist of *Luisa Miller*, who was preparing a libretto for *Il trovatore* just then. Verdi apologized to his librettist for his presumptuousness and then proceeded to propose major changes anyway. Verdi was unhappy with Cammarano's slow progress and wondered whether the subject matter was not congenial to his collaborator. Should they change track? 'I have', Verdi wrote, 'another subject which is *simple and tender* and almost ready made, you might say. If you like, I'll send it to you and we won't think any more about the *Troubadour*.'[12]

Some commentators suppose that Verdi may here be alluding to *La Dame aux Camélias* and the future *La traviata*.[13] If so, it would be proof that he encountered the raw material for the opera as a result of reading the novel or hearing about it from Strepponi, that is, well before seeing the play at the Vaudeville. But a leading authority on Verdi, Julian Budden, disagrees by adducing Cammarano's deeply engrained conservatism: since Verdi's librettist was already struggling with the historical iconoclasm of *Il Trovatore*, how could he be expected to tackle a contemporary, modern dress opera with a prostitute heroine? Moreover, would Verdi refer to the story of *La traviata* as 'simple and tender' rather than something more akin to 'bold and rather shocking' (Budden) to someone as nervous about the censor as Cammarano?[14]

But these are questionable conjectures. It is true that Cammarano—he died before completing the libretto for *Trovatore*—might well have balked at the idea of writing a libretto based on Dumas's *La Dame aux Camélias*. Cammarano possessed highly attuned antennae with regard to the censors of the various jurisdictions in which Verdi's operas were performed. As for the assumption that for Verdi 'bold and rather shocking' and 'simple and tender' would be antonyms, this does not stand up to scrutiny; not after *Luisa Miller*, and certainly not after *Rigoletto*. The reason why the moralists of the time took such umbrage at *La traviata* was because, far from casting a stone at this particular Mary Magdalene, the composer deploys his immense lyrical gifts to exalt her. And he does so with a certain defiant relish. That much is clear from a letter written by Verdi to his friend, the composer Cesare de Sanctis, after the initial failure of *La traviata* at La Fenice: 'Ah, so you like my *La traviata*—that poor sinner who was so unfortunate in Venice. One day I'm going to make the world do her honour. But not at Naples where your priests would be terrified of seeing on stage the sort of thing they do themselves at night on the quiet.'[15]

The reported confidence by the composer to his adopted daughter and the music critic Escudier's independent testimony suggest, as we saw, that *La traviata* originated in an immediate visceral response to the intense sorrow and loneliness portrayed in *La Dame aux Camélias*. Was there another catalyst in the composer's life that helped shape his vision in *La traviata*? If the play triggered the opera, Verdi's unconventional relationship with Strepponi is sometimes adduced as the real life underpinning of *La traviata*. Thus, Mary Jane Phillips-Matz notes that

> the general tone and feeling of the opera, its intensely personal and compassionate atmosphere, its setting as a family drama, is not unlike the very situation Verdi lived through just before he wrote it. Life bettered art in this case...and out of their [Strepponi's and Verdi's] hour of strife came *La traviata*, which is perhaps Verdi's finest tribute to the human condition.[16]

There is indeed a superficial similarity between Marguerite and Armand and Peppina and Giuseppe, while Verdi's father-in-law Antonio Barezzi could be said to resemble Germont *père*, particularly since Barezzi did not, at first, approve of Strepponi. But apart from disapproval in their own home town, Verdi and Strepponi never experienced the kind of suffering portrayed in the opera. If the intensity of *La traviata*, its searing struggle to wrest beauty from sorrow, did grow out of a personal experience of the composer, we may need to look elsewhere for its origins. The roots of *La traviata* may instead reach down into the most traumatic inner recesses of Verdi's life, a series of events that would haunt him until, perhaps, their ghost was laid to rest at last with this opera, the ultimate anthem to youth doomed by illness and sorrow.

What probably connects the opera most profoundly to Verdi's life is not his liaison with Strepponi but his grief over the loss of his wife Margherita. It is inconceivable that the calamitous scene of Margherita's dying moments would not have echoed in Verdi's heart and memory every waking hour. Now, at the time of the January letter to Barezzi he was poised to enshrine that pain and sorrow in the transcendent music of the final scenes of *La traviata*. The last act of the opera, set in Violetta's bedroom, probably evokes Margherita's dying at least as much as it does the play and novel by Dumas. How could it not since Verdi and Barezzi were present at her death as were probably, too, a doctor and chambermaid nurse, a real life tableau that eerily anticipates the end of *La traviata* thirteen years later. If the opera's flouting of conventional morality reflects the sexual anarchy of Dumas's novel and also Verdi's unconventional relationship with Giuseppina Strepponi, its rapturous elegiac music may be the composer's final leave-taking from the young mother of his dead children. Margherita was only three years older than Dumas's heroine when she died. Like Violetta, but unlike the orphaned Marie Duplessis, she was surrounded in her final moments by her family who loved her.

It may all have started with a name. Until quite late into the composition of the opera, Violetta was called Margherita, after Dumas's heroine Marguerite Gautier. The name Margherita must have been indelibly precious to Verdi whose wife had been named after the same flower as Dumas's heroine. Verdi may have been drawn to the story partly by this coincidence. *La traviata* is Verdi's most intensely private opera and time and again Violetta's suffering is stressed in the libretto, her 'corsi affanni' that will be healed at last by Alfredo's love, or so she hopes as does he: 'Nowhere in Italian opera is grief more beautifully transfigured than here', remarks Budden, identifying one of the salient reasons for the opera's enormous success, its ability to generate transcendent beauty from topics as distressing and sordid as consumption and prostitution.[17] The opera is sublimely adept at internal moral and imaginative ambiguities. Thus, when Germont sings about his daughter, 'pura siccome un angelo', he is in truth singing to Violetta about her own unsullied soul, while overtly extolling the stainless virtues of Alfredo's sister whose prospects of marrying well look to be destroyed by her brother's relationship with Violetta. As the opera draws to a close, Violetta is held by Alfredo while Germont *père* is leading the chorus in 'As long as Heaven has tears to shed, I shall weep for you; let your soul soar free to the angels; God is calling you home',[18] blessing this fallen daughter of Eve while begging her forgiveness for having tragically misunderstood her sweet nature and hurting her great heart ('perdonami lo strazio recato al tuo bel core').

The months between Verdi's and Strepponi's return to Sant' Agata in March 1852 and the premiere of *La traviata* in Venice a year later were taken up by the composer conducting his usual round of detailed negotiations with various opera houses, particularly the Teatro Apollo in Rome, for the premiere of *Il trovatore*, and La Fenice in Venice for *La traviata* (Figure 21.3). His attention seems to have been equally divided between the two operas, both giving him more than their share of headaches: *Il trovatore* because Cammarano would not deliver on the deadlines for the libretto—Verdi was

Figure 21.3 Giuseppe Verdi at the time of *La traviata*.

unaware of how ill Cammarano was at the time—and *La traviata* inasmuch as the very opera itself was in limbo for several months after Verdi had signed a contract with La Fenice for an opera in March 1853.

Piave would be the librettist for the new opera (Figure 21.4). His track record was singularly impressive. He and Verdi had already collaborated, sometimes stormily, on among others *Macbeth* and *Rigoletto*. And, since 1842, Piave had been La Fenice's chief poet-in-residence. In a letter to Verdi on 26 February 1853, shortly before the premiere of *La traviata*, Strepponi referred to Piave affectionately as 'il Gran Diavolo', a nickname that she and Verdi clearly used for Piave, a tribute presumably to the Murano-born librettist's maverick resourcefulness.[19] Piave in return called Verdi 'Bear', perhaps because of his fractious temperament and larger-than-life

Figure 21.4 Francesco Maria Piave, Verdi's brilliant librettist and collaborator on *La traviata*.

presence. The two men had grown close enough over the years to disagree vehemently with each other without rancour. Verdi invariably triumphed in these encounters, most famously perhaps during the composition of *Macbeth* when, time and again, he remonstrated with Piave over his long-windedness and lack of 'fire and sublimity'. But that was to measure Piave against the genius of Shakespeare, which the Venetian poet inevitably found intimidating, not least because of Verdi's virtual adulation of the world's most acclaimed dramatist. This was not the case with Victor Hugo, the author of the play that inspired *Rigoletto*, and Dumas. In dealing with them Piave could give free rein to his talent and creativity. His poetic gifts, diplomatic skill, and nose for business made him the ideal go-between for Verdi and the opera house.

From a letter by Piave to the Fenice's secretary Guglielmo Brenna dated 20 October 1852, we learn that when Piave stayed with Verdi that autumn to work on the new opera for Venice, at the behest of La Fenice, who were anxious about the lack of progress on the promised work,

> suddenly Verdi got carried away by another idea and I had to throw away what I'd done and start all over again. I think that Verdi will write a fine opera now that I've seen him so worked up.

The maestro changed his mind even though Piave had, apparently, already almost completed a new libretto. It is not known what that jettisoned libretto consisted of. Instead, according to Piave, Verdi was 'in love' with the *new* opera, which was called *Amore e Morte* ('Love and Death') at this stage, perhaps in homage to the great poet Leopardi's homonymous Canto.[20] No-one knows what changed Verdi's mind about the opera and the libretto quite as dramatically as Piave indicated. Also, if we are right to surmise that he was already considering an opera based on *La Dame aux Camélias*, to follow *Il trovatore*, as early as April 1851, then why would he and Piave have embarked on a still-born libretto in the first place? Piave's silence on the subject matter of the earlier libretto is intriguing. It is not inconceivable that librettist and composer were colluding to cover their tracks vis-à-vis La Fenice, and that the libretto to which Piave refers was only ever a phantom, perhaps a sketch for an opera. Verdi may all along have been holding off because he wanted to work on the Dumas story, more than ever since he saw it at the Vaudeville and discovered more parallels between it and his own situation, with regard both to the spurning of Strepponi by the Bussetans and also the terrible loss of his family.

While Verdi and Piave were working on a libretto based on Dumas's play and novel, Brenna tried to clear the passage of the opera with the censor based on a sketchy synopsis Piave had submitted to him. It is a tribute to La Fenice's skills and tenacity that they succeeded in persuading the censor to pass the opera at its crucial first hurdle. Its name would be changed from the provisional working title of *Amore e Morte* to something else. Who first proposed *La traviata* is not recorded, but by January 1853 Verdi was writing to his composer friend de Sanctis, announcing that

> For Venice I'm doing *La Dame aux Camélias* which will probably be called '*La traviata*'. A subject for our own age! Another composer wouldn't have done it because of the costumes, the period and a thousand other silly scruples. But I'm writing it with the greatest of pleasure. Everyone cried out at the idea of putting a hunchback on the stage; well, there you are. I was very happy to write *Rigoletto*.[21]

Verdi was evidently well aware of the provocative character of *La traviata*, declaring peremptorily that he would be vindicated with the new opera just as he had been with the 'hunchback' opera *Rigoletto*, which had turned a deformed court jester into the protagonist. The respective premières of the two works, in the same theatre in Venice, are separated by almost exactly two years. Their obvious differences of plot and subject matter notwithstanding, they are musically as profoundly linked as they are in their imaginative visions. They are the most melodic operas Verdi ever composed; many years later he cited them as his two favourites. Each in its own way is dynamite, as both operas wrestle with the soul-destroying bourgeois complacencies of their time. In this respect they are as iconoclastic as the plays of Ibsen or the novels of D. H. Lawrence.

To grasp the lure of pleasure in *La traviata* in relation to love and tenderness, one of the opera's greatest challenges, it is illuminating to look at Verdi's exploration of love and sex in *Rigoletto*, particularly its portrayal of the Duke of Mantua, Verdi's near neighbour in his own 'paese' of Emilia Romagna. The rampant Duke is a brilliantly immoral creation, a daring tribute to eros and music. He is Verdi's answer to Mozart's Don Giovanni. When he proposes to a prostitute tellingly called Maddalena, he does so with the jaunty concession 'un mostro son', meaning 'I *am* a sex monster'. Without warming up, he plunges into the opera's orgiastic opening scene with a full-throated aria, the 'ballata' in which he proclaims that to him all women are fair game: 'Questa o quella per me pari sono' ('this one or that one, to me they are all alike'). Not surprisingly the scene is ocasionally played as a Neronic orgy. In Jean-Pierre Ponnelle's film of *Rigoletto*, the Duke of Mantua (Luciano Pavarotti) appears as a cross between Nero and Bacchus, bedecked with vine-leaves and laurels, while David McVicar's dazzling 2001 production for the Royal Opera House Covent Garden opened with a riot of nudity and sexual chaos. The Duke ends the opera as he began, with an aria, the legendary 'La donna è mobile', the best-known tune of nineteenth-century Italian opera. Rather than being held to account, the Duke is singing his strutting signature song in post-coital ecstasy, unaware of the fact that the jester's innocent daughter Gilda has had herself murdered to save his life. Convention and morality do not resonate with the Duke of Mantua; instead he equates with the glorious tenor part written for him by Verdi. The sybaritic Mantuan court of wine, women, and song is evidently recalled in the ballroom scene that opens *La traviata*, as if Verdi wished to signal a reprise of the earlier opera's exuberance, but in a setting in which the sixteenth-century court of

Rigoletto has been transposed to a sumptuous contemporary Parisian drawing room of the late 1840s.

But ultimately it is the tragic story of Gilda's self-sacrifice for love that
provides the most intimate link with *La traviata*. Her aria 'Caro nome' tran-
scends even Luisa Miller's deliquescent cabaletta for purity of sounds and
resonant *tessitura*, paving the way for Violetta's stunning 'Forse è lui' ('Perhaps
he is the one'), in which the courtesan Violetta, like the virginal Gilda, sings
of a new-found love. Piave's eight short verses for 'Caro nome' carry Verdi's
most lyrical *tinta*. It is mapped onto a downward curve of lilting tenderness
of woodwinds and voice which eventually soars in exultation as Gilda
expresses her boundless love:

Caro nome che il mio cor	Beloved name that my heart
festi primo palpitar,	first moved to beat,
le delizie dell'amor	of the bliss of love
mi dèi sempre rammentar!	you must always remind me.
Col pensiero il mio desir	In my thought my desire
a te ognora volerà,	will ever fly to you
e pur l' ultimo sospir,	and my last breath
caro nome, tuo sarà.	beloved name will be you.

Few composers can match Verdi's virtuosity at pulling out all the stops of
sentiment and pathos to tug at our heart strings. The two solo violins that
accompany Gilda's aria are echoed later in the harmony of faintly audible
violins and violas that float her dying lines 'Up there in heaven, next to my
mother' ('Lassù in cielo, vicino alla madre') about the kind-hearted woman
who saw beyond her jester father's physical deformity into his soul and
thereby secured his love and loyalty.[22]

Gilda's mother, unlike Violetta's who is never mentioned, looms large in
Rigoletto. She died and now, Gilda tells her father, she is watching over father
and daughter as their guardian angel. Gilda never knew her mother and she
does not know her father's name either. When he refuses to tell her who he
is, she pleads with him that he should at the very least tell her about her
mother: 'If I am not allowed to know you, at least let me know my mother.'
('Se non di voi, almen chi sia / fate ch'io sappia la madre mia.') Later, as Gilda
lies dying in her father's arms at the unwitting hand of his thwarted act of
revenge, she assures him that her mother is waiting for her in heaven. At last
she will see the woman whom she has missed all her life and, reunited with
her mother, she will pray for her poor father: 'Up there, in heaven next to
my mother, in eternity I will pray for you ... I will pray ... I will pray for

you.' ('Lassù in cielo vicino alla madre / in eterno per voi pregherò...pregherò...per voi pregherò...') It is pure melodrama and, for Verdi, the truest, for in spite of his fiercely held atheistical views, it seems that he too may have clung to the hope that human losses were not final. That the confirmed anti-cleric longed in a hidden corner of his heart to be reunited one day in the hereafter with his wife and their two children we need not doubt. He certainly did not seem to rule out the idea of life after death when his adored benefactor Antonio Barezzi died. Verdi told his friend, the Risorgimento journalist and editor Opprandino Arrivabene:

> Poor Signor Antonio! If there is a life after death, he will see whether I loved him and whether I am grateful for all that he did for me. He died in my arms; and I have the consolation of never having made him unhappy.[23]

In the Verdi canon the two father–daughter operas, *Luisa Miller* and *Rigoletto*, the latter in particular, are as seminal for *La traviata* as the Dumas works that directly inspired it. Gilda's sentiments about her mother would have been instantly recognized by Marie Duplessis, probably never more potently than on the day in 1845 when Lady Anderson presented her with her mother's portrait. In the role of Violetta, the short lives of Marie Duplessis and Margherita Verdi, and the responses to the two women's tragedies by a novelist and composer, coalesce. The motifs of fathers and daughters, sex, self-sacrifice, and exploited young women are shared between *Rigoletto* and *La traviata* and may reflect an intensely personal, intimate involvement in each opera by the maestro. As far as ground-breaking compositions were concerned, *La traviata* continued where *Rigoletto* left off. It would be just as irreverent as its predecessor but domestic, not political, and 'a subject for our own age', including with regard to 'costumes'. Verdi singled these out in his letter to de Sanctis because he was adamant that the opera required contemporary dress, that is, the true costumes of the story's real-life period, Paris in the 1840s.

An opera about a courtesan, a prostitute by another name, certainly gave the censor food for thought, and its aim to hold up a mirror to the contemporary underbelly of a major European capital proved unacceptable. Try as he might to retain the modernity of the setting, Verdi was firmly rebuffed by the board of La Fenice. Piave had suggested to Verdi that the opera be set back in the time of Cardinal Richelieu in the seventeenth century. It so happens that Richelieu's real name was Armand du Plessis. Marie Duplessis might have appreciated the irony and so perhaps did Piave. It is not impossible that the brilliant poet-musician from Murano imagined that a Richelieu link, however tenuous and inspired by the real life heroine's name, would add an additional frisson to the opera. In the end La Fenice forced Verdi to settle for '*Paris and its neighbourhood around 1700*' for his original '*Scene: Paris and its neighbourhood around 1850. The first act happens in August, the second in January, the third in February*'.[24] It was not until 1906, over fifty years after its first performances, that *La traviata* was at last staged, as originally intended, at La Scala in Milan, with Rosina Storchio, the first ever Madama Butterfly, as Violetta. By then the contemporary costumes of the 1850s had themselves become historical mementoes.

If Verdi lost his battle over period and costumes, his other chief concern regarding the new opera was the soprano who would sing the part of Violetta. He was adamant that he needed an exceptional singer ('una donna di prima forza') because the scope and scale of the role are staggeringly ambitious. No other soprano parts of Verdi's and none in Italian nine-teenth-century opera, apart from *Norma* and *Lucia di Lammermoor*, make such arduous demands of their lead singer. One of the legendary Violettas of our time, the full lyric soprano Renée Fleming—her 2006 Los Angeles *La traviata* conducted by James Conlon ranks among the greatest recordings ever of the opera—commented in an interview:

> There is no more perfect role in the entire soprano lexicon than Violetta.... I wanted to contribute on the basis of her vulnerability, rather than her hero-ism...Vocally, her challenges are many and are probably impossible to over-come completely, since she really does require three different voices: wild coloratura for Act One, Italian *verismo* for the first scene of Act Two, and limpid lyricism for the rest.

The scale of Violetta's part will be considered presently. Not only are the vocal demands exceptional, but much of the opera's imaginative action revolves around the young woman's frail state of health. As late as 3 February 1853, just over a month before the premiere, Piave was reporting that Verdi needed a singer 'with an elegant figure, who is young and sings passion-ately'.[25] He might have been describing the 29-year-old Angela Gheorghiu in the 1994 Royal Opera House production conducted by Sir Georg Solti. Verdi was almost obsessively insistent about the casting of Violetta. La Fenice did everything possible to meet his demands, but in the end circum-stances thwarted his wishes. In the meantime Piave had written a powerful

libretto for the new opera, laying the surest foundations for what was to
follow. In the words of one of the most perceptive students of the opera,

> Piave's Violetta, idealized as she is, becomes in Verdi's hands intensely human
> and yet heroic as well; and no one need feel the loss of the novel's realistic
> detail. In *La traviata* the myth achieves its most perfect form. Dumas's play
> remains a faded period drama needing the talents of a great actress to restore
> it to life; *La traviata* is an undying masterpiece.[26]

Proust similarly acclaimed the opera while comparing it to Dumas's novel
and play, remarking that 'it was Verdi and *La traviata* who gave a style to *La
Dame aux Camélias*. Better still, they gave it a soul' and by so doing succeeded 'in raising *La Dame aux Camélias* to the level of Great Art'.[27]

22

La traviata 1853–4

The apotheosis of Marie Duplessis

From Verdi's letter to de Sanctis we know that *La traviata* had acquired its now legendary name by January 1853 at the latest. While the *Amore e Morte* of the working title conveys key motifs of the opera, the vowel sounds of *La traviata* are forever linked inextricably to the lyricism of the music. Its mundane signification of 'the woman led astray' is largely lost, even on modern Italian ears. The dichotomy between the euphonious Italian word and the raw reality behind it did not go unnoticed by the London *Times* reviewer of the first British performances of *La traviata* in 1856: 'It was contended', he noted,

> that, although *La traviata* was a very pretty sounding word, it might be rendered into a much stronger English expression without incorrectness, and that damsels to whom the expression would apply were not fit objects for the admiring contemplation of aristocratic young ladies. Did this kill *La traviata*? Not a whit!

Tis Pity She's A Whore, the title of John Ford's classic Caroline tragedy about sibling incest, comes to mind. Would Ford's play be less effective if it were called *Giovanni and Annabella*, after its two incestuous lovers who conduct their doomed affair in language borrowing heavily from Shakespeare's *Romeo and Juliet*? One may well wonder how much the subject matter of Verdi's opera is rendered more palatable, or at least commercially viable, by its euphemistic lyric title.

Although the meaning of *traviata* as 'woman led astray' was obviously current enough in the Italian of the period for Piave to use and Verdi to approve, the word has been almost exclusively identified with the opera since the mid-1850s. Even native Italian speakers find it hard to separate the

feminine past participle of the now obscure verb *traviare* from the music that
has given the word an autonomous life. Today its meaning is universally
identified above all with a musical mood and feeling, whether the melancholy tidal ebbings of the overture and prelude or perhaps, more often in
the popular perception of the opera, the effervescence of the tenor's drinking song in its opening scene, as beloved as the Duke of Mantua's 'La donna
è mobile' from *Rigoletto*. For most people the sparkling brindisi, a fast valzer
in 3/8, marked *allegretto* by Verdi on the score, and the plaintive melodic
mood of the opera converge to capture the quintessence of the Verdian
meaning of *La traviata*.

If great works of art generate the terms on which they are experienced,
in this case a term of moral obloquy has been transfigured, never more fittingly, into intoxicating beauty and pathos verging on ecstasy. Verdi not only
composed sublime music for the opera, but by doing so he almost inciden-
tally reinvented an aspect of the Italian language and its moral coding. It is
this tour de force of the imagination, and of the heart, that propelled the
opera to the forefront in the struggle against cant and bigotry. The opera
urges its audiences to think again about who they are, the sexuality that
drives so much of their actions, and the young women who practise the
oldest profession in the world, and all that while they are enjoying the music
and spectacle. Verdi had already trumped conventional morality with the
prancing Duke of Mantua, whose libertine energy soars beyond good and
evil on wings of musical magic. It is similarly impossible to cast a stone
at Violetta, who is present embryonically in the 'bella figlia' prostitute
Maddalena in *Rigoletto*. Verdi knew this and so, as we will see, did Liszt.

The word traviata occurs only twice in the opera, during Violetta's last act
aria 'Addio del passato'. Violetta is alone in her apartment. She has just read
Germont's letter explaining that Alfredo survived the duel with the baron
who was injured but is recovering. Germont has told Alfredo the truth
about Violetta's self-sacrifice and Alfredo is on his way to Violetta to implore
her pardon. Germont too will join him in asking her forgiveness, begging
her in his letter to get better for a life of future happiness that she so deserves.
The words of Germont's letter are spoken by Violetta, 'in a low voice, not
singing but timed' ('con voce bassa senza suono ma a tempo') to the haunting accompaniment of 'Di quell' amor', led here by the two first violins
shadowed by the gentlest subterranean echo of viola, violoncello and contrabasso. The passage, with the violins in G-flat major, is marked *andantino* in
the score, with an additional double *pp.* for *pianissimo*. It forms a tender

variant of her earlier duet with Alfredo. This lead melody, with its sonorous dying fall, perfectly renders Violetta's pure nature, which sings in harmony with the true love that Alfredo had called 'the heartbeat of the universe'. The identical motif, again *andantino*, occurs also at the very end of the opera, this time in the key of A major and starting on A rather than the lower G of Germont's letter. Verdi marked it *double pianissimo*, without even the faint *contrabasso* of the letter; this gentlest, most lyrically diaphanous, rendering of 'di quell'amor' anticipates the heavenly harmonies as Violetta's soul yields to Germont's prayers to join the angels in Heaven.

Violetta's reading of the letter culminates in her anguished exclamation that it may be too late: 'E tardi!' She briefly rallies before realizing that it is all in vain. She starts to weep for her prematurely wasted life and dreams, before commending her soul to Heaven and asking for forgiveness in one of the greatest arias in all Italian opera, 'Addio del passato':

Addio del passato bei sogni ridenti,	Farewell, past of sweet smiling dreams
le rose del volto sono già pallenti;	the bloom on my face has faded already;
l'amore d'Alfredo pur esso mi manca	I so desperately miss the love of Alfredo,
conforto, sostegno dell'anima stanca…	comfort and support of my weary soul…
Ah, della **traviata** sorridi al desio;	Oh grant this fallen woman her desire;
lei, deh, perdona; tu accoglila, o Dio,	forgive her, Lord, take her to You, o Lord
Or tutto finì!	or may everything finish.
Le gioie, i dolori tra poco avran fine,	My joys and sorrows will soon be over,
La tomba ai mortali di tutto è confine!	the grave for mortals is the end of everything;
Non lagrima o fiore avrà la mia fossa	no tear or flower will adorn my tomb
Non croce col nome che copra	no cross with my name on it will cover
quest'ossa!	my bones.
Non croce non fior	no cross, no flower
Ah, della **traviata** sorridi al desio	Oh grant this fallen woman her desire
A lei, deh, perdona; tu accoglila, o Dio	forgive her, Lord; take her to You, o Lord
Or tutto finì!	or may everything finish.

Violetta's anguish over her 'fossa', a desolate mass grave, with no-one to mourn for her, is rendered more poignant by our knowledge that far from being anonymous and forgotten, Marie Duplessis's tomb is honoured to this day because of Marguerite and Violetta. For 170 years it has been among the most visited sepulchres in Paris.[1]

While Piave and Verdi follow Dumas's play very closely at key moments, Violetta's insistent reverting to her grave is missing from both novel and play. It may be that it was the increasing magnetism of Marie Duplessis's final resting place that inspired Verdi to work it into his opera for dramatic effect, and he may have done so quite possibly after visiting the tomb of the lady of the camellias in Montmartre. Weaving the grave into the opera allowed Verdi's heroine to share in her own myth-making, by importing into *La traviata* a tension between Violetta's fears about her memory and the sure knowledge of many in the audience that they were unfounded, that far from being forgotten the woman who had inspired her character had instantly become one of the most revered figures in Paris. And *La traviata* would in turn significantly enhance the status of Marie Duplessis's grave. During the course of one of several visits to the Cimetière de Montmartre over the years, in March 2011 when the trees were bare and the camellias burgeoning, I photographed the flowers left for her. Roses and camellias were vying for attention. Her name was of course 'Rose Alphonsine', and in her short life of glamour in Paris was inundated with roses by her admirers. One of the flower pots, of roses, said it all: 'A Marie Duplessis, dite la traviata, La Dame aux Camélias, Nous t'aimons Alphonsine.' All that was missing, from the grave and the adulatory flowers, was her first name Rose, but then the anonymous admirer may have felt that the roses in the pot spoke for themselves in this regard.

Names are important in Verdi's operas as in the case of the Duke of Mantua's fantastical pseudonym of Maldè, which closely echoes the name of Margherita Verdi's mother's maiden name.[2] They are never more so, per-haps, than in *La traviata*. Not only did the title of the opera come about quite late, but the heroine's name too changed, from Margherita, after Marguerite Gautier, to Violetta. It so happens that the opera was in some places—in Rome and Naples for example—initially performed under the title of *Violetta*. This may have been in deference to pockets of strong local clerical presence that objected to an opera which alluded to prostitution in its title, moreover using an apologetic past participle that would seem to lay the blame at someone else's door. Even in Paris, vastly more conservative than its saturnalian image of the period suggests, the opera was also at first trailed as *Violetta*, with *La traviata* as parenthetical subtitle.

Exactly when the Margherita of *La traviata* became Violetta is not known. The heroine was still called Margherita in Verdi's original sketches ('schizzi') for the opera in the course of 1852 before Piave was even involved in a libretto. It is tempting to imagine that the *tinta* of the music eventually and organically turned 'Margherita' into another flower with the same syllabic count and cadence, 'Violetta', but one that could be more lyrically expressive when sung. The name had to be floral because Margherita/Violetta was the lady of the camellias and her flowery name serves to underline her beauty and vulnerability. Verdi's hero Shakespeare describes a traditional characteristic of the violet, its transient doomed beauty and its association with youth: Laertes warns his sister Ophelia to beware of the attention paid to her by Hamlet, because his love may be no more than 'a fashion and a toy in blood, / A violet in the youth of primy nature, / Forward, not permanent, sweet, not lasting, / The perfume and suppliance of a minute. / No more'.[3] Quite apart from not wishing to use his wife's name for a courtesan, Verdi may have preferred Violetta to Margherita because daisies ('marguerite') are white while purple or violet harmonize much more suggestively with the erotic milieux and décors familiar to Parisian demi-mondaines. Moreover, in the play Armand's sister, who is unnamed in *La traviata*, is called 'Blanche' by Duval *père* ('ma fille, ma Blanche bien-aimée') to make the point even further.[4]

Flower motifs thrive in the garden of colour-coded camellias and their apparent messages about the sexual availability of the lady who wore them. Claudin recorded this and Dumas acknowledged it in his *faux-naïf* remark about the mystery of Marie Duplessis's habit of exhibiting red and white camellias at different times of the month. The alternating camellia colours may not be entirely a myth, although it is hard to believe that Marie Duplessis would have acted quite so brazenly; she was hardly a streetwalker touting for custom. Nevertheless, the potent sexual symbolism of flowers is echoed in *La traviata* when in the first Act Violetta plucks a flower from her bosom ('Si toglie un fiore dal seno') and passes it to Alfredo, urging him to return to her when the flower has faded ('Quando sarà appassito'), adding that this meant tomorrow.

The flower is not specified—is it a camellia or a rose?—but its erotic connotation is evident in Violetta's plucking it from between her breasts. While the fading itself could be neutral, the fact is that the flower will eventually blanch and thus deliver Violetta to her new lover. She can have sex again and, in the arms of true love, she, like the flower, may recover her lost whiteness or innnocence. Piave and Verdi could never have hoped to secure the censor's blessing for the raw sexuality of Dumas's flower symbolism, but they were not going to shirk it either. And the opera returns to flowers again at its most dramatic musical moment when Violetta parts from Alfredo at the end of Act 2. At this point in the opera Germont *père* has just departed, after extracting from Violetta her promise to leave Alfredo for the sake of his innocent younger sister whose marriage prospects and future would be jeopardized by her brother's liaison with a courtesan. Violetta is not at liberty to tell Alfredo why she is leaving him. Desperately she asks him to reassure her that he loves her: 'We shall be happy, because you love me, Alfredo, don't you?' ('sarem felici... Perché tu m'ami, Alfredo, non è vero?'), to which he replies 'O, how much!' ('O, quanto!'). But Violetta is crying, and when he asks her why she is weeping, she rallies by telling him that she will always be close to him in among the flowers that surround them: 'I will be there, among those flowers, forever close to you...' ('Sarò là, tra quei fior, presso a te sempre...').

Her embrace of flowers and death triggers Violetta's transcendent 'Amami Alfredo', an epiphany during which she pours out her love and passion. The full score, which gives the entire text as sung, reads 'Amami Alfredo, amami quant'io t'amo, amami, Alfredo quant'io t'amo, quant'io t'amo... Addio...' ('Love me, Alfredo, love me as much as I love you, love me, Alfredo, as much as I love you, as much as I love you... Goodbye'). It takes approximately 90 seconds to sing 'Amami Alfredo', a swell of music that strains to breaking point the outer reaches of the soprano voice: the protracted 'a's of 'Amami' and 't'amo' are expected to quiver in perfect harmony with the rise and fall of the strings, anticipating the exquisite chiming with the music of 'spenta ancora' ('already dead') in Act 3 of the 1854 revised version of 'di questo core'.[5] The pathos and romantic intensity of this moment raise it out of time. Even the 'Liebestod' in *Tristan und Isolde*, yet to be composed in 1853, may not soar more gloriously than this 'ardent outburst introduced by a Rossini-like crescendo of unparalleled pathos' in 'La traviata'.[6] Verdi launched the core Violetta melody of 'Amami Alfredo' in E-major in the elegiac adagio of the prelude, before embedding it into a valzer, a dance beat that chimes with what Violetta calls 'il tempo mio giocondo', her 'life of pleasure'. The opening chords of the opera thus grant us a haunting orchestral glimpse of Violetta's soul. Verdi composed the prelude in the Hôtel de l'Europe after arriving in Venice for final rehearsals, only a few days ahead of the premiere. Clearly for him the melodic line of 'Amami Alfredo' distilled the essential *La traviata*. In the words of the leading Verdi scholar Roger Parker, the opera's prelude becomes nothing less than a 'three-stage portrait of the heroine, but in reverse chronological order... First comes a musical rendering of her final decline in Act 3, with high, chromatic strings dissolving into "sobbing" appoggiaturas; then a direct statement of love, the melody that will in Act 2 become "Amami, Alfredo"; and finally this same melody repeated on the lower strings, surrounded by the delicate ornamentation associated with Violetta in Act 1.'[7]

If Marie Duplessis inspired the young Dumas's novel, as the whole of Paris believed, her story now may have merged with that of Verdi's wife Margherita, who had been dead for over twelve years when Verdi started to compose *La traviata*. The opera may be nothing less than Verdi's attempt to universalize his own experience of loss and grief. At last he could share with the world the enormity of his private sorrow, now that his musical powers of expression were at their apogee. Inasmuch as most audiences of great *La traviata* performances are usually left in tears, not just once but repeatedly, the maestro succeeded resoundingly.

While Violetta's name may be accounted for with reference to flowers and Verdi's wife, there would seem to be no such reason to change Dumas's Armand and his father Georges Duval to Alfredo and Giorgio Germont. Even allowing for the fact that 'Armando' might sound less convincingly Italian than 'Alfredo', Germont is no more indigenous a name in Italy than Duval. Verdi and Piave may have wanted to distance their work from its original, but why would they then retain the father's first name 'Giorgio' and replicate other names from the play, such as Annina ('Nanine') and Gastone while the play's 'Olympe' becomes 'Flora Bervoix', in keeping with the leitmotif of the opera that links women and flowers through beauty and its transitory glories and rewards. Could it be that 'Germont' is Verdi's rendering of 'Gramont', after Agénor de Guiche Gramont whose family had been so anxious to part their scion from his siren that they dispatched him to Britain? Here would seem to be proof that Verdi ventured beyond the story of the Dumas play into the real world of Marie Duplessis to authenticate his opera by grounding it more deeply in historic events. From his visits to Paris, from Strepponi's living in the city during the last full year of Marie Duplessis's life, and above all from their many friends on the inside of the Parisian world of artists, writers, and musicians, Verdi knew full well that the two Duvals could not possibly be based on Dumas *père* and *fils*. The idea that the old rogue would have objected to his son's sinning with a courtesan was patently ridiculous. Rather, as we saw, the two Dumas shared their women when it suited them, and may, just possibly, have 'shared' Marie Duplessis too, at least according to some writers on this story.

Why though would Verdi use Gramont rather than Perrégaux? He must have heard about her relationship with Perrégaux from his Parisian circles—it was impossible not to after the latter's near collapse at her funeral—but Verdi would have known too that Édouard de Perrégaux had lost his father the year *before* his affair with Marie Duplessis. And he did not have the benefit of Vienne's memoir, published in 1888, which specifically states that it was Perrégaux who stayed at Bougival with Marie Duplessis.[8] So, of the two, it was Gramont/Germont rather than Perrégaux who became the lover of *La traviata*. Verdi, it seems, wanted the story of his opera to be as true to the facts as it could be and therefore requested that Piave change these names. That it was the maestro rather than his librettist who suggested the changes we need hardly doubt given the composer's repeated sojourns in Paris. Apart from a wider fastidious concern with the truth of his art, Verdi was evidently well aware of the opera's real-life characters and their complicated lives and liaisons.

As regards the wider adaptation of the novel and play for the libretto, Piave freely transposed, rewrote, and transcended Dumas, probably in close consultation with Verdi. He would do the same with Verdi's early sketches. While Piave revered the maestro for his musical gifts, after witnessing at close quarters what Verdi was capable of achieving with *Rigoletto*, the master's writing was a different matter. One of Verdi's 'abbozzi', or early drafts, for the final duet of Germont and Violetta in Act 2 survives. It occurs immediately after Germont has embraced Violetta; she asked him to hold her in his arms just once as a daughter ('Qual figlia m'abbracciate'), now that she has agreed to sacrifice her only chance of happiness to that of his pure and innocent child. Overwhelmed, Germont asks what he can do for Violetta to thank her, as she moves to her eccritoire to write her parting letter to Alfredo. More than any other word, the adjective 'generosa' links Violetta to Marie Duplessis. Germont first uses it here: 'You are indeed generous!', he exclaims, 'what can I do for you?' (Generosa! e per voi che far poss'io?').

In the opera this particular duet involves the most complex orchestration as Violetta and Germont converge halfway through her aria, to the extent that he cuts into her aria before she starts on her second stanza. Up until this point, which occurs shortly before Germont's departure from Violetta's drawing room, father and lover have fought for Alfredo. Now Violetta has surrendered. She is dying, she exclaims, and pleads with Germont not to let Alfredo curse her memory but to tell him one day of her sacrifice, to let him know that it was her undying love for him that made her do it. Germont replies 'No, generosa, vivere, / e lieta voi dovrete, / merce' di queste lacrime / dal cielo un giorno avrete', which translates as 'No, generous woman, you must live, / and be happy. / The reward for these tears / Heaven will grant you one day.' But Verdi's sketch for the same passage reads 'No non morrete o misera / se le preghieri ardenti / d'un vechio padre possono', which translates as 'No, you will not die, wretched woman / if the ardent prayers / Of an old parent can...' The remainder of the last line, marked by dots, is not legible, but it presumably read something like 'sway the will of the Almighty', or 'intercede for forgiveness with Heaven'.

Compared to Verdi's, Piave's choice of words could hardly be more felicitous. The maestro's leaden verse and paternalistic arrogance is replaced by a silky paean to Violetta's sweet nature, her tears, and the certain promise of redemption at the hands of Heaven. Verdi's words cast Violetta as a sinner who may, or may not, be reprieved by the intervention of an upright old father's prayers. Piave's Violetta, on the other hand, may expect to live and be happy because the heavens are bound to embrace her generous and wounded soul. Verdi's lines condense the opera to a cameo morality play while Piave's resonate with the grace and beauty of the Violetta of *La traviata*. Verdi was well aware of his friend's superior poetic gifts, which is why in the end he set Piave's poetry, and not his own words, to the music of *La traviata*.

Perhaps the reason why the words after Verdi's 'vechio padre possono' are not legible is because Verdi could not quite bear to spell out to Violetta her fate as imagined by Germont *père*. After all, since the music and mood of the opera probably existed in his mind long before the libretto, it is hard to see how Violetta could provoke such a blunt, if not crude, response from Alfredo's father who, in any case, is a kind, if misguided, man, and not a villain. To cast him as a parochial bigot goes against the grain of the opera, even though, to judge from his sketch, Verdi had at first clearly considered polarizing Violetta and Germont much more than he would eventually do. It is after all Germont who refuses to acknowledge Alfredo as his son in the great scene at Flora's party after Alfredo has, unforgivably, hurt and shamed Violetta by flinging money at her in public, as a whore whom he is paying off with his recent gambling gains. The role of the father in the opera is immensely complex, both musically and psychologically. How else could the opera sustain the intensity of the second act where the chief confrontation is between Violetta and Germont, the courtesan and the upright disapproving father of her young lover? Chemistry between characters and performers is required just as much in opera as in a Shakespeare play.

The pitfalls of interpreting Germont as a punitive philistine were exposed in the 2013 English National Opera's *La traviata*, an inventive and challenging production, directed by Peter Konwitschny, and starring Corinne Winters as one of the most seductive and lyrical Violettas of recent times. Alfredo was sung by Ben Johnson while the part of Germont fell to Anthony Michaels-Moore. As well as radically cutting the opera—gone for example is the ballet interlude at Flora's party—Konwitschny stripped it of its poetic period aura. By doing so he rode the fashionably minimalist tailwind of the 2004 Fenice production, directed by Robert Carsen, and of Willy Decker's 2005 'hard-edge' Salzburg *La traviata* which featured Violetta as a scarlet woman (she was dressed in violent red), sung by Anna Netrebko partnered by Rolando Villazón as Alfredo and Thomas Hampson as Germont. Decker turned *La traviata* into a parody of *The Threepenny Opera*, more Weill and Brecht than Verdi and Piave, with a breezy contempt for the opera's *tinta*, the libretto's verse, and its stage directions.[9] Carsen's production, the first opera at the newly reborn Fenice in November 2004, dispensed with all but the barest necessities to produce Verdi's lavish classic. Only a Visconti or a Zeffirelli, ardent lovers of *La traviata*, could produce hugely lavish sets to recreate Paris in the 1840s or 1850s and add value to the music by doing so. They understood the importance in the opera of what has been identified as its innovative use of a 'rich musical colouration that conjures up a particular geographical location'.[10] La Fenice's 2004 production, on the other hand, was worthy at best, while the singing was superb. The love affair between the legendary opera house in the lagoon and its greatest ever premiere opera continues to be fraught 150 years on.

The 2013 English National Opera production cut the score drastically and Ben Johnson's nerdy Alfredo, complete with glasses, cardigan, and duffle coat, looked woefully incongruous among the guests at Violetta's party. This was of course the intention as he and his family are bourgeoisie rather than aristocracy. Even so, he seemed an impossible partner for Violetta whose love affair with Alfredo specifically involves erotic intimacy as well as the love that binds the universe together. But the most radical departure from

Verdi and Piave concerned the introduction into Act 2 of Alfredo's little sister in a mime part. Every audience of the opera knows about Alfredo's virginal sister who may not marry if her brother persists in keeping a courtesan. To have her on stage poses huge challenges. What Konwitschny gives us is a gawky teenager in spectacles who is marched in by her father, to show that he has indeed 'due figli', words repeated by a puzzled Violetta who had not been told by Alfredo about his sister.

Konwitschny's Germont is a self-righteous tyrant who not only strikes his teenage daughter but who does so on stage to put pressure on Violetta. Gone, it seems at first from his entry, is all the tenderness and melodic magic of the great encounter in Act 2 of the opera. Not so, for by a stroke of brilliant inventiveness, Konwitschny's Violetta and Alfredo's sister, the 'Blanche' of La Dame aux Camélias, played by Kitty Fry in the production that I saw on 3 March 2013, are magnetically attracted to each other. The two young women cling together in solidarity and love as they cower before a menacing Germont, oblivious to the alleged pollution that infects one of them. The scene must rank among the most genuinely creative moments in any recent performance of La traviata. In the English National Opera's production the tension at the heart of Verdi's masterpiece is visually enacted for us on the stage during the encounter between Germont and the two women who are both victims of his rigid beliefs. To the extent that this strategy rescued a controversial production by turning it from a wilful interpretation into one that was as inventive as it was maverick, Konwitschny's La traviata was a wrongheaded triumph: it was as if his only way of making his interpretation palatable was to stand Verdi's opera on its head and undermine its quintessential radicalism.

Verdi's short Germont sketch was probably drafted soon after he saw the play in Paris and came under its spell. The play ends with Marguerite's girl friend Nichette kneeling next to her dead mistress, saying 'Rest in peace, Marguerite. Much will be forgiven you because you loved much'.[11] This irenic ending of the play caused consternation among the self-apppointed guardians of Paris's public morality. The lady of the camellias was let off too lightly, they judged: a pious pardon offered by one putte to another appeared, at the very least, unseemly. Piave and Verdi went further than that once they had moved out from under the shadow of Dumas. Whereas in the play Marguerite dies with the love and blessing of a fellow fallen woman, who takes comfort from the fact that her friend's capacity for love will secure her forgiveness in the hereafter, in the opera Violetta moves far beyond this. In death she is no longer a fallen woman in need of forgiveness, but a saint called home by her Maker to join the angels in Heaven: 'Iddio ti chiama a sé', Germont says even as he is begging *her* forgiveness, a pardon that Violetta granted spontaneously when she told Annina that she was dying surrounded by friends, Alfredo, his father, the doctor, and Annina herself. In the opera it is the men, and above all that pillar of the respectable bourgeoisie, Germont *père*, who need forgiveness from a prostitute; it is Violetta who pardons and blames herself.

While the opera's hostile treatment of family and respectability gave it teeth, its polemic forms part of a wider tapestry that the composer weaves around the mysterious ecstasies of love. The leitmotif of 'Di quell'amor' is first articulated in a rapturous duettino by Alfredo and Violetta in the opera's third scene and is marked *andantino* on the score. They are momentarily alone and Alfredo seizes the moment with his famous profession of love, 'Un dì felice', the aria in which he tells her that he has silently worshipped her ever since she crossed his path and inspired his love a year earlier. Its melodic line is destined to haunt and comfort her throughout the opera; and when she dies, the violins play 'Di quell'amor' for her with tender delicacy. It is the most important musical motif in the opera. My text for both aria and cabaletta follows the full Ricordi score, which includes the sung repetitions:

ALFREDO	ALFREDO
Un dì felice eterea,	One happy day, ethereal
mi balenaste innante,	You lit like lightning across my path
e da quel dì tremante	And since that momentous day
vissi d'ignoto amor.	I have lived of an undeclared love,
Di quell'amor, quell'amor ch'è palpito	of a love, of a love that is the heartbeat of the
dell'universo, dell'universo intero,	universe, of the whole universe
misterioso, misterioso, altero,	mysterious, mysterious, proud,
croce, croce delizia,	torment, tormenting delight
Croce e delizia, delizia al cor.	torment and delight, delight of the heart.

In *La Dame aux Camélias*, Marguerite asks Armand about the origin of his devotion to her. It stems, he says, from an irresistible 'sympathy' that draws him to her. When she asks how long he has felt this way, he replies 'For two years, since that day when I saw you walk in front of me, beautiful, proud, smiling. Since that day I have followed your life, from afar and silently.'[12]

Compared to the dramatic rendering of the same moment in Piave's libretto, Dumas's text is a somewhat inert circumlocution for love at first sight. It is also of course in prose, unlike *La traviata*, whose libretto consists almost entirely of verse, mostly rhyming couplets and frequently ending in 'o', consolidating the mournful ambience of the opera. Alfredo's love for Violetta not only happens at first sight, but Piave compares it to a bolt of lightning that flashed across Alfredo's path ('mi balenaste innante'). The power of 'balenaste innante' resides in this ultra-kinetic image—nothing is literally more phenomenal or sudden than a flash of lightning—while tying Violetta into it through the word 'eterea'. By her 'ethereal presence' she is herself a phenomenon of nature, hence the use of 'tremante', which means 'earthquake'. The love evoked by Alfredo is not mere sexual love but encompasses the very pulse and lifeblood at the core of all life in the universe: 'quell'amor ch'è palpito / dell'universo, dell'universo intero'. For Piave and Verdi, the young man's love is as effortlessly poetic and philosophical as it is intense and erotic.

If the imaginative poles of *La traviata* are love and death, as in its original title, the opera also defiantly celebrates life. Much of its tenderness and melancholy mood depends on Violetta's passionate vitality, her zest for life in the full knowledge of her fatal illness. Her last two lines in the opera are 'Ah, io ritorno a vivere, / o gioia!' ('Ah, I am starting to live again, oh joy!').[13] It is a measure of Verdi's range and instinctive grasp of the need for his art to entertain, in order to reach people, that an opera shaped by its melancholy *tinta* should in the popular imagination often be identified by one tune, the iridescent aria of the drinking song that is 'Libiamo nei lieti calici'. It became an instant hit. Why this should be so can be glimpsed from a twenty-first-century event, a planned 'impromptu' performance recently filmed in 2013 (for the ARTE television network) in the Mercato di Porta Palazzo in Turin. The flower market was in full swing when suddenly the opening orchestral bars of the song thundered out over the tannoy. People were startled momentarily until the tenor, Dario Prola, disguised as a flower seller, launched into song. At that point the wider market realized that singers were in their midst. As Prola moved down the serried ranks of floral stalls, the Goan soprano Maria de Lourdes Martins was waiting for him, as was the chorus of guests from Violetta's party. While cameras and mobile phones flashed, the two singers wandered among a crowd of admirers swaying to the rhythm of one of the most gorgeous pieces of music ever composed.[14]

This party piece par excellence owes much of its perennial appeal to its use of the *valzer*, the triple-time dance that pulsates throughout the opera. By its sheer exuberance the brindisi pitches Violetta's life of luxury and pleasure as Paris's leading courtesan to the audience. Rather than setting her up only to be cast down, it expresses the extent to which she is intoxicated by life, wealth, and sexual freedom. The valzer specifically anchors the opera in the 1840s, thereby creating an obviously incongruous tension with nineteenth-century productions that set it in 1700. In that respect, and ever since the premiere at La Fenice, the drinking song guaranteed the work's imaginative integrity in spite of the lame betrayal of locating it so far back in the past. If the brindisi is oddly uncharacteristic of Alfredo, it agrees perfectly with the company he is keeping at that moment. The dramatic point of the song is to provoke a reaction from Violetta, eliciting from her a credo of pleasure and indulgence as clear and lucid in its own way as Iago's Manichean prayer in *Otello* many years later.

The opening scene of *La traviata* elevates it far above the tawdry episode that launches the affair of Armand and Marguerite in the novel where, after the theatre, the young men repair to her apartment for dinner and sex. This coarseness is toned down considerably in the play while in the opera Violetta presides over a grand Parisian soirée, one which anticipates the ball at Flora's in Act 2. Everything is on a grander scale than in Dumas.[15] Verdi and Piave insisted on high decorum in the full knowledge of the opera's defiance of moral complacency in almost all other respects. To stand their wishes on their head, as Decker's 2005 Salzburg production did, ironically misses the point of Verdi's radical approach while trying to make it more effectively.

The world of aristocratic boulevard gamblers, lions, and luxury concubines such as Violetta Valéry could hardly be further removed from the grimy lofts and studios of Puccini's *La Bohème* and its source, Henry Murger's semi-autbiographical 1851 *Scènes de la vie de bohème*. Troubling moral issues certainly underlie Violetta's existence, but her glitzy life of glamour and baroque ballrooms outstrips anything in Dumas. Where the novel and play are furtive, the opera is open and public, just as Dumas's small-scale interior settings are blown up into the huge stage of an opera house which, in the case of the Royal Opera House Covent Garden, can invite 2,256 people to the party on any given night. Far from being prim or coy, the opera runs with the glamour without moralizing it. After all, it is only because Violetta is the queen of parties that her initial resistance to Alfredo's invitation to join him in domestic bliss rings true. The brindisi not only instantly creates a

joyous atmosphere of dancing, drinking, and loving, but also sets up a courting tension, because Alfredo's youthful burst of singing shows up Violetta's
current protector, Barone Douphol (usually referred to as barone in the
opera), as a spoilsport. He is based on Count Stackelberg, as a lover who
keeps and pays her for sex without being able to match her zest for life.

The atmosphere before the song is charged and mischievous because
Violetta's guests relish the prospect of a confrontation between the two men
of different generations and they enjoy toying with Alfredo, who does not
fit in with them. The scene is set for a sexual contest between a young and
idealistic bourgeois and an ageing aristocratic *roué*. In some ways it recalls
the gladiatorial opening of *Rigoletto*, but the dissolute sexual universe of the
court of Mantua is not quite reprised in the drawing room of *La traviata*,
even if we hear an echo of it as the guests pour into Violetta's home after
gambling earlier during the night at Flora's. The brindisi is artfully woven
into the fabric of the party, turning Alfredo's initiation into the upper class
ball into its mood setter. In the most luxuriant *La traviata* of recent years, the
stylish 2006 Los Angeles production starring Renée Fleming (Violetta),
Rolando Villazón (Alfredo), and Renato Bruson (Germont), Violetta grace-
fully waltzes with one of her guests between 'Tra voi, tra voi saprò dividere /
il tempo mio giocondo' ('Among you, among you I shall know how to
divide / my times of pleasure and play') and her return to her solo singing
with the provocative 'Life is joyful abandon' ('La vita è nel tripudio'). By
then the chorus of *Tutti* have eagerly echoed her sentiments. The song orig-
inates in Dumas's play which freely interweaves its dialogue with various
kinds of music, including the polka (at which Doche excelled), piano playing and the popular folk song 'Marlbrough s'en va-t-en guerre', though not
quite to the point of becoming a musical.

The first verse of the song in *La Dame aux Camélias* pokes fun at Arab
culture, which preoccupied Paris intensely in the 1840s because of the protracted French campaigns in Algeria where they encountered fierce resistance from local Muslim warlords, notably Abd al-Qâdir. This conflict
touched the lives of several of the characters in this story, including Marie
Duplessis and her rival Alice Ozy, both of whom knew men who had served
in this colonial venture. The Arab part of the song is local and of no particular interest to Verdi, but it does provide a launch pad for his more generic
wine, women, and fun tune. In the novel the drinking song falls to Gaston
Rieux, who becomes Gastone, Visconte de Letorières in the opera. It is suggested by Prudence, Marguerite's procuress, in response to Gaston's remark

that Armand is 'as melancholy as a drinking song'. When Prudence presses him to sing, Gaston jauntily replies 'Always the old traditions! I am convinced that the middle-aged Prudence had a steamy encounter in a wine cellar'. Rejecting a dry paradise of virgins in favour of a decadent Paris drawing room surrounded by prostitutes, Gaston proposes instead to worship 'the sparkle of two eyes / Reflected in my glass'. After all, he continues, 'The good Lord created love and wine good / Because he loved the earth': if only the 'strict censor' were less of a killjoy!

The version of the song in *La traviata* differs significantly in tone from Dumas's barbed lyrics:

ALFREDO	ALFREDO
Libiamo ne' lieti calici	Let us drink from the joyous cups
che la belezza infiora	bursting with beauty,
e la fuggevol ora	and let the fleeting hour
s'innebrii a voluttà	freely intoxicate itself.
Libiam ne' dolci fremiti	Let us drink to the sweet tremors
che suscita l'amore	that love provokes,
poiché quell'occhio al core	for those eyes
(indicando Violetta)	(*pointing to Violetta*)
onnipotente va	conquer the heart irresistibly.
...	...
VIOLETTA	VIOLETTA
(s'alza)	(*rising*)
Tra voi, saprò dividere	Among you all I shall know how to pass
il tempo mio giocondo;	my days of gaiety;
tutto è follia nel mondo	Everything is folly in this world
ciò che non è piacer.	that is not pleasure.
Godiam, fugace e rapido	Let us enjoy; fleeting and swift
è il gaudio dell'amore;	are the joys of love,
è un fior che nasce muore,	a flower that blossoms and dies
né più si può goder	and can no longer be enjoyed.

Piave's verse sings with an abundance of vowels, an ode to the sounds and colours of Italian, and affords Verdi scope for one of his most rapturous tunes. The piece captivates the transience of life and love, while granting wine its due: the link in Italian between the infioria of the calici of wine and the ephemeral pleasure of love, a flower that blossoms and dies, harmonizes the wider flower motif that pervades the opera and encompasses the heroine's very name. The ebullience of the brindisi instantly traces the opening of

La traviata back to the percussive surges of *Rigoletto*. Verdi was aware of this, even going so far as to warn La Fenice that he might only be able to offer them a rehashed version of *Rigoletto* at best if they did not agree to his detailed demands. Both operas overflow with pent-up energy, constantly arching upwards towards release, in a manner characteristic of Romantic music as, for example, in Tchaikovsky's 'Polonaise' in *Eugene Onegin*. No sooner has the brindisi finished than an off-stage banda starts playing a valzer for the guests to dance through the night. At that moment Violetta is taken ill and so she and Alfredo stay on stage, which then allows him to declare his love to her in 'Un dì felice'. At no point is there a break in the pulse of the music. Verdi was determined to hook his audience in Venice early on, just as he had done with *Rigoletto* when he launched the Duke of Mantua into the opera with a glittering aria.[16]

For Verdi and Piave working away at Sant'Agata during the last weeks of 1852, the challenge was steeper even than with *Rigoletto*. The intimacy of the story, its subject matters of love, sex, and death, and the composer's almost monomaniacal determination that the setting needed to be *contemporary*, all underline his personal stake in it. While the two men worked on the script Verdi repeatedly tested some of the music on Piave, who knew better than anyone how to write verse set to music. Piave's close links with La Fenice provided the opera house with a guarantee that the composer was indeed giving it his all. His origins in Murano, an island in the Venetian lagoon, meant that Piave knew Venice's public, panjandrums, and Habsburg masters very well indeed and that he was expert at pleasing the first two and circumventing the others.

On 6 March 1853, a little over a year after the premiere of *La Dame aux Camélias* at the Vaudeville, *La traviata* opened at La Fenice (Figure 22.1). Verdi would have appreciated the irony that Dumas's *La Dame aux Camélias* was playing in Italian in Campo San Luca at the same time. This might have been construed as a good omen. Moreover the lead singers were all accomplished, contrary to Verdi's caustic assertions in the immediate aftermath of the opening night: after all, Felice Varesi, the first baritone ever to sing Germont *père*, had been the star of *Rigoletto* in the titular role of the hunchback, while Lodovico Graziani, the tenor who undertook Alfredo, was a fine singer who would appear in a number of Verdi parts in the course of his life.

But performances of *La traviata* in the end stand or fall by their Violettas. The honour of the first Violetta ever belongs to Fanny Salvini-Donatelli

Figure 22.1 The now famous poster from the Teatro La Fenice in Venice, advertising the premiere of *La traviata* on 6 March 1853.

(Figure 22.2). She was by all accounts a highly effective soprano. Verdi knew her well: ten years earlier he had conducted her as Abigaille in *Nabucco*. Even so, Verdi had been emphatic in his notes to La Fenice that he did not want the 38-year-old Salvini-Donatelli to sing Violetta. He objected to her mostly, it seems, on account of her size: she would simply not be credible in the part of a vulnerable woman in her twenties dying of a wasting disease. In fact she performed very well on the night of 6 March and was more acclaimed than the two men. Even so, as the performance progressed that evening, neither the singing nor the acting generated the momentum that Verdi had hoped for. Later that very night of 6 March 1853 Verdi fired off furious missives to various friends about the 'fiasco', including one to his friend, the conductor Angelo Mariani. It is the most interesting of his letters on the subject and extends a proud challenge to the doubters:

> *La traviata* was an immense fiasco, and worse, people laughed. Still, what do you expect? I am not upset over it. I'm wrong or they are wrong. As for myself,

Figure 22.2 The soprano Fanny Salvini-Donatelli, the first ever Violetta in 1853.

> I believe that the last word on *La traviata* was not said last night. They will see
> it again, and we shall see! Anyway, dear Mariani, mark down the fact that it was
> a fiasco.[17]

La traviata ran for another eight nights and did well at the box office, earning
considerably more than some of Verdi's other operas; moreover Salvini-
Donatelli was lauded by one of Venice's leading reviewers for some of the
most melodious singing heard in Venice for a long time.[18] Verdi had overre-
acted and, by doing so, hurt the feelings of the cast. The fact that his damning
letters were written on the very night of the premiere shows the depth of his
hurt and the perceived slight to his masterpiece. He knew better than anyone
what an extraordinary opera he had composed and therefore had every right
to expect at least the plaudits and laurels showered on him on the opening
nights of *Rigoletto* and *Il trovatore*. Moreover, Verdi's personal sentimental invest-
ment in *La traviata* was probably much higher than in any other opera so far.
His angry outbursts caused the baritone Felice Varesi to respond in an open
letter. This must have rubbed salt in Verdi's wounds, not least because Verdi's

high opinion of the tenor was well attested, a fact of which Varesi reminds us. Varesi stopped short of blaming the opera itself while asserting that Verdi had failed to use the full potential of his cast, and that he in particular, the singer of grand parts like Macbeth and Rigoletto, had been short-changed.[19]

On 6 May 1854, a little more than a year after its allegedly tepid premiere, *La traviata* was staged again in Venice. The venue was the Teatro San Benedetto in Campo San Gallo, at the insistence of its manager Antonio Gallo, who had persuaded a reluctant Verdi to relent and let Venice have another go at the opera. The San Benedetto was a much loved Venetian opera house and had been the city's favourite until it was superseded by La Fenice in 1792. Piave personally took charge of the production, his professional affiliation with La Fenice notwithstanding. The role of Violetta was sung by the wholesome soprano Maria Spezia, who was 26 at the time and certainly looked the part of Violetta much more than Salvini-Donatelli had done (Figure 22.3). She was partnered by Francesco Landi as Alfredo and the great baritone and Verdi veteran Filippo Coletti as Germont. This time *La traviata* caused a sensation.

The opera's march into legend started there and then and the world's favourite musical melodrama would never again look back. If Verdi was elated by its success, he did not show it, protesting instead against the well-founded suggestions in the press that he had extensively revised the opera. This he vehemently denied, chiding the critics in yet another letter to his friend, the composer de Sanctis:

> You should know that the *La traviata* which is currently playing at the San Benedetto is the same, exactly the same as the one that was staged last year at the Fenice, with the exception of a few transposed keys and a few changes to notes and register [*puntutura*] that I implemented specifically to adapt them for these particular singers' needs. These changes to tone and register will stay in the score because I consider the opera to have been written for this cast. Apart from that not a single piece has been altered, not a single piece added or removed, not one musical idea was changed. Everything that existed for La Fenice does too for the San Benedetto. Then it was a disaster; now a triumph. You draw your own conclusions.[20]

Verdi was still smarting from the slight endured by *La traviata* and himself a year earlier. He had known all along that the opera was exceptional, even by his own standards, and now he felt vindicated; except that the critics were hinting that he might have got it wrong the first time, that the reason why the opera succeeded in 1854 was due, in part at least, to his rumoured revisions. There was no chance in 1854 to wind back the clock to compare the

L'ILLUSTRATION, JOURNAL UNIVERSEL.

Mlle Spezia, rôle de Violetta dans la *Traviata*.

Figure 22.3 Maria Spezia, the first truly successful Violetta in 1854.

two versions so Verdi could afford a certain amount of bluster. In actual fact, his revisions to the 1853 score were rather more extensive than he admitted to de Sanctis and only partly in response to a cast he found more congenial. All the same, not many of the changes to keys and register would be noticed in performance by any but a handful of musicians and music scholars among his audience; and of course by Verdi himself, who was blessed with an ear that picked up the slightest nuance of a misplaced note or less than felicitous key in his score.

The actual extent of the alterations can be gauged from two sources: Verdi's dealing with his publisher Ricordi in Milan and the original 1853 score of *La traviata*, which survives in the archives of La Fenice. When Ricordi asked to publish the score of the opera, Verdi held back five pieces for several weeks before submitting them in a redrafted form. The bulk of the revisions occur in Act 2, with a few in Act 3. Unlike most modern interpretations of the opera, which divide it into four distinct tableaux, Verdi thought of *La traviata* as a three-act work.[21] The most striking rewriting occurs in the *Largo del Finale* of Act 2, the great ensemble scene that immediately follows on from Violetta's humiliation and collapse. Alfredo's reason for acting with such insensate cruelty is that Violetta has just told him that she returned to her former protector, Baron Douphol, because she 'loved' him. This falsehood seemed the only way to alienate Alfredo's affection from her, which she promised his father she would do. Alfredo knows nothing of this and acts out of a sense of utter betrayal and anger.

In front of the entire cast the deeply hurt Violetta, recovering from her faint, now sings the intensely moving 'di questo core' ('of this my heart'), in which she tells him openly, in public, how much she loves him, vowing to do so beyond the grave. Her lines launch a choric ensemble as gorgeous and moving as the 'bella figlia' quartet of *Rigoletto* while preparing the way for the revised *Finale ultimo* in which Violetta, one last time, again sings of her love for Alfredo in terms that echo 'di questo core':

VIOLETTA (riavendosi)	VIOLETTA (*reviving*)
Alfredo, Alfredo, di questo core	Alfredo, Alfredo, of this my heart
non puoi comprendere tutto l'amore...	You cannot grasp the depth of love...
tu non conosci che fino a prezzo	You do not know that even at the cost
del tuo disprezzo – provato io l'ho.	of your contempt I have proven it.
Ma verrà tempo, in che il saprai...	But in time to come you will know it...
com'io t'amassi confesserai...	How much I loved you, you will know...
Dio dai rimorsi ti salvi allora...	May God save you then from remorse
io spenta ancora – pur t'amerò.	In death I will still love you.

When the chorus joins in with Violetta, it does so by repeating 'Quanto peni! fa cor!' ('How you suffer! But take heart!') and 'rasciuga il pianto che t'inondò' ('wipe the tears that flood your face'). While the chorus assures her that she is among friends who love her and share her suffering, Alfredo, Germont, and the barone pursue their own musical line, with the barone vowing to avenge the insult to Violetta and Germont torn by his knowledge of Violetta's self-immolatory love.

There may be no better way to understand Verdi's evolving Violetta from 1853 to 1854 than to compare two outstanding interpretations of the different versions of 'di questo core': the now legendary 1994 Royal Opera House Covent Garden *La traviata*, conducted by Georg Solti, with a young Angela

Gheorghiu as Violetta, and the 2004 *La traviata* at La Fenice, with Patrizia Ciofi in the title role. Verdi's classic was chosen above all others to mark the rebirth of La Fenice after the disastrous fire that destroyed it in 1996. Perhaps to pay homage to the opera and to atone for its failure in 1853 to recognize the enchantment of the world's favourite opera, La Fenice put on the original, rarely performed, 1853 score.

Audiences all over the world are familiar with the revised 1854 *La traviata* score of the San Benedetto production, which was also the one conducted by Solti at the Royal Opera House. The production's star had been talent-spotted as a potential Violetta two years earlier by Georg Solti, when she sang Mimi in *La Bohème* at Covent Garden. Solti suggested to Richard Eyre, a friend and at the time the director of the National Theatre, that he go and observe her as Mimi in Vienna. Eyre was instantly won over by her instinctive ability to synchronize her acting and voice; it was as if her entire body sang, he later said. It would be the first opera Eyre directed. Together with Solti and the house's designs director, Bob Crowley, he created one of the most glorious and lasting productions in Covent Garden's history. The opera was broadcast live by the BBC, whose expert camera work enhanced the production's focus on Violetta. Angela Gheorghiu possessed all the qualities Verdi had longed to see in his heroine 142 year earlier: fragile beauty, an exquisitely lyrical soprano voice, and a spontaneous intimacy with the role of the vulnerable heroine. The costumes for the opera require the same care and intelligent attention as the rest, and the Royal Opera House got this absolutely right too. In the end the lyrical presence of Gheorghiu, Solti's sensitive conducting, Eyre's brilliant directing and the cameras' dance of love around the heroine, dressed in exquisite black lace of the period, all converged to turn this particular recording of 'di questo core' into the miracle that it is.

The finale of Act 2 starts with Violetta painfully rising from the floor until she stands upright, with her hands delicately poised akimbo on her hooped skirt, an echo of the fashionable crinolines of the 1840s. The effect is to underline Violetta's intense fragility and isolation as she starts to sing of her undying and self-sacrificing love, 'in a supremely weak voice and with passion' ('con voce debolissima e con passione'). Angela Gheorghiu breathed soul and sorrow into the music, with the camera synchronizing its zooms with the musical emphases and colours of 'di questo core'. At appropriate moments it not only picked her out of the crowd, but repeatedly homed in on her upper body, face and mouth. Her posture throughout the scene supported her voice, and she used her mouth to project visual beauty into her singing, an extraordinary feat in a live performance with no retakes.

The lilt of 'di questo core' accords with the distinctive tidal music of the opera, until she reaches the penultimate line, 'Dio dai rimorsi ti salvi allora...' ('May God then save you from remorse'). At the repeat pass of 'salvi allora', the voice arches upwards on the second vowel of 'allora' before ebbing back down for 'io spenta ancora—pur t'amerò', Violetta's vow that her love will transcend death. At this precise moment, in the close-up of the camera's lens, Gheorghiu's features and body seamlessly blend into the music to form a tableau of almost ineffable beauty. The surrounding cast, including all the chief singers and also orchestra, respectfully attentive to Violetta's solo song, now come in and join her in *crescendo* without drowning her out. As the ensemble surges and retreats on a valzer-like roll towards the final bars, an ocean of music surrounds the mortally ill Violetta while granting her a breathing space after 't'amerò'. At this precise point Eyre's production intro-duced a touch of directing genius that arises organically out of the undulat-ing rhythm of the music and its worshipping of Violetta. Such is her weariness in the wake of her solo effort in 'di questo core' that she can no longer stand up unsupported in the surf of voices and orchestra. As she starts to sway, her arms opening in a Christ-like gesture, Flora first and then the doctor, Grenvil, each gently take one of her hands in both of theirs so that she is held as she prepares for the two last peaks in this extraordinary scene.

At the ebbing away of the first wave now shared between Violetta and the ensemble, the trumpets join in E flat, an hosannah of homage to Violetta.[22] The rich sound of the brass chimes with the visual intensity of Gheorghiu's Violetta here: a Bellini Madonna dressed as a demi-mondaine, with the entire scene turning into a virtual 'adoration' of Violetta; the trumpets, which are missing from the original 1853 version of 'di questo core', resonate above all other instruments in the final bars of this scene.

The final peak comes with Violetta's last 'io spenta ancora—pur t'amerò'. In the 1994 Royal Opera House production Gheorghiu's anguished singing of 'spenta ancora' was immeasurably enhanced by the intensity of her facial expression, the gentle sway of her body, with her mouth rounding out the vowels to perfection. These few seconds deserve to rank among the most inspired moments in the history of *La traviata* recordings, fleeting glimpses from a live performance of genius that inspired camera work managed to freeze for all time. In the 1854 version of 'di questo core' Violetta is wel-comed back into her social set. The words 'spenta ancora' fittingly mark her

final surrender just when her solo singing is gradually overtaken and sub-
merged by chorus and orchestra. Eyre's production understood better than
any other that this constituted a key passage of pathos in the opera. In this
final, public moment of epiphany, in the arching forward of Angela
Georghiu's body with her hands and arms held by her friends, Violetta
becomes a Madonna of love and sorrow.

Violetta's renunciation and readmittance into society constitute the
major difference with the 1853 version of 'di questo core' in which she is
isolated instead. La Fenice's 2004 rerun of its most celebrated premiere was
a remarkably courageous one and the production's Violetta, the outstanding soprano Patrizia Ciofi, a stalwart of the house, fired on all cylinders as
she reached 'di questo core'. By then members of the audience would have
been aware of nuanced differences between the opera they were hearing
and the one they were used to. But nothing could have prepared them for
the dramatic 'del tuo disprezzo' ('of your disdain') in the fourth line of the
aria, in which the notes jump high off the stave on an almost strident 'tuo'.
The effect is stunning: not the disdain itself but the fact that it is *Alfredo's*
contempt which hurts Violetta. The intimate use of 'tuo' in public would
have been bold enough—the libretto is the same in both 1853 and 1854
versions—but casting it up, literally, in this manner serves to stress Violetta's
anger and the intensity of the clash between her and Alfredo. In the 1853
opera 'tuo' is an anguished accusatory apostrophe; in 1854 it has become a
mere possessive pronoun. In some classic productions of the 1854 *La traviata*, Violetta is invited to over-emphasize the word 'disprezzo', in spite of
the fact that in the full score Verdi marked the entire passage from 'conosci'
through 'disprezzo' and 'provato io l'ho' as *ancora pianissimo* ('still very gently'). Even the most brilliant Violetta of the post-war era, Renée Fleming,
stresses 'tuo disprezzo' too dramatically in the sumptuous 2006 Los Angeles
production.

The point of the 1854 revision of the music was to rein in Violetta, to turn
even initial anger and outrage into love, forgiveness, and sacrifice, and to
mellow the melodic line. As the soprano Ciofi reaches 'salvi allora' in 'Dio
dai rimorsi ti salvi allora' on the second pass of the line, her voice soars up
before eventually reconnecting with the familiar musical line of 'di questo
core'. Whereas the 1854 Violetta gradually succumbs to the chorus of voices
around her, Ciofi twice more pulls away from the chorus's consensual harmonies, refusing to yield her own 'sempre libera' melodic line. In the original
score of 'di questo core' the heroine struggles with her destiny rather than

meekly embracing it; the Violetta of 1853 rises one last time, free on the wings of a solo melodic line, while the 1854 Violetta sinks under the waves of the ensemble.[23]

In the twelve months or so since *La traviata*'s first short run at La Fenice, Verdi had probably heard the opera a hundred times in his head. He must have wondered time and again how it could conceivably have failed to enthral audiences when its immediate lyrical cousins, *Rigoletto* and *Il trovatore*, had provoked nearly riotous adulation. By softening his heroine in this crucial scene, he seems to want to canonize her even more than before. It is hard not to see in the 1854 revision of 'di questo core' a fiercely personal engaging with the opera and Violetta in particular. Far from standing back and toning down the radical character of the work, Verdi instead breathed further vitality into it. Above all, the emphasis on surrender in the 1854 version of 'di questo core' paves the way for the glorious vision of Violetta in the immediately following Prelude to Act 3.

The first orchestral chords of the Prelude, marked *estremamente piano e assai legato* on the score, replay the opening bars of the opera's overture, though now in C minor, the key of Beethoven's great Symphony No. 5, before diverging from the overture at the 10th bar. Violetta is in full view on the stage as indicated in the libretto: 'Violetta sleeping on her bed and Annina, sitting next to the fireplace, also asleep'. There now follows probably the most transcendent moment in the opera as the rich tones of the violins start to wrap themselves around the heroine, tentatively at first but on an ever-increasing tide of sound. On bars 19 and 21 the violins begin an upward surge (marked *cres. poco a poco*) but at the last moment resist resolving the chords. A second ascent follows and this time, at bars 23–4, the music breaks through the sound barrier, as gloriously as it does in the finale of *Tristan und Isolde*. It retreats one more time before soaring all the way up to A-flat after which it ebbs away gently to the final two bars marked as a 'fading pianissimo' (*pppp morendo*) by the composer. According to the Verdi expert Fabrizio Della Seta, 'If therefore no.1 [the overture] can be interpreted as a retrospective account of Violetta's life, the brief orchestral prelude to the third act describes for us her tragic epilogue.'[24] But also perhaps her apotheosis, for the poignant orchestral preamble to Act 3, as tender as Mozart's 'Contessa perdono' from *Figaro* or the adagio of his Violin Concerto No. 3 in G Major, seeks to render nothing less than Violetta's soul.

The fragile beauty of this musical representation of Violetta in the prelude to Act 3 was captured perfectly in James Conlon's 2006 Los Angeles *La traviata.* Violetta, resting on her bed, comes into view only at the 19th bar, just as the music prepares its first upward flight. Conlon absolutely understands the brilliant dialogue between the music and the libretto's stage direction as the notes gently lap around Violetta. Under his baton the violins strive to make us hear the heartbeat of an angel at the first peak of bars 23–4; it may be the most sensitive and intuitive realization of those two bars in the recorded history of the opera. The barely detectable presence, in the darkened bedchamber on either side of Violetta, of altarboys with censers completes the homage to the sinner turned saint, Marie Duplessis of the Madeleine turned into the Madonna of the boulevard; not a socially constructed angel like Alfredo's sister but one who is destined to occupy her rightful place in Heaven as a reward for her purity of heart, as Germont tells her in the opera's final moments.

In the Conlon Prelude to Act 3, Violetta's bed becomes the shrine of a saint; the scene is, as Verdi probably intended, one of worship. At the same time the ebbs and flows of the music are profoundly sensual, fitting for Violetta whose life revolved around Eros while her dying happens to the sound of 'di quell'amor', which blends human and divine love. Any interpretation that fails to see this duality and integration inevitably shortchanges the opera's radical achievement. To portray Violetta instead as a tough and vulgar courtesan may well chime with the modish needs of twenty-first-century productions intent on hardening the edges of the opera. Robert Carsen made this point forcefully in an interview for *Passion Verdi*, first broadcast by ARTE in 2013, narrated by an outstanding Violetta (Natalie Dessay) and written, produced, and directed by Olivier Bellamy and Michel Follin. Carsen stressed the intended contemporaneity of the opera, the fact that Verdi wanted people to recognize themselves in the setting and the issues raised by the work; hence, in his view, the absolute necessity to play the opera in a modern context.

While such an attitude sounds commendably loyal to Verdi in principle, it may well misread the 1840s and 1850s, which are crucial to the context of the opera. The grittiness of street prostitution in the period was as raw as it is today, but a chasm of decorum separated that from the world of upper-class demi-mondaines. Directors who give us sluttish Violettas not only go against the grain of the music but fundamentally misconceive the rituals of the period in which it was written and set. To the majority of Verdi's contemporary audiences the high-society world of *La traviata* would have been no more familiar than the period costumes of Mario Lanfranchi's 1967 film of the opera, featuring Anna Moffo, or Zeffirelli's 1982 version of the same with Teresa Stratas, are to us.

The scale of the achievement of *La traviata* is as patent as that of a major Shakespearian tragedy. It likewise never looked back, at least not after 1854. To say that it took *La traviata* a year to establish itself as a classic would be misleading. It simply needed another theatre, another cast, and a handful of brilliant revisions to deliver to the world one of its best-loved works of art. In fact, the justly acclaimed San Benedetto production of 6 May 1854 was only the opera's tenth official staging in its entire life. Verdi need not have worried, the more so since the Fenice performances had not really been nearly as disastrous as he had hastily claimed the night of the world premiere of *La traviata*.

Not that the opera's path would run all that smoothly from then on. Verdi's lifelong anticlericalism and his aversion to censorship made him refuse productions of it until he was satisfied that the opera could be staged just as he desired. Thus, the idea of *La traviata* fending for herself in a house as much under the thumb of conservative censors as the Teatro San Carlo in Naples was not to be entertained. It was however in the reputedly enlightened city of Bologna, host to the oldest university in Europe, alma mater of Italy's national poet Dante Alighieri, that Verdi's opera suffered perhaps its most egregious cut, when a canon of the cathedral removed the word 'croce' from 'croce e delizia' substituting 'pena e delizia', because he would not contemplate the cross being used in the context of prostitution. He also saw fit to rewrite Violetta's exuberant and defiant 'La vità è nel tripudio' to 'Mia vità è nel tripudio', that is changing it from 'Life is joyful abandon' to 'My life is joyful abandon'. He wished to restrict her statement to the character of the courtesan, lest the Bolognese audience assumed that this was the maestro, composer of *Nabucco*, talking *in propria persona*.[25]

In the meantime, London and Paris were waiting for *La traviata*, with the British capital first off the mark by a few months in May 1856. By now the opera was flourishing across Italy, the Church's sporadic sniping and objections notwithstanding. If Violetta had already been consecrated one of the great heroines in opera, the young soprano who undertook the role in the two great capital cities gave her class and pedigree. Not even the Church could object to the new golden girl. Her name was Marietta Piccolomini (Figure 22.4). She had first sung Violetta the year before at the tender age of 21. A year on, and at exactly the same age as Marie Duplessis in the last year of her life, Marietta Piccolomini, progeny of one of the most illustrious

La prima donna Maria Piccolomini. Rôle de la Traviata.

Figure 22.4 Marietta Piccolomini, who sang the role of Violetta at the London and Paris premieres and made *La traviata* famous throughout Europe.

Siennese dynasties, descended from popes, cardinals, and condottieri, propelled *La traviata* into legend. Of course audiences flocked to see her as much as they wanted to hear Verdi's opera. But because the opera *is* Violetta—and indeed was sometimes known by that name in the early years—it was impossible to love and admire the young Piccolomini without responding to the power of the role she inhabited with such grace and panache.

La traviata premiered at Her Majesty's Theatre in London on 24 May 1856 and predictably caused consternation.[26] As yet though, the reviewers were suitably respectful given Piccolomini's blue-blood credentials. The first *Times* review of the opera appeared on 26 May 1856. The writer was inevitably drawn to the legendary Piccolomini name of the soprano and clumsily alluded to Juliet's 'What's in a name?', addressed to Romeo in the balcony scene of *Romeo and Juliet*. For Juliet a name is just that, letters without substance, a convention: 'a rose by any other word would smell as sweet', she reasons, so why should Romeo's surname of Montague mean that he has to be her sworn enemy? The reviewer, not blessed with Juliet's, or Shakespeare's, moral intelligence, begs to differ: 'some names', he remarks, 'are so exceedingly big that one cannot hear them with indifference.' Certainly no true snob could. In his review he offers a detailed exposition of the plot of the opera before concluding: 'We have been thus minute with the plot because the book is of far more consequence than the music, which, except so far as it affords a vehicle for the utterance of the dialogue, is of no value whatever, and, moreover, because it is essentially as a *dramatic* vocalist that the brilliant success of Mademoiselle Piccolomini was achieved.... For the present it will be just sufficient to treat *La traviata* as a play set to music.'

The Times was not done with *La traviata*. To its chagrin, the opera ran and ran at Her Majesty's Theatre in the Haymarket, seemingly unstoppable. So, on 7 August 1856, the paper's leader writer took time out from covering the Empire to demonstrate why his paper was known as the 'thunderer'. This opera posed 'a grave question of public morality', he contended stentoriously, excoriating the work, its composer, and those who were involved in staging it, for their offence among others to English womanhood:

To come to the point, for some months past an opera bearing the name of *La traviata* has been represented at Her Majesty's Theatre ... This opera is founded upon a tale as profoundly immoral as itself [*sic*], called *La Dame aux Camélias*, which was published not very long since in Paris ... Suffice it to say that all the interest is concentrated upon the death struggles of this wretched girl. It is for her that pity is asked, and it is to her that pity is given. The novel is the apotheosis of prostitution, and upon the stage is practically added a clinical lecture upon consumption in its direst form. Now, we say that, morally speaking, this is most hideous and abominable.

The writer is exercised by the 'paid strumpets' and 'the brothels and abominations of modern Paris' that populate the opera while audiences too need to look to their moral compass:

> Deep and unmitigated censure should be the portion of an audience who could sit out such a spectacle, especially when that audience is for the most part composed of women. Surely, in order to entertain an English lady it is not necessary to take her for a saunter in the Haymarket at midnight, and to conduct her about 4am to the consumptive ward of an hospital that she may see a prostitute finish her career....

To its credit *The Times*, in the same issue of 7 August 1856, published a letter containing a spirited defence of the opera and of the way Piccolomini had interpreted Violetta. The letter was written by an actor whose final broadside was that the libretto of *La traviata* contains 'not a single impure expression'. Opinion in the country about the opera was, to say the least, divided, and the pendulum was rapidly swinging towards Verdi's magnanimous music and vision. So *The Times* returned to the charge a few days later, this time deploying the fire and brimstone language of seventeenth-century Puritan sermons, and again using the inclusive 'we' of the righteous:

> we renew our indignant protest against this exhibition of harlotry...upon the public stage...The image of the weeping Magdalene is one of the most touching which has been handed down to us even in the pages of Scripture, but who can wish to see the story of Magdalene dramatized, and presented to the public with all the soft allurements of music and song?...A dirty story is the ready resource of every vulgar fellow who can do no better...[then, responding to the defence of the opera by B. Lumley, the manager of Her Majesty's Theatre at the Haymarket, the *Times* columnist grandly notes]...we leave it to the public to decide whether we or Mr Lumley and the Satanic dramatists are the truest friends of the stage.
>
> (*The Times*, 11 August)

The fire-breathing rhetoric of the crusader stooped so low as to call Verdi, Piave, Dumas, and their fellow dramatists 'Satanic'. On 27 October 1856 *The Times* finally capitulated when its music reviewer took on his own paper, noting that 'As the son of Alcmena strangled the serpent in his cradle so did the *Dame aux Camélias*, in defiance of the Lord Chamberlain's edicts, grow up into *La traviata*, and firmly establish itself on the boards of Her Majesty's Theatre.'[27] The review constitutes a robust defence of the opera on all counts, and particularly against the narrow moralists. The writer notes with considerable glee that the huge theatre was packed night after night and that people had to be turned away from the doors. In London *La traviata* soon exceeded *Il trovatore* in popularity, primarily because of Piccolomini who sang the role at both the Haymarket and then the Royal Opera House.[28]

With *La traviata* a sensation in London, it was time for Paris. Violetta would at last go home, as it were. In December 1856 Marie Duplessis had been dead for nine years although she had hardly been out of the public's awareness for any length of time, due to the continuing success of Dumas's novel and play. Since the Paris premiere of *Nabucco* in October 1845, Verdi had joined the pantheon of giants of Italian opera. But Paris was also profoundly sensitive to the way it was portrayed in the two Verdi operas based on French works, *Rigoletto* and *La traviata*. Thus, while *The Times* was fulminating against *La traviata*, the bold impresarios of the Haymarket cocked a snook at the censors and staged both *La traviata* and *Rigoletto* ahead of Paris. The hunchback opera had earlier premiered to rapturous applause in London in 1853 but Paris, perhaps out of deference to Victor Hugo whose *Le roi s'amuse*, the source for *Rigoletto*, was still banned, only staged it four years later.

La traviata opened in Paris on Saturday 6 December 1856. Verdi's greatest supporter in the city on the Seine had long been the critic Léon Escudier. On 14 December 1856 he wrote a stunning review of the Parisian première of *La traviata* in *France Musicale*. His review pays tribute to the recent London run of the opera where, he remarks, applauding tramplings of feet, hurrahs, and showers of flowers accompanied every performance. The fact that Piccolomini again starred as Violetta was noted in Paris too, but her pedigree did not unduly colour Escudier's view of her abilities which he thought also considerable but not always perfect. Nevertheless, he waxes rhapsodic at her beauty and stage presence, her instinctive talent for acting, the flair, elegance, even grace of her deportment on stage, a perfect match for the role, 'quite simply an untutored genius' that moved the audience from joy to tears. What raises Escudier's review above the pack is its immediacy and sheer modernity. His is an instinctively visceral response to the opera's drive and its power to move. Apart from Verdi and Piave, he may have been the first person to realize that *La traviata* was nothing short of a musical miracle, that no opera had ever struck such chords quite so deeply in the human heart. At the Paris premiere the part of Alfredo was sung by de Candia ('Mario') who, Escudier thought, had never performed as beautifully as he did in the brindisi in Act 1. Marie Duplessis had probably seen him in *Don Pasquale*. Germont was sung by the baritone Francesco Graziani, brother of the tenor Lodovico Graziani, who had undertaken Alfredo at the world premiere of *La traviata* in Venice.

If Escudier was irked by the clumsiness, as he saw it, of the production, unworthy of the 'master of Busseto', individual musical numbers soared on this night as they do in all great *La traviatas*: 'the music of *La traviata* is not for ordinary audiences; for all its pellucid clarity, it is profoundly spiritual', Escudier wrote. His description of the orchestral prelude, a 'delicious instrumental page', noted that 'it is as if a ray of hope were born and nurtured in a heart in love'. He was ravished by the bacchanalia of 'Libiamo' ('such sensuality in its melodical contours…it felt like a musical intoxication') while 'Un dì felice' held the audience spellbound. Time and again Escudier found the *mot juste* to render the feel of a particular cavatina or aria, as when describing Germont's great aria 'Di Provenza il mar, il suol' as irresistible elegiac poetry, 'a melody in the manner of Bellini'.[29] Escudier recognized the plaintive beauty of the prelude of Act 3 before offering up an incisive decription of Act 3 of *La traviata*:

> In the third act it is all suffering. The parties and pleasures of youth have been succeeded by sadness and repentance. La traviata, broken, pale with shame, resigned and dying, cries and sobs. From delirious passion she has passed to the delirium of fever. The act opens with an instrumental page of adorable poetry. La Piccolomini is no longer this fresh-looking bright young woman, with the smile of a woman in love, and ardent eyes. The shadows of death hover over her face. She rises as if she were wrapped in her shroud, sings of her regrets and cries for her lack of respectability. How moving that melody punctuated by sobs ['Addio del passato bei sogni ridenti'] sung sighingly in an agonizing voice. And here now is her partner of her lost former pleasures. She sees him one last time and it is here now that we get that famous duet which is one of the most acclaimed masterpieces of modern music ['Parigi o cara noi lasceremo']. Who could fail to be moved by hearing these last melodies of love, intangible echoes of earthly joys forever lost? Where could one possibly find its peer since it is peerless even in all of Verdi's repertoire. It is a drama of sublime integrity. One feels as if one's heart had been possessed while one's eyes flood with tears. The orchestral part certainly matches the singing, constantly following its most capricious turns with an exquisite touch, an inexhaustible wealth of musical colours. The composer thus sustains his opera until the very end. Violetta dies in the arms of her lover on the final, fading note of the orchestra.

Where, Escudier wondered in December 1856, would *La traviata* go from here? He was certain it would prevail in the future because, he averred, even the maestro Verdi had never written more gorgeous melodies. Not since Rossini had such music been heard or, for that matter, divided critical opinion in Paris so profoundly. But the doubters were soon forgotten.

With *La traviata* the story of Marie Duplessis reached for the skies. From inauspicious beginnings at la Fenice in Venice it spread across the cities of Italy, Europe, and the Americas. In New York it premiered at the 'Old Met' on 5 November 1883, barely two weeks after the opening of the Metropolitan Opera itself, alongside *Faust*, *Lucia di Lammermoor* and *Il trovatore*, all of which were meant to launch the new house to stardom; as indeed they did. If *La traviata* has universally supplanted the literary work that engendered it, nevertheless Dumas's play remains a milestone work for its frankness about sex. Its adult acceptance of a libertine world of licence anticipates the mores of the 1960s. Even today its changes of register, as in its uses of 'tu' after sex for the much more common 'vous', resonate powerfully in French. Ever since the 1850s the novel and play have glowed with the aura of *La traviata*, an echo of the *tinta* that long ago rose to the surface from Verdi's musical unconscious during a performance of Dumas's play. What he heard were the initial chords of a music that millions of people around the world have since experienced as one of the most sublime products of human creativity.

23
Epilogue
Memory and myth

Cold in the earth and the deep snow piled above thee,
Far, far removed, cold in the dreary grave!
Have I forgot, my only Love, to love thee,
Severed at last by Time's all-severing wave?

(Emily Brontë, 'Remembrance')

Marie Duplessis had only just turned 23 at the time of her death so that many, if not most, of her friends, were inevitably young men and women like Dumas *fils* or Judith Bernat, to mention only two who feature in this story by name. While there was no youth culture in the middle of nineteenth-century France any more than in Dickens's England, her Parisian set of lions, dandies, writers, artists, and musicians consisted mainly of young people most of whom survived her. If they had been minded to forget her they were not allowed to do so. All Paris knew that Dumas's novel was intimately based on real life. What did the lovers and friends, men and women, who had been close to Marie Duplessis think as they read the novel, or when they sat through the play at the Vaudeville? How odd it must have seemed to them that their friend was becoming a legend and so quickly. Not only that, but they will have witnessed the power of her story to move as people wept and succumbed to the sheer pull of the melodrama. Then came *La traviata* whose reputation preceded its arrival at the Italian theatre in Paris. By the time it was first performed in December 1856, *La dame aux camélias* with Eugénie Doche had been enjoying one of the epic runs of the Parisian dramatic scene while the illustrious Judith Bernat was exporting the role of the heroine beyond the capital. It was clear to all who had known the young woman behind *La traviata* that the opera idealized not just the original young woman but also the heroine of both novel and play. Few of Marie Duplessis's friends have left records of their responses to the play. The fact that Morny licensed it within a few days of taking office may show quite how affected he was by it. And Dumas? His published response in the 1867 preface to the novel mostly expatiates on the licensing, the cast, and the first performances of his play. He had said everything he wanted to say in the novel and play themselves. The adulatory reviews of his play must have been gratifying. But what did he make of *La traviata*, and were there any contractual negotiations over the rights to *La Dame aux Camélias* granted to Verdi, Piave, and La Fenice?

We may be reasonably confident that Dumas *père et fils* and many of their friends and other acquaintances of Marie Duplessis's would have been at the Paris premiere of *La traviata* in December 1856. Did they too, like Escudier, melt over the sounds of the opera, or did the fact that they had known its subject restrain their emotions? Escudier makes no reference to the real life Mary Magdalene but, as a major player on the Parisian music scene and not much more than two years older than Marie Duplessis, he must have known all about her, both during her life and subsequently by attending one of the Vaudeville performances of the play. It is not impossible that Escudier, who first met Verdi in Milan in May 1845, suggested Dumas's novel to Verdi and that this was why Escudier's sister sent it to the composer.[1] It is tempting to wonder whether he accompanied Verdi and Strepponi to a performance at the Vaudeville, given that he was probably Verdi's closest professional friend in the city.

Writing in his memoir *Parisine*, published in 1869 not long before his death, Nestor Roqueplan, the kingpin impresario of Paris who had once bought Marie Duplessis chips on the Pont-Neuf, recalled his first visit to the tomb in Montmartre. It was the time of life, he noted ruefully, when visits to cemeteries became ever more frequent. He entered the cemetery's lodge with the intention of finding the graves of two Prussian officers, one of which carried a Latin inscription that he particularly desired to see. He asked for help in finding it and was referred to a 55-year-old warder of the cemetery whose family had been employed there since its inception eighty years earlier, when it was founded to cater for the dead of the Revolution. After showing Roqueplan the German tombs, the warder offered to show him another one, 'of a beautiful woman', unaware of Roqueplan's acquaintance with the dead woman. As they stood before the sarcophagus of Marie

Duplessis, Roqueplan, who had never visited it before, pondered the pride his companion took in being the guardian of the legendary courtesan:

> I recalled the pretty Marie Duplessis, who became the lady of the camellias and then La traviata, surviving herself through the love of a poet and the genius of a musician. If I were to write the novel *The Lady of the Camellias*, I would divide it into three parts: 1. Fried Chips; 2. Camellias; 3. Phthisis.

Her life story came back to him then. Nearly thirty years after meeting a hungry Alphonsine Plessis on a Paris bridge, his memory was as sharp as one might have expected from the leading theatre and opera impresario of the era. His memoir precedes Vienne's by nearly twenty years and therefore has independent authority from his. He remembered (he must have heard this at the time as he was not present) that her coffin was filled with camellias and that during the first year after her death women who had envied her wealth and success started the trend of visiting her tomb to pay homage by laying bunches of camellias on it.

If Roqueplan's memory serves, then it would seem that Marie Duplessis's tomb became a place of pilgrimage almost at once. That it was women who thus honoured her tallies with other reports that referred to some of the fallen girls of Paris, who mourned for their sister by following the cortège on that February day in 1847; or perhaps, as seems more likely, by making their way discreetly to the cemetery in Montmartre, far from the gazing crowds but spotted by the staff at the cemetery. Roqueplan's information about the women's camellias would seem to come from the very warder who showed him the grave. This man ought to know; he was 38 when Marie Duplessis was buried here and may well have been a gravedigger at the time, if not one of the very men who dug her up for her second burial.

When Roqueplan visited her grave, the man who first rendered Marie Duplessis famous was very much alive. A rumour, allegedly emanating from the gravediggers of the Montmartre cemetery, had it that Dumas never visited his lover's tomb.[2] This is demonstrably untrue. Not only did he, as we saw, visit it on 1 January 1850, but in the 1867 preface to the play of *La Dame aux Camélias* he showed that he knew her tomb well and was all too aware of its iconic status in Paris: 'If, in the cemetery of Montmartre, you ask to see the tomb of the lady of the camellias, the guardian will take you to a small square monument which carries under the name Alphonsine Plessis a crown of white artificial camellias, fastened to the marble under a glass case. That grave now has its legend. Art is divine: it creates and it resurrects.'[3]

If Dumas saw *La traviata*, he could hardly fail to be moved by it but so far no response by him to the opera has come to light. He would have known that his novel and play could never climb the giddy heights of Verdi's masterpiece, which wrenched the story of Marie Duplessis from its local context and exported it to the entire world. Henceforth the young woman whom Dumas had sought to honour had acquired wings of a kind that perhaps only music can gift. One of her biographers records that at some point after her death the premises of 11 boulevard de la Madeleine were occupied by a tailor, one M. G. Malsis. He was, or became, Dumas's tailor. Apparently visits to his tailor in the Madeleine invariably upset Dumas. While this is quite possible, it may also be the case that Malsis attracted Dumas's custom precisely because his shop was the old apartment of Marie Duplessis; Dumas's attachment to the physical space that had been hers, and which he briefly shared with her, may have remained as strong as it was in *Péchés de Jeunesse* and the first edition of *La Dame aux Camélias*.[4]

When Dumas died on 27 November 1895 he was interred in the cemetery of Montmartre a mere hundred yards from the woman he had loved in the 1840s. In his testament he had expressed the wish to be buried in Père-Lachaise. Perhaps his daughter Jeannine felt that her father ought in death, and for all eternity, to be close instead to the girl from Normandy who had made his fortune and his fame; maybe. Jules Claretie, the director of the Comédie-Française, attended his funeral and afterwards drifted across to the tomb of Marie Duplessis. So did others. In his own words written a few days after the interment, 'Our people of Paris are essentially sentimental, as they use their free Sunday to visit, in the Montmartre Cemetery, the grave of Marie Duplessis, the lady of the camellias, after saluting the provisional grave where Alexandre Dumas rests under his flowers.' Dumas's novel had made her the incarnation of love in the nineteenth century. Writing towards the end of that century, Claretie maintained that if a statue were erected to the younger Dumas, the crowds of Paris would be bound also to adorn the tomb of Marie Duplessis with white or pink camellias.[5] As late as the 1920s Marie Duplessis's grave was looked after by one Mr Bourdon on behalf of Mr Ernest d'Hauterive, 'son-in-law of Alexandre *fils*'.[6] Dumas *fils* and, eventually, his widow and daughter had discussed the lady of the camellias in later years. Dumas's daughter, Jeannine Alexandre d'Hauterive, proudly wore the necklace that her father had originally presented to Marie Duplessis during their liaison in 1844–5 and which he had subsequently bought back from whoever purchased it at the Madeleine auction in February 1847.[7] In 1943 she was buried with it.

Having secured a perpetual concession in Montmartre for his wife, Édouard de Perrégaux was bound to visit her tomb. He may have done so regularly. No-one doubted his grief at the time of her death. How he responded to the almost universal notion, after 1848, that the chief lover of the lady of the camellias had been the younger Dumas, we will never know. Perhaps he and Dumas had come to an understanding on this during the period of his temporary return to Alice Ozy after Marie's death. In 1852 he must have seen the play with Eugénie Doche. It it is not impossible that Horace de Vieil-Castel's broadside against the 'gull' who regularly turned up at performances of La Dame aux Camélias was directed at Perrégaux, even though he alleged that the dupe had been jilted by Doche with whom Perrégaux had never been linked. Perrégaux owned a copy of Dumas's novel. In it he seems to have kept one of Marie's letters, the one in which, as we saw, she appears to refer to him as 'my very own stallion'. He may in fact have collected all her letters. According to Julie Claudine de Perrégaux, in 1915, when she was 15, her grandfather Frédéric de Perrégaux 'gave her two packets of letters—one tied with a pink ribbon, the letters of Alphonsine—the other with blue ribbon, the letters of Édouard'. He told her to burn them, saying 'These are the letters of a whore who brought dishonour upon our family.'[8]

Perrégaux's loyalty to Marie Duplessis after her death, which started with the second burial in Montmartre, probably continued over the years that followed. Perhaps all the way to 1889 when, in the village of Saint-Cyr near Versailles one evening, at the age of 73, the widower of Marie Duplessis walked into his garden and died probably of a stroke. Saint-Cyr is not far from Bougival where over forty years earlier he and Marie had spent so many happy hours. When La traviata opened in Paris, did Perrégaux, an inveterate visitor to the opera, go and see it, to witness for himself the ultimate apotheosis of his young wife? Once again he needed to confront the fact that she had been taken from him, twice over because now her lover's father was probably named after Gramont. He knew Guiche Gramont. The two men met, if not before, then during Marie Duplessis's funeral at the latest. Perrégaux, Gramont, and Morny all lacked the creative gifts of Dumas, Verdi, and Piave but in their own ways, and largely unwittingly, by loving Marie Duplessis they each played a crucial role in a trajectory that in the end transported her to glory and immortality as Violetta Valéry.

The tributes to the young woman from the Orne did not stop there. No-one in the world could be better placed than Liszt to appreciate the scale and achievement of *La traviata*. His elegiac letter about Marie Duplessis on learning of her death eloquently expressed his love for her and later he vouched for the authenticity of her portrayal by Dumas, whom he had once met, it seems, in Marie's apartment at 11 boulevard de la Madeleine.[9] It may not be his only tribute to her, because his great piano sonata in B minor, in draft within a year of her death and completed in 1853, the year of *La traviata*, may also be about Marie Duplessis. At least that is how it was interpreted in 1963 by Frederick Ashton, who used it to create his ballet *Marguerite and Armand*, after the protagonists of Dumas's novel and play.

What Liszt made of *La traviata* is not recorded. As one of the greatest musicians of the nineteenth century, his views on the opera would be of enormous intrinsic interest; they would be even more so because the opera wholeheartedly celebrates a young woman whom he himself had adored to distraction. It is inconceivable that he did not see *La traviata* in the course of his long life, particularly as the opera's triumphal march through the capitals of Europe became unstoppable within a year of its premiere. More than anyone Liszt would have grasped the extent to which the music captured the quintessence of the young Marie Duplessis. Perhaps he regretted that in the end it was a stranger who had so brilliantly celebrated her legacy; who had breathed into her a memory and soul beyond anything imagined by Dumas. No correspondence on the opera between Liszt and Verdi, or Liszt and anyone else for that matter, exists. The fact that Liszt was closely tied into the Wagner circle may account partly for this. He had been Wagner's sponsor and his daughter Cosima became Wagner's wife. The musical world of nineteenth-century opera tended to divide between Verdians and Wagnerians, with most musicians well aware of the fact that they were the contemporaries of two equally impressive musical titans.

But Liszt was a great adaptor, and one of several pieces of Verdi's music that he rescored for piano is the tenor aria 'Bella figlia dell'amore' ('beautiful daughter of love') by the swaggering Duke of Mantua from *Rigoletto*. The aria, which is launched by a bold orchestral gallop—it anticipates the surgings of *La traviata*—leads into the great quartet of the Duke, Rigoletto, Gilda, and Maddalena that concludes the third scene of Act 3 of *Rigoletto*. Liszt composed his version, *Rigoletto: Paraphrase de Concert* (S.434), in 1859, six years after *La traviata*. The young woman who is serenaded with 'Bella figlia dell'amore' is a beautiful prostitute by the name of 'Maddalena'. She is the sister of the murderer Sparafucile whom the hunchback has hired to kill the Duke to avenge his daughter's violated honour. Is it too fanciful to wonder whether Liszt set this particular piece of Verdi to music because of his own love affair with the Maddalena of the Madeleine, Marie Duplessis being both Gilda and Maddalena? In *Rigoletto* Maddalena pleads with her brother to let the Duke of Mantua live, because the cocky singer of 'La donna è mobile' is the most irresistibly seductive of young men. Sparafucile gives in to her wishes but on condition that another body can be substituted. Overhearing this, Gilda offers herself as a human sacrifice, to take the place of the Duke of Mantua whom she loves in spite of the hurt he has caused her.

Many years later Liszt confided in his former pupil and secretary, Janka Wohl, about Marie Duplessis. Her memoir, *François Liszt: souvenirs d'une compatriote*, was published in 1887, a year after Liszt's death. In it she recalls how

> Sometimes, particularly during the last years of his life, a melancholy note crept into the recollections of the master. He loved to linger over former missed opportunities, over occasions he had spoiled, over everything that had eluded him, like the rich man even harder to please than the gourmet. This feeling of regret became laced with extreme frankness one day when he spoke to us about Mlle Duplessis.

She then records Liszt's own recollection of their first encounter in the lobby of the Ambigu-Comique and how the following day a friend of Marie's offered to take him to 'the beauty in fashion'. This 'friend' may well have been Lichnowsky, if the latter had returned to Paris by then. Wohl continues:

> In her home Liszt found brilliant company, the best in Paris... writers, artists of the very first order, etc. He returned to her home frequently. She wanted to accompany him to Weimar, 'but I assumed that there would be certain problems with putting her up', said Liszt and made her understand that she would not like it. She demurred, claiming that she would not have the time to get bored because she rose at two in the afternoon, before going to the Bois [de Boulogne] for an hour or two and at night she went to the theatres. That was her life! They came to an agreement: they would meet up the following year in Pest [Budapest] from where they would travel together to Constantinople. Liszt left. Sixteen months later he heard the news of her death. She was already suffering from consumption at the time of their relationship. Liszt found her very graceful, high-spirited, and full of childlike abandon.[10]

In the same year that Wohl's book appeared, Verdi received a letter and article from Gérard de Contades, who had just completed his ground-breaking
essay on the portraits of Marie Duplessis. Not only was Contades well connected among the upper echelons of Parisian society, and therefore enjoyed
the widest possible access to the men who had known his subject four
decades earlier, but he had known the young artist Charles Chaplin and had
consulted him about his painting sessions with Marie. Above all he had
enjoyed the benefit of Dumas *fils*'s good will who shared his pictures of
Marie with him, notably the Olivier watercolour; which is why we know
so much about its pedigree and eventual migration into the home of the
novelist. Contades loved *La traviata* and desired Verdi to have a copy of his
article because it contained two images of Marie: Chaplin's Comédie-
Française one and the one of an 'ingénue' Marie in her bathrobe, which
Contades oddly misattributes thinking it might be the 'lost' one painted by
Vidal. Verdi probably already knew what she had looked like anyway.

Until the end of the nineteenth century, and over many years beyond,
Marie Duplessis's grave was lovingly tended, at first by one Comtesse Néra
de la Jonchère. Was she from the Château de Jonchère in Bougival? The
main artery of the town to this day is the avenue de la Jonchère. If there is
indeed such a link here, she may have been someone whom the lovers had
known during their brief interlude in the bend on the Seine; or else she
may have been a friend of Dumas whose links with this western edge of
Paris lasted many years. Subsequently the daughter of Dumas *fils*, Jeannine
de Hauterive, also retained an interest in the grave, which lay after all not far
from her father's. Following her death during the Second World War, others
took over. As late as 1950, the concierge of the Paris building inhabited by
one of Dumas's biographers set off every Sunday to the grave of the lady of
the camellias with a bunch of azaleas.[11] Violetta's dreaded 'fossa' of the opera
has become a place of homage. Far from being a shadowy presence behind
the opera, the young woman in Montmartre has been virtually canonized.
It is impossible to stand in front of her grave without hearing chords from
La traviata or imagining the many people who over the years have squeezed
through the narrow gaps between the tombs, to stand in front of the sarcophagus to remember Marie Duplessis, the real-life woman who, through
La dame aux camélias, inspired the glory that is *La traviata*.

Verdi reverts repeatedly to Violetta's 'past sufferings and sorrows' ('corsi
affanni') that the love of Alfredo was destined to redeem. He knew the
humiliation and loneliness endured by young women like Marie Duplessis.

This is why he poured all his prodigious musical gifts into *La traviata*, in which Violetta's extraordinary presence indubitably resonates with his grief over the death of his wife and two little children many years earlier. As a small boy Giuseppe Verdi had depended on the kindness of a stranger, the father of the woman he married. He was forever grateful. As his genius came to be toasted all over the world in the long years that followed, he more than anyone imagined the hardships and privations of that other road he never needed to take because of the trust and generosity of Antonio Barezzi.

His compassion for Marie Duplessis may stem from there, and so may his instant recognition of her inner beauty from Dumas's portrayal of her. Every time *La traviata* is performed or its peerless tunes are sung at La Scala in Milan, the Met in New York, the Royal Opera House in London, the Staatsoper in Vienna, in public squares in Italy, in the markets of Turin, or in the cafés of Verdi's native Busseto, the world is left a slightly kinder place. Verdi, who later composed a haunting opera called *La Forza del Destino*, shared his own destiny with Marie Duplessis. His origins and his terrible early losses were in the end compensated, as much as they could be, by a productive longevity that allowed him to grant her the only possible redemption for her suffering. The creation of Violetta, known universally as 'traviata' and descended from the tragic existence of Marie Duplessis, was ultimately an act of love that has echoed around the world since that first night of 6 March 1853 at La Fenice in Venice. *La traviata* constitutes Verdi's supreme musical expression of 'the still sad music of humanity', as William Wordsworth put it in his poem 'Tintern Abbey'. Like *King Lear*, the opera seeks to redeem adversity by grace, beauty, and intensity; like Shakespeare's masterpiece, *La traviata* too is suffused by tears.

Main Characters

Marie Duplessis, alias Rose Alphonsine Plessis, *alias* 'la dame aux camélias'

Agénor de Gramont, Duc de Guiche, lover of Marie Duplessis

Alexandre Dumas fils, author of *La Dame aux Camélias*

Alexandre Dumas père, author of the *Three Musketeers* and *The Count of Monte Cristo* and impresario

Alice Ozy, an actress and mistress of Édouard de Perregaux, drawn by Chassériau and Théophile Gautier

Antonio Barezzi, Verdi's father-in-law who first spotted his genius

Charles Chaplin, a young artist who repeatedly drew Marie Duplessis

Charles de Morny, half-brother of Louis-Napoléon Bonaparte; he licensed Dumas's play *La Dame aux Camélias* in 1852

Clémence Pratt, fashionable hat designer and procuress from the Madeleine

Clotilde, chambermaid and travel companion of Marie Duplessis

Count Gustav von Stackelberg, a rich and retired diplomat in Paris

Delphine Paquet, née Plessis, elder sister of Alphonsine

Duchesse de Raguse, née Hortense Perrégaux, aunt of Édouard de Perrégaux

Édouard de Perrégaux, lover of Marie Duplessis and Alice Ozy

Eugénie Doche, the first actress to play la dame aux camélias in 1852

Fanny Salvini-Donatelli, the first Violetta at La Fenice on 6 March 1853

Felice Varesi, the first Germont at the world premiere of *La traviata*

Felix von Lichnowsky, a close friend of Liszt

Fernand de Montguyon, intimate friend of de Morny's and equerry to the heir to the French throne

Francesco Maria Piave, librettist of *La traviata*

Franz Liszt, the greatest pianist of the age

Giuseppe Verdi, composer of *La traviata*

Giuseppina Strepponi, Verdi's mistress and second wife

Judith Bernat, actress at the Variétés and Comédie-Française theatres, befriended by Marie Duplessis

Jules Janin, a leading arts and theatre reviewer of Paris in the 1840s

Lady Charlotte Anderson Worsley Copley, an English baroness and friend of the mother of Marie Duplessis

Léon Escudier, a Paris music critic and friend of Verdi's

Lodovico Graziani, the first ever Alfredo

Lola Montez, dancer, adventurer, and friend of Marie Duplessis

Maria Spezia, first sang Violetta in the 1854 revised score of *La traviata*

Margherita Verdi, née Barezzi, Verdi's first wife and mother of his two children

Marie Deshayes, alias Marie du Plessis, mother of the future dame aux camélias

Marietta Piccolomini, the admired Violetta of the London and Paris premieres of *La traviata*

Marin Plessis, a pedlar from the Orne and the father of Marie Duplessis

Nestor de Roqueplan, director of the Variétés theatre and Paris Opéra

'Nollet', a restaurant owner from Palais-Royal who took Alphonsine as his mistress

Olympe Aguado, a rich photographer and lover of Marie Duplessis

'Plantier', a septuagenarian from Exmes who abused the teenage Alphonsine

Richard Wallace, Anglo-French founder of the Wallace Collection and chronicler

Romain Vienne, friend and chronicler of Marie Duplessis

Théophile Gautier, poet, novelist and journalist whose obituary of la dame aux camélias may have inspired Dumas's novel

Tony, a French-speaking English provider of horses from the Champs-Élysées

Marie Duplessis's life at a glance

15 January 1824	Rose Alphonsine Plessis born in Nonant in Lower Normandy.
20 January 1824	Christened at the church of Sainte-Blaise, Nonant.
6 January 1828	Her father nearly kills her mother.
7 January 1828	Last sight of her mother who goes into hiding and then flees the region.
30 September 1830	Death of her mother in Châtelard (Clarens) on Lake Geneva.
spring 1833	Takes her first communion in Saint-Germain-de-Clairefeuille.
1834–6	Homeless and drifting in the hills around Nonant.
August 1837	Taken to the paedophile Plantier's house in Exmes.
October 1838	Removed by her father from the Denis home in Exmes.
autumn 1838	Works in a factory in Gacé.
c. Christmas 1838	Withdrawn by her father from Gacé and abused by him.
January 1839	Taken by her father to work in Paris.
summer 1839	Becomes the mistress of a wealthy restaurant owner from Palais-Royal.
January 1840	Meets a grand nobleman, her 'Pygmalion'.
1840	A year of 'schooling' during which the country girl becomes the first lady of Paris's demi-monde; moves to 28 Mont-Thabor, Paris.
May 1841	Gives birth in Versailles to a baby boy who dies shortly afterwards.
10 July 1841	Returns to Nonant to recover from the birth and to visit her family and guardian.
13 July 1842	Issued with her first passport to travel abroad.
22 July 1842	Arrives in Baden-Baden where she is wooed by her future protector, Count Stackelberg.

15 October 1842	Moves into a new apartment at 22 rue d'Antin, Paris.
autumn 1842–spring 1843	Is the mistress of Agénor de Gramont, Duc de Guiche.
February 1843	Visits London.
21 May 1843	Appears with Édouard de Perrégaux at the Prix du Jockey-Club at the Chantilly races.
June 1843	Visits London again with, probably, Perrégaux.
summer 1843	Rents a cottage in Bougival to the west of Paris; lives there with Perrégaux.
25 July 1843	With Alexandre Dumas *fils* she encounters the elder Dumas in the Comédie-Française.
2 December 1843	Attends a charity show at the Variétés in which a rival, the actress Alice Ozy, performs.
c. February 1844	Moves into a mezzanine apartment at 11 boulevard de la Madeleine, Paris.
c. April 1844	Starts an affair with Liszt's friend Lichnowsky.
September 1844	Meets Dumas *fils* at (probably) the Variétés theatre; their affair launched that same night.
1 January 1845	Receives extravagant gift of oranges wrapped in 1000-franc bills.
spring 1845	Becomes the lover of the rich Olympe Aguado.
October 1845	Paris premiere of Verdi's *Nabucco*; her sister Delphine Plessis marries a local weaver by the name of Louis Paquet.
27 October 1845	Meets Liszt in the foyer of the Ambigu-Comique theatre; they become lovers.
December 1845	Sees the portrait of her mother and Lady Anderson Copley; becomes friends with a rising star of the theatre, Judith Bernat.
25 January 1846	Acquires her second (extant) passport.
21 February 1846	Marries Édouard de Perrégaux in London.
19 April 1846	Appears at the steeplechase at La Croix-de-Berny outside Paris.
May 1846	Joins Vicomte Théodoric Narbonne Pelet at La Roche-Nonant near Exmes.
12 June 1846	Stays in Spa.
19 June 1846	Dazzles onlookers with her dancing at the grand inaugural ball in Spa.
26 June 1846	Stays in the Europäischer Hof in Baden-Baden.

first half of July 1846	Stays in the Englischer Hof in Bad Ems.
autumn 1846	Drawn and painted repeatedly by the portrait artist Charles Chaplin; constantly attended by doctors as her tubercular condition deteriorates.
20 October 1846	Romain Vienne calls on her; it is the last time he sees her alive.
November 1846	Visited in her apartment by Henry Lumière.
end of December 1846	Attends her last show in Paris, *La Poudre-coton: Revue de l'année 1846*, at the Palais-Royal theatre.
3 February 1847	Marie Duplessis dies at 11 boulevard de la Madeleine.
5 February 1847	Her funeral at the Madeleine, followed by burial in the unconsecrated section of the cemetery of Montmartre.
16 February 1847	Reinterment in a perpetual concession in the new part of the Montmartre cemetery.
24–27 February 1847	Auction of her belongings at 11 boulevard de la Madeleine.
1847	Dumas *fils* writes *Péchés de Jeunesse*, a poem about his relationship with Marie Duplessis.
1848	First publication of Dumas's roman-à-clef *La Dame aux Camélias*.
2 February 1852	Premiere of Dumas's play *La Dame aux Camélias* at the Vaudeville theatre in Paris.
6 March 1853	Verdi's *La traviata* premieres at la Fenice.
6 May 1854	The revised *La traviata* staged at the Teatro San Benedetto in Venice.
24 May 1856	London premiere of *La traviata* at Her Majesty's Theatre.
6 December 1856	Paris premiere of *La traviata* at the Théâtre-Italien, Salle Ventadour.

Notes

CHAPTER I PROLOGUE: A WEEKEND IN THE COUNTRY

1. *La Presse*, Sunday 28 February 1847.
2. 'cet épiderme de camélia fait pour la toile de Hollande, la batiste et les dentelles'.
3. Gros 1929, 138 reproduces the list, with all its grammatical idiosyncrasies: '9 pot de fleurs; 2 grappe de [fleurs?]; 4 Camellia monté [*sic*]; 2 grappe de Camellia; 2 Camellia blancs monté; 1 Bouquet à la mains; 1 fleur de Camellia impérialiste; 2 fleurs de Camellia monté; 1 Bouquet à la main et 4 fleurs Camellia monté; 5 azaleat; 2 Roses du Roy; 1 Bruere; 1 pot de yacinthe de hollande; 1 Bouquet à la mains; 2 grappes de Camellia; 9 pot to yacinthe de hollande', adding up to a grand total of 164 francs. A partial facsimile of the Ragonot bill is reproduced in Issartel, 37.
4. Gros 1929, 136, although one of Graux's bills of fare notes that she ordered claret and champagne when she took a party of guests to a nearby restaurant.
5. *Archives et état civil de l'Orne*.
6. Choulet, 116, notes that Alphonsine Plessis returned to Nonant to deal with inheritance matters in the wake of her father's death, now that both her parents were dead as well as her grandfather Louis Deshayes, who had died on 22 April 1840. The reason why she did not attend her father's funeral is because she was heavily pregnant at the time.
7. Vienne, 73.
8. It is no. 138 on the 1811 *Plan Cadastre de Nonant* (part of the *Archives et état civil de l'Orne*).

CHAPTER 2 A MOTHER AND DAUGHTER: 1824–1837

1. No. 78 on the 1811 *Plan Cadastre de Nonant*.
2. Vienne, 5–6.
3. It is clearly marked on Institut Géographique National (IGN) 1715 OT, but no Duponts are recorded in the Exmes registers.
4. 'Le premier d'octobre, mil huit cent trente, le Sieur médecin Buenzot, visiteur des morts de la paroisse de Montreux, a déclaré que Marianne Deshayes, agée de trente-trois ans, femme de chambre de Courménil Département de l'Orne en France, fille des Deshayes, femme Duplessis, est décédée dans la commune de Châtelard le trente Septembre mil huit cent trente, à huit heures et demie du soir.' Bridel pasteur (registre des décès de la paroisse de Montreux).

5. Vienne, 162–3.
6. Marchand, 81.
7. Gonthier, 23.
8. At that point they were superseded by the first proper hotels to open on the Lake Geneva Riviera in anticipation of the railways, which reached the area itself in the late 1850s (Bettex, 301).
9. Marchand, 97–8.
10. Byron carved his name into one of the pillars supporting the vault of the dungeon, close to the pillar to which Bonnivard was chained; see also Ellis, 'Chillon, Clarens and Ouchy', 60–8.
11. See e.g. Cardwell, 77–9.
12. Rambert, 119–20.
13. He was born six years after Byron's death at the age of 36.
14. 'Un de nos premiers hôtes étrangers fut Lady Compton, soeur du duc de Northampton, qui logea chez le ministre Dufour, ancient précepteur dans la famille du Duc; et le petit salon du ministre devint, grâce un peu à la présence de Lady Compton, un centre de réunions pour les premiers habitués de Montreux…Les deux premiers hôtels s'ouvrirent vers 1835' (Bettex, 299).
15. Deirdre Le Faye (198), has Jane Austen on 4 August 1797 refer to Spencer Compton, with 'in his way to school'.
16. The Du Hays account (*Récits Chevalins*) suggests that Augustin died in Paris before 1828 and that his widow lived there and presumably also died there at some point after 1828. It would have been in Paris that Mrs Augustin acted as '*lectrice*' to baroness Anderson. This mysterious couple may be the Joseph Matthew Augustin who died in Paris in the 11th arr. on 30 September 1829 and Louisa Eulalie who died in the 11th arr. on 27 June 1840.
17. *L'Illustration*, 27 December 1845.
18. 'Ma mère est morte de la poitrine': Dumas *fils*, *La Dame aux Camélias* (ed. Raffalli, 1974), 281.
19. His parents' names are given in the *Registre des décès, Commune de Châtelard 1877–1918*. They were John Thomas Pelham and Henriette, and Herbert's profession was of 'pasteur' (*Archives Vaudoises*).
20. *Archives Vaudoises*, 'Police des étrangers', K-VII-H, June 1828.
21. Vienne, 12; Marie Duplessis's rival Alice Ozy similarly referred to her 'première communion' at the age of ten: Vaudoyer, 14.
22. 'est décédée dans la commune du Châtelard (Montreux), Des Hayes, femme Duplessis, Marianne / Profession: femme de chambre / Originaire de Curménil (Department de l'Orne, France) / Domiciliée à (Domicile non indiqué) / Âgée de trente-trois / Fille de Des Hayes / Et de…..Etat-civil: femme Duplessis' (Gros 1929, 75).
23. The *Table Décennale* for Courménil (*Archives et état civil de l'Orne*) duly records 'Deshayes Marie Anne décédée en la Commune de Montreux districte de Vevey 30 7ᵇʳᵉ 1830'. Nine entries further down on the same page is recorded her

father's death, 'Deshayes Lucien 21 April 1840.' The full entry of the *état civil* correctly gives his name as 'Louis'. He was 73, 'propriétaire', widower, and is listed under 'Section Duplessis', a place in Courménil. 'Le Plessis' is clearly marked on the 1811 *plan cadastral* of Courménil as is the track leading to it, the 'chemin du Plessis'.

CHAPTER 3 L'AFFAIRE PLANTIER: EXMES 1837

1. Choulet, 81. Jean-Pierre Plessis Chéron died in October 1863 at the age of 64 but nothing is said about where he lived other than that he was the son of an identically named father and that he was a widower. The fact that Chéron was locally called 'Plessis' might point to a family connection between Marin Plessis and the Chérons. Could Plantier be an alias for one of the Chérons?
2. Boudet, 39, notes that Alphonsine was paid 60 francs a month by the Denis family to do the washing, make the beds and serve at tables.
3. Tardieu, 'Observation VII', *Étude Médico-Légale*, 88–90.
4. Parent-Duchâtelet's book was called *Essai sur les cloaques ou égouts de la ville de Paris* (1824).
5. Parent-Duchâtelet, I, 203.
6. Mogador, I, 119–250.

CHAPTER 4 WORKING GIRLS IN PARIS: 1839–1841

1. His brother Camille was a society painter and one of the extant paintings of Marie Duplessis, showing her at the theatre, is attributed to him, although in truth this well-known picture of a chubby, teenage Marie Duplessis may not be of her at all. By the time she had become notorious enough to attract the attentions of painters she had become the epitome of flair and elegance.
2. Claudin talks about the Pont-Neuf in 1838 and seeing the royal princes being taken to school: 'Tous les matins, à huit heures, je partais pour l'Ecole et, arrivé au Pont-Neuf où il y avait alors des baraques, je prenais du café au lait. Tandis que je mangeais, je voyais passer régulièrement une carrosse jaune et bleue de la cour, conduisant au Collège Henry IV le Duc d'Aumale et le Duc de Montpensier' (Claudin, 4).
3. Roqueplan, *Parisine*, 64–6. There are different versions of this incident, but the one related here is the earliest and probably the most reliable. A later one occurs in Roqueplan's reminiscence in the *Figaro* of 6 October 1878. In *Sylphide* of March 1847, de Villemessant tells yet another story of a starving Marie Duplessis, about how she asked a friend of his for a bowl of cherries, which she wolfed down the moment it appeared. This would seem to be a variant of Roqueplan's apple and chips story. The Villemessant piece, written a few weeks after her death, concludes with 'At her deathbed not one friend held that same exquisite hand that she had shared with so many lovers, none wept for her

with the exception of her guardian angel in heaven, and she did not hear him' (93).

4. *Paris Dansant...le bal Mabille, La Grande-Chaumière, le Ranelagh* (1845), 15. Its proximity to the Bois de Boulogne meant that the Ranelagh was to all intents and purposes only accessible by carriage, hence particularly exclusive.

5. 'Il était neuf heures quand nous arrivâmes Allée des Veuves...Mabille avait été un petit bal champêtre, éclairé avec des quinquets à l'huile...On payait dix sous d'entrée...C'était le rendez-vous favori des valets de chambre, des femmes de chambre, dans le temps où ils étaient moins élégants que leurs maîtres....C'était un jardin modeste!...Les calicots, les grisettes, les modistes, pourraient nous renseigner à cet égard...Le bal était en progrès...On payait un franc d'entrée.'

6. The review appeared in *L'Éclair* in 1852.

7. A term used at the time for a type of coquettish working-girl.

8. Baldick, 349.

9. Parent-Châtelet, I, 205–6.

10. Claudin, 16. Of the famous restaurants of Palais-Royal, only the Véfour, now the Grand Véfour, survives.

11. Véron, II, 4.

12. Stendhal, 89–92.

13. The Jack the Ripper murders shone a spotlight on the plight of poor women in East London, many of whom customarily supplemented their meagre income from factory work and hop-picking by casual prostitution. In October 1888 the Metropolitan Police estimated that there were some 62 brothels in Whitechapel and 1,200 prostitutes, 'mostly of a very low condition' (MEPO 3/141,158–63, cited in *The Ultimate Jack the Ripper Sourcebook*, by Stewart P. Evans and Keith Skinner (2000), 315).

14. Bernheimer, 29.

15. Claudin, 20; *An Englishman*, I, 125.

16. *Les Filles Publiques*, 57–9; 63. It would in fact not be until the arrival of penicillin that syphilis would finally be mastered.

CHAPTER 5 A FAIR LADY MEETS PYGMALION: 1840–1841

1. In *Le Pilori des Communeux* (1871), 238, Henry Morel claims that Marie Duplessis was taught elocution by Achille Ricourt, a sought-after voice master at the École des Jeunes Artistes in Paris, who also happened to be the director of the literary review *L'Artiste*.

2. Claudin, 218.

3. Alton-Shée, II, 9.

4. Bronne, 12.

5. Choulet, 126, identifies the rooms immediately above the main entrance as her apartment while suggesting that it was her lover Agénor de Guiche who moved her here.

CHAPTER 6 THE BABY OF A TRAVIATA: VERSAILLES, MAY 1841

1. After the Queen of Tahiti, Pomaré IV, who between 1843 and 1847 waged war against French attempts to colonize her islands.
2. Simond, 252.
3. Mogador, I, 310.
4. Mogador, I, 307–15.
5. Mogador, I, 315.
6. Soreau, 100.
7. The four Versailles foundlings (out of 56 babies) in May 1841 were: 10 May 1841: Charles Doloire; 20 May 1841: Félix Époulier; 27 May 1841: Clare Étibois; 28 May 1841: Jean Frontal. The corresponding figure for May 1840 was six, out of a total of 70 babies: 4 May 1840: Marie Athanase; 11 May 1840: Louise Elgin; 14 May 1840: Angélique Lattin; 16 May 1840: Françoise Minden; 18 May 1840: Achille Habert; 28 May 1840: Philip Néri. In 1839, four out of seventy babies were foundlings.
8. Carmona, 7–11.
9. While pulmonary tuberculosis is a contagious rather than hereditary disease, the fact is that Marie Duplessis, her mother and, it seems her son, may all have died of it. In this respect they tragically resemble their English contemporaries, the Brontës, a family in which all six children of Patrick Brontë, and their mother too, probably died of tuberculosis.
10. Vienne, 81.

CHAPTER 7 STALLIONS AND FLANEURS ON THE BOULEVARD DES ITALIENS: 1841–1842

1. The reason why September is cited in some of the literature is because she signed her dates as 9th, which denotes November rather than the ninth month of September, which in French is commonly abbreviated to 7th.
2. Morny had four legitimate children from his late marriage to Sophie Troubetzkoï, but there may have been in addition as many as four, if not five illegitimate children, all from different women, including Louise Le Hon and Sarah Bernhardt.
3. Marville, 468–9, shows the passage, a sort of Burlington Arcade.
4. Gibert, 88.
5. See Loviot, 25–6; on p. 87 Loviot reproduces a signed 1849 drawing of a fully dressed Alice Ozy by Chassériau.
6. Roqueplan, *Parisine*, 309–10; Claudin, 34.
7. Claudin, 39–41.
8. Graux, 17, preserves copies of her bills at the Maison Dorée for the nights of 23 and 27 August, and also for 30 August, the very night Dumas separated from her (she was probably entertaining a lover at the restaurant at the time) as well as 17 September.

9. *An Englishman*, I, 144–5.
10. Janin, *735 Lettres*, I.
11. Girardin, *Lettres Parisiennes*, I, 159.
12. Texier, I, 34.
13. *Sylphide*, 24 June 1843, 58.
14. Simond, 207.
15. Loviot, 30.

CHAPTER 8 AN OLD COUNT IN BADEN–BADEN: JULY 1842

1. Whitelocke, 47.
2. The splendiferous 'Grande Salle' of the Maison de la Conversation and its elegant matinée venue, the 'Salon des Fleurs', are evoked in some detail by Arlincourt ('partout un luxe asiatique' (157)), who knew Baden-Baden very well. The closest comparable modern venue to both would be the Musikverein in Vienna.
3. Emilio Sala notes that the 'polka came into vogue in Paris at a specific time—in the winter of 1843–4. This was the time when Alphonsine Plessis became Marie Duplessis, the sparkling attraction of rue d'Antin. In the same winter, Madame Doche danced the polka at the Vaudeville...' (*The Sounds of Paris in Verdi's* La traviata, 70).
4. *Sylphide*, 1843, spring issue, 192.
5. It was Brididi who gave Élisabeth-Céleste Veinard the nickname 'Mogador', a *nom-de-guerre* to rival her fellow dancer's moniker of 'Pomaré'.
6. Mogador, I, 284–5.
7. Boudet, 158; in the first edition of *La Dame aux Camélias*, Dumas stated that Stackelberg first met Marie Duplessis at 'Bagnères'. He later changed this to 'Bagnères-de-Bigorre', when he may have meant 'Bagnères-de-Luchon', because a stamp in her first passport firmly places her in Bagnères-de-Luchon during the 1842–3 period. A contemporary visitor comments on its popularity with the English and found that in the morning the town's central Allée d'Étigny, leading to the baths, was packed with people trotting about in dressing-gowns and slippers, so much so that 'one might think oneself in Constantinople' (*Sylphide*, July–December, 1846, 130). Dumas *fils* stayed at Luchon as did Lamartine, Flaubert and many of the chicest people in nineteenth-century France, including Marie Duplessis and probably also Stackelberg and his family.

CHAPTER 9 PARTYING IN PARIS AND LONDON WITH ANTINOUS: 1842–1843

1. Vienne, III, 114.
2. Plancy, 65–6.

3. Guiche's biographer Constantin de Grunwald similarly muses that 'To judge by that letter, the two lovers were caught in the act by an old protector, whom she calls "the general"', who was probably, Count Stackelberg (Grunwald, 14).

4. *La Dame aux Camélias*, 31; Marguerite is Dumas's name for Marie Duplessis in the novel.

5. The *Times* of 13 September 1842 reports Guiche's presence at the races in Doncaster that September. It seems likely that he would have met the Copley-Andersons of nearby Sprotborough Hall there as they had a keen interest in horse racing. At that stage Lady Anderson's daughter was still alive.

6. Balabine, 137–8.

7. *An Englishman*, I, 55.

8. Vienne, 265–7; Judith, 243–4.

9. 'L'hiver à Paris', *Sylphide*, 1843, spring issue, 76.

10. Vienne, 105–6.

11. Balabine, 86 ff.

12. It houses the British embassy to this day.

13. *Sylphide* 1843, spring issue, 112.

14. *Sylphide* 1843, spring issue 126.

15. Karlsruhe, Baden *Standesbuch* (Landesarchiv Baden-Württemberg), image 491, no. 53.

16. In addition, on 1 April 1843, Marie Duplessis paid an invoice to Lacoste, and on 22 May 1843 she settled a bill with the jewellers Révillon (Graux, 46).

17. Grunwald, 14.

18. Vienne, 84–5, 89.

CHAPTER 10 A SUMMER IDYLL ON A BEND IN THE RIVER: 1843

1. Two days earlier the Prix de Diane, to become the most prestigious of all the races, and endowed with the king's ransom of 6,000 francs (only the Jockey-Club prize fetched more at 7,000), was run for the first time.

2. Vienne, 125.

3. *La Dame aux Camélias*, 191.

4. Adolphe, 325. The official web pages of Bougival note that 'Le cénacle des pay-sagistes s'attable chez Souvent (futur restaurant de l'Hôtel de l'Union): Corot et ses amis, Célestin Nanteuil, patriarche du canotage, et Louis Français qui se dit 'élève de Bougival', sont à l'origine de cet engouement.' <http://www.tourisme-bougival.com/Ville-des-impressionnistes and http://www.tourisme-bougival.com/Louis-Français>

5. Goncourt, I, 98–9.

6. The 1891 Bougival tourist guide by Alexis Martin also lists 'Ternaute, Hérault, Meissonier et bien d'autres' (Martin, 142).

7. *An Englishman*, I, 76 reports that the three years that Dumas *père* spent running the theatre at Saint-Germain-en-Laye earned the railway company that ser-viced it a princely 20,000 francs a year in exta revenue, simply because so

many Parisians flocked out there to patronize a venue run by the great man himself.

8. *Adolphe*, 138.

9. The pont de Bougival, painted by Monet, was built in 1858: it was not there when Marie Duplessis and Dumas briefly lived here; the modern bridge dates from 1969.

10. It can be glimpsed in a painting by Berthe Morisot and its shell survives today at 23 Quai Georges Clemenceau.

11. Martin, 142–3.

12. The online archives of the Yvelines include an old photograph (Archives Départementales Yvelines: ref 3Fi35 70) called 'Fête au bord de la Seine', which shows the vastly expanded former Auberge Souvent, called Hôtel de l'Union, in a picture taken from the site of the 'Grenouillière' on the opposite bank.

13. Dumas calls the chaperone 'Prudence Duvernoy', the name of Marie Duplessis's real-life procuress Clémencè Pratt, but it is not clear whether at this time the two women had already met to do business together.

14. 'Nous ouvrions les fenêtres qui donnaient sur le jardin, et *regardant l'été s'abattre* [my italics] joyeusement dans les fleurs qu'il fait éclore sous l'ombre des arbres...' (202–3).

15. Choulet, 125 n.11, notes that Marie Duplessis's two trips to London, in February and June 1843, were until recently unknown to her biographers.

16. Judith, 200.

17. The 'big clock' refers to the Galerie de l'Horloge which connected the Boulevard des Italiens to the Opéra area itself in the rue Chauchat. Along with its parallel gallery, the Galerie du Baromètre, it was photographed by Marville. Here people gathered during the opera's masked balls. It was a favourite place for assignations.

18. Dumas *père*, 152–5.

19. Dumas *père*, 158.

20. *Les archives de la police de Spa, Fonds Albin Body* (*Archives de la Ville de Spa*).

21. <http://www.spa-entouteslettres.be/dameauxcamelias.html> See also Fonds Body, Ville de Spa: revue *Histoire & Archéologie spadoises* n° 93 (mars 1998), n° 97 (mars 1999), et n° 98 (juin 1999). In an email to the author, 24 January 2012, Peeters clarifies moreover that 'la Comtesse du Plessis qui est présente à Spa en 1844 n'est pas la Dame aux Camélias ; il s'agit d'une veuve de 50 ans, domiciliée à Saint-Domingue...' and stresses that Count Stackelberg did not visit Spa, contrary to what has sometimes been alleged.

22. *Le Journal des Théâtres*, 23 September 1843.

23. 'Mon cher Édouard, ayez la bonté de remettre au porteur mes papiers dont j'ai le plus grand besoin. Vous m'obligerez de prier M. Breton de ne pas me faire attendre plus longtemps après mes bijoux : car vous le savez, je désire partir le plus tôt possible, et je ne le puis sans eux, puisqu'ils me sont nécessaires pour terminer mes affaires. Comme vous pourriez ne pas être chez vous, ayez l'obligeance de faire la réponse, et je l'enverrai chercher ce soir.

Comme vous ne venez pas avec moi en Italie, je ne sais pourquoi vous avez dit à beaucoup de monde que vous vienderiez [*sic*] plus tard me me [*sic*] retrouver. Vous avez donc bien envie de me faire du mal? Vous n'avez jamais ignoré que cela pouvait me nuire dans mon avenir, que vous voulez absolument faire triste et malheureut [*sic*]. Je vous pardonne cela de bon coeur, mais je vous prie de ne pas oublier le sujet de ma lettre.

Toute à vous, Marie

22. rue d'Antin'

24. 'Ta lettre m'arrive à cinq heures; il m'est impossible, cher Édouard, de me *trouver* au rendez-vous de M. Breton; puisque M. Redel sera très pressé, je ne le trouverai plus (et ma course sera inutile); une autre fois cher Édouard écrit moi une demi h. à l'avance j'espère te voir bientôt. Je t'embrasse mille fois sur tes yeux.'

25. 'Mon cher coeur,
Voilà un siècle que tu es parti, je t'ai écrit deux lettres et tu ne m'as pas répondu. Si tu as un peu d'amitié pour moi ne m'oublie pas si longtemps tu veux savoir ce que je deviens? je vais souvent au théâtre je vois très peu de monde et je t'aime de tout coeur. toi cher donne moi de tes nouvelles aime moi bien et envoye moi du chevreuil je veux dire un chevreuil dis moi si monsieur mon cheval se porte bien. Je veux recevoir souvent de long lettre de toi et si non ferai t'arracher les yeux et dieu sait si je te les ménage cette fois-ci adieu mon cher bibi. Malgre ma colère je te baise longtant toujours et de toute mon âme.

leundi [*sic*] 23 Octob(re) 1843'
See Gordon, 72–7.

26. Blois, 107.

27. 'Combien je suis fâchée, mon cher Édouard, de n'avoir pas eu ta lettre une heure plus tôt! Zélia m'a écrit pour me demander si je pouvais passer la soirée avec elle; j'ai promis, n'ayant rien de mieux à faire. Si tu le veux, nous dînerons demain ensemble; fais-moi dire si tu acceptes. En attendant, cher petit frère, je baise mille fois tes yeux bleus, et je suis toute à toi de coeur. Marie.'

28. 'Mon Ned chéri,
On donne ce soir, aux Variétés, une représentation extraordinaire au bénéfice de Bouffé. On commencera par Le Dîner de Madelon, Le Père Turlululu, Phèdre par Audry, Les Armes de Richelieu, Le Solitaire mélodrame par Audry, Le Gamin de Paris, un peu de La Sylphide quadrille d'artistes, enfin soirée charmante; tu me feras grand plaisir si tu peux m'avoir une loge. Réponds-moi, bien cher ami, moi je t'embrasse mille millions de fois tes yeux, si tu veux bien me le pernettre.   Marie [*c*. Saturday 2 December 1843].'

29. *Journal des théâtres*, 7 December 1843.

30. Gros 1923, 167:
'Vous me ferez grand plaisir, cher Édouard, si vous voulez venir me voir ce soir (théâtre du Vaudeville, n° 27). – Impossible de dîner avec toi, je suis très souffrante.

Mille tendresses,   Marie.'

31. Gros 1923, 266–7.

32. *Sylphide*, December 1845, 283.
33. *Sylphide*, June 1846, 94.
34. Gros 1929, 61.
35. Graux, 49–50.
36. On the other hand, Pratt may have been Marie Duplessis's procuress already at the time of her trysting with Perrégaux in Bougival in the summer of 1843 because in his novel, the source for most of our information about Bougival (apart from Vienne's memoir), Dumas calls the lovers' chaperone 'Prudence Duvernoy', his name for Pratt. If Pratt was working for Marie Duplessis by 1843 then it is likely that she was the one who triggered the courtesan's move to the apartment next to hers.
37. The premises of no. 11 were ocupied by 'Choppin (Ant.), *rentier*, Belbeuf (Mis de). G.O. *pair*, Morel-Vindé (vic. De), O, pair, and Merinville (de), *rentier*.'
38. The apartment at 11 boulevard de la Madeleine was rented from Mr Charles Hautoy, whom the 1846 *Almanach* of addresses describes as 'entrepreneur de bâtiments', who lived at 7 avenue de Marigny on the Champs Elysées. The rent was 3,200 francs a year, payable in four three-monthly instalments of 800.

CHAPTER 11 SIN AND LUXURY AT 11 BOULEVARD DE LA MADELEINE: 1844–1847

1. Graux, 59.
2. The popular view of Mary Magdalene as a prostitute may not strictly correspond to the accounts of her in the Gospels and she is not, as is sometimes assumed, the woman taken in adultery about whom Jesus said 'He that is without sin among you, let him first cast a stone at her.' (John, 8.7)
3. From the table of corresponding values in 'Livre tournois' (French Wikipedia), extrapolated from Robert C. Allen's article 'The Great Divergence in European Wages and Prices from the Middle Ages to the First World War' (2001). Boudet (127) estimates that the cost was the equivalent of 45,000 EUR ('300,000 de nos francs actuels') in 1844 when, as she points out, a bottle of champagne cost just one EUR; in other words, assuming that the average bottle of champagne costs 20 EUR in 2013, the real cost today of refurbishing Marie Duplessis's apartment might come to roughly 900,000 EUR. The '*Mémoire* du tapissier' survives in the Noel Charavay/Octave Halbout dossier and was consulted by Gros, who refers to it in both his 1923 and 1929 books on Marie Duplessis. Unfortunately he muddies the waters, twice. In his 1923 book (67) he notes that the refurbishment memoir refers to the Madeleine apartment (correct) where she moved from the 'rue du Mont-Thabor' when in fact he means d'Antin; in the 1929 revised version (117) he claims that she moved from Mont-Thabor to d'Antin (correct) while implying, mistakenly, that the inventory refers to the d'Antin apartment.
4. Its baroque beauty is captured perfectly in the 1967 Mario Lafranchi film of *La traviata* featuring Anna Moffo as Violetta.

5. The Madonna motif is even more accentuated in the 1872 Lérat engraving deriving from this original.

6. It fetched 375 francs at the auction where it was bought by one Mr Vialla (Catalogue, 394).

7. Contades 1887.

8. Gros 1923, 155, and Boudet, 93, both cite the Montjoyeux piece.

9. *Almanach*, 1846.

10. Contades 1887, 132.

11. In the *Revue Encyclopédique* (1896), 741–7: the Olivier image is on p. 741.

12. *La Dame aux Camélias*, 95.

13. Boudet, 182–3.

14. Texier, II, 60.

15. Quite how much of a literary lioness she was can be gleaned from a simple invitation of 16 June 1846 to Théophile Gautier, in which she almost casually invites a leading writer of Paris to dine at her home with three literary giants of nineteenth-century Paris: 'Voulez-vous venir dîner chez nous aujourd'hui avec M. de Lamartine, Balzac et Victor Hugo?'

16. Launay, IV, 31.

17. Vienne, 202–3.

18. The Pleyel piano premises and the Jockey-Club were at 18 boulevard de Montmartre. The brilliant pianist Camilla Pleyel, who was briefly married to Berlioz before marrying Camille Pleyel (!), the piano builder whose pianos were Chopin's favourites, was a friend of Liszt's who performed with her in Vienna. Both he and Chopin dedicated works to her.

19. Vienne, 205. On Lichnowksy's friendship with Liszt, see also Saffle, *Liszt in Germany* (126). Liszt later wrote a powerful letter about Lichnowksy's murder by a mob in 1848. There is an impressive series of sketches of him in volume 2 of *Le Pélerin* by le Vicomte d'Arlincourt (120 ff.), where d'Arlincourt describes Felix de Lichnowsky as 'much in demand in Paris' and as 'jeune, beau, et de haute naissance'.

20. Dolph (27), whose book appeared in 1927, claims that he was able 'to locate the very rooms she occupied one summer at [Bad] Homburg', but does not speci-fiy which summer and whether or not this information derived from a *Fremdenliste* of the spa town.

21. Among Lady Copley's possessions at her death and sold with the rest of the property after the First World War featured the emblems of Yarborough (DY DAW 13/1 & 4).

CHAPTER 12 ALEXANDRE DUMAS *FILS*, LOLA MONTEZ, AND OLYMPE AGUADO: 1844–1845

1. See Dumas *fils*'s witty verse letter cited in André Maurois, *Les Trois Dumas* (1957), 187–8, in which he invites his friends for dinner in Saint-Germain-en-Laye, including references to the Henri IV pavilion and street directions to his father's

home: 'Pour ne pas vous causer une course incongrue, / Je vais vous indiquer la maison. Dans la rue / De Médicis, au fond; la dernière maison, / Ayant la porte verte et fermant l'horizon.'

2. Dumas *fils*, *Théâtre Complet* 3rd edn., vol. 8 ('Notes') (1898).

3. Graux, 63–4. Amant is listed alongside Eugénie Doche, the first Marguerite Gautier, among the 'Artistes' of the Vaudeville in the 1846 *Almanach* of 25,000 Paris addresses. The original French text of Marie Duplessis's letter, with spelling mistakes, reads: 'Mon petit monsieur Amant. Encore pour moi une loge. Je n'ose vous la demander de premier rang. Vous n'auriez qu'à m'envoyer à tous les diables. Cependant, si vous voulez être un de ces diables, mais bon, vous me feriez ce plaisir. Autrement une bonne loge de façe de 2e. Laure Cogniot vous a-t-elle fait demander, pour elle-même, une loge de 1er rang? Si elle ne l'a pas fait, veuillez, je vous prie, lui en faire parvenir une et quand [*sic*] à moi, je vous en supplie, pensez-y et envoyez-la-moi de suite. Je vous en serai très reconnaissante. Vous devez bien faire quelque chose pour moi. Je suis allée chez vous sans vous y trouver. Mes amitiés et tous mes remerciements. M. Duplessy.'

4. Dumas *fils* 1898, 'Note A'.

5. *La Dame aux Camélias*, 121.

6. Dumas waxes lyrical when reminiscing about Ravelet's stables in his letter to Calmann-Lévy in the 1886 preface to *La Dame aux Camélias*. The stables stood here until 1860 and boasted an exceptional cherry tree, on which Dumas nearly conducted a romantic flirtation.

7. Peigné's note confirms that she must have been with Perrégaux until late spring 1844 when the original debt was incurred.

8. Gros 1929, 176.

9. Balabine, 185.

10. Vienne, 195–6.

11. The *Journal des Débats*, 30 March 1846, gives a detailed account of the events, including verbatim reports of the dinner conversations in Palais-Royal, that led up to the fatal duel.

12. *An Englishman*, I, 146–7.

13. *Sylphide*, June 1846, 201–2.

14. Vienne, 236.

15. Walker, 424.

16. Graux, 17.

17. 'Cher Adet, pourquoi ne m'as-tu pas donné de tes nouvelles, et pourquoi ne me parles-tu pas *franchement*? Je crois que tu devrais me traiter comme une amie. J'espère donc un mot de toi et je te baise bien tendrememt comme une maîtresse ou comme une amie, à ton choix. Dans tous les cas, je te serai toujours dévouée. Marie.' The letter is reproduced in Brisson, 199, who spotted it in Jules Janin's copy of *La Dame aux Camélias*, an extensively annotated and illustrated copy that Dumas *fils* left in his will to Eugénie Doche, who in turn kept an entire sideboard full of *La Dame aux Camélias* memorabilia.

18. 'Ma chère Marie,

Je ne suis ni assez riche pour vous aimer comme je le voudrais ni assez pauvre pour être aimé comme vous le voudriez. Oublions donce, tous deux, vous un nom qui doit vous être à peu près indifférent, moi un bonheur qui me devient impossible.

Il est inutile de vous dire combien je suis triste, puisque vous savez déjà combien je vous aime. Adieu donc. Vous avez trop de coeur pour ne pas comprendre la cause de ma lettre, et trop d'esprit pour ne pas me la pardonner.

Mille souvenirs.

A.D.'

A facsimile of Dumas's parting letter is reproduced by Issartel, 61.

19. 'Ma chère Marguerite,

J'espère que votre indispositon d'hier aura été peu de chose. J'ai été à onze heures du soir demander de vos nouvelles, et l'on ma répondu que vous n'étiez pas rentrée. M. de G... a été plus heureux que moi, car il s'est présenté quelques instants après, et à quatre heures du matin il était encore chez vous.

Pardonnez-moi les quelques heures ennuyeuses que je vous ai fait passer, et soyez sûre que je n'oublierai jamais les moments heureux que je vous dois.

Je serais bien allé savoir de vos nouvelles aujourd'hui, mais je compte retourner auprès de mon père.

Adieu, ma chère Marguerite, je ne suis ni assez riche pour vous aimer comme je le voudrais, ni assez pauvre pour vous aimer comme vous le voudriez. Oublions donc, vous, un nom qui doit vous être à peu près indifférent; moi, un bonheur qui me devient impossible,

Je vous renvoie votre clef qui ne m'a jamais servi et qui pourra vous être utile si vous êtes souvent malade comme vous l'étiez hier.'

20. Images 224–5, 'marriages', *Archives et état civil de l'Orne*, Saint-Germain-de-Clairefeuille.

CHAPTER 13 THE PIANIST, THE BARONESS, AND THE ACTRESS: OCTOBER 1845–FEBRUARY 1846

1. In a gesture characteristic of him, the elder Dumas carried out an impromptu revision of the 7th tableau of the play after he spotted the theatre's 'pompier' leave because he was bored by it: an hour and a half later the elder Dumas had successfully revised the scene to his (and the 'pompier's') satisfaction (*An Englishman*, I, 73–4).

2. Blaze de Bury, 211–12.

3. In the summer of 1845 Jules Janin wrote a 'cantate pour Mr Liszt'.

4. Janin 1975, I, 134.

5. Janin's two accounts of the encounter of Marie Duplessis and Liszt in *L'Artiste* 1852 and his *Histoire de la Littérature Dramatique* vol. 4 of 1854 differ slightly. *Histoire* reports parts of the alleged conversation between them, including her telling Liszt that she heard him play his 1844 '*Marche hongroise in E flat minor*' and his 1841 'Réminiscences de *Don Juan*' at a concert.

6. *Sylphide*, December 1845, 288.

7. 'très gracieuse, pleine d'esprit et "d'abandon enfantin"...Elle avait beaucoup de coeur, un entrain tout à fait idéal, et je pretends qu'elle était unique dans son espèce. Dumas l'a très bien comprise, il n'a pas eu grand'chose à faire pour la créer de nouveau; c'était bien l'incarnation la plus absolue de la femme qui ait jamais existée' (Liszt to Janka Wohl: Wohl, 172–3).

8. Simond, 271.

9. 'Je ne vivrai pas. Je suis une singulière fille et je ne pourrai y tenir à cette vie que je ne sais pas ne pas mener et que je ne sais pas non plus supporter. Prends-moi, emmène-moi où tu voudras; je ne te gênerai pas: je dors toute la journée; le soir, tu me laisseras aller au spectacle et la nuit tu feras de moi ce que tu voudras!'

10. 'Ce voyage à Constantinople, dont la perspective la ravissait, est une de ces étapes évitées à grande peine que j'ai toujours regrettées' (Wohl, 173).

11. Vienne, 159.

12. Vienne, 161.

13. Vienne calls the baroness 'veuve d'un général anglais' (162). This is intriguing, because at no point does Lady Charlotte refer to a husband. Copley was not a general.

14. The Copleys' books included also a *Guide du Voyageur en France* (1840), Murray's *Handbook to Switzerland* (1854), and *Carlsbad* by Rudolf Mannl (1850).

15. In the Sprotbrough papers (Doncaster Archives), the Copleys' possessions are classified under DY DAW 13/1–8, the most important of which are DY DAW 13/1 & 4; 13/4 lists everything that was left to Copley's sister, including the books in the library and a copy of the 1852 edition of *La Dame aux Camélias*, with Janin's preface about Marie Duplessis.

16. Sprotbrough papers, DD/CROM/13/1.

17. *Le Mercure des Théâtres*, 4 January 1846, refers to her replacement after playing the role.

18. Judith, 236.

19. Judith, 92–7.

20. Judith, 238–9.

21. Judith, 242.

CHAPTER 14 A REGISTRY WEDDING IN LONDON: 21 FEBRUARY 1846

1. Thus *L'Illustration* noted that 'Tout le monde a été frappé de la douceur de la température à Paris pendant le mois de décembre dernier' (*Illustration*, 17 Jan. 1846).

2. The wedding licence is reproduced in Issartel, 32.

3. Gros 1923, 272–3, cites Charavay and gives as source Charavay's pamphlet, *L'amateur d'autographes, no. de novembre 1910*. He also refers to Montjoyeux's *Lanterne* piece of 1892 in which Montjoyeux refers to the Kensington wedding. Montjoyeux knew her of course and accompanied her coffin.

4. Gros 1923, 266.
5. *La France Théâtrale*, 22 March 1846.
6. Janin 1851–2.
7. 'Mon cher Édouard,
     Dans tout ce que vous m'écrivez, je ne vois qu'une seule chose à laquelle vous
     voulez que je réponde, la voici: Vous voulez que je vous dise par écrit que vous
     êtes libre de faire ce que bon vous semble. Je vous l'ai dit moi-même avant-hier,
     je vous le répète et je le signe:
     Marie Duplessis'
     The text of the letter is printed by Gros 1923, 273–4.
8. See Gros 1929, 205–6, *La Gazette des Tribunaux*, 3 April & 19 July 1846, and
     Sylphide, June 1846, 180, which reports Marie Duplessis's appearance in court:
     'L'autre jour, au tribunal de première instance, on demandait à une de nos plus
     jolies lionnes de la Chaussée d'Antin [she was in fact in the Madeleine by then],
     Marie Duplessis: "Etes-vous dame ou demoiselle?" "Qu'importe," répondit-elle,
     "cela ne fait rien à l'affaire; prenez que je suis demoiselle.'''
9. *Sylphide*, June 1846, 201–2.
10. Boudet (146) wonders whether Narbonne did not first possess Marie Duplessis
     as a child before Marcel, in a seigneurial *ius primae noctis* fashion, with shades of
     Figaro; Boudet dates Marie's visit to Cochères to 1843.
11. Vienne, 285.

CHAPTER 15 A SUMMER SUNSET IN THE SPAS OF EUROPE: 1846

1. 'Ne m'en veuillez pas, cher ami, de ma négligence à écrire et n'augurez pas de
     là oubli ou indifférence pour vous. Je suis bien heureuse de votre amitié; mais
     vous savez, parmi mes nombreux défauts, la paresse n'est pas au dernier rang;
     vous comprenez bien que les longues promenades à la campagne diminuent
     encore mon goût pour le style; et loin de m'accuser, vous me devez gré de
     l'effort que je fais en ce moment pour surmonter le sommeil qui m'accable.
         Adieu, cher Tony, je m'arrête ici, car je n'en finirais pas de vous ennuyer;
     encore adieu et mille amitiés.

     Marie Duplessis
     Spa, le 12 juin 1846'
     [Postscript] 'Mille remerciements pour votre complaisance pour moi. Cher, ne
     vendez pas ma voiture. J'aurai bientôt le plaisir de vous voir, je l'espère du
     moins. M.D.' (Graux, 24)
2. Gautier, *Correspondence*, III, 1846–8.
3. Turner's *Promenade de Sept-Heures* (1839), now hangs in the Tate Britain Gallery
     in London.
4. In his preface to *La Dame aux Camélias*, first printed in the December 1851 issue
     of *L'Artiste* (August 1851–January 1852), Janin talks about her appearance in
     the famous Allée des Sept-Heures in Spa and her brilliant horsemanship: 'on

la vit quelque temps après, ivre et folle d'une joie factice, franchissant à cheval, les passages les plus difficiles, étonnant de sa gaïeté cette allée de *Sept-Heures* qui l'avait trouvée rêveuse et lisant tout bas sous les arbres.'

5. Graux, 24.

6. In an essay in *Le Mercure de France* of 1890, Johannès Gros argues that she visited Baden-Baden, Wiesbaden, Bad Ems, and Spa for her health in the summer of 1846. Graux, 24, also notes that she proceeded from Baden-Baden to Wiesbaden and Ems. On Liszt in Bad Ems, see Michael Saffle, *Liszt in Germany 1840–1845* (1994); on Bad Ems, see H. A. Sarholz's magisterial 1996 *History of Bad Ems*, which lists the *Englischer Hof, Die Vier Türme, Russischer Hof, Europäischer Hof, Darmstädter Hof,* and *Die Vier Jahreszeiten* among the pre-eminent places to stay.

7. 'Pardonnez-moi, mon cher Édouard, je vous en prie, à deux genoux: si vous m'aimez assez pour cela, rien que deux mots, mon pardon et votre amitié, écrivez-moi poste restante à Ems, duché de Nassau. Je suis seule ici et très malade. Donc, cher Édouard, vite mon pardon. Adieu.

Marie Duplessis'
For a facsimile of this letter, see Issartel, 33.

CHAPTER 16 AGONY AND DEATH OF A MAIDEN: OCTOBER 1846–3 FEBRUARY 1847

1. For example on 13, 17, 18, 19, 20, 22, 24 October 1846: see Graux, 26–7.

2. After the death of Marie Duplessis, Koreff submitted a request to her estate for 1,400 francs in payment for 280 visits to her. He failed to convince the tribunal of his claim that his visits were medical rather than social in character (Gros 1929, 265–6 and *Gazette des Tribunaux*, nos 24 & 26, November 1847). Liszt's long letter, dated Weimar, 12 February 1847, supporting Koreff's claim to have acted as her physician, pays tribute to the doctor's allegedly warm and caring friendship for Marie Duplessis. It is reproduced in Gros 1929, 216–17.

3. Contades 1887, 132.

4. Vento, 120–2.

5. Vento, 121.

6. Issartel, 36, also attributes this one to Chaplin but Gros 1923 gives it to Vidal.

7. Choulet, 180. Gros 1923, 94, gives a Mr Évrard of Lignières (Orne) as the name of the owner in the 1920s. In the 1929 version of his book, Gros (178) notes that by then the painting was in a parlous state. The same Évrard at the time also owned the miniature of the mother of Marie Duplessis, which is today in the Musée de la Dame aux Camélias in Gacé.

8. 'Moutier arrive à Madrid et me dit que, quand il a quitté Paris, vous étiez malade. Voulez-vous me permettre de m'inscrire au nombre de ceux qui s'attristent de vous voir souffrir?

Huit jours après que vous aurez reçu cette lettre, je serai à Alger.

Si je trouve, à la poste restante, un mot à mon nom, et qui me pardonne une faute que j'ai commise il y a un an environ, je reviendrai moins triste en France, si je suis absous – et tout à fait heureux, si vous êtes guérie.

Ami.[tiés]

A.D.'

Maurois 1957, 205, n. 3 notes 'Cette lettre inédite et capitale m'a été communiquée par Mme [Georges] Privat.'; Coward xiv also refers to this letter.

9. In her correspondence with Théophile Gautier in 1847 Alice Ozy refers affectionately to her relationship at the time with Perrégaux.

10. Eventually his father rallied and became mayor of Nonant in 1851.

11. The Russian consular official Balabine (244) notes that the Duc de Guiche Gramont was present at the Tuileries palace on 28 January 1846, when Corneille's *Horace* was staged. His presence at court was the talk of all the guests because it gave notice of a thaw between Guiche and Nemour (Guiche had been a childhood friend of a pretender to the French throne, the Duc de Bordeaux).

12. Gros 1923, 329.

13. Gros 1929, 61.

14. Moreover, his later behaviour, with regard particularly to longing to look on her face one last time after death, may suggest that he did not after all see her between the time she died and the sealing of her coffin.

15. Gros 1929, 257 agrees and notes that 'Installé au chevet, Charles Chaplin fixa, à la lueur du cierge funéraire, l'image de la belle trespassée sous l'aspect de l'éternité.'

16. The *Catalogue de la vente* of the estate of Chaplin mentions as lot no. 60, *La mort de La Dame aux Camélias*: Gros 1923, 344.

17. Janin 1851–2, in Neuschäfer and Sigaux, 492.

18. Gros 1923, 256 records Clotilde's entry in her account book of the two francs that she disbursed for the priest's ham: 'Jambon pour le *praître* [*sic*]: deux francs'.

CHAPTER 17 TWO WINTER FUNERALS IN MONTMARTRE: FEBRUARY 1847

1. Martin-Fugier, 111.

2. Judith, 247.

3. Gros 1929, 260 lists and cites the relevant documents for the reinterment. On the legal mechanisms for acquiring a grave in perpetuity and the need to involve the prefecture and the bureau of the *état civil*, see *Almanach 1842*, 476. The law states that there is a choice of cemetery only in the case of perpetual concessions, but of course Marie Duplessis had already been moved into Montmartre.

4. Vienne, 302. The porter's direction suggests that they were standing in the path or track that is now the avenue Saint-Charles from where the grave can be glimpsed some twenty feet or so away. In the 1840s the cemetery was leafy (it is again today) but the paths in it were somewhat hazardous and unmetalled.

5. 'La poussière volait / Au ciel! Chaque caillou devenait éteincelle! / Le vent est moins léger, moins prompte l'hirondelle! / C'etait, sous la feuillée, une ombre qui sifflait! / O Marie, où vas-tu fouler le serpolet?' (Gros 1923, 183).

6. 'Qui n'a vu Duplessis, la belle courtisane, / Assise sur sa couche, et les cheveux flottants, / Le front encore plus blanc qu'une fleur de liane, / Ses lèvres de chair rouge et ses yeux éclatants, / Larges perles d'azur sous un flot diaphane, / Et son beau cou de cygne et ses seins irritants.'

7. Houssaye, 303–4.

CHAPTER 18 AUCTION AT 11 BOULEVARD DE LA MADELEINE: FEBRUARY 1847

1. 'They vanished in the great fire of San Francisco along with my own much treasured correspondence and my complete literary papers, the fruit of ten years' labour, including various poems and collections, plays and comedies, two librettos that Donizetti had commissioned from me, newspaper articles and so on the whole running to something like ten volumes' (Vienne, 315).

2. Vienne, 301.

3. Gros 1929, 264.

4. This account follows Gros 1929 (270), who refers to Gautier's 28 February 1847 piece in *La Presse* and to *An Englishman in Paris*. Gros is usually as rigorous as he is scrupulous and here *quotes* both Gautier and refers to Wallace. But it has not been possible to verify this: while the Gautier *La Presse* piece of 1847 contains a version of these lines, it does not refer to Richard Wallace, nor does Wallace talk about the auction. Gros seems to have constructed an imaginary dialogue between Gautier and Gros, perhaps because they agree on the essentially innocent nature of the lady of the camellias.

5. *An Englishman*, I, 2, 82, and 153.

6. *Almanach de Paris*, I, 1842.

7. The will is quoted in the Lisburn biographical entry on Wallace which notes that 'The clue to the identity of his mother is found in the will of the fourth Marquess of Hertford, made in 1837, where he refers to "Richard Jackson (son of Agnes) now of the age of twenty or thereabouts and residing at No. 1 rue Taitbout, Paris"'. 'The life and work of Sir Richard Wallace Bart. MP', *Lisburn Historical Society*, vol. 5, pt. 2 (1996).

8. The source of this information is the 1890 volume called *The Lady Wallace's Inventory of Contents of Hertford House*, held by the library of the Wallace Collection, which itemizes all the possessions in each and every room and space in the mansion.

9. *Lisburn Historical Society*: 'The life and work of Sir Richard Wallace Bart.' He had himself re-baptized on 21 April 1842 in the Anglican Church in the rue d'Aguesseau, the same street where many years later he cared for the wounded of the Siege of Paris.

10. *An Englishman*, II, 322.

11. The clock was decribed in the catalogue as '1 magnifique pendule en bronze doré or moulu, avec vases et plaques en porcelaine, pâte tendre, décors fond bleu turquoise à médaillons, sujets pastoraux, oiseaux et fleurs' while the chandelier was '1 lustre à 24 lumières en porcelaine, décors fond bleu turquoise, à médaillons de fleurs et d'oiseaux, monture en bonze doré or moulu'. The piece of rosewood furniture appears in the catalogue as '1 très beau coffre sur son pied en bois rose, avec riches ornements en bronze doré et plaques en porcelaine tendre, décors fond bleu turquoise à médaillons, sujets pastoraux.'

12. Gros 1923, 378.

13. According to Dickens, as quoted in Maurois (211), 'l'enthousiasme n'a plus connu de bornes lorsque Eugène Sue a acheté le livre de prières de la courtisane.' But Maurois, 211 n. 2, cautions that the original of this letter does not seem to be extant and that the editors of Dickens's correspondence are sceptical about it. It may be that the letter about the Madeleine auction, quoted in the *Inimitable Boz*, is not authentic. This suspicion is consolidated by the fact that Sue is *not* recorded as bidding at the auction of Marie Duplessis's effects.

14. Gros 1920, 79.

15. Graux, 77.

16. Graux, 56.

17. On the family of Delphine Paquet-Plessis, see Choulet 178–83, who notes that Marie Duplessis's last surviving relative died in 2010. A Mr Évrard from Lignières (Orne) had a stash of materials relating to the Dame aux Camélias, including the famous image of Marie Deshayes. In 1923 Gros (1923, 94) called him the last surviving member of the family of the family of Marie Duplessis. He must have been been the son of a Plessis-Paquet daughter, as the Paquets had three children, a boy and two girls who both married (Vienne, 322); in other words, Évrard would have been a grandson of Delphine's.

CHAPTER 19 *LA DAME AUX CAMÉLIAS*, BY ALEXANDRE DUMAS *FILS*: 1848

1. Letter to Calmann-Lévy published in the 1886 edition of *La Dame aux Camélias*.

2. This is double bluff and smokescreen. Posing as a recognizable generic fictional preface, it asserts that this is a true story when in fact it really is just that.

3. *The Times*, 27 October 1903. The most rigorous, scholarly writer on the lady of the camellias, Johannès Gros, also categorically attributes *An Englishman in Paris* to Richard Wallace (Gros 1923, 364).

4. *An Englishman*, II, 211.

5. *Athenaeum*, 13 August 1892, 219–20.

6. *An Englishman*, II, 299.

7. *An Englishman*, I, 280.

8. *An Englishman*, I, 238–9.

9. *An Englishman*, I, 236.
10. *An Englishman*, II, 334.
11. *An Englishman*, II, 42.
12. It was during the Commune that he had the idea of making 'some rough memoranda...They are among the papers that I have preserved.' *An Englishman*, II, 330–1.
13. *An Englishman*, I, 44–5.
14. The uncertain use of 'distinction' here, correct in French but not wholly idiomatic in English, a *faux-ami* in other words, would be just the sort of mistake a bilingual English-French speaker like Wallace might make.
15. *An Englishman*, I, 159–66. The author of the *Memoir* continues here with an account of that other lover of camellias, the then legendary 'Gentleman of the Camellias' whose fame with respect to the flower preceded that of Marie Duplessis. This former dandy, an eccentric who spent a fortune on camellias, is long forgotten but camellias were his badge during his lifetime. His name was M. Lautour-Mézerai. He never appeared in public without a camellia in his button-hole and 'always occupied the same place at the Opéra'.

CHAPTER 20 *LA DAME AUX CAMÉLIAS* AT THE VAUDEVILLE:
FEBRUARY 1852

1. From Dumas's preface to the 1852 edition of the play in *Théâtre choisi des auteurs contemporains*, which followed shortly after the Vaudeville premiere of *La Dame aux Camélias*. The music and scores of Dumas's play, a 'pièce mêlée de chant', and the way they relate to Verdi's opera, are fully discussed by Sala, 113–39.
2. Dumas *fils*, 1867 preface to *La Dame aux Camélias*, in *Théâtre Complet avec préfaces inédites* (1898).
3. Brisson, 193.
4. Brisson, 195–6.
5. Brisson, 19.
6. Brisson, 201.
7. Sala, 125.
8. Dumas *fils*'s chapsodic response to his first dramatic success, in the 1852 preface to *La Dame aux Camélias* in *Théâtre choisi des auteurs contemporains*, further demonstrates his closeness to his father and his desire to impress him.
9. This claim would seem to be borne out, partly at least, by Marie Duplessis's 1843 extant order of flowers from Ragonot, which contains almost exclusively camellias and azaleas which, if evergreen, have no scent unlike the deciduous variety.
10. Horace de Vieil-Castel, *Mémoires*, II, 34 ff. Vieil may, unintentionally, give the game away here: the character in the play is called 'Saint-Gaudens' but may be based on the real life Comte de Gervilliers; unless 'Saint-Gaudens' stands for Saint-Geniès who knew Marie Duplessis in Baden-Baden and purchased some

of her belongings at the Madeleine auction. Whoever he was, he did not seem to mind Dumas's portrayal, if the novelist's later reminiscence about meeting 'Saint-Gaudens' can be believed: 'It's me, yes me, whom you have represented in Saint-Gaudens. I am not cross with you over it. I find it so entertaining that I go to hear myself every night' (Dumas *fils* 1898, Note A).

11. Phillips-Matz 1993, 303.

12. According to Grove, Verdi sometimes associates particular keys with particular characters, as for example Macbeth and Lady Macbeth, who are in flat while the witches are in sharp.

13. The valzer, from the German Walzer, was in the air and Verdi's sparkling valzer in F major, composed in the late 1850s and famously used for the dance of Claudia Cardinale and Burt Lancaster in the film *Il Gattopardo*, demonstrates just how accomplished he was at writing valzers. Verdi and the Viennese 'Walzerkönig' Johann Strauss II overlapped for seventy-four years in the nineteenth century, with Verdi the elder by twelve years.

14. Budden 1992, 128.

15. In one of the greatest *Luisa Miller* productions of modern times, staged in 1979 by the Royal Opera House Covent Garden, conducted by Lorin Maazel and featuring Katia Ricciarelli as Luisa Miller, with Placido Domingo and Luciano Pavarotti alternating as Rodolfo, Richard Van Allan as Wurm and Renato Bruson as Miller, Ricciarelli's crystalline staccatos and pianos blended perfectly into the orchestral accompaniment, the soprano voice and the instruments chiming in exquisite harmony. Further specific links between *La traviata* and *Luisa Miller*, Verdi's 'Alpine' opera inspired by Schiller's *Kabale und Liebe*, are discussed in '*Luisa e Violetta: eroine borghesi*' by Michele Girardi in the libretto programme for the 2006 spring production of the opera at La Fenice, starring Darina Takova as Luisa Miller (Fenice *Luisa Miller*, 13–32).

16. Phillips-Matz 1993, 304, 306.

CHAPTER 21 VERDI AND THE BAREZZIS—THE GENESIS OF *LA TRAVIATA*: 1823–1852

1. Phillips-Matz 1993, 312.

2. 'Voi sapete che a lui devo tutto, tutto, tutto, Ed a lui solo.'

3. Phillips-Matz 1993, 18.

4. Phillips-Matz 1993, 20; for a detailed account and Verdi's narrow escape that day—he was meant to be in the same church—see http://santuariomadonna prati.it/itasmp/storia.htm. Phillips-Matz 1993's pages on Verdi's early childhood in Roncole (11–23) are as informative as they are sensible about, for example, Verdi's relatively privileged (*and* humble) background: against sleeping above the stables needs to be set his education from the age of four and the present of a spinet. In the same chapter Phillips-Matz 1993 (16) repudiates the story, which is still current, about Verdi's younger sister Giuseppa suffering from Down's

syndrome. It was repeated as fact to the author of this book in Verdi's birthplace in August 2013. Giuseppa Verdi died in Le Roncole on 9 August 1833. Verdi had seen her two months earlier on his return home after a year spent in Milan, where he was enrolled as a pupil of the talented music teacher and composer Vincenzo Lavigna.

5. Phillips-Matz 1993, 208.
6. Phillips-Matz 1993, 207.
7. Phillips-Matz 1993, 183, 767.
8. Phillips-Matz 1993, 101.
9. Phillips-Matz 1993, 101.
10. Phillips-Matz 1993, 103.
11. Phillips-Matz 1993, 301.
12. Letter dated 9 April 1851, *Copialettere*, 121: 'Io tengo pronto un altro soggetto semplice, affettuoso, e che si può dire quasi fatto: se voi lo volete io ve lo spedisco, e non pensiamo più al *Trovatore*.'
13. Notably Carlo Gatti in his ground-breaking 1931 two-volume study of the composer, *Verdi*.
14. Budden 1992, 62, 115.
15. Budden 1992, 124.
16. Phillips-Matz 1994, pp. 226–7 in Nicholas John's *Violetta and her sisters*.
17. Budden 1992, 144.
18. 'Finché avrà il ciglio lacrime / io piangerò per te; / vola a' beati spiriti; / Iddio ti chiama a sé.'
19. Abbiati, II, 222. In the same letter, when discussing Nestor Roqueplan's unlicensed putting on *Luisa Miller* at the Le Peletier Opéra, Strepponi urges Verdi to write Roqueplan a letter of thanks for the privilege: his failure to do so she attributes to Verdi's underestimating French vanity: 'Vedo che non conosci ancora bene fin dove arriva la vanità francese'. Unlike Meyerbeer, she notes, who would at once have penned a fawning note. She uncharitably refers to Meyerbeer as 'la *mummia*'. Her penchant for monikers extends to Verdi whom she usually addresses as 'Caro Mago' ('Beloved Wizard') while also using the musical word *pasticcio* (as in pastiche) as a term of endearment, perhaps playing on the word's associations with food.
20. Rutherford detects 'shades of Leopardi's poem' in an opera which may itself be 'effectively an essay in *death*' (Rutherford 2013, 186).
21. Budden 1992, 116; see also Phillips-Matz 1993, 322.
22. La Fenice *Rigoletto*, 66, 105.
23. Phillips-Matz 1993, 529.
24. *Parigi e sue vicinanze, nel 1700 circa...Parigi e sue vicinanze, nel 1850 circa. Il primo atto avviene in agosto, il second in gennaio, il terzo in febbraio.* La Dame aux Camélias bluntly indicates that 'La scène se passe vers 1845'.
25. Letter of 30 January 1853 (Kimbell, 298–9).
26. Budden 1992, 121.

27. 'C'est Verdi et *La traviata* qui ont donné un style à *La Dame aux Camélias*. Mieux encore, ils lui ont donné une âme...à élever *La Dame aux Camélias* au niveau du Grand Art.'

CHAPTER 22 *LA TRAVIATA* 1853–4: THE APOTHEOSIS OF MARIE DUPLESSIS

1. The American rock star Jim Morrison's grave in Père-Lachaise too occasionally lays claim to the accolade of the most visited tomb.
2. Maldè is the 'caro nome' of Gilda's aria. She has been duped by the Duke of Mantua into believing that he is a poor student by the name of 'Gualtier Maldè'. Margherita Verdi's mother was Signora Maria Demaldè, that is de-Maldè. This may be a coincidence, but given Verdi's attention to detail and the fact that the name Maldè triggers one of the greatest soprano arias in the repertoire, the choice of name may be a deliberate gesture of solidarity towards the composer's dead wife and her family.
3. In Sonnet 12 Shakespeare refers to 'the violet past prime' as a symbol of time's forward march and the inevitable decline of the beauty of nature's proudest displays.
4. Act 3 scene 4: *La Dame aux Camélias*, in Neuschäfer and Sigaux, 350.
5. The count of seconds follows the 1994 Royal Opera House production conducted by Georg Solti. Perhaps no-one has ever interpreted 'Amami' with greater lyricism than Angela Gheorghiu in that production. As she moves towards Alfredo on the first *Amami*, her entire frame is shaking from the vocal effort to capture in her notes the inner sublimity and generosity of the 'traviata' she is playing.
6. Christopher Wintle, 'A Tragedy of Affliction', Royal Opera House *La traviata* programme, May 2010.
7. Roger Parker, *The New Grove Dictionary of Opera*, vol. 4 (1992), 800.
8. Vienne, 126 ff. refers explicitly to 'Robert Saint-Yves' (Edouard de Perrégaux) and his eloping to Bougival with Marie Duplessis: 'Il acheta, pour elle, à Bougival, une maison de campagne entourée d'une prairie, de jardins et de bosquets, et la fit meubler magnifiquement. Ils s'y installèrent ou plutôt s'y enfermèrent.' ('In Bougival he bought her a cottage surrounded by meadows, gardens, and groves and had it furnished magnificently. They took up residence there or, rather, they shut themselves away in it.')
9. Naturalistic productions casting Violetta as a whore have in the past evoked Verdi's indignant letter to a friend after the Roman censor ruined *La traviata* in 1854 by a series of preposterous rewritings, which included turning Violetta into an wealthy young orphan who loves to party: 'He has made la Traviata *pure and innocent*. Many thanks! Thus he has ruined all the situations, all the characters. A *whore* must always be a *whore*. If the sun shone at night, there would be no more night. In short, they don't understand anything' (Rutherford 2013, 133). Verdi's point is that Violetta is pure and innocent *and* a courtesan.

10. Abbate and Parker, 377.

11. 'NICHETTE : Dors en paix, Marguerite! Il te sera beaucoup pardonné, parce que tu as beaucoup aimé!'

12. 'ARMAND : Depuis deux ans, depuis un jour où je vous ai vue passer devant moi, belle, fière, souriante. Depuis ce jour, j'ai suivi de loin et silencieusement votre existence.'

13. Kate Hopkins calls this final affirmation of Violetta 'Verdi's greatest gesture of sympathy to "the fallen woman"', her reward for remaining true throughout to her ideals' ('Transgressive Women', English National Opera programme for *La traviata*, 3 March 2013, 30–4).

14. In the ARTE film made for television, *Passion Verdi*; although this excellent programme deals with Verdi's whole *oeuvre*, tunes from *La traviata* inevitably predominate because no other opera of Verdi's has quite the same lyrical and melodic reach.

15. In 'Verdi and *Verismo*: the case of *La traviata*', Roger Parker stresses that *La traviata* resists the 'nascent Realism' of Dumas's fiction and that Violetta is partly characterized through 'ambience' which sets her apart firmly from the twilight world of Marguerite Gautier: Cassaro, 215–22.

16. Budden 2008 notes the interaction of the voices and the 'pounding of the banda' (222) in the opening scene of *Rigoletto*; the hectic, insistent pulse of the banda is an important musical feature linking *Rigoletto* and *La traviata*.

17. Phillips-Matz 1993, 323.

18. Phillips-Matz 1993, 322–4.

19. Varesi's letter of 10 March 1853 is quoted in full in Budden 1972–3, 44–5.

20. Letter to De Sanctis of 26 May 1854 (Luzio, *Carteggi Verdiani*, I, 24–5).

21. Act 2 consisted of four separate scenes: (a) the country scenes of Alfredo, Violetta, and Germont, (b) the ball at Flora's, including the scene with the masked gypsies and matadors, (c) Alfredo's flinging money at Violetta as a prostitute, and (d) the grand finale of that act, which Verdi called '*Largo del Finale*'. In his own words, the revisions concerned *Scena e duetto* (Violetta/Germont), Act 2; *Aria* (Germont) and *Largo del Finale*, Act 2; *Duetto* (Violetta/Alfredo), *Finale ultimo*, Act 3.

22. Marked 'Tr^{be}' in 'Mi^{b}' on pp. 334–5.

23. Commenting on Violetta's defiance of communal harmony here, a leading authority on *La traviata* regrets the loss of it in the revised 1854 version: 'The second part of each phrase at present sung by Violetta and Alfredo was originally a solo for the tenor with occasional broken interjections...for Violetta of a purely harmonic character. By way of compensation the melody ended with an expansive phrase of four bars in place of the present two, *with the soprano queening it in vocal splendour*. It is difficult not to regret the loss of this phrase despite its parallel octaves....The reason for its removal probably lies in Verdi's determination to keep the part within more modest vocal bounds than before and avoid anything that smacked of the *prima donna*' (Budden 1972–3, 61–2) [my emphases].

24. La Fenice libretto of *La traviata* (2011), 84.
25. Budden 1992, 163.
26. Rutherford notes that the opera 'provoked the kind of moral outrage in the British press that would perhaps be later matched elsewhere by only two other operatic heroines: Carmen and Salome' (Rutherford 2003, 588).
27. This refers to the office of the Lord Chamberlain who censored all stage performances in Britain until 1968.
28. Budden 1992, 164.
29. Escudier, 399 (14.xii.1856); an almost equally admiring review of the opera had appeared in *Le Constitutionnel* of Monday 8 December 1856.

CHAPTER 23   EPILOGUE: MEMORY AND MYTH

1. *France Musicale* 1845, 164; Phillips-Matz 1993, 303–4.
2. Soreau, 8, writing in the late 1890s, reports a gravedigger who, at the time, had been working in the cemetery for eighteen years, saying that he never saw Dumas at her grave 'even though he came here fairly frequently, because many members of his family rest here and he himself is buried in this cemetery today'. Dumas *fils* died in 1895.
3. Dumas *fils*: 'Si, au cimetière Montmartre, vous demandez à voir le tombeau de *La Dame aux Camélias*, le gardien vous conduira à un petit monument carré qui porte sous ces mots, *Alphonsine Plessis*, une couronne de camélias blancs artificiels, scellée au marbre, dans un écrin de verre. Cette tombe a maintenant sa légende. L'art est divin. Il crée ou ressuscite' (*Théâtre Complet d'Alexandre Dumas Fils* (1868)).
4. Dolph, 39.
5. Claretie, 376–8.
6. Gros 1929, 260.
7. Gros 1920, 83.
8. John, 75. Julie Claudine de Perrégaux was in fact 20 in 1915, the year in which her grandfather died; Frédéric de Perrégaux was a second cousin of Édouard de Perrégaux's.
9. Wohl, 173.
10. Wohl, 169–70.
11. Coward, 19.

A bibliographical note

All biographies of Marie Duplessis are heavily indebted to a book by her friend and chronicler Romain Vienne, *La Vérité sur la Dame aux Camélias*. There is as yet no translation of this memoir, which was published over four decades after her death. Vienne's eye for detail and a highly polished style should range him alongside some of the best journalists of the age, including the poet and novelist Théophile Gautier and the theatre critic Jules Janin. Both Gautier and Janin knew Marie Duplessis and wrote about her; both feature in this book at key moments in her life. If Vienne is at times self-righteous, boastful, and proud to flaunt his intimate acquaintance with the lady of the camellias, he is also highly accurate. In his own words, he only ever wanted to record her story faithfully because she was so different from other courtesans of her day; her beauty and kindness, he claimed, made her shine with a lustrous intensity in that shadowy world. For the purpose of this book it was essential to establish Vienne's credibility by repeatedly testing his claims against other sources such as newspaper reports, contemporary columnists' accounts, the extensive *état civil* of France, and Dumas's memoir novel *La Dame aux Camélias*. In almost every instance where Vienne could be cross-checked—and there are plenty—he turned out to be reliable, which means that he can, at least in principle, be trusted to tell the truth also in a number of instances, such as for example Alphonsine Plessis's predicament in Exmes, for which he is our sole source.

Vienne's reputation was unfairly dented subsequently by the scholarly, but barbed, Johannès Gros, whose publications on Dumas and Marie Duplessis remain seminal. Gros assiduously searched through countless nineteenth-century French newspapers and a number of archives, notably military ones, to consolidate his chronology with regard to several characters in this story who enjoyed intermittent careers in the army. He also was granted access to private collections that have since been dispersed at auctions, including the important Noel Charavay / Octave Halbout one, which contains significant materials relating to the refurbishment of Marie Duplessis's Madeleine apartment. He moreover lived close enough to the tail-end of the generation who had overlapped with the last survivors of this story and their descendants, including the son-in-law of Dumas *fils* who shared information with him about the necklace which Dumas had presented to Marie Duplessis. Gros's visceral animosity towards Vienne's memoir, because of its self-inflated tone and actions such as Vienne's destruction of Marie Duplessis's correspondence, prevented Gros from grasping the achievement of the latter's endeavour.

A major boon to the twenty-first-century researcher of this Parisian story from the 1840s and its creative aftermath is *Gallica*, the vast and constantly expanding digital database of the holdings of the Bibliothèque Nationale in Paris. Even the most obscure publications from the 1830s and 1840s emerge from the mists of time at the press of a button when the same endeavour might have taken weeks only a generation ago. Local archives in Alençon, Paris, Versailles, Lausanne, Montreux, Doncaster, Baden-Baden, and Bad Ems, contained vital information on the life of the mother of the lady of the camellias and the family who adopted her. Major research libraries in London, Paris, Venice, and New York, proved invaluable resources for the story of Marie Duplessis and for Dumas, Verdi, and *La traviata*.

Memoirs, journals, and collections of letters from the period, including *An Englishman in Paris* and accounts by others who were there such as Balabine, Claretie, Claudin, the Goncourts, Houssaye, Janin, Lumière, Mogador, Roqueplan, Véron, and Vieil-Castel, to mention some of the more prominent ones in this book, transport us to the heart of nineteenth-century Paris, a hive of creative and political activity, constantly in ferment. Its boulevards, cafés, and the Arts and Fashion scenes of the time are richly documented in the buoyant newspaper culture of the age, notably in the *Journal des Débats* and *La Sylphide*. Their contributors and reviewers included some of the best writers of the age, among them Janin, Gautier, and de Villemessant. In addition to covering the grand winter balls and latest fashions of the capital, a number of the major metropolitan papers also reported on the summer seasons in various resorts such as French-speaking Baden-Baden, the favourite haunt of the Paris glitterati. The Almanachs of Paris and France helped authenticate the real lives of the characters in this story by, among others, providing their addresses. One of the leading Paris papers of the time was *L'Illustration* which, as its title suggests, was extensively illustrated. Its sketches of the grand boulevards, from Place de la Madeleine in the west to Bastille in the east, are almost as true as photographs of the same. A number of buildings, including several theatres, survive intact today from the 1840s; others such as the famous Café Anglais, on the boulevard des Italiens next to the Italian Opera at Favart, were repeatedly photographed before they were demolished. They demonstrate just how accurate the drawings in *l'Illustration* are. This matters here particularly because the paper reproduced a detailed drawing of the boulevard and block of buildings that included the final apartment of Marie Duplessis.

The interval between the revolutions of 1830 and 1848 marked a golden age of dramatic and musical reviewing in Paris, which at the time boasted more theatres and opera houses than any other city in Europe. The novels, plays, and poems of Balzac, Dumas *père et fils*, Hugo, Sue, Nerval, and Musset, and the music of Rossini, Donizetti, Bellini, Chopin, Liszt, Thalberg, and Verdi created the heady brew that was the Paris of Marie Duplessis. Balzac's daring novel *La Cousin Bette* immerses us more deeply in her world, morally and topographically, than any other work from the period, while Sue's *Les Mystères de Paris* proffers a Gothic version of the same. The medical studies and sociological surveys of the period, by Béraud,

Parent-Duchâtelet, and Tardieu make for grim, at times shocking, reading, while bearing faithful witness to the morass of child prostitution and sexual violence that Marie Duplessis inhabited.

The creative afterlife of Marie Duplessis in Dumas's novel and play and in Verdi's *La traviata* has attracted a substantial secondary literature over the years. With regard to Dumas, it is somewhat surprising therefore that not more attention has been paid to the important differences between the first and second editions of *La Dame aux Camélias*, with the former providing indispensable information about the Madeleine apartment. As yet there is no biography of Dumas *fils* comparable to Mary Jane Phillips-Matz's vast tome on Verdi, not to mention the monumental studies by Carlo Gatti. But many of Verdi's letters remain unpublished so that much more may emerge in due course, even about the genesis of *La traviata*. In addition to reviews of the opera in, among others, the London *Times* and *France Musicale*, I drew on the critical, biographical, and musical studies of Budden, Matz, Parker, and others, including the programmes of the Royal Opera House Covent Garden and of La Fenice in Venice. The full score of *La traviata*, published by Ricordi, was invaluable as were Fabrizzio Della Seta's edition of the 'Abbozzi' and his illuminating annotations in La Fenice's libretto of *La traviata*. One of the joys of researching and writing this book were the many productions of *La traviata* that I attended or watched over the years, as often as not on my pc with the score to hand. Time and again it is the sheer delicacy of the musical line in the opera that makes one sit up, when the orchestra almost falls silent as it lets the human voice perform its magic. Verdi's close attention to detail on the score, a 'partitura' that was moreover produced at great speed, is astonishing; the maestro knew exactly what he wanted at any given time in every single bar.

References

I. ARCHIVES

Archives de la Paroisse de la Madeleine
Archives de la Ville de Spa
Archives du Cimetière de Montmartre
Archives et état civil des Yvelines (Bougival and Versailles)
Archives et état civil de l'Orne
Archives et état civil de Montreux
Archives et état civil de Versailles
Archives of Bad Ems
Archives of Baden-Baden
Archives Vaudoises et état civil, Lausanne
Badeblatt
Doncaster Archives
Emser Kurlisten
Landesarchiv Baden-Württemberg
Registre du Cimetière Saint-Louis, Versailles
The Wallace Collection

2. NEWSPAPERS

Galignani's Messenger
L'Argus des Théâtres
L'Artiste
L'Éclair
L'Entr-acte
L'Époque
L'Illustration, Journal Universel
La France Musicale
La France Théâtrale
La Gazette des Tribunaux
La Lanterne
La Presse
La Semaine

La Sylphide
Le Constitutionnel
Le Courrier de Paris
Le Figaro
Le Gaulois
Le Journal des Débats
Le Journal des Théâtres
Le Mercure de France
Le Mercure des Théâtres
Le Siècle
Paris Élégant
Revue et Gazette musicale de Paris: 1835–1880
The Athenaeum
The Times

3. BOOKS AND ARTICLES

Abbate, Carolyn, and Parker, Roger, *A History of Opera: the Last Four Hundred Years* (2012)
Abbiati, Franco, *Giuseppe Verdi*, 4 vols. (1959)
Adolphe Joanne, *Les environs de Paris illustrés: itinéraire descriptif et historique* (1856)
Allen, Robert C., 'The Great Divergence in European Wages and Prices from the Middle Ages to the First World War', *Explorations in Economic History* 38 (2001), 411–47
Almanach de Paris, 2 vols. (1842)
Almanach des 25,000 adresses des principaux habitants de Paris pour l'année 1846
Alton-Shée, Edmond d', *Mes Mémoires, 1826–1848* (1869)
An Englishman in Paris, ed. Albert Dresden Vandam (Richard Wallace), 2 vols (1892)
Ariste, Paul d', *La Vie et le monde du boulevard, 1830–1870. Un dandy: Nestor Roqueplan, etc.* (1930)
Arlincourt, Charles-Victor Prévot, Vicomte d', *Le Pélerin*, vol. 2 (1842)
Arvin, Neil C., *Alexandre Dumas Fils* (1939)
Baldick, Robert, *Pages from the Goncourt Journal* (1962)
Balabine, Victor de, *Journal de Victor de Balabine secrétaire de l'ambassade de Russie 1842–1846* (1914)
Bauër, Gérard, *Chronique* (1964)
Béraud, F. F. A., *Les Filles publiques* (1839)
Bernat, Julie (Judith), *La vie d'une Grande Comédienne, Mémoires de Madame Judith de la Comédie Française* (1911); afterwards *My autobiography* (1912)
Bernheimer, Charles, *Figures of Ill Repute: Representing Prostitution in Nineteenth-Century France* (1989)
Bettex, Gustave, *Les Alpes suisses dans la littérature et dans l'art* (1913)
Blaze de Bury, Henri, *Alexandre Dumas* (1885)

Blois, Jules, 'La Dame aux Camélias', *Revue Encylopédique* (1896), 105–8

Body, Albin, *Le théâtre et la musique à Spa, au temps passé et au temps présent* (1885)

Boudet, Micheline, *La Fleur du Mal* (1993)

Boulenger, Marcel, *Le Duc de Morny, Prince Français* (1925)

Brisson, Adolphe, *Portraits Intimes* (1897)

Bronne, Carlo, *La Comtesse de Hon* (1952)

Budden, Julian, *The Operas of Verdi*, vol. 2 (1992)

Budden, Julian, 'The Two *Traviatas*', *Proceedings of the Royal Musical Association* 99 (1972–3), 43–66

Budden, Julian, *Verdi*, 3rd edn. (2008)

Bulletin société historique et archaéologique de l'Orne (1907)

Burgard, G., *Notice sur l'Hôpital-Hospice de Versailles* (1908)

Burger, Ernst, *Franz Liszt: Eine Lebenschronik in Bildern und Dokumenten* (1986)

Cabanès, Augustin, *Une Allemande à la cour de France: La princesse Palatine* (1916)

Cardwell, Richard A. (ed.), *The Reception of Byron in Europe* (2004)

Carmona, Michel, *Morny: le vice-empereur* (2005)

Cassaro, James P. (ed.), *Music, Libraries, and the Academy* (2007)

Charavay, Noël, *L'amateur d'autographes* (November, 1910)

Choulet, Jean-Marie, *Promenades à Paris et en Normandie avec la Dame aux Camélias*; préface de Leontina Vaduva (1998)

Claretie, Jules, *La Vie à Paris 1895* (1896)

Claudin, Gustave, *Mes Souvenirs: Les Boulevards de 1840–1870* (1884)

Conati, Marcello, *La Bottega della Musica: Verdi e la Fenice* (1983)

Contades, Gérard de, 'Les Quartiers de la Dame aux Camélias', in *Le Livre* (1885)

Contades, Gérard de, 'Les portraits de la Dame aux Camélias', in *Portraits et Fantaisies* (1887), 129–35

Corbin, Alain, *Les filles de noce: misère sexuelle et prostitution au XIXe siècle* (1978)

Coward, David, *La Dame aux Camélias* (1986)

Deschaumes, L., 'Un ami et biographe de la dame aux camélias', *Revue Encyclopédie* (1896), 741–5

Dolph, Charles A., *The Real 'Lady of the Camellias'* (1927)

Du Hays, Charles, *Récits chevalins d'un vieil éleveur, l'Ancien Merlerault* (1885)

Dumas, Alexandre *fils*, *La Dame aux Camélias*, 1st edn. (1848); 2nd edn., with a preface about Marie Duplessis, by Jules Janin (1851–2); illustrated by Alphonse de Neuville (1865); with Dumas *fils*'s letter to Calmann-Lévy (1886); éd. établie et annotée Bernard Raffalli, préface d'André Maurois (1974)

Dumas, Alexandre *fils*, *Péchés de Jeunesse* (1847)

Dumas, Alexandre *fils*, 1886 preface to *La Dame aux Camélias*, *Théâtre Complet avec préfaces inédites* (1898)

Dumas Alexandre *fils*, *Théâtre Complet*, vol. 8, 'Notes' (1898)

Dumas, Alexandre *père*, *Les Mohicans* (1855)

Ellis, David, *Byron in Geneva: That Summer of 1816* (2011)

English National Opera programme for *La traviata*, March 2013

Esquiros, Alphonse, *Les vierges folles* (1842)

Garibaldi, Luigi Agostino (ed.), *Giuseppe Verdi Nelle Lettere di Emanuele Muzio ad Antonio Barezzi* (1931)

Gatti, Carlo, *Il Teatro all a Scala* (1964)

Gatti, Carlo, *Verdi* (1931; 2nd edn. 1951)

Gatti, Carlo, *Verdi nelle imagini* (1941)

Gautier, Théophile, *Correspondance générale*, ed. Claudine Lacoste-Veysseyre and Pierre Laubriet, vol. 12 (1872)

Gautier, Théophile, *Portraits Contemporains* (1874)

Gibert, Alcée and Massa, Philippe de, *Historique du Jockey-Club français depuis sa fondation jusqu'en 1871 inclusivement* (1893)

Girardin, Émile de (alias Vicomte Charles de Launay), *Lettres parisiennes* (1857)

Goncourt, *Le Journal des Goncourt*, vol. 1, 1851–1861 (1888)

Gonthier, Albert, *Montreux et ses hôtes illustres* (1999)

Gordon, Douglas, 'A letter from La Dame aux Camélias', *The Journal of the Walters Art Gallery*, vol. 12 (1949), 72–7

Graux, Lucien, *Les Factures de la Dame aux Camélias* (1934)

Gribble, Francis, 'The Real "Dame aux Camélias"', *Fortnightly Review* (September 1924), 393–402

Gros, Johannès, *Alexandre Dumas et Marie Duplessis: documents inédits* (1923)

Gros, Johannès, *Une Courtisane Romantique: Marie Duplessis* (1929)

Gros, Johannès, 'La Fin de la Dame aux Camélias', *Mercure de France* (1920), 33–85

Grothe, Gerda, *Der Herzog von Morny* (1966)

Grove, George, *The New Grove Dictionary of Music and Musicians* (2nd edn., 2001)

Grunwald, Constantin de, *Le Duc de Gramont. Gentilhomme et diplomate* (1950)

Guinot, Eugène, *L'été à Bade* (1859)

Hartoy, Maurice d', alias Maurice Hanot, *Dumas fils inconnu, ou le Collier de la Dame aux Camélias* (1964)

Hillairet, Jacques, *Dictionnaire Historique des Rues de Paris*, 2 vols. (1963)

Hillairet, Jacques, *Les 200 Cimetières du Vieux Paris* (1958)

Houssaye, Arsène, *Les Confessions: souvenirs d'un demi-siècle, 1830–1880* (1885)

I Copialettere di Giuseppe Verdi, pubblicati e illustrati da Gaetano Cesari e Alessandro Luzio e con prefazione di Michele Scherillo (1913)

Issartel, Christiane, *Les Dames aux Camélias: de l'histoire à la légende* (1981)

Janin, Jules, *Un hiver à Paris* (1843)

Janin, Jules, *Histoire de la littérature dramatique*, vol. 4 (1854)

Janin, Jules, *735 Lettres à sa femme*, ed. Mergier-Bourdeix, 3 vols. (1975)

Janin, Jules, 'Mademoiselle Marie Duplessis', Préface de Jules Janin au roman, 1851–2, in *Dumas Fils: La Dame aux Camélias: le roman, le drame, La traviata*, ed. Hans-Jörg Neuschäfer and Gilbert Sigaux (1981)

John, Nicholas, *Violetta and her sisters: The Lady of the Camellias: Responses to the Myth* (1994)

Judith: *see* Bernat, Julie.

Kimbell, David, R. B., *Verdi in the Age of Italian Romanticism* (1981)

La Fenice programmes for *Luisa Miller*, *Rigoletto*, and *La traviata*

La poudre-coton, revue de l'année 1846, en quatre actes et un entr'acte mêlé de couplets, par MM. Dumanoir et Clairville (1846)

Launay: *see* Girardin, Émile de.

Lazare, Félix, *Dictionnaire des rues de Paris* (1844)

Le Faye, Deirdre, *A Chronology of Jane Austen and her Family: 1700–2000* (2006)

Le Page, Auguste, *Les cafés politiques et littéraires de Paris* (1874)

Les Hôtels de Baden-Baden: lithographs (1858)

Lisburn Historical Society, vol. 3, pt. 2: 'The life and work of Sir Richard Wallace Bart. MP' (1996)

Loviot, Louis, *Alice Ozy* (1910)

Lumière, Henry, *La dame aux camélias. Une lettre inédite de Marie Duplessis* in *Revue normande* (1900)

Lurine, Louis, *Les Rues de Paris 1843: Paris Ancien et Moderne* (1943)

Luzio, Alessandro, *Carteggi Verdiani*, 4 vols. (1935–47)

Marchand, Leslie A., *Byron's Letters and Journals*, vol. 5: *1816–1817* (1976)

Martin, Alexis, *Promenades et Excursions dans les environs de Paris* (1891)

Martin-Fugier, Anne, *Comédienne: de Mlle Mars à Sarah Bernhardt* (2001)

Marville, Charles, *Paris*, ed. Marie de Thézy (1994)

Massa, Philippe de, *Souvenirs et impressions, 1840–1871* (1897)

Masson, Frédéric, *Charles Chaplin, Art et Lettres* (1888)

Maurois, André, *Les Trois Dumas* (1957)

McCormick, John, *Popular Theatres of Nineteenth-Century France* (1993)

Mogador: *see* Veinard, Élisabeth-Céleste, Comtesse de Chabrillan.

Montebianco, Roland, *Sir Richard Wallace* (2007)

Morel, Henry, *Le Pilori des Communeux* (1871)

Musset, Alfred de, *Rolla* (1833)

Neuschäfer, Hans-Jörg and Sigaux, Gilbert (eds.), *Dumas Fils: La Dame aux Camélias: le roman, le drame, La traviata* (1981)

Normandy, Thomas, *The White Death* (1999)

Parent-Duchâtelet, Alexandre Jean-Baptiste, *De la Prostitution dans la ville de Paris: considérée sous le rapport de l'hygiène, de la morale*, 2 vols. (1836)

Parent-Duchâtelet, Alexandre Jean-Baptiste, *Essai sur les cloaques ou égouts de la ville de Paris* (1824)

Paris Dansant…le bal Mabille, La Grande-Chaumière, le Ranelagh (1845)

Parker, Roger, in *The New Grove Dictionary of Opera*, ed. Stanley Sadie, vol. 4 (1992)

Phillips-Matz, Mary Jane, *Verdi: A Biography* (1993)

Phillips-Matz, Mary Jane, 'Art and Reality: the *Traviata* of Verdi's Private Life', pp. 219–27 in John, Nicholas (1994)

Pieri, Marzio, *Verdi: l'immaginario dell' Ottocento* (1981)

Plancy, Baron de, *Souvenirs et indiscrétions d'un disparu* (1892)

Prasteau, Jean, *C'était la dame aux camélias* (1963)

Rambert, Eugène, *Montreux* (1877)

Rondelet (Dr), 'La Médecine dans le Passé', 'Tuberculeuses Célèbres: "La Dame aux Camélias"', *La Médecine Internationale* (1913), 13–31

Roqueplan, Nestor, *Nouvelles à la main 1840–1844* (1844)

Roqueplan, Nestor, *Parisine*, 4th edn. (1868)

Rouart, Jean-Marie, *Morny. Un voluptueux au pouvoir* (1997)

Rounding, Virginia, *Grandes horizontales* (2003)

Royal Opera House programmes for *Luisa Miller, Rigoletto, La traviata,* and *Marguerite and Armand*

Rutherford, Susan, 'La Traviata or the "Willing Grisette"', *Verdi 2001* (2003), vol. 2, 585–600

Rutherford, Susan, *Verdi, Opera, Women* (2013)

Saffle, Michael, *Liszt in Germany 1840–1845, a Study in Sources, Documents, and the History of Reception* (1994)

Sala, Emilio, *The Sounds of Paris in Verdi's* La traviata (2008; English tr. by Delia Casadei 2013)

Sarholz, Hans-Jürgen, *Geschichte der Stadt Ems* (1996)

Saunders, Edith, *The Prodigal Father: Dumas Père et Fils and 'The Lady of the Camellias'* (1951)

Seta, Fabrizio Della, *Giuseppe Verdi, La traviata schizzi e abbozzi autografi* (2000)

Simond, Charles, *La vie parisienne à travers le 19ᵉ siècle: Paris de 1800 à 1900 d'après les estampes et les mémoires* (1900)

Sommer, Hermann, *Zur Kur nach Ems* (1999)

Soreau, Georges, *La vie de la Dame aux Camélias* (1898)

Stendhal, alias Henri Beyle, *Souvenirs d'égotisme, Documents Biographiques, Oeuvres Complètes*, ed. Victor Del Litto vol. 36 (1970)

Sue, Eugène, *Les Mystères de Paris* (1843)

Tardieu, Auguste Ambroise, *Étude Médico-Légale sur les Attentats aux Mœurs* (1857)

Texier, Edmond, *Tableau de Paris*, 2 vols. (1852)

Toussaint, Patrick, *Marie Duplessis: La vraie Dame aux Camélias* (1958)

Vaudoyer, Jean-Louis, *Alice Ozy ou l'Aspasie Moderne* (1930)

Veinard, Élisabeth-Céleste, Comtesse de Chabrillan, alias Mogador, *Mémoires de Céleste Mogador*, 4 vols. (1848)

Vento, Claude, *Les Peintres de la Femme* (1888)

Verdi, Giuseppe, *La traviata, Partitura* [complete score] (*nuova edizione riveduta e coretta* (Ricordi, 1999)

Vérel, Charles, *Le marquisat de Nonant . . . Nouvelle édition revue et corrigée par l'auteur* (1908)

Véron, Louis-Desiré, *Mémoires d'un bourgeois de Paris*, 6 vols. (1853–5)

Vieil-Castel, Horace de, *Mémoires du Comte Horace de Viel-Castel sur le règne de Napoléon III, 1851–64* (1883)

Vienne, Romain, *La Vérité sur la Dame aux Camélias* (1888)

Walker, Alan, *Franz Liszt: The Virtuoso Years 1811–1847* (1983)

Weerth, Georg, *Leben und Thaten des berühmten Ritters Schnapphahnski* (1848)

Whitelocke, R. G., *The City of the Fountains, or Baden-Baden* (1840)

Wintle, Christopher, 'A Tragedy of Affliction', Royal Opera House *La traviata* programme, May 2010

Woerth, Eric, *Le Duc d'Aumale* (2006)

Wohl, Janka, *François Liszt: souvenirs d'une compatriote* (1887)

Yung, Emile, *Montreux et ses environs* (1898)

Picture credits

Frontispiece: unattributed water colour of Marie Duplessis, perhaps by Charles Chaplin. (© Archives of the Comédie-Française)

1.1 The site and remains of the Viennes' home in Nonant. (© René Weis)

2.1 Nonant in the Orne, the home village of Marie Duplessis as it is today. (© René Weis)

2.2 The hamlet of Clarens near Montreux, famous through Rousseau and Byron, where Marie Duplessis's mother died. (© The British Library C.115.t.5)

2.3 The church in Saint-Germain-de-Clairefeuille, where Alphonsine Plessis took her first communion. (© René Weis)

2.4 *The Little Beggar Girl* ('Petite Mendiante') by William-Adolphe Bouguereau. (© Sotheby's/akg-images)

3.1 The close of 'Four Banal' in the village of Exmes. (© René Weis)

3.2 The Denis inn, Exmes. (© René Weis)

4.1 A rare photograph of Paris in 1852, five years after Marie Duplessis's death. (© TopFoto/Collection Roger-Viollet)

4.2 *Rolla* by Henri Gervex. (© akg-images/Jean-Claude Varga)

5.1 Charles Duc de Morny, a Bonaparte and half-brother of the President-Emperor Napoleon III. (© TopFoto/Collection Roger-Viollet)

5.2 No. 28 rue du Mont-Thabor, a street parallel to the rue de Rivoli, close to the Tuileries and place de la Concorde. (© René Weis)

6.1 No. 9 rue du Marché Neuf, Versailles where Alphonsine Plessis gave birth to her baby. (© René Weis)

6.2 The Cimetière Saint-Louis in Versailles, where Alphonsine Plessis's little boy, Charles-Yves, is buried. (© René Weis)

7.1 Alice Ozy in the *Baigneuse endormie près d'une source* by her lover Théodore Chassériau. (© TopFoto/Collection Roger-Viollet)

7.2 The boulevard des Italiens, north side, the hub of 1840s Paris, from a drawing of the period. (© The British Library 574.m.13)

7.3 The Maison Dorée at night from a contemporary lithograph by Eugène Lami. (© TopFoto/Collection Roger-Viollet)

8.1 The luxury Hôtel de l'Europe (Europaïscher Hof) in Baden-Baden, as it was in the 1840s. (© The British Library 10231.a.72)

8.2 The legendary staircase in the Hôtel de l'Europe in Baden-Baden. (© René Weis)

8.3 Map of Baden-Baden as it was in 1842. (© Bibliothèque Nationale de France)

9.1 No. 22 rue d'Antin, a slim, flat-iron building occupied by Marie Duplessis in October 1842, courtesy of her old protector, Count Gustav Ernst von Stackelberg. (© René Weis)

9.2 Agénor, Duc de Guiche Gramont, one of Marie Duplessis's most prestigious lovers. (© Beinecke Library, Yale University)

9.3 The famous Ventadour theatre, a favourite venue for presenting Italian opera throughout Marie Duplessis's life in the city. (© René Weis)

10.1 A rare photograph of the Café Anglais, opposite the Maison Dorée. (© TopFoto/Collection Roger-Viollet)

10.2 Renoir's *Dance at Bougival*. (© akg/De Agostini Picture Library)

10.3 A tureen with countess Marie Duplessis's crest on it. (© Musée de la Dame aux Camélias, Gacé)

11.1 The five windows of Marie Duplessis's last and most famous home, the mezzanine apartment at 11 boulevard de la Madeleine. (© René Weis)

11.2 The south side of the boulevard de la Madeleine as it was in 1845. (© The British Library 574.m.13)

11.3 The Olivier portrait of Marie Duplessis, painted in the salon at 11 boulevard de la Madeleine. (© The British Library P.P.4283.k)

11.4 The best-known portrait of Marie Duplessis, by society artist Édouard Vienot. (© akg-images)

12.1 Alexandre Dumas *fils*. (© Bibliothèque Nationale de France)

12.2 The 'Grande Terrasse' at Saint-Germain-en-Laye. (© René Weis)

12.3 Lola Montez, future Countess of Landsfeld. (© akg-images)

12.4 Olympe Aguado. (© Jean-Marie Choulet)

13.1 The Ambigu-Comique theatre. (© TopFoto/Collection Roger-Viollet)

13.2 Franz Liszt, the greatest pianist of the age, at the time of his involvement with Marie Duplessis. (© Franz-Liszt-Museum der Stadt Bayreuth)

13.3 Marie Deshayes, the mother of Marie Duplessis, in a drawing commissioned by her employers in Chamonix. (© Musée de la Dame aux Camélias, Gacé)

13.4 An early painting attributed to Camille Roqueplan of, probably, Marie Duplessis, at the theatre or opera. (© TopFoto/Collection Roger-Viollet)

14.1 The Salle Favart, much patronized by Marie Duplessis and her set. (© akg/De Agostini Picture Library)

14.2 The auditorium of the Salle Ventadour. (© akg-images)

15.1 Formerly the 'Englischer Hof' in Bad Ems. (© René Weis)

15.2 The legendary Kursaal in Bad Ems. (© René Weis)

16.1 The first of several drawings of Marie Duplessis by the young artist Charles Chaplin. (© The Bridgeman Art Library)

16.2 A copy of a Chaplin drawing, sketched by Riffaut and engraved by Marie Duclos. (© Bibliothèque Nationale de France)

16.3 The 'bathrobe Madonna' picture of Marie Duplessis. (© Musée de la Dame aux Camélias, Gacé)

16.4 A famous picture of Marie Duplessis on her deathbed. (© Royal Opera House, Covent Garden)

17.1 The sarcophagus grave in Montmartre, Marie Duplessis's final resting place. (© René Weis)

18.1 Sir Richard Wallace. (© By kind permission of the Trustees of the Wallace Collection)

19.1 The former Auberge du Cheval Blanc in which Dumas *fils* wrote the memoir novel that made Marie Duplessis famous. (© René Weis)

20.1 The Vaudeville theatre where *La Dame aux Camélias* premièred in 1852. (© TopFoto/Collection Roger-Viollet)

20.2 Eugénie Doche as Marguerite Gautier in *La Dame aux Camélias*, by Richard Buckner.

20.3 Sarah Bernhardt, the greatest lady of the camellias after Doche. (© Bibliothèque Nationale de France)

21.1 Margherita Barezzi, the young wife of Verdi, who died of encephalitis at the age of 26. (© akg-images)

21.2 Giuseppina Strepponi as Violetta from *La traviata*. (© Photo SCALA, Florence)

21.3 Giuseppe Verdi at the time of *La traviata*. (© Photo SCALA, Florence)

21.4 Francesco Maria Piave, Verdi's brilliant librettist and collaborator on *La traviata*. (© Photo SCALA, Florence)

22.1 The now famous poster from the Teatro La Fenice in Venice, advertising the premiere of *La traviata* on 6 March 1853. (© akg-images)

22.2 The soprano Fanny Salvini-Donatelli, the first ever Violetta in 1853. (Wikimedia Commons)

22.1 Maria Spezia, the first truly successful Violetta in 1854. (© Bibliothèque Nationale de France)

22.1 Marietta Piccolomini, who sang the role of Violetta at the London and Paris premières. (© Bibliothèque Nationale de France)

Index

Bold entries refer to illustrations.